EGO PSYCHOLOGY AND THE PSYCHOSES

EGO PSYCHOLOGY
AND THE PSYCHOSES
PAUL FEDERN, M.D.

EDITED and with an INTRODUCTION by
EDOARDO WEISS, M.D.

MARESFIELD REPRINTS
LONDON

ISBN 0 9501647 3 9

PRINTED IN GREAT BRITAIN
AD/CRP/HD/77

ACKNOWLEDGMENTS

I wish to express my thanks to those who helped me in making this volume possible:

Gertrud M. Kurth, New York, and Mrs. Marjorie Lawson, Chicago, materially assisted me in the editing; Walter Federn is responsible for the compilation of the author's writings; and Ernst Federn rendered invaluable service by coordinating the work of editor, coeditor, and publisher between Chicago and New York.

I also wish to thank the editors of the following journals for permission to reprint, in edited form, material which first appeared in their publications:

International Journal of Psychoanalysis: "Some Variations in Ego Feeling," "Narcissism in the Structure of the Ego," and "The Awakening of the Ego in Dreams"; *Psychoanalytic Quarterly:* "Ego Feeling in Dreams"; *Psychiatric Quarterly:* "A Dream under General Anesthesia"; and *American Journal of Psychotherapy:* "Principles of Psychotherapy in Latent Schizophrenia." The reader will find the exact citations in the bibliography of Federn's Writings at the end of this book.

Edoardo Weiss, M.D.

Chicago

CONTENTS

CONTENTS

INTRODUCTION

BY EDOARDO WEISS, M.D.

The publication of Paul Federn's original contributions to ego psychology fills an important gap in the study of mental health. It will enable psychologists, psychiatrists, and other workers in this field to become better acquainted with the findings and viewpoints of an outstanding scholar who threw new light on the psychodynamic phenomena on which rest not merely the ego functions but the ego experience (*Erlebnis*) itself. In his last will, Paul Federn entrusted me with the editing of this book. This trust I consider a sacred obligation toward my first teacher in psychoanalysis with whom I had maintained a close association of friendship and exchange of opinions for more than forty years. I shall never forget Federn's words at our last meeting, Christmas, 1949. Aware that his days were numbered, he said to me: "Don't grieve when I am gone, I have put down in writing what I had to say in the field of ego psychology."

He felt *his* work completed, but still the task remained to collect and organize his original contributions into one volume. In working on this book, I wholeheartedly complied with his "hope and desire . . ." as expressed in his last will.

The present volume contains, in addition to articles which were previously published in various British and American journals, several hitherto unpublished papers and the first English translation of two of his contributions to theory: "The Ego as Subject and Object in Narcissism," and "On the Differentiation of Normal and Pathological Narcissism."

1

For many years the findings of Paul Federn did not awaken the interest which they deserved on the part of psychoanalysts. In one of his seminars, he referred to this as the period in which he worked in a state of "splendid isolation." Gradually, however, his new and startling concepts were assimilated by a steadily increasing number of students.

Paul Federn's absolute loyalty to Sigmund Freud was apparent to everyone who knew him personally. In all his lectures and writings he expressed his great admiration for Freud as a person and as a scientist, comparing him with the outstanding geniuses of history. He was fascinated by whatever Freud had to say and took great pains to interpret correctly every phrase of his writings. Whenever new experience and more mature scientific investigations induced Freud to modify earlier concepts and formulations, Federn worked his way through to them; this holds true especially for Freud's early and later conceptualization of the "instinct dualism." When Freud replaced the concept of the ego and the sexual drives with that of the life and the death instinct, Federn concurred with these concepts enthusiastically.

However, Federn's admiration for Freud by no means prevented him from following his own course in research and from formulating his own problems, thereby revealing great originality of mind. Nevertheless, he preferred to consider his findings only as confirmations and elaborations of Freud's.

Only hesitantly, and after lengthy discussion, did Federn admit the existence of some discrepancies between his and Freud's theories concerning the dynamic structure of the ego. But he hinted at them only occasionally in his writings, as at the very few errors of Freud. Conversely, he frequently referred his findings and formulations to Freud's basic dynamic concepts.

Although Federn remained a firm believer in the death instinct, in discussions with me—I did not agree with him in this respect—he recognized that this drive theory did not do justice to all observable mental and physiological phenomena. In his mind the idea was developing that in addition to libido and mortido (as he called the dynamic expression of the death instinct) a third kind of cathexis may exist—namely, a neutral one manifesting itself in every biologic function. He admitted still other possibilities, on which, however, he did not feel ready to elaborate; hence his "drive tri-alism" has not been dealt with in his writings. At any rate, he remained firm in his conviction that constructive (life) and destructive (death) tendencies operate in every living being.

Apart from theoretical considerations, Federn's findings and concepts concerning ego psychology are of paramount practical importance for every psychiatrist. They constitute an indispensable equipment of knowledge, not only for the understanding of pathologic phenomena such as depersonalization and estrangement, and the psychoses in general in the great variety of their manifestations, but also for the adoption of proper attitudes in the treatment of neuroses and psychoses.

Consider the implications of the statements that the impairment of the ego and its functions as it occurs in psychoses is due not to an enrichment of ego cathexis at the expense of object libido, but, on the contrary, to an impoverishment of ego cathexis; and that hallucinations and delusions do not constitute unsuccessful attempts to re-establish an emotional rapport with the external world but indicate lesions of the ego itself (the breaking down of the sense of reality), which manifest themselves prior to, and independently of, the ego's loss of interest in the external world. The knowledge of the basic theory of ego psychology is essential for the successful treatment of psychotics, for it determines every practical therapeutic approach.

Thus Federn has demonstrated that a strong transference can be established in the psychoses and has shown the means to accomplish it. Hence, with every patient the psychiatrist must gauge "ego strength" and "ego weakness." These concepts, however, have a different meaning in the light of Federn's ego psychology inasmuch as some functions of the ego may be weak while other functions remain strong, or the entire ego may be weak, and therapy must be governed by the specific constellation.

The full importance of Federn's ego psychology will become evident if one focuses on two points: first, his individual approach to the study of ego phenomena in all their complexity; and, secondly, the fact that Freud himself never extended his revised libido theory, in all its consequences, to the concept of narcissism which he had formulated earlier. It is known that in his earlier (instinct) dualism, Freud considered the self-preservative drive of the ego, its integrative function, its defenses and development, as non-libidinal. The "ego drives" were powered, in his conception, not by libido but by a biologically different kind of cathexis, the "ego drive cathexis," which could not be turned into libido, just as libido could never become ego drive cathexis. Freud energetically defended the concept of this instinct dualism, the economic implication of which is self-evident, especially in his polemic against Jung's "monistic" concept of the libido, in the fundamental paper "On Narcissism—An Introduction." [1] At that time, Freud made a strict, uncompromising distinction between "libido" directed toward the ego, a condition which he called "narcissism," and the non-libidinal self-preservative cathexis, to the operation of which all ego functions were due. In his earlier writings, he also formulated the neurotic conflict in terms of a discrepancy between the demands of the libido (sexual drives) and the ego (self-preservative drives). Later he described the neurotic conflict in structural terms: as an incompatibility between the organization of the ego and certain demands of the id.

Later, Freud abandoned his earlier distinction between libidinal and non-libidinal self-preservative drives of the ego.[2] On this, as on many previous occasions, the outstanding scientific and flexible quality of Freud's mind became very apparent. He realized that scientific concepts are largely provisional and must be modified progressively as a result of new experiences and more matured thinking. Freud's love for truth outweighed by far any scientific ambition, so that no strong emotional commitments to previously expressed opinions could establish themselves in him. With the new point of view, the whole concept of narcissism had to be revised, and ego psychology in general had a fresh opportunity for further development.

. . . .

[1] Freud, *Collected Papers* (London: Hogarth Press, 1941), IV, 30.
[2] Freud, *Beyond the Pleasure Principle* (London: Internat. Psychoanalytic Press, 1922).

It remained for Paul Federn to demonstrate that ego libido participates in the actual structural formation of the ego. His theory is based on accurate descriptions of the subjective experiences of healthy as well as diseased persons. He himself was endowed with an exceptional introspective capacity. Federn expresses the fact that the ego is an *Erlebnis*—that is, a subjective experience—by equating the ego with the actual sensation of one's own ego, which he calls ego feeling. Freud used the latter term two or three times, but did not examine the concept indicated by it. The phenomenon of self-experience itself, of the specific *Erlebnis,* cannot be explained.

Prior to psychoanalysis, psychology dealt only with the ego, and the subjective phenomenon of ego sensation was called "ego consciousness." By the term ego *feeling* Federn gives expression to the fact that one's own ego is actually *felt.* Paul Schilder, who elaborated on the concept of body scheme or body image, and who described the manifestations of depersonalization and estrangement (but only in severe pathological conditions), spoke of consciousness of one's personality and its somatic organization. Those psychiatrists and psychoanalysts who became increasingly interested in depersonalization and estrangement considered them as expressions of derangement, loss, or frustration of interest in objects. Federn studied the manifestations of these phenomena not only in severely pathological cases but also in certain ego states within the range of normality, as he could observe them in himself and as they were communicated to him by his patients. He recognized them clearly as ego disturbances *per se,* although they may be provoked by withdrawal or frustration of object libido, as Nunberg, Hartmann, and other psychoanalysts correctly observed. However, the contention that it is not the decrease of object libido, but of a part of ego libido, which is responsible for an ensuing feeling of estrangement from external objects is proved by the fact that an individual can still feel strongly interested in objects which he experiences as estranged.

As long as the ego functions normally, one may ignore, or be unaware of, its functioning. As Federn says, normally there is no more awareness of the ego than of the air one breathes; only when respiration becomes burdensome is the lack of air recognized. The ego feeling is the feeling of unity, in continuity, contiguity, and causality, in the experiences of the individual. In waking life the sensation of one's ego is omnipresent, but it undergoes continuous changes in quality and intensity. Slight disturbances and variations of ego feeling are a matter of common experience and subside unnoticed. When we are tired or drowsy, we feel numb; upon waking from a refreshing sleep, or upon receiving exciting news, we sense an invigorated ego feeling.

Ego feeling is not the same as consciousness, because there are object representations which refer to data that do not belong to the ego and which are also conscious. The ego feeling is the discriminating factor between ego and non-ego. Federn recognized that the ego is an actual continuous mental experience, and not merely a mental abstraction. Neither is the ego the sum of all conscious, interrelated phenomena, nor is it the integrative function of the mind. The ego is a reality as *Erlebnis,* as subjective experience, and science does not yet explain how this phenomenon comes into being.

It is meant as an exact description of actual experience, and by no means mere theory, when one speaks of investment of continuously changing contents with the unifying, coherent ego feeling. Although the ego experience passes from one state to another, it is felt as continuous and is re-established after transitory interruptions, as during dreamless sleep. The discrimination between the data which are *felt* as pertaining to the ego and those which are *felt* as belonging to the non-ego is a matter of a particular *sensation,* of the "sense of reality," and does not rest on the functioning of "reality testing." Hallucinations and delusions of psychotic patients, as well as the dreams of healthy people, consist of mental products which are *sensed* as external realities *independently* of any "reality testing." One understands clearly the difference between consciousness and ego feeling when one considers that mental phenomena which come to the individual's consciousness without being invested with ego feeling are *sensed* as being real; that is, as belonging to the *external* world. It is also clear that this phenomenon is not identical with recognition of reality by means of reality testing.

Federn is in agreement with Jaspers when he distinguishes between "sense of reality" and "reality testing." In his discussions with me, he clarified the expression of the phenomena of the investment of mental contents with ego feeling, and their divestment from it, by using the terms *Ver-ichung* and *Ent-ichung*—which could be translated as "egotization" and "de-egotization."

Federn applied the term ego feeling only to those contents that are sensed as participating in the coherent ego unity; that is, in a distinct entity, something opposed to external reality. It is the feeling of bodily and mental relations in respect to time and content, the relation being regarded as an uninterrupted or restored unity. From an accurate study of the dreaming ego, it appears evident that mental ego and bodily ego are felt separately, but in the waking state the mental ego is always experienced as being inside the bodily ego.

This ego is not identical with the body image or body scheme described by Schilder. Only when the body image is completely invested with ego feeling does the actual feeling of bodily ego correspond to the entire body image. Conversely, the bodily ego can disappear without involving the somatic organization, which allows proper use of the body, with the unity of correctly ordered perceptions of one's own ego.

The ego phenomenon presents the problem of its specific nature and can also be studied in its dynamic, economic, and topographic aspects—in other words, from a metapsychological point of view. To account for the fluctuating intensity of the ego feeling, Federn postulated the existence of a specific ego cathexis, thus passing from mere description to theory of the ego phenomenon. However, it has to be borne in mind that he never asserted that his theories could explain the actual phenomenon of the ego *Erlebnis*, the ego experience. He only provided dynamic and economic orientations which were valuable in this field of research, and which also proved to be very helpful in the therapeutic approach to psychoses.

A varying amount of mental energy is employed in the individual for the establishment of ego feeling and for the various functions of this entity which is felt as such. Federn assumes that it is a particular cathexis which is experienced as ego feeling, no one knows how. His adoption of metapsychological considerations in the study of the ego is as justified as was Freud's introduction of such formulations in the general field of psychoanalysis. In describing the ego defenses and all kinds of ego accomplishments, Freud also considered these to be manifestations of ego cathexes—which, however, in his earlier concept of the drive-dualism, he did not consider to be libidinal.

Correlating the ego cathexis to the ego experience, Federn assumes that the metapsychological basis of the ego is a coherent cathexis unity. To account for various specific qualities and manifestations of the ego, he further assumes that the ego cathexis must be a compound of libido and that energy which dynamically expresses Freud's death drive. Of course, not every energetic manifestation in the individual is an expression of ego cathexis; the drives which have to be mastered by means of ego cathexis represent a task imposed upon the ego. Only a variable portion of the total cathexis produced by the organism, a portion which can be exhausted and restored, illuminating the ego to various intensities and being at its disposal for its dynamic functioning, constitutes the ego cathexis.

Federn's definitions of the ego were often misunderstood. To repeat, for clarity, Federn describes the ego as an experience, as the sensation and knowledge of the individual of the lasting or recurrent continuity, in time, space, and causality, of his bodily and mental life. This continuity is felt and apprehended as a unity. The *metapsychological basis* of the ego is a state of psychical cathexis of certain interdependent bodily and mental functions and contents, the cathexes in question being simultaneous, interconnected, and also continuous. The nature of these functions and the center around which they are grouped are felt as familiar for the experiencing ego.

Federn's analysis of the various forms in which the ego libido—that is, the libidinal component of the ego cathexis—manifests itself and of the economic conditions which constitute ego strength and ego weakness, together with his concept of narcissism, led Federn to certain views which are at variance with some statements of Freud.

Federn calls our attention to the fact that the ego is subject and object simultaneously. As subject it is known by the pronoun "I," and as object it is called "the Self." [3] The ego is the bearer of consciousness, yet the individual is conscious of his own ego—a circumstance which Federn characterizes as a "unique paradox" by which the ego differs from all other existing institutions.

The ego as subject is experienced in various modes which can be indicated in terms made familiar by grammar. The *active* ego cathexis is experienced in the ego's planning, thinking, acting, and, in its most elementary form, in the phenomenon of attention. The *passive* ego cathexis determines the need for stimuli. The *reflexive* cathexis is manifested in self-love or self-hate. However, in its original and most primitive form the ego cathexis, or rather the corresponding ego feeling, can be classified, not according to these three categories, but by the middle voice as it is used in the classical Greek language. Federn termed this neutral, *objectless* form of ego cathexis *"medial"* cathexis. In English grammar the middle voice is expressed by certain intransitive phrases such as "I grow," "I thrive," "I live," "I prosper," "I develop," and, in the case of a predominant destructive component, by "I perish," "I age," "I die."

Federn considers as *primary narcissism* only the original manifestation of the ego libido, the "middle voice" type. This he regards as the very source of the ego's sense of gratification in its own actual existence, the reason for which prospering, growing, and living are felt to be pleasurable in themselves. In this concept of "primary narcissism" Federn is stricter than Freud, who uses this term to indicate the reflexive as well as the medial ego libido in the sense of the "middle voice."

In Federn's opinion, it is the "medial" libido component of the ego cathexis which is responsible for the feeling that everyday life, with its sensations, and its motor and intellectual functions, is not an empty, dull, or disagreeable experience, but a pleasantly *familiar* one. Body and mind combine to procure for the ego this enigmatic enjoyment of life in it-

· · · · · · ·

[3] This ought not to be confused with the concepts expressed by George H. Mead in *Mind, Self and Society* (Chicago: Univ. of Chicago Press, 1934).

self. Every ego function, bodily as well as mental, carries some of the self-enjoying primary narcissism. Furthermore, external libidinal interests are continuously added, through the experience of life, to this original narcissistic cathexis.

If the libidinal component of the "medial" ego cathexis is withdrawn, or is not supplied in the organism in sufficient quantities, then the individual feels a disagreeable change in his vitality and self-unity. As long as only the libidinal component is lacking, the integrative function of the ego persists, but the *familiar feeling* of an integrative balance is impaired. Federn regards the morbid ego feeling which characterizes depressive states as the most convincing proof of the existence of a death drive. When the destructive component of the ego cathexis becomes predominant, the patient is unable to enjoy anything, nor does he recall pleasant experiences of the past. His ego is in a state of hopelessness. He dislikes everything in his existence and has the urge to cease to exist. As every psychiatrist knows, this destructive component also overflows into object relationships. In Federn's opinion the destructive component of the ego cathexis, when it is well fused with an adequate amount of libido, manifests itself in will power and determination.

Federn explains the sense of reality and its disturbances, such as the feeling of estrangement for external objects and loss of reality, as well as the phenomena of hallucination and delusion, on the basis of one of his most important concepts, that of the *ego boundary*. Unfortunately, this concept has not been well understood by many of his readers.

Healthy individuals are not conscious of the potential ego boundaries of their bodies and minds. In the beginning, self-observation in this respect requires some practicing under proper guidance. Federn's concepts of the ego as a dynamic entity and the ego boundary as its peripheral sense organ are new, and are not contained in Freud's theory.

Egotized data are accessible to introspection, while the perception of data pertaining to the field of the non-ego—that is, the external world—is called extraspection. The difference between introspection and extraspection is related to the dividing plane between what Federn aptly termed "inner mentality" and "external reality." If, in waking life, a healthy individual directs his attention simultaneously inside and outside his mind, he *senses* clearly what is only his thought, memory, or imagination and what is a *real* object or event of the external world. The whole field of what is sensed as "inner mentality" participates in the coherent ego experience unity. All the perceived data which lie outside the boundary of this experience unity are *sensed* as external reality, as *non-ego,* and are accessible to extraspection. Furthermore, as we know, not only the external world but also all the psychic phenomena which remain excluded from the preconscious ego—as, for instance, all repressed material—pertain to the non-ego and are felt as such. *Therefore, they too are accessible to what we call extraspection.* Freud's introduction of the term *id,* which is *non-ego,* for this field of mental dynamics clearly expresses this state of affairs. In fact, Freud speaks of an *inner* and an *outer foreign country* in respect to the ego.

Whatever enters the ego boundary from without (all data which are unegotized, as the stimuli from the external world as well as those from the repressed unconscious) is perceived by what we call extraspection and is felt as external reality. Thus the dynamically invested ego boundary, the ego's periphery, assumes the role of a sense organ of the ego which discriminates real from unreal.

The assertion that the contents of repressed material are accessible to extraspection needs clarification. Correctly stated, it reads as follows: *If* such contents are perceived in general, they are perceived by extraspection; but in the waking life of the healthy ego, repressed material does not reach the ego. The boundary toward the repressed unconscious is dynamically strong enough to prevent the entrance of repressed material; what we call counter- or anti-cathexes participate in and strengthen the inner ego boundary.

The ego boundaries are very flexible. At different times various egotized data lose their ego cathexis. Federn's "geographical" description of the ego boundary gave many readers the impression that he conceived the ego and its boundaries to be static. Nothing could be more alien from Federn's teachings. The geographical connotation of the term "boundary" is unfortunate. It must be borne in mind that the concept indicated by this term is an exquisitely *dynamic* one, and that Federn has always emphasized the flexibility of the ego boundaries.

Their dynamism can be experienced by any one in the process of falling asleep. As sleep approaches, the ego and its boundaries lose their cathexis, so that unegotized mental phenomena can reach the drowsy ego by entering its weakened boundary. Thus hypnagogic images ensue; one starts hallucinating, or dreaming. However, when one makes an effort to awake completely the ego boundaries are re-established to their full strength and the hypnagogic images disappear. Some contents may be recognized again as one's own previous thoughts which had become de-egotized in the process of sleep and egotized again upon awakening. Other contents may have derived from the repressed unconscious (id) and have broken through into the ego from without, upon the weakening of its inner boundary (countercathexes).

The dynamic ego boundary toward the stimuli of the external world is different. It includes the physical sense organs, which are conceived by Federn, as by many neurologists, as apertures or windows, so to speak, embedded in the external wall of the organism, thus providing paths of communication between the external world and the central nervous system. However, the *sensation of reality* which one has for the perceived external world is not due simply to the fact that the stimuli enter the physical sense organs but that they enter the external dynamic ego boundary, which includes the sense organs. The latter are pervious to external stimuli and constitute the normal organs of extraspection in the waking life of the ego. When the external ego boundary loses its cathexis, the external objects, however distinctly perceived, are sensed as strange, unfamiliar, or even unreal. In some ego disorders the feeling of estrangement may be the first stage of the loss of reality. The environment is felt as lifeless, like changing pictures on a screen. In the process of recovery the slightest increase of libido cathexis on the boundary is recognizable: the perception of objects becomes warmer and the objects themselves are sensed as having obtained a pleasantly increased vividness. An object is sensed as *real, without the aid of any reality testing,* when it is not only excluded from the ego but also when its impressions impinge upon a well-cathected ego boundary. As long as a normally cathected ego boundary is not stimulated, one is not aware of it.

In the psychological chapter of his *Interpretation of Dreams,* Freud also based the original "reality testing" of the infant on the distinction between "within" and "without." Such testing is performed by bodily movements. When the infant continues to perceive some object upon turning his head or closing his eyes, he eventually *learns to recognize* what he perceives as being due to inner stimulation, or, rather, as being *unreal;* whereas, if the perceived elements change direction, or disappear and reappear in relation to given movements, they are eventually recognized by him as being real—that is, as existing in the external world.

If one draws a parallel between Federn's explanation of the "sense of reality" and this primitive form of "reality testing" indicated by Freud, one must consider two points. In the first place, the act of "testing" the "inside" and the "outside" is related to the whole organism, while the "sense of reality" discriminates between "within" and "without" in relation only to the ego, not even to the whole mind, for the id is excluded. Federn's explanation of delusions and hallucinations is quite consistent with Freud's characterization of the id as the *inner foreign country* in respect to the ego. The weakening of the inner ego boundary is responsible for delusions and hallucinations. Secondly, this primitive testing through movements is a means for the first orientation in the establishment of ego boundaries. Counter- or anti-cathexes, which belong to the inner ego boundary, are progressively mobilized in order to check inner stimuli. Thereby the ego-syntonic stimuli are included in the ego itself, and are then no longer *sensed* as external, as are the objects perceived by extraspection; and the repressed mental stimuli are excluded from the ego.

Once the dynamically efficient ego boundaries are established, this primitive form of reality testing loses its function of orientation. What is sensed as real can no longer be reversed by any reality testing or reasoning. This is also the case in delusions and hallucinations. The individual has, very early, given up using movements as a means of discriminating between "real" and "imagined." In further development, reality testing becomes much more complex and serves the purpose of *obtaining knowledge* of realities. Remembering and learning are the basic functions at the service of reality testing. The individual achieves different degrees of certainty and doubt.

Psychotic individuals sense the contents of their delusions and hallucinations as real because they arise from mental stimuli which actually entered consciousness without obtaining ego investment, not because of a defective reality testing. In order to create an agreement between his "false realities" and the correctly recognized data of the external world, the psychotic person may construct proper rationalizations and resort to secondary elaborations of the original unconscious contents which invaded the ego from without its inner boundary. This activity constitutes a mental function compensatory for the omitted reality testing for which the patient felt no need. It is an attempt to mend the disturbed integration of the ego.

Federn emphasizes the flexibility of the ego boundaries, which undergo progressive changes from birth on, and include, at various periods, various contents. Some changes of the dynamic ego boundaries also occur during the everyday life of the individual, in different situations. Throughout these changes, however, the ego constitutes a continuity and struggles to establish and maintain, in every state, its coherence and integration. The specific contents which are at any given time included within the ego boundary determine the specific ego state. Different ego boundaries are correlated with different ego states.

The repression of ego states is one of the most important findings of Federn. It can be experimentally proven that ego states of earlier ages do not disappear but are only repressed. In hypnosis, a former ego state containing the corresponding emotional dispositions, memories, and urges can be reawakened in the individual. In Federn's opinion, the unconscious portion of the ego consists of the stratification of the repressed ego states. Double and multiple personalities, as well as somnambulism, ensue when different ego states are alternately reawakened.

The phenomenon of identification consists in the inclusion in the ego of an object or its autoplastic duplication, so that the ego feels that object as part of itself: that object becomes egotized. Mere imitation is not internalization of the object in question. Only when the ego cathexis extends itself over the product of imitation can we speak of identification of the ego with an object. In mental conflicts, distinct ego feelings are associated with the ego and the superego respectively.

Identification has an economic implication. The more identifications an ego maintains, the more ego cathexis is used up. Therefore, identifications which are too numerous and too strong may cause a relative ego weakness. Conversely, when the afflux of ego cathexis diminishes, fewer identifications can be maintained. With the onset of sleep, the superego loses its ego cathexis prior to the nucleus of the ego, and in the process of awakening, the superego awakens after the ego.

The cathexis of the core of the ego was discussed by Freud in his papers on the preconscious, the secondary mental process, as well as on the various defenses of the ego, including its dynamic *Reizschutz*, its defensive barrier. This cathexis was thought to be non-libidinal—ego drive cathexis—in Freud's earlier drive dualism. Federn considers this ego cathexis, as has been said, to be a compound of libido and mortido; he characterized it as an indispensable support of the personality. He describes the feeling of depersonalization as "ego atony" or as a "loss of the ego's inner firmness." Libidinal deficiency of the ego boundary causes feelings of estrangement for external objects, while such deficiency of the ego nucleus brings about feelings of depersonalization.

Freud first conceived the structure of the "mental apparatus" in terms of *Ucs, Pcs,* and *Cs.* Later he abandoned this formulation, because the unconscious comprised not only drives but also portions of the ego and superego, and substituted his structural concept in terms of id, ego, and superego.

According to Federn, the inclusion of a mental element in the coherent ego unity coincides with its participation in what Freud had described as the preconscious in his earlier structural concept of the mind. The preconscious is the territory over which the ego extends itself. In fact, Federn asserts that the very ego feeling extends itself permanently over the preconscious, although only few elements are conscious at any given moment. Precisely on this basis, the extension of the integrating ego over the preconscious, rests the confidence of every healthy individual in his ability to behave and express himself in a coherent way. We have the subjective sensation that we are disposing coherently of our preconscious data. When we want to go to a familiar place, we have the confident feeling of knowing, at any turn, which way to take, although the single landmarks along the route will not be simultaneously conscious to us. We *sense* whether the behavior or utterances of other people are consistent or not, although the perceived impressions steadily disappear in a continuous flow from consciousness, and new impressions continuously enter our consciousness. It is not consciousness but the ego cathexis, experienced as ego feeling, which expands itself permanently over the preconscious and permits us to function mentally in a coherent and integrated way.

Federn's view on the checking function of the ego cathexis corroborates Freud's statements concerning the dynamic working patterns of the preconscious. Federn frequently refers in his writings to the early concepts of Breuer and Freud concerning the free-floating or mobile and the fixated or resting energies. The process of "fixing" the free-floating cathexis, which Freud called the secondary mental process and which is characteristic for the preconscious, is performed by the ego cathexis. It is the investment of *id* elements by ego cathexis whereby the primary process is put to an end and the elements concerned are integrated in time, space, and causality. Rational thinking, which checks the emotions to some extent, is due to the secondary mental process. The stronger the binding capacity of the ego cathexis, the better can the ego resist frustration and postpone and renounce gratification. The countercathexes, of which the inner ego boundary consists, and which maintain repressions, belong to the ego, according to both Freud and Federn. But for Federn, these cathexes contain libido.

Federn's description of the dynamics of the state of sleep and of the schizophrenic process is, in some respects, at variance with Freud's concept in this regard. Federn holds that sleep and schizophrenia are marked by a deficiency rather than an excess of ego libido. As far as the phenomenon of sleep is concerned, this contradiction could perhaps be considered as only formal. In dreamless sleep the ego fades away; its cathexis is withdrawn, perhaps into the id or the biological organism. Therefore, if one accepts Freud's assertion that in the state of sleep the ego regresses to the primary narcissism, one extends the concept of narcissism to include the libido invested in the whole organism and not only that invested in the *ego structure*. One would adopt, as it were, an egomorphic concept of the whole organism, including the physiological organism and the id, and the very topographical (structural) concept of the mind would be lost.

Mental contents which form the dream only partially awaken the ego, the dreaming ego, and sometimes awaken it only to some of its former states. Many old and recent memories, the ego's rational capacity, and other functions may remain dormant. Federn's discovery that ego states can be repressed is also proved by the fact that they can be rearoused in dreams. Much attention has been given by Federn to the dreaming ego. In waking life, mental and bodily ego cannot be easily distinguished because they are permanently inherent in the ego. Conversely, in retrospect one can recognize that in most dreams one's body was not felt. Just as many ego functions were not awakened in the dream, one's body was not awakened. In waking life a bodiless ego feeling would be a dreadful sensation. Nevertheless, some affects, and the will, can arouse certain bodily sensations even in the dream, although too strong or too persistent bodily feelings put an end to the state of sleep. But usually the dreaming ego passively perceives its dreams, while the will is, in Federn's opinion, the very concentration of active ego cathexis toward an action or a thought, and not a mere "foreknowledge" of the action, thought, or planning that is going to occur.

Dreams during general anesthesia are especially apt to prove the distinction between mental and bodily ego, since the body cannot be awakened. The feeling of one's identity concerns only the mental ego, since upon awakening one feels oneself to be the same as during dreaming. In dreams with complete absence of bodily ego feelings, some dream figures always represent some parts or states of the dreamer's own ego. Such portions or situations of the ego, remaining excluded from the dreaming ego, which has retracted boundaries, appear as external objects; that is, they are projected on dream persons. As early as the *Interpretation of Dreams,* Freud had recognized that some dream persons must be interpreted as the dreamer's ego or part of it.

Among the functions of the ego, Federn acutely analyzed that of conceptual or abstract thinking, a function which, as Kurt Goldstein and other psychiatrists observed, is impaired in schizophrenia. Federn characterizes the psychopathology of schizophrenia as a narcissistic disturbance *not* because of an *increase,* but rather a *deficiency, of ego libido.* Ego weakness is due to deficiency of ego cathexis resources, of which the ego libido plays the most important role. Federn asserts that the dreaming and the schizophrenic egos are both weak. There is a dynamic deficiency; the reduced ego cathexis in the schizophrenic thus leads to a devastation of all kinds of mental functions and to the characteristic psychotic quality of mental production. Federn does not share Freud's opinion that delusions and hallucinations constitute restitution phenomena for the loss of emotional contact with the world of objects. He observed hallucinations and delusions in his patients long before they withdrew object cathexis. In his opinion, these phenomena result from veritable lesions of the ego, and are not attempts at restitution. As is the case with the dreaming ego, they are due to a lack of cathexis at the ego boundary, wherefore fusion of false and actual reality ensues. This fusion is only one of the reasons for the impairment of the patient's thinking function. In addition, deficiency of ego cathexis also deprives him of the ability to use one of his most important tools: controlled conceptual thinking.

Abstract concepts are formed from elements common to various experience situations, that is, to different ego states. These elements must be isolated, sensed, recognized as such, and purified from all other additional contents of the concrete ego states which were their source. For this process of isolation and purification a certain amount of energy—specifically, ego cathexis—is employed. Therefore, deficiency of ego cathexis deprives the individual of the ability to think of *a* tree, *a* house, or *a* table; he will be able to reproduce in his mind only the memory of concrete, really seen trees, houses, and tables.

When there is a deficiency of ego cathexis, a highly developed and organized ego cannot maintain adequate cathexis of all its boundaries, and it is therefore exposed to invasion by the unegotized unconscious. In such a case, regression to an earlier ego state, requiring less expenditure of ego cathexis, can be used as a defense against false realities. Upon return to a former ego state, the boundaries will be reduced in extent to those of that state, but as such they will be intact. Invasion by false realities, regression to former ego states, and loss of the ability for abstract thinking are the main pathological features of schizophrenia.

Not only does the "mental apparatus" as a whole present a mental structure, but so also does the ego itself, which Freud and other analysts considered an "organ" of the total personality. When speaking of ego strength and weakness, therefore, one should indicate which specific ego functions are impaired. True, there are cases of a general ego weakness which lead to complete disintegration of the ego in all its functions. But in most cases some ego functions are strong while others are weak. The process of identification is an ego function; all kinds of defenses—the capacity for controlling drives, for postponing and renouncing gratification, for maintaining the ego boundaries at a sufficient strength—require specific dynamic exertions. So does thinking, and, in particular, conceptual or abstract thinking. An example of a specific structural weakness of the ego is presented by certain paranoic patients who have a defective sense of reality, due to a weakly cathected inner ego boundary, while at the same time they may be very good thinkers. Reality testing would be very efficient if it were used by such patients in order to discriminate between real and unreal.

Paul Federn's illuminating studies of the functional patterns of the ego lead, through their dynamic and economic implications, to a new orientation in the treatment of psychotic patients. While the neurosis expresses, for the most part, the ego's defense against ego-alien impulses, whereby the ego integration as such is maintained, the psychosis represents a defeat of the ego.

Once this concept is acknowledged, the guiding principle in dealing with psychotic patients becomes to help them to conserve mental energy and not to waste it. The deficiency of ego cathexis can be due either to lack in its supply or to its uneconomic apportionment. The patient's positive transference to the therapist, who must affectionately dedicate himself to the patient's problems, is even more important than it is in the classical method of psychoanalysis with neurotic patients. In the treatment of psychotics only the positive transference, which should not be interpreted to the patient, can be used, and every kind of negative transference should be avoided. Complete sincerity toward the patient is imperative; under no circumstance should he be deceived. In addition, he should be helped to solve the impending problem of his current life with the aid, not only of the therapist, but mainly of his family and of a disciplined environment. No treatment of psychotics can be successful without a skilled woman helper, a mother or sister figure. A mother transference of a psychotic patient on the male therapist confuses him, because he is unable to distinguish this feeling from a homosexual one.

In dealing with the patient's unconscious and his resistances, one must proceed in a way opposite to that adopted in the analysis of neurotic patients. The broken down counter-cathexes of the psychotic patient must be re-established; resistances must be encouraged; repressions should not be lifted but produced. Too much unconscious material has already invaded the psychotic ego, more than it can deal with. Every sort of claim must be lowered, emotional hardship must be reduced, and so far as possible the patient must be released from responsibilities.

It is imperative not to take the anamnesis, the history, of a psychotic patient, since the memories of former psychotic episodes may produce a relapse.

Psychotic patients are often very accessible to explanations of their psychotic mechanisms. In the case of recently arisen delusions, the therapist can often succeed in strengthening the patient's weakened ego boundary between the mental and the real, thus enabling him to rectify his "false reality." The method consists in inducing the patient to make correct use of the omitted reality testing. One helps him to recognize the data which he actually perceived, as distinct from the data which were distorted or added to account for the facts he falsely sensed as real.

I hope that this brief clarifying summary of Paul Federn's original contributions to ego psychology, and their therapeutic use, will better prepare the reader to follow his expositions, which are very rich in content but are often complex and not always easy to comprehend at one's first approach. It always takes time and needs repetition to extend one's ego boundaries over new concepts, thus assimilating them with what has already an integrated position in one's store of knowledge.

The reader, as he progresses through this volume, will note certain repetitive material. Such repetition can be avoided in a single unified manuscript, but is inevitable in a book of collected papers. Yet, as I have just said and as Federn himself notes, repetition is a prerequisite for achieving complete egotization of new concepts. Furthermore, each new paper has its own wealth of content and connotation, so that even those quite familiar with Federn's basic concepts will find ample reward for their attentive reading. To read Federn is indeed an adventure in understanding.

PART I

ON EGO PSYCHOLOGY

1

SOME VARIATIONS IN EGO FEELING

The manifold self-experiences in waking life and dreams are described. The distinction between the bodily and the mental (psychic) ego feelings is clarified, and the relationship between the bodily ego feeling and Schilder's "body scheme" is outlined.—E. W.

Until the advent of psychoanalysis all psychology was psychology of the ego. A raising or lowering of ego feeling was included, although called by other names, among the common emotions. Since psychiatrists have turned their attention to the phenomena of depersonalization, there have been numerous investigations of disturbances of ego feeling. In his work on self-consciousness, consciousness of the personality and the somatic organization, Schilder in particular has described this condition in some detail, but he has been concerned mainly with its manifestations in grave pathological conditions. The present communication deals with certain states bordering on normality, and is based on my own self-observation and on the self-observations communicated to me by patients.

All definitions of the ego come to grief owing to the fact that they represent the ego as a distinct entity, something opposed to external reality. "Ego feeling" can be described as the feeling of bodily and mental relations in respect to time and content, the relation being regarded as an uninterrupted or a restored unity.

Concerning the time relation, we know from Freud that for

the Ucs time does not exist. In so far as we can recall dream experiences by self-observation, the "dream ego" very rarely has any feeling of its unity in time, although this is not invariably absent. Nevertheless, events occurring in dreams are felt to follow some chronological order. This does not contradict Freud's view, since in dreams the system Cs is to some extent awake. When in waking life the feeling of unity in the ego in regard to time is absent, there arises the well-recognized condition of depersonalization (also of *déjà-vu*). Whereas normally the present is regarded as existing somewhere between the future and the past, in such states the present is constantly experienced as beginning *de novo*. This depends on ego feeling and not on the faculty for perceiving the passage of time, since time orientation still persists.

As regards content, we can distinguish in the ego a mental from a bodily ego feeling. The phrase *cogito ergo sum* is a rational formulation of mental ego-feeling. Since Freud has differentiated the superego and defined its unconscious components more clearly, many psychoanalysts have tended to regard this distinction as a mere formulation or construction, linking together several already recognized institutions in the ego exercising a censoring function. Self-observation shows that in every case of mental conflict there are distinct ego feelings associated respectively with the ego and with the superego which can be distinguished from one another. (An accurate description of these ego feelings has not yet been published.) In some cases, the ego feeling associated with the superego is purely mental and without any body content. This is in keeping with the fact that normally the superego has no approach to motility. It does not seem to apply to melancholia, which accounts for the closer association of suicide with this disease than with other forms of depression of equal intensity. Moreover, we can tell from self-observation that the superego has no direct access to volition, but is able to inhibit it and can influence the voluntary direction of attention. All this may not, however, be the same in other people, and doubtless it would be possible to discover differences in this form of ego feeling. As far as obsessive impulses, thoughts, or ideas derive from the superego, like all compulsions they are accompanied by a feeling which varies according to the intensity of the unconscious cathexis, that is, the feeling that they are almost on the verge of motor discharge, although without actually attaining it. Their accentuated motor character and, with thoughts, intentional character bring about an increase of inhibitions and feelings having an opposite tendency, and stimulate a constant anxiety lest the ideas should really be carried into action.

On the other hand, the ego feeling belonging to the ego, as distinct from the superego, has access to motility and to the bodily sensations of the ego. In view of the fact that, in the neuroses, mental processes can be projected (using the word in an extended sense) into the body, i.e., "converted," whilst in the psychoses they can be projected (in the usual sense) outside the body into the external world, we can describe the mental ego as an "inner ego," thereby adopting a topographical point of view which has, of course, no immediate connection with the topography of levels of consciousness.

The bodily ego feeling is a compound feeling including all motor and sensory memories concerning one's own person. It is not, however, identical with these memories, but represents rather a unified feeling of libido cathexes of the motor and sensory apparatus. The bodily ego feeling is not identical with the somatic organization, with the unity of correctly ordered perceptions of one's own body. The one can disappear without involving the other. The bodily ego feeling could be regarded as a part of the mental ego feeling, and any distinction drawn between the two as useful only for simplicity of presentation. This view is contradicted, however, by observations of states in which the two are quite distinct. This occurs in the case of the "dream ego" and also in loss of consciousness, falling asleep, and waking up. Scherner, the most acute observer of dream-manifestations before Freud, described these states, using a terminology which nowadays sounds unfamiliar.

The simplest process is that where a person in a somnolent condition suddenly falls into a dreamless sleep without hypnagogic symptoms. Here the intensity of all ego feeling is almost at once reduced to zero. This must be emphasized, since Freud's description of sleep as a narcissistic state might give rise to the misunderstanding that the ego is specially invested with narcissistic libido during sleep. All that he implies is that the libido in the Ucs is turned to more narcissistic account, although not exclusively. The fact that displacements, withdrawal of libido, and fresh cathexes in the Ucs also concern object representations, shows that these are occasionally completely altered after a short dreamless sleep. We could be more certain of this if it were possible to demonstrate the dreamlessness of a state of sleep.

However that may be, it is usually possible to observe that in a withdrawal of cathexes with sudden falling asleep, bodily ego feeling disappears sooner than mental ego feeling or superego feeling. The body ego (for the sake of brevity I shall sometimes use the term "ego" instead of "ego feeling") can disappear entirely while falling asleep and can be freshly invested and awakened by the "mental" ego which has remained awake. In this way, we can succeed in postponing sleep voluntarily. It is probable that with most people who fall asleep suddenly, the superego loses cathexis before the ego. Even when the superego has disappeared, the ego may, as the result of some memory or an external stimulus and with a perceptible feeling of voluntary effort, recathect the body ego. Only then do bodily innervations appear; movement precedes the return of the body ego only in the case of waking up in terror.

Similar to the normal process of rapid falling asleep, there exists a normal process of waking which occurs, apparently, spontaneously and unaccompanied by awakening dreams, through external and somatic stimuli, including those of inner rhythm. The body ego and the mental ego awaken almost simultaneously. At the same time, one can often observe a certain precedence of mental ego feeling unaccompanied by any feeling of strangeness. We rediscover ourselves at the beginning of a new day. The superego awakens as a rule only after the ego.

On the other hand, even when we wake up from a dream, it is possible to distinguish very clearly between the body ego and the mental ego (a particular example of this will be adduced later). Awakening dreams arise partly from bodily or external stimuli and partly from the superego. When we dream that we have finished some disagreeable task, or that we have looked at the time only to find that it is too late to do anything effective, the ego will nevertheless successfully protect itself from the superego by waking up in time. On the other hand, when a person whose identity relates to superego control appears in a dream at the moment of waking, or when the dreamer is reminded in a dream of the duties awaiting him, the superego has been in time and has regained cathexis first.

In an attack of fainting, where the loss of consciousness occurs gradually, the distinction between body ego and mental ego is clearer than in falling asleep. Here the body ego is felt to slip away from one and slide downwards in the strangest manner; sometimes the distal extremities go before the proximal parts; for a short space of time the mental ego alone is felt in a definite way, an experience which never occurs under any other conditions. It may be that it accompanies states of ecstasy and is responsible for the self-evident dualistic conviction of the separate existence of body and soul. The ascension-myth is a projected representation of such experiences. A completely opposite condition is found in states of extreme mental fatigue where bodily ego feeling alone is present.

In gradual falling asleep, both ego feelings are present, and hypnagogic manifestations lead gradually to the dream state. Here the mental and the body ego undergo varying modifications which remind us of waking states of a similar kind. During a state of somnolence, the pleasure principle overcomes the reality principle in the mental ego. Many people invariably fall asleep in the midst of wish phantasies. These become more active because the regression to centrifugal cathexis of sensory function gives rise to the well-known hypnagogic visions; more attention is directed to vegetative processes; motility and volition recede. Hence, falling asleep is disturbed by any thought which involves the reality principle, by external sensory stimuli which tend towards centripetal cathexis of sensory function, and, in the last resort, by processes of the vegetative organs of so slight an intensity that they pass unobserved during waking life. These modifications correspond to another mental ego feeling, the ego feeling of the child. The fact that many individuals, as they grow older, find it more difficult to fall asleep is largely due to increasing difficulty in relinquishing the reality principle.

Phantasies which formerly enabled them to fall asleep have lost their pleasurable character; these people are no longer childish, nor can they express childish wishes.

Regression to the childish stage of bodily ego feeling is less familiar to us. We may assume that the child's original ego feeling extended only to sensations arising from the less vegetative erotogenic zones, whereas bodily ego feeling similar to that of the adult is gradually developed later. This adult ego feeling corresponds to Schilder's somatic organization. Normally, all ego feeling extends to the whole body. In gradual falling asleep, however, the body ego regresses to the stage when the various parts of the body first came to be included in the ego.

This regression proceeds in very different ways. The body ego often completely loses all dimensional sense: it becomes warped and distorted in every direction. The most bizarre representations of modern portraiture can be observed on oneself when falling asleep: the symmetrical parts of the body often appear of unequal length, or spatial dimensions become entirely out of proportion. If two or three parts of the body are correctly apperceived, the rest becomes a more or less vague mass, magnified or reduced on one side of these parts, or lying round them. The planes of the body are displaced in every direction. Occasionally the modification is simply in the nature of curtailing: the bodily ego feeling may go no farther than the trunk or down to the knees, or middle parts of the body may lose bodily ego feeling. Frequently the body loses outline in some direction, and one feels instead a movement of these parts in this direction which is not transmitted to the body as a whole. Here we have an actual loss of ego boundaries.

The bodily ego feeling relating to the face and head remains unaffected by these modifications longest of all. The parts of the body acting as supports in the recumbent position are also more stable, although these too can be involved in the disappearance of bodily feeling. It was not a coincidence when a patient who fell asleep with the feeling that his skull had become enlarged in one direction experienced, on the following day, a feeling of depersonalization precisely in regard to his voice, i.e., an auditory sense of strangeness.

The modifications of bodily ego feeling we have described are not associated with any feeling of strangeness. They do not attract our attention unless we direct attention to them, and if we do observe them, we feel certain that we need only direct more attention to the bodily shape. Sometimes we need only make the slightest movement, in order to dispel the illusion. This exercise of will, to be sure, prevents us from falling asleep, but normally it restores the entire body ego. We are unable to say whether similar distortions of the body ego exist in childhood during the process of its formation.

When the body ego habitually becomes unstable in this way in people who fall asleep with difficulty, the remarkable fact can be observed that erotically significant zones or parts are more resistant than others and they are more resistant with these individuals than with others. For example, a person with a marked degree of oral libido does not lose the bodily feeling of the mouth; a patient who in his youth had had a strong interest in exhibiting his buttocks, and several masochists for whom the back was of erotic significance, retained the cathexis of these erotically important parts of the body. In an analogous way, the fact that in everyone the subjective body feeling of the face is least modified can be accounted for by its strong libidinal cathexis.

In the case of delayed falling asleep, we are unable to say whether hypnagogic visions and hypnagogic modifications of ego feeling are always continued into a dream when sleep finally comes, because the memory of the falling asleep dream does not last until the following morning. In normal persons we seldom hear of dreams in which distortion of the bodily ego feeling occurs. Such dreams have their special significance.

On the other hand, even when the dream ego has a definite bodily contour, it is generally less complete than that of the whole body ego. If we refrain from influencing the subject and ask him to draw the dream scenes, the complete figure of the dreamer is seldom sketched; frequently it is only vaguely indicated, perhaps only by the head or bust. In most instances the dreamer only indicates where he stood; sometimes he doesn't even know that. (Skilled draughtsmen are very willing to complete the figure of themselves in the interests of secondary elaboration, and we have to explain to them the origin of this impulse.) At all events we see that the dream ego has very often an incomplete bodily feeling. In other cases, however, this is quite complete, often indeed accentuated. In such dreams the feeling of well-being is frequently very marked.

In dreams with characteristic sensations, painful as well as pleasant, the bodily feeling is always increased, but often incomplete. It is both accentuated and complete in flying and swimming dreams, which are accompanied with a marked feeling of well-being. There are, however, dreams with a similar content without any feeling of well-being and with only a vaguely outlined body ego. If the latter is entirely absent, the dream cannot be given the customary interpretation. In anxiety and inhibition dreams, bodily ego feeling is always marked but is often concentrated in special parts of the body. Since these dreams are quite typical and are repeated in the same person without any alteration, it is easy to note any variation in the accompanying ego feeling.

As further evidence that the extent of the bodily ego feeling in dreams is determined by the erotic constitution, a typical dream of a masochistic person who had a special liking for exhibiting his legs is worthy of mention. It was that characteristic form of flying dream which consists of floating downstairs, but in this case only the lower extremities were represented in the body ego. In normal persons we seldom hear of dreams in which distortion of the bodily feeling occurs. Such dreams have their special significance.

In contrast to such dreams in which bodily ego feeling is more marked than in waking life, the majority of remembered dreams have a complete lack of any body feeling. The "dream ego" is in such instances the mental ego only. The libido which has been withdrawn from the body on falling asleep, or rather has retreated into the id, has not been redirected to the body ego. The regression leading up to the dream meets with object presentations and activates them to the point of reality, and often beyond that point; yet in spite of the most vivid dreaming, the dreamer feels nothing of his own body. Preservation of his identity and the feeling of it depends on mental ego feeling. The dream character of dreaming in these instances lies precisely in this absence of bodily ego feeling. The fact that patients describe their states of depersonalization as "dreamlike" relates to this defect in bodily ego feeling.

The vividness of isolated dream elements depends on concentration of libido cathexis by condensation, as Freud has stated. Dreams which are remembered as complete and specially vivid can be divided into two groups. In one of these it is observed that the element of personal participation is accentuated, the affect is marked, the body ego is clear, and often vivid sensations of a typical sort are present, whereas the accessories and setting are often merely suggested, colourless, and transient or hardly tangible. In the second group, on the other hand, the representation of these latter elements is unusually vivid. Clear and detailed pictures of town or country appear as large as in a panorama, brightly lit up, and the actors too are sharply defined. In this group the bodily ego feeling is often entirely absent or is limited to the head or lower limbs. It would appear that the libidinal cathexis is insufficient for both object presentations and the body, consequently either mental or bodily ego feeling must be deficient in dreams; if both were fully invested, the dreamer would wake.

A patient who did not suffer from depersonalization in waking life has reported to me a remarkable example of the distinction between the mental and the bodily ego. He had an unusually complete and vivid sexual dream with very vivid object presentation and ego feeling of a pleasurable sexual nature. The dream was enacted in his bedroom but not in his bed. He woke up suddenly and found himself in bed in a state of complete depersonalization; he felt that his body was lying beside him and that it did not belong to him. His mental ego awakened first. Bodily ego feeling had not awakened along with the mental ego because the libido available for narcissistic use is essential for the awakening of bodily ego feeling, and in the foregoing dream all the libido had invested the very vivid presentation of the object. This unusual occurrence clearly shows that cathexis of the ego stands in a compensatory relation to cathexis of a sexual object.

It is easy to understand that in dreams where bodily ego feeling is present, the dreamer is represented by himself, and only fragmentary objects or allusions to them by other figures can come into the dream. In dreams with complete absence of bodily ego feeling, some figure in the dream always represents the dreamer's ego; this shows that to the mental ego the body ego always constitutes one element of the dream, even if it is not experienced in person.

We have given above so many examples of the variations and limitations of ego feeling in dreams of normal persons, that we cannot be surprised to find similar conditions in their waking life. In all conditions of extreme fatigue, especially where the person is prevented from falling asleep only by external forces and interests, bodily ego feeling loses some of its intensity and extent. It is often concentrated solely in the fatigued parts of the body. In all depressions following fatigue the bodily ego becomes incomplete.

This applies also to every endogenous or exogenous depression and to melancholic depression: in the intervals of anxiety neuroses, disturbed bodily ego feeling is present. It is frequently limited to the head and face. It requires, however, only an effort of will to bring back the entire bodily feeling. Some activity will bring this about, or a conversation with some second person, or even meeting someone, especially if he does not belong to the accustomed milieu. Real depersonalization, on the contrary, commences just when the subject is alone, or feels lonely on meeting with strangers or in social situations which are not flattering to his vanity. The slight disturbances of ego feeling we have described differ from states of depersonalization, first, in that in depersonalization the reduced body ego cannot be invested with more libido, and secondly, in that, when the attempt is automatically made to do this, perception of an object arouses in the patient a feeling of strangeness. The variations we have described are hardly ever noticed spontaneously; depression varying in degree and often quite slight is present, but no strangeness is felt, and the complete body ego can always be recovered. In certain prodromal states of schizophrenia, however, limitation of the body ego is experienced spontaneously, and the patient complains that in spite of vigorous efforts of will it cannot be extended, although he has nevertheless no feeling of strangeness.

Persons who find when falling asleep that special parts of the body resist limitation of the body ego, particularly those parts invested by component sexual instincts, also show similar peculiarities in waking life by analogous variations in their ego feeling. When extreme cases of perversion are required to observe their body ego, even when not actively engaged in sexual practices, one finds that the erotogenic zones are permanently accentuated in their bodily ego feeling. There is a striking contrast in the ego feeling of sadists and of masochists: in the former, the organ of cohabitation is included in the body ego; in the latter it is excluded. In extreme cases of sado-masochism, ego feeling swings in alternate directions. The mental ego feeling of sadists also includes genito-sexual feeling: with masochists the latter is felt only in a bodily way and as outside the ego.

All these manifestations can be explained by reference to the development of ego feeling. Mental ego feeling, corresponding to inner perceptions, is the first to be experienced by the child; ego feeling related to the body and to perceptions conveyed through the body comes only gradually. Thereafter, the feeling of cathexis of object presentations is distinguished from that of cathexis of the body itself, and at the same time the perceptual content of the external world is differentiated from that of the body. The appearance of any new part of what is later ego feeling in its entirety represents one fixation point in development, the most important of which is the distinction between body ego and mental ego. When violent separation from the body occurs, as in temporary loss of consciousness, the ego feeling regresses to this fixation point. Partial regressions are also seen in the waking state as the result of libido frustration, which in turn gives rise to states of depression. In complete depersonalization, ego feeling regresses permanently to this fixation point.

In most instances, ego feeling regresses to stages of development at which the various organs of bodily perception are gradually incorporated into the ego, and as the body ego becomes consolidated, ego feeling becomes more and more complete. My view of the cause of depersonalization is, accordingly, as follows: when external objects are perceived by means of organs, all or part of which have not yet been included in the body ego, such objects are regarded as strange. This is not because the object is recognized with more difficulty, but because the object has impinged on a part of the ego boundary which has not been invested with narcissistic libido. All cases of depersonalization complain that they can neither "get at" the object nor can the object "get at" them.

This also accounts for the fact, first observed by Nunberg and confirmed by me in every case, that symptoms of depersonalization are present in every transference neurosis. When deprivation of the object occurs suddenly, object libido is withdrawn from the object, and narcissistic libido is withdrawn—at any rate temporarily—from the part of the ego boundary concerned with its perception. As a rule, in the transference neuroses this narcissistic libido cathexis is soon renewed. In obsessional neurosis the ego boundaries, if we are sufficiently familiar with the fixation points, can probably be found in the mental ego feeling. In conversion hysteria they are to be found between the body ego and the mental ego.

The distinction between mental and bodily ego feeling, the fact that either one or the other retains libidinal cathexis in dreams, and, lastly, the fact that bodily ego feeling is most marked in dreams with typical sensations, enable us to understand the mechanism of conversion. Here a libido cathected process in the Ucs regresses to a fixation point between the mental and the body ego and is projected from this into the body ego. But where projection of bodily processes into the external world occurs (a regular occurrence in dreams and a permanent symptom in the waking life of psychotics), regression breaks down the boundary between the feeling of the body ego and the perception of objects. It might be said that many apparently healthy people work off their conversion neuroses during sleep by means of typical bodily dream sensations. In a similar way, an anxiety neurosis can be discharged in anxiety dreams.

We can understand many cases of depersonalization by paying attention to the variations of the body ego. It is probable that all of the numerous stages of depersonalization can be traced to some fixation point or other in the development of ego feeling.

The variations of ego feeling we have detailed above constitute a territory in which the dynamic conception of the mind is confirmed almost entirely by means of self-observation of the outflow and withdrawal of *libidinal* cathexes. It is striking how clearly the identity of the narcissistic cathexis of the ego and of sexual energy appears. Variations in ego feeling are endopsychic symptoms which can be investigated by means of psychoanalysis and are amenable to psychoanalytic treatment.

2

NARCISSISM IN THE STRUCTURE

OF THE EGO *

Through an accurate study of ego disturbances such as deper-
sonalization and estrangement—which are caused by the invest-
ment of excessive amounts of object libido at the expense of
ego libido, by deficiency of the latter without that of the former—
a clear separation of ego libido from object libido is achieved.
The actual existence of narcissism is thus verified; it is nor-
mally felt in the healthy bodily ego feeling, which is absent
or altered in states of estrangement. Libidinal conditions at both
the core and the periphery of the ego in various emotional
states are discussed from the dynamic, the economic, and the
*topographic points of view.—*E. W.

Although the disturbances which I propose to consider are experienced in a mild transient form even by healthy people
from time to time, disturbances which you yourselves have all
shared, I fancy that you have not paid them much attention.
For they are not striking, and it was only a particular occasion
that led me to take that path of inquiry along which I am
asking you to accompany me. You will probably feel an inner
resistance against this, for we would all rather leave untouched
our own undisturbed ego feeling, that precondition of all happiness. Because of this resistance, the observation of the components of the ego has been ignored by those authors who
would see in the ego only an abstraction of the distinction be-

. . . .

* Read before the Tenth International Psychoanalytical Congress, Inns-
bruck, September 1, 1927.

tween subject and object, and also by those who have attributed to the ego a "homogeneous wholeness," so that for them the term "ego" was almost synonymous with the old term— "the soul."

Consequently, psychoanalysis must disown both these conceptions. The structure of the ego, i.e., its division into institutions, the dynamics of these, their relation to the instincts, to the unconscious, even to the body, occupies us all. Here lies the test of Freud's theory of narcissism: Does the libido merely actuate the ego, or does it build it up?

I

One might have expected that, even if the observation of our own mild disturbances did not prompt us to the psychoanalytic investigation of the ego, nevertheless those severe cases of illness, depersonalization and estrangement, which long ago aroused the interest of psychiatrists, would have done so. They have been treated extensively in the writings of Janet and Schilder. These distinguished works, however, were written without any acknowledgment or application of the libido theory. It is only recently that psychoanalysts have attempted to apply this theory in order to explain depersonalization. It is my aim here to test the libido theory on this task, and by this test to demonstrate its correctness anew.

And here I take my stand on Nunberg's work. From his psychoanalytic observations he has conclusively proved that depersonalization and estrangement originate in the loss of an important libido object, in the traumatic effect of the withdrawal of the libido. Nunberg has also drawn attention to the ubiquity of these disturbances in the beginning of neuroses. I myself go still further and believe that all psychoses and neuroses are preceded by a disturbance of the ego in the form of estrangement, but that, for the most part, this has disappeared by the time a neurosis or psychosis has been established, for it has often occurred in early childhood and has been forgotten. Moreover, it is not always recollected during analysis, especially as psychoanalysts so far have not paid it sufficient attention. Thus, our experience that the initial disturbance of the ego cannot in every case be proved, must not prevent us from assuming its ubiquity. I hope that further inquiry will succeed in demonstrating its occurrence as essential to the libido theory.

Now, since the frequency of its occurrence is unquestioned, I have previously described "estrangement" as the most frequent "transitory narcissistic actual psychosis." [1] I wish to justify this nomenclature. First of all, I will draw your attention to the fact that this nomenclature involves me in a certain opposition to Nunberg's discovery that we are concerned with an injury to the ego through the withdrawal of the object libido from an object, for I have in mind a direct actual disturbance of the narcissistic libido. This divergence brings into relief the most important fact from which my further conclusions proceed: We are not concerned with distinguishing the ego libido from the object libido only theoretically, but with marking off their limits by means of observation.

From our practice and from the literature on the subject, we all know the earnest, and always somewhat uncanny, complaints with which severe cases of depersonalization describe their condition, or rather their changing conditions. The outer world appears substantially unaltered, but yet different: not so spontaneously, so actually, near or far; not clear, warm, friendly, and familiar; not really and truly existing and alive; more as if in a dream and yet different from a dream. At heart the patient feels as if he were dead; and he feels like this because he does not feel. His feeling, wishing, thinking, and memory processes have become different, uncertain, intolerably changed. And yet the patient knows everything correctly, his faculties of perception, of intellect, and of logic have not suffered at all. He knows, too, how his capacity for feeling is diminished. As Schilder, using a term of Husserl, so rightly says: "The evidence" (or "le sentiment du réel," as Janet plastically calls it) is lacking. In still more severe cases even the unity of the ego has become doubtful; in its continuity the ego is only perceived, not felt. Time, place, and causality are

. . . .

[1] "The Most Frequent Narcissistic Psychosis," a paper read before the Hungarian Psychoanalytic Association on Feb. 19, 1927.

recognized and properly applied to finding one's bearings, but they are not possessed spontaneously and self-evidently. It is only in the very worst cases that the core of the ego, which Hermann rightly pointed out is connected with the sense of equilibrium, is lost.

With cases of average severity, there are more of those who complain only of estrangement of the outer world than of those who have also lost the evidence for their affects and the rest of their inner life. Now, applying the libido theory, we should assume that where the self-evident experiencing of the outer world has been lost—object libido is lacking; contrariwise, where the ego feeling and the inner life have been disturbed—narcissistic libido is lacking.[2]

I have found this assumption to be incorrect. For we learn from our patients that in every case of estrangement, even in those which are supposed to be exclusively external, the ego feeling is disturbed. It is true that the patients themselves do not notice this. Indeed, that portion of the ego feeling is disturbed which I have described in my communication about the variations in ego feeling as bodily ego feeling. This compares with the "body scheme" discovered by Schilder, as "evidential experience" perception. The corporal ego feeling is the evidential sensation of the whole body, not only of its weight (as Schilder and Hartmann found), but also of its size, extension, and sense of fullness. This feeling, always a characteristic one, indeed our most characteristic one, we pay no attention to at all, not even when it is disturbed. However, once one's attention has been drawn to a change in this sensation (e.g., after a state of fatigue), the healthy person no less than the patient is easily in a position to distinguish and pursue its variations. I myself discovered this when, several years ago, I wished to observe how ego cathexes are withdrawn from the body and

. . . .

[2] We are not concerned here with what happened to it in a particular case, whether and whither it was withdrawn, whether it has disappeared or been transformed, any more than we are with the pathological conditions in which the estrangement takes place, that is to say, the previous history of the estranged ego. My inquiry is not concerned with the clinical picture of estrangement, but only with the diagnosis, the phenomenology, and the theory of its dynamics.

mind at the time of falling asleep. Those who have lost the happy capacity for going off to sleep at once like a child, or those who are ready from time to time to deny themselves in this respect, will confirm the fact that the corporal ego feeling is subject in this connection to simple or complex alterations.

With the help of this piece of knowledge let us return to our cases of estrangement of the outer world. We find that with them the bodily ego feeling, this psychical representation of the bodily ego boundary, is always disturbed during the estrangement. It is then no longer coterminous with the correct "body scheme."

Now, diminutions and distortions of the bodily ego feeling often occur, even in a state of complete wakefulness, in people when they are not in a very good mood, although they do not suffer from estrangement and consider themselves perfectly healthy. They are very frequent in so-called neurasthenia. The disturbance vanishes, however, as soon as attention is drawn to the representation of the total configuration of the body, which happens of its own accord when movements are intended or carried out. Then the complete bodily feeling is immediately restored. The whole symptom appears so harmless that it may seem to you not even significant enough for conclusions to be drawn from it. But, in spite of its harmlessness, it is not vague, it is surprisingly precise. If, for example, a neurasthenic's ego feeling ends at his armpits due to fatigue, when he presses his arms to his breast, the latter, quite remarkably appears to him too narrow, although he perceives and knows how broad his thorax is. I have been able to produce in myself a still odder feeling when, through work and lack of sleep, I have felt the bodily ego feeling of my head disturbed. In such a state, when I clasp my skull with my hands, in spite of my perception of the hard bone between the outstretched fingers, I feel as if it was without extension.[3]

I found that with those suffering from estrangement of the outer world the bodily ego feeling is not only temporarily lacking, limited, or diminished, it is unadjusted by half an

. . . .

[3] Such symptoms are even of practical importance because, being the earliest failure of the ego feeling, they warn one not to go on overtiring oneself.

hour's sleep and it obstinately remains in a state of disturbance. Nor can it be restored solely by drawing attention to it, or by movement, so long as the estrangement lasts. These particulars can be obtained quite exactly from those suffering from estrangement, for introspection is a constant necessity for these patients. This has caused some authors wrongly to explain the estrangement itself by the increased introspection, or, as Hesnard has recently done, by an increase of narcissism. In contradistinction to this, my explanation emphasizes the reduction of narcissistic cathexis.

Hence we have arrived at the firm conviction that the evidence of the bodily ego boundary must be retained in order that the outer world may remain evident. We possess therefore—quite apart from Freud's reality test, through which the outer world is recognized by its independence of the ego by means of search and comparison—a permanent evidential feeling of the outer world which originates in the fact that impressions from the outer world pass a bodily ego boundary charged with a particular quality of sensation and bodily ego feeling. The psychical representation of the bodily ego boundary, the evidential feeling of the same, is sometimes lacking only for parts of it, e.g., for the legs when walking, or for the organs of hearing, sight, or taste. Mild stages which represent simply a deadening of an ego boundary can still be overcome by exertion. This exertion accompanies the reality test so familiar to us, and the evidential feeling is restored simultaneously with it. The normal person with a completely healthy ego, on the contrary, uninterruptedly possesses his full feeling for bodily boundaries which permanently and unobtrusively demarcates the outer world.

From all this we are led to the certain conclusion that the estrangement of the outer world consists in a disturbance of the ego periphery in relation to a feeling cathexis. This must be distinguished from the cathexis of objects. In particular, this peripheral ego feeling is by no means identical with the sense of touch and the other sense functions. Many authors have established in great detail the fact that all these functions have remained intact even in the most severe cases of estrangement.

Nunberg's observations have already shown us that this cathexis of the bodily ego boundaries is libidinal in its nature.

I, too, have definitely been able to ascertain, just as Nunberg stated some time ago without mentioning ego cathexis, the direct connection between the origin and disappearance of the peripheral ego cathexis and actual sexual processes. I will here give some examples from my experience.

For two years I observed and analyzed daily a case of estrangement of the outer world which was temporarily extremely severe. It turned out that my patient always reacted to his sexual claims by losing the corporal ego feeling. In addition, his lasting condition of estrangement had begun after a period of excessive sexual indulgence. (Numbers of such cases, moreover, are to be found in nonpsychoanalytical literature, though the authors do not assign to them the importance that is their due.) This case supplied me with a quite special proof of the derivation from sexuality of the cathexis of bodily ego feeling. This patient recollected the former evidential feeling of the bodily periphery in his bath quite well, but had now entirely lost it. However, during occasional masturbation in the bath, the full bodily ego feeling was restored, only to be succeeded by more intense estrangement as sexual tension was eased.

A convincing proof of another kind was a dream of which I have already given particulars. It is quite peculiar because it ended with a very high degree of temporary estrangement of the bodily ego. The man dreamed very vividly, and in an unusually intense sexual way, that he had coitus outside his bed with a strongly desired sexual object. The whole process was described by the dreamer as the most vivid dream he ever remembered. One may say that all the libido aroused during sleep had become object libido. This use of the libido was retained for a short while in waking, for he awoke from the dream (this gives renewed interest to the problem of awaking from dreams), and then he felt himself aware only of the awakened mental ego feeling, while the bodily ego feeling in the periphery and depths was at first completely lacking. It was an uncanny experience; beside him in the bed lay his body, and he himself felt as though still with the loved sexual object, whose absence he felt with surprise and regret. If we picture to ourselves continuous states of this kind, we get some idea of that degree of estrangement in which all narcissistic cathexis of the bodily ego is lacking. Similar conditions are reported of narcotized patients. Such stages of estrangement are frequently described in the literature.

I could produce still more examples of how immediately the bodily ego feeling is dependent on the sexual instinct, but the above example is enough to let us draw this conclusion: The evidential feeling is based on the libido directed on to the ego, or better, on the libido employed for ego feeling. The libido only establishes the ego. Here narcissism is not a theoretical conception, but observed as it were in *statu nascendi*. The actuality of narcissism is thereby demonstrated.[4]

With what I have said so far I have justified my description of estrangement as a narcissistic actual psychosis. I have devoted so much space to the actual sexual cause only for the purpose of demonstrating my point, not because I wish to describe it as the only cause of states of estrangement. Estrangement takes place not only on account of actual disturbances in the economy of the actual sexual processes, i.e., on account of exhaustion of the libido reserves; much more frequently the narcissistic cathexis of the bodily ego boundaries disappears from all the complicated psychoneurotic mechanisms by which the libido is repressed or displaced. Especially important, and at the same time empirically demonstrable, is the narcissistic cathexis due to the identification of the ego with the male genital and, likewise, the disturbance of the one by the disturbance of the other, as in pathoneuroses according to Ferenczi's description. Thus the narcissistic cathexis may be interfered with either from the side of the ego or from that of the sources of the libido in the id.

I will repeat what I said before in Budapest, because it has since then been put forward by Reik in Vienna: The first estrangement in childhood is due in most cases to a shock. (The fact that in many people the ego remains permanently weakened, so that afterwards depersonalization processes are prom-

. . . .

[4] It is empiricism, not belief in authority or partiality for a theory, which prevents us from following Rank's psychology and throwing the libido theory overboard, or from conceiving of sexuality, as Adler does, as an accessory and a mere field of activity of the whole individual psyche.

inent, does not belong to the question of the nature of depersonalization, but to its etiology and clinical picture.) This connection between shock and depersonalization draws our attention to an essential distinction between the dynamics of anxiety and the dynamics of shock. In anxiety, the bodily ego boundary retains its narcissistic cathexis; moreover, owing to the tense expectation and the libidinal stressing of the ego connected with it, which consciously or unconsciously is threatened with danger, it is probably even more strongly charged with narcissistic cathexis. This narcissistically libidinal cathexis explains in part the existence of anxiety pleasure. However, in shock, the ego loses its narcissistic boundary cathexis. Every shock is accompanied by the feeling of alienation. Into this new context, I shall reintroduce Freud's explanation of the traumatic neurosis.

One should not feel surprised that the outer world is estranged when the ego boundary is deprived of its narcissistic cathexis, which we regularly feel in the shape of healthy bodily ego feeling. The phenomena which correspond to the lack of object libido have indeed long been known to us as indifference and callousness in regard to objects. This impoverishment in the libidinal cathexis of objects and object representations often occurs long before the estrangement. We describe the world, or the person no longer loved, as strange, that is, strange in the sense of being "as indifferent to one as a stranger." But the completely indifferent stranger who is unworthy of any interest or any transference does not seem in the least "estranged." When we speak of the fixation of the whole object libido on one person, of love, we notice that if this suddenly cools, our ego abates its ardor and alters, while the object becomes a matter of indifference to us. But neither of them, the ego nor the object, is estranged in the sense of depersonalization. I think that we are not sufficiently surprised by the fact that in general, as we have repeatedly found, the ego and the world can become changed, indeed completely changed, if sexuality is thwarted or repressed. Before Freud, sexuality scarcely belonged to the mind, only to the body. Before psychoanalysis, we conceived of love only as an experience of the ego, as happy or unhappy. But—as we now know—it is love that first creates the ego and sustains it. The question that the great and pious poet put to his God, "Was love woven by you in the weft of the world, or was it merely a miscalculation that slipped from you unawares?" [5] was first answered by psychoanalysis. But as soon as we reflect and consider the marvel of the building up of the ego by the libido, we must admire the greatness of Freud's concept whereby he first inferred the existence of narcissism from a schizophrenic's withdrawal from the world.

II

The psychical representation of the perceptive organs, the bodily ego boundary, is charged with bodily ego feeling from narcissism. We have already heard that this narcissistic covering, and along with it the corporal ego feeling, varies normally and pathologically, according to its strength, extension, and power of resistance.

We will now turn to the phenomena of morbid variations of bodily ego feeling, that is to say, to the pathology of peripheral narcissism. The strength of the cathexis differs with individuals and forms an important component in the temper or mood of a person. When increased to a pathological degree we have the difference between manic and melancholic states. The maniac feels his breast and limbs to be sound and filled out, the melancholiac feels them to be unsound and as if emptied out. States of estrangement are particularly frequent in melancholia.

We will now consider without theoretical preface some examples of the pathological differences in the extension of bodily ego feeling. I found with a hysterical patient that in the periods in which he was free of his symptoms the bodily ego feeling was normal; when his mood got worse, it was reduced especially at those parts of the body where hysterical symptoms showed themselves; but immediately before the appearance of the symptoms, it was intensified.

We find that in other pathological cases, either the bodily

. . . .

[5] Mickiewicz, *Forefathers' Eve* (*Dziady*)—classical Polish poem.

ego feeling is withdrawn towards the head (often not extending beyond the forehead or the mouth, or extending only down to the neck or halfway down the breast, etc.) or its general intensity is reduced. In the first instance the parts that have remained in a state of cathexis have, from time to time, an intensified bodily ego feeling. The eyes remain charged with cathexis unless optical impressions are intensively estranged. The mouth zone is still more resistant.

In male psychical impotence the genitals are for the most part without any bodily ego feeling. In cases of fixation where, along with the repression of the genital libido, the entire libidinal personality seems to have remained in the pregenital stage, while the intellect is fully developed, the bodily ego feeling also is ready to regress to a reduced extension. Thus, in the bodily ego feeling we have an ascertainable symptom of ego regression. It is as if the narcissistic cathexis of the bodily ego boundary, i.e., its psychical representation, has continued at an earlier stage or else easily withdraws into it. At our congress in Homburg, Pierce Clark investigated such cases among narcissistic neuroses and psychoses by means of his phantasy method, and he also spoke, though with no special emphasis, of the bodily ego feeling.

As an example I will describe a case with varying bodily ego feeling. The patient was being treated by me for homosexual impotence and depressive inhibition. In those periods when his attitude was actively homosexual, or was heterosexual, he possessed a full bodily ego feeling and adapted well to reality in respect to object libidinal gratification in his professional and social life. In those periods when his attitude was passively homosexual, which corresponded to his puberty period, the bodily ego feeling did not reach beyond the middle of his body; at such times he also felt a resistance against picturing to himself more than the upper part of other people's bodies. Thus the rejection of genital activity went along with a reduction of the narcissistic cathexis. But there were also periods of severe estrangement, and in these the bodily ego feeling invested only the mouth and the pharynx. This limitation, which must correspond to the period of infancy, was accompanied by depression and libidinal indifference. Finally, there were periods in which the attitude was corresponding to that of the third and fourth year of life, in which he felt his bodily ego as corresponding to this age. Here the libido was directed passively towards the father and actively towards the mother. For these periods one would have to assume not only rejection and repression of mature genital activity, but also the affirmation of genital infantile sexuality. The real outer world was estranged and the mood was excited, almost ecstatic, with anxiety-preparedness. All these particulars came to me as a surprise and were uninfluenced by me.

Another problem is whether there are qualitative differences in the bodily ego feeling and whether these differences are dependent on the quality of the component instincts, whose libido feeds the narcissistic cathexis. You will understand me better if I remind you of Freud's "From the History of an Infantile Neurosis." [6] Freud tells us of a patient who alleged that he always saw the world as if through a veil. Though the author does not say so, this complaint clearly betrays the state of estrangement. Freud lays stress on the fact that until the treatment this condition used to yield only when the patient had an enema. As we are concerned with an anal character and passively homosexual fixation, this case is analogous to the case mentioned above, in which the patient lost his estrangement only during masturbation in his bath. The difference is that in my case the restoration of the narcissistic cathexis was provoked by genital excitation, and in Freud's case by anal passive excitation.

We can understand that two people are bound to feel and behave differently if their bodily ego feeling comes from such different sources. Nevertheless, I consider it to be still uncertain whether one can assume a different quality in the narcissistic cathexis itself. Even without so bold an assumption, we can explain the distinction in the bodily ego feeling according to its component source in the following way: When we observe in perverts the distribution and extension of the bodily ego feeling, and also its intensity, we find the narcissistic cathexis distributed with unequal strength on the surface of

. . . .

[6] Freud, *Collected Papers*, III, 473.

the body, with a preference for the erotogenic zones. With male sadists the specifically erotogenic zones, the mouth with the teeth, the eye, hand, and penis, are not only more strongly sexualized during sexual excitation but have a permanent increase in ego intensity. The masochist, on the other hand, has not incorporated his genital in his corporal ego feeling at all. People who blush have invested their particular exhibitionistic zones, such as face, genitals, buttocks, and, in the case of women, the breasts, with a permanently stronger ego feeling. Thus the influence of the component instincts, which come to the fore in narcissism, is manifest in the distribution of cathexis. This perverse ego feeling also explains—apart from the wishes that are only dormant—how it is that such individuals regularly feel their perversity and are always prepared to be recognized or persecuted as perverse.

It is self-evident, but for the sake of clarity it should once again be expressly stated, that no variation of the sense functions accompanies all these changes; only by some one or other conversion mechanism may physiological functional changes supervene.

III

We will now leave the estrangement of the outer world and turn to the estrangement phenomena of the ego—to real depersonalization. In estrangement of the outer world, we could always establish the narcissistic cathexis, or its lack, through the patient's bodily ego feeling. We lack this index for our inquiry into estrangement of the inner world, and need to develop a working hypothesis.

All feelings of estrangement have something so specific in common that we must assume for all of them one and the same specific cause, whichever psychical function the alienation may attack. Since we have ascertained that in regard to the external perceptions, the cause lies in the loss of a normal narcissistic cathexis, we are bound to assume a loss of narcissistic cathexis in every case where estrangement occurs, thus in the estrangement of feeling, thinking, remembering, wishing, etc.

The evidence of a function is only regularly lost, i.e., estranged, when its narcissistic cathexis is lost. But in order for it to have got lost it must have been present in the normal state. We can only infer, we cannot observe, at least so far, the part played by narcissism in normal functions. By its absence in pathological states we learn where in the normal state an ego boundary with a narcissistic cathexis permanently exists. By this method we are able to find narcissism in the ego structure even within the external ego periphery, that is, the psychical representation of the periphery of perception. To put it briefly: Where estrangement occurs, a narcissistic cathexis exists at that point in the normal ego structure.

We shall hold all the more firmly to this hypothesis in proportion as it is confirmed by existing psychoanalytic conclusions regarding the theory of the ego libido. Where it leads to other conclusions, further inquiry is called for.

We may go still further and say: Where estrangement never occurs, there should not be any question of the participation of narcissism in this function. We can now demonstrate the existence of narcissism, but of narcissism alone, as it were, through a reagent. We must not actually decide from our results that it alone builds up the ego; perhaps where any estrangement is lacking, our attention will be drawn to yet other factors in the ego structure.

I think that our working hypothesis promises us an extensive program of work, which with severe ego disturbances, psychoses, will take us into the depths of the ego structure. Certainly in the case of severe narcissistic ego disturbances, we must be prepared to encounter the great difficulty that severe cases of insanity will not supply us with as clear an account of their estrangement feelings as do the intellectually intact victims of depersonalization whom I have so far examined. A similar difficulty exists with regard to dreams, for self-observation during dreams is difficult and is still more difficult to retain correctly in memory.

At present we will only test by our method, in a quite general way, the estrangement of some psychical functions. We will turn first to the affects. Estrangement seldom extends in the same degree to the whole emotional life. The patient behaves like a person who possesses feelings and yet he complains of an impoverishment of his feelings. This is a symptom of "pathological" mourning that has not yet been noticed; estrangement of the mourning affect always occurs in this case. Yet, self-reproaches, complaints, and guilt feelings hold entire sway over the patient who, however, often complains even of them that he does not feel them, and who accuses himself of being blunted in feeling. Similarly, in all other cases of estrangement of affects, these feelings of the patient do not seem to him genuine or evident; he feels them to be different, just as he feels his perceptions to be different. But the affects are not in any way unconscious, for the patient observes and laments the affects (e.g., shame, ambition, and love) which he feels not to be genuine.

Thus, we conclude that the ego normally admits the affects with a narcissistically charged boundary, cathexis of which is lacking in the case of the affectively estranged. This conclusion is in complete accord with Freud's theories, both in that the specific quality of every affect is determined by the quality of its dispersal in the psychical, and that they are memories of repeated experiences in the far past. We are not yet able to say whether the estrangement of an affect is due to the fact that, centrifugally, in the process of dispersal, it leaves an ego boundary no longer charged with narcissism, or that the sensation of the affect, centripetally, meets such a boundary. In any case, every feeling that is received by the ego without narcissism is a cold nothing in feeling-experience, no matter how intense it would be in itself if it were to impinge upon the Cs as "part of the ego," i.e., at a narcissistically charged boundary. This conception confirms also the opinions and statements of many non-psychoanalytical authors who speak of "inactivity" feeling in the case of estranged feeling and of "activity" feeling in the case of normal feeling; even the libido theory implies by the word "cathexis" an active reception. "Active reception" sounds like a contradiction in terms; yet it corresponds to the actual process. It will require much individual work to distinguish the particular boundaries for the modes of feeling or to demonstrate the homogeneity of the ego boundary for them. A difficulty in the way of understanding these conditions lies in the fact that this encounter with the narcissism of the ego is itself homogeneously experienced as feeling-quality together with the feeling, whereas the perceptions, being experiences of a fundamentally different kind, can more easily be separated from it. It resembles the difference between certain goods on which customs duty has to be paid directly and separately, and other goods where the duty disappears in the total price paid for them.

We mentioned before that the affects are subject to estrangement precisely because they are memories of experiences. That is to say, with many cases of estrangement memory participates in the disturbance. The memories enter the Cs rapidly and correctly and they are also clearly differentiated, but yet they enter, if one may so express it, in a remarkably "unegolike" manner. Among psychoanalysts Reich has laid particular stress on the memory feeling. In accordance with what we have been saying we must assume that the memory feeling is lacking when a narcissistic cathexis which is too weak or else nonexistent is set up or re-established where the memories enter the Cs. This connects with Ferenczi's remarks on affirmation.

It is remarkable that on its entry into the Cs, what has been truly repressed never, so far as I have observed, possesses the character of estrangement. Here the narcissistic cathexis of the ego boundary is already present. But one must not suppose that an estranged memory is not conscious, that in fact narcissistic cathexis is identical with that mental cathexis which constitutes consciousness. On the contrary, one may here point out the essential distinction between the narcissistic cathexis in question and the object libidinal cathexis that is attached to the remembered representation. In repression, the object libidinal cathexis of the object representation in question was either present in the Ucs and withdrawn from the connecting elements, or else it was withdrawn from the repressed representation itself. The emerging associations restore the object libidinal cathexes. The ego boundary itself may be narcissistically overcharged—in the obsessional neurosis—or else undercharged or uncharged. The memory ego feeling depends only on this narcissistic cathexis or recathexis.

The condition of *déjà-vu*, for which Freud postulated a connection with an unconscious displacement, as far as its economics and contents are concerned, has been rightly attributed to depersonalization by all writers except Freud himself. In this process, which is always felt as a violent disturbance of the self-evident stability of the feeling of one's own existence, an experience, as is well known, is suddenly apprehended as having happened once before; at which point the time feeling is so lost that one does not know whether this "once before" was immediately previously or unimaginable ages ago. With many depersonalization patients, this phenomenon is always recurring and is diagnosed by them as a feeling of estrangement; as these patients are experts in diagnosis, I have no doubt that the *déjà-vu* consists in a very short estrangement. The state of affairs is as follows: quite transitorily a memory in the form of an emerging experience passes the ideational ego feeling boundary, or a perception passes the perceptive ego feeling boundary, in the first place at a moment when the boundary is without narcissistic cathexis, and immediately afterwards when it has again received a narcissistic cathexis. I cannot decide whether in some cases of *déjà-vu* the experience simultaneously passes two ego feeling boundaries of which one is charged with narcissistic cathexis and the other is deprived of it, or whether the same boundary is passed in rapid succession. Thus it resembles the state of diplopia, which can be induced by looking through a prism with one eye or by looking through an amblyoscope (with two indices of refraction). The narcissistically blunted boundary takes away the feeling of the present and the evidential feeling, whereas the narcissistically excited boundary imparts them. Thus the *déjà-vu* appears to be a particularly good illustration of our assumptions. It also confirms the connection with internal shock, for in varying measure this often precedes the *déjà-vu* or appears with it.

We learn from *déjà-vu*, too, that the time feeling may be estranged. Many depersonalized patients complain of this estrangement. Thus, we must assume that there is also an ego feeling boundary with a narcissistic cathexis which is directed against the time perception. This assumption coincides with the libido-theoretical explanations given by Freud in his paper on the *Wunderblock*,[7] and by Hollós, of the double course of cathexis that takes place in the Pcs, or else in the Ucs or Cs, according to whether conscious or unconscious time perception is in question. The real orientation in time, the knowledge of the passage of time, as with all other depersonalization phenomena, is unaltered. An exact inquiry into time alienation should give us still more exact knowledge of *déjà-vu* and of the narcissistic cathexis between Pcs and Cs.

IV

Our new discoveries make a problem in psychosis more intelligible. When an idea which otherwise possesses only an intellectual or imaginative force is felt as real in the outer world, we describe it as a hallucination; a complete projection has taken place. This process is explained by assuming that, just as we found that the bodily ego feeling may regress to an earlier condition (smaller size), so even ego boundaries otherwise abandoned may be charged anew with narcissistic cathexis. The voice, which once really was heard through an ego boundary, lost the character of reality when this ego boundary was enlarged or else replaced by one of wider compass. But if the old smaller ego boundary is once again partially charged with narcissistic cathexis, then the voice again acquires the reality feeling. We do, in fact, find psychotic hallucinations that occur simultaneously with ego regressions. But even without regression an ego boundary, e.g., in delirium, may be transiently charged with a fresh cathexis.

I can do no more than mention here that estrangement processes do occur which lead us to infer a narcissistically charged boundary between ego and superego: the conscience can be estranged.

In connection with the ego-superego boundary, reference must be made to the narcissistic psychoses and neuroses, whose dynamics and topography can probably be much more exactly

. . . .

[7] Freud, "A Note upon the Mystic Writing Pad," *Intern. J. of Psycho-Analysis*, XXI (1940), 469-474.

investigated by taking into account the ego boundaries revealed by estrangement feelings. States of depersonalization do not constitute a disease entity but vary clinically in form and intensity in almost normal people, in so-called psychasthenia and other actual neuroses, and in the mild and the most severe cases of schizophrenia and manic-depressive psychosis. I believe that the word "narcissistic" will be used less and less as merely a description of a direction of libido, but will be used to denote qualitatively different typical links in the psyche.

Our further task will consist in the more exact investigation of that psychosis which only the most healthy person avoids during sleep, i.e., dreams. At present I must content myself with stating that the "ego in dreams," so far as bodily ego feeling as well as mental ego feeling are concerned, varies with the individual in different dreams, even in the same night, and varies with different people. These variations have to do also with the dynamics of dreams and with the habitual narcissistic cathexis of the sleeper in his waking condition; the laws governing these matters await further research.

Consideration of dreams suggests many as yet unsolved problems in our present theme, but I shall introduce them into the inquiry only insofar as they have some bearing on the last subject with which I propose to deal: the estrangement of the will. Many of these patients complain of the automatism of their actions, as if they were not aware of any volition. They say that they act as if in a dream. In other contexts, depersonalized patients describe the alienated world as dreamlike. In actual dreams, however, there is no estrangement feeling. Even if the reality test is roused and the dreamer recognizes a process to be altogether surprising and contradictory to his usual experience, e.g., that his dead father is alive, he still submits to it against his better knowledge. Thus, all dream pictures are perceived with a narcissistically charged ideational feeling boundary, if we may in general assume for the dream ego the same ego structure as we do for the waking state. These are questions which have been answered by Freud's theory of dreams, but which ought to be confirmed by fresh observations.

With most dreams, as with estrangement, bodily ego feeling is either lacking or much reduced and time feeling is usually

lacking; in ordinary dreams volition, especially, is lacking—
apart from a scanty residue that seldom appears.[8] Freud has
referred to this in his *Traumdeutung*. Janet too, calls *aboulia*
the first common element of dreams and estrangement. The
estranged patient notices this peculiar kind of *aboulia*, which
is not a real one. The dreamer experiences it naively, without
noticing it, and without comparing it with volition in the
waking state.

It does not contradict our explanation of estrangement that,
in dreams, the corporal ego feeling is so often lacking without
estrangement being felt by the dreamer. The dreamer is not
faced with an outer world; however insofar as he dreams, he is
awake and receives the emerging representations with a narcissistically charged boundary which precisely determines the relative evidence of the dream-images. We are bound to assume that
it is not the perceptive boundary with which he receives the
images. We do not know whether the feeling that one is dreaming, which so often occurs, corresponds to the awakening of this
boundary and to a feeling of estrangement. Nor do I yet know
whether the bodily ego feeling appears in such dreams. We
psychoanalysts are accustomed to recognize small indications in
the manifest dream as representing important processes paralyzed by sleep. Now we find one such indication in a dream
when an action of the will has occurred without the dreamer
being aware of the will. Instead of his volition, the dreamer has
a quite momentary accentuation of the bodily ego boundary, i.e.,
of a part of the bodily ego feelings which has hitherto been
lacking. In a dream in which there is no memory of any bodily
ego feeling at all, the arm is felt when it carries something. This
bestowal of narcissistic cathexis is what corresponds in the dream
to an act of will. Similarly, in the case of an estranged person
who succeeds in feeling the voluntariness of his action, the bod-

. . . .

[8] Even in such typical dreams, for example, as one in which the dreamer
wants to catch a train, we seem to have to do with, not an exceptional
awakening of the will, but only with will-memories. Even these will-
impulses run off uncontrolled in the dream. Somnambulists' dreams need
to be more particularly investigated. In any case, the above remarks do not
relate to such abnormal dreams nor to the rare dreams in which volition
is experienced.

ily ego feeling for the parts concerned is likewise re-established.

Thus we see that for an act of will, as for attention, the narcissistic bodily ego boundary cathexis, apart from the libidinal object cathexis, is necessary. But neither the object libidinal cathexis alone, nor it and the narcissistic bodily ego cathexis together, suffice for the act of will; indeed these are present even in dreams and yet no volition appears. Nor are they—as we have already learned—specific for volition. We find object libidinal cathexis in every wish, as well as in passive predilection; narcissistic bodily ego feeling cathexis belongs to the normal complete ego, even when the will is not felt.

It is self-evident that in the experiencing of the will, the mental representation of muscle action supervenes. But there is also volition with deferred innervation. For volition to take place, a particular process is essential which is invariably absent in dreams and is disturbed in those more severe states of ego disorder which exceed mere estrangement in the volition and increase into the "dreamlike" character of the action. Freud has revealed this process in his theory of consciousness in the *Traumdeutung*. We may describe it as a regulation of the dispersal of quantities of object libido.

Let us consider in what the real dream quality in dreams consists: usually, the images pass by the sleeper who is not in a position to retain or call back a dream image, as he can in waking. In dreams, the ego is at the mercy of the dream elements which have emerged from the Ucs; there is no "backwards," no tarrying, in dreams. Thus, this act of tarrying, which is common to thought and will, belongs to a part of the psyche that is paralyzed in dreams. As this latter does not pertain to the already familiar narcissistic cathexis, the retention of the object libido in the waking state must proceed from another source of power. As volition belongs unquestionably to the ego, this force proceeds from the non-libidinal part of the ego, from that instinct which Freud has called the death instinct. (Not only because it ultimately leads to death, but also because, as the instinct of attack and defense, it would in the first place like to kill.) Thus, by a process of elimination we have arrived at the point where we can recognize the will as a non-libidinal part of the ego. As psychoanalysis has occupied itself chiefly with the unconscious and the libido, the investigation of the will has so far played only a small part in it.

v

Now that we have found confirmation even for the bisection into love and death instincts, we will point out, in a brief retrospect, what seems to be the nature of the advance we have made in this inquiry. We have found those ego disturbances through which the psyche is rendered unable to withstand the traumatic or otherwise injurious effect of the demands on the libido. They are: the shock experience and the withdrawal of the narcissistic ego boundary cathexis. We have thus given a quite specific metapsychological content to Janet's *"fonction du sentiment du réel"* as well as to Minkowski's *"notion de perte de contact vital avec la réalité."* By observing the actual psychosis which appears in the guise of estrangement, we have demonstrated anew the function of the libido in building up the ego. Our observations seem, too, to open a new path for investigating the ego structure.

3

EGO FEELING IN DREAMS

Federn was the first to study extensively and intensively the actual states and changes of ego feeling in falling asleep, in dreaming, and in awakening. He discusses such neglected yet evident phenomena as the absence of bodily ego feeling in most dreams. The mental ego, in its passive rather than its active state, carries on in the dream; only exceptionally does the bodily ego participate, and when such participation becomes too intense, the sleeper awakes, the dream is ended. Active bodily ego feeling in dreams represents volition.–E. W.

EGO FEELING

I cannot assume that every reader interested in this study of the dream will care to read or reread my previous communications; therefore, by way of introduction, I should like to review the more important results of my previous studies of ego feeling and outline the conception of the ego which grew out of them.

Ego feeling is the sensation, constantly present, of one's own person—the ego's own perception of itself. This statement reaffirms the idea, emphasized especially by Oesterreicher, that "the ego" is not a mere abstraction devised to convey in a single word the idea of the "ego participation" (*Ichbezogenheit*) of actions and events. Neither is the ego solely the sum of these ego participations, nor do I regard it merely as the sum of the ego functions (Nunberg), nor yet simply as the "psychic representation" of that which refers to one's own person (Sterba): these are all aspects of the ego—they represent functions performed by the ego or which belong within the ego.

The ego, however, is more inclusive; more especially, it includes the subjective psychic experience of these functions with a characteristic sensation. This self-experience is a permanent, though never equal, entity, which is not an abstraction but a reality. It is an entity which stands in relation to the continuity of the person in respect to time, space, and causality. It can be recognized objectively and is constantly felt and perceived subjectively. We possess, in other words, an enduring feeling and knowledge that our ego is continuous and persistent, despite interruptions by sleep or unconsciousness, because we feel that processes within us, even though they may be interrupted by forgetting or unconsciousness, have a persistent origin within us, and that our body and psyche belong permanently to our ego. Many authors have therefore used the term "ego consciousness" (*Ichbewusstsein*) to designate this phenomenon. The expression "ego feeling" has occasionally been used by Freud and by other psychologists and also, as a self-explanatory term, by laymen. If I prefer this latter expression to the term "ego consciousness" and single out "ego feeling" to mark the integrating part of the ego, I do so not because of an arbitrary preference for this designation but for the following reasons. The ego's experience of itself does not consist simply in the knowledge and consciousness of the qualities of the ego mentioned above; the experience also includes a sensory element for which the words "feeling" or "sensation" are appropriate, and the term "ego consciousness" ignores this feeling quality. Not only in clinical pathology but also in the psychopathology of everyday life—in sleep, fatigue, distraction, and daydreams—we can distinguish, often accurately, between ego *feeling* and ego *consciousness*. Ego consciousness, in the pure state, remains only when there is a deficiency in ego feeling. And the mere empty knowledge of one's self is already a pathological state, known as estrangement[1] or depersonalization. The term "ego consciousness," then, would cover our ego experience only if "estrangement" were the normal state of all human beings.

. . . .

[1] There is no exact English equivalent for *Entfremdung*. This phenomenon is usually described as "sense of unreality," which does not convey the meaning of *Entfremdung*. The word is therefore translated literally.

It is also incorrect to identify ego feeling with consciousness, though numerous authors, of whom I believe Janet was the first, have described and defined "becoming conscious" as becoming attached to the ego. At the present time, we know that the property of belonging to the ego may become, be, or remain conscious or unconscious; and from the study of pathological states, we know that ego feeling may disappear from previously conscious portions of the ego and later reappear. In every psychological process, ego feeling may or may not accompany consciousness. When ego feeling does not accompany consciousness, the individual is only aware that an experience—which may be the perception of a somatic or external reality, a memory, or merely an affect—is or has been taking place within, but this knowledge is accompanied, under these circumstances, by a sense of strangeness; or, in other words, a feeling of estrangement appears instead of ego feeling. That the cardinal feature of "ego experience" (*Icherlebnis*) is not thought or knowledge but sensation was first noted in cases of pathological disturbances in ego feeling. The symptom of estrangement, since it was first discovered, has always been referred to as a *feeling* of estrangement, never as a *knowledge* or *consciousness* of estrangement.

Ego feeling, then, is the totality of feeling which one has of one's own living person. It is the residual experience which persists after the subtraction of all ideational contents—a state which, in practice, occurs only for a very brief time. This total ego feeling is always a combination of changing and unvarying elements, and the total subjective experience of one's ego orientation toward an act is qualified by the ego feeling that is present at the time. I consider it more correct to speak of the "ego orientation *toward* an act" than of the "ego orientation of an act," at least in a discussion of ego feeling.[2] Consideration of the fact that ego feeling constantly fluctuates in extent, so that its content is constantly shifting, and of the fact that it nevertheless is constantly uniting all relations and parts of the ego into a single whole, leads us to the conclusion

. . . .

[a] This statement does not imply a dispute with Schilder, who referred to the "ego orientation of an act" for other purposes.

that the "ego" always includes both total and partial experience and must always be investigated both analytically and synthetically. These conceptions of ego feeling cause us to reject as misleading the temptation to distinguish between viewing a thing exclusively as a whole or exclusively as a part. Psychoanalysis has always sought to comprehend the parts as well as the whole, laying more stress, however, on analysis than on synthesis. My study of ego feeling further emphasizes this double orientation of psychoanalysis.

A theorist might still query whether what we have here designated as ego feeling is not merely the intellectual experience of that which remains constant while ever-changing experiences, relations and reactions pass through consciousness; that is, whether it is not merely a *knowledge* on the part of the ego, the content of which escapes attention because it does not change. This question is answered conclusively by the observation that even the clearest *knowledge* of one's own ego is experienced as something insufficient, uncomfortable, incomplete, and unsatisfying, even akin to fear; and that even for the purest "self experience" something affective in quality is requisite for normality.[3]

Ego feeling, therefore, is the simplest and yet the most comprehensive psychic state which is produced in the personality by the fact of its own existence, even in the absence of external or internal stimuli. As has been said, it is true that unmixed ego feeling can form the whole content of consciousness for a very short time only, as there are always too many stimuli ready to enter consciousness. To repeat our formulation: combined with the consciousness of the self, there is also an affective sense of the self, which we designate briefly as "ego feeling." In other articles,[4] I have studied "ego feeling" more intimately and have shown in pathological and normal cases

. . . .

[3] To designate the feelings themselves as perceptions of autonomic processes, and to consider such perceptions as equivalent to those with intellectual content (Behaviorism), does not touch the problem. For we are basing our investigation on the empirical fact that there is a difference between intellectual and affective experiences.

[4] See Chapters 1, 2, and 15.

that *somatic* and *psychic* ego feeling may be separate from each other, and that we must distinguish within the varying extensions of ego feeling a nucleus of ego feeling which remains constant; and, in particular, that we have a precise sense of the degree to which our psychic processes and our body are invested with ego feeling. Whenever there is a change in ego feeling cathexis, we sense the "boundaries" of our ego. Whenever an impression impinges, be it somatic or psychic, it strikes a boundary of the ego normally invested with ego feeling. *If no ego feeling sets in at this boundary, we sense the impression in question as alien.* So long as no impression impinges upon the boundaries of ego feeling, we remain unaware of the confines of the ego. Psychic and bodily ego feeling can both be active or passive. In different persons the quality of the ego feeling depends also upon what special instinctual forces (e.g., tender, sadistic, masochistic, exhibitionistic) exercise a continuous dominance over the personality or else are ready at all times to find expression. Further, we have confirmed Nunberg's finding that all neuroses and psychoses begin with a condition of estrangement of shorter or longer duration. We also found that the withdrawal of ego feeling from an ego boundary can be a defensive measure of the ego, which can occur with or without repression, or which can initiate repression and itself disappear. The development of the individual is accompanied by a development, qualitative and quantitative, of ego feeling, the stages of libido development also being characterized by various types of ego feeling. Therefore, ego feeling is capable of fixation at, or regression to, an earlier stage, in respect to both quality and extent.

The hypothesis based on these points, which is useful as a psychoanalytic conception of ego feeling, states that ego feeling is the original narcissistic investment of the ego. As such it has at first no object; I designated it intermediate (*medialer*) narcissism. Not until much later, after the object libidinal cathexes have reached the ego boundary, or have invested it and again been withdrawn, does reflexive narcissism arise.

This hypothesis is supported by numerous clinical observations. If it is correct, the study of "ego feeling" has furnished us with a working method of adding to our knowledge of cathexes with narcissistic libido and also, indirectly, of the functioning of object cathexes.

Dreams, considered as topics for study, are met with so regularly in healthy individuals that it is difficult to say whether they should be included in normal or in abnormal psychology. In any case, as regards the ego in dreams we are dealing with a disturbed condition; hence, the study of "ego feeling" in dreams must logically follow a clinical investigation of estrangement. Therefore, using mainly data derived from patients suffering from estrangement, I shall first discuss the relations between estrangement, dreams, and sleep, and only then present our subject proper, the quality and the quantity of ego feeling during dreams.

ESTRANGEMENT AND DREAMING

Very many persons who are suffering from estrangement state that they see reality as in a dream, or, that they feel as if they were in a dream. This is a surprising statement which re quires explanation. This statement would not have been surprising if our feeling in regard to a dream, while we are dreaming, were similar to the one which the estranged individual has in regard to reality. This is not the case, however. The dreamer subjectively feels that his dream is real. The surprising, incomprehensible, even absurd, character of much that is dreamed does not prevent the dreamer from believing in the reality of his dream as long as he is dreaming, even though what he dreams may be inconsistent with whatever knowledge of reality remains over from the waking state in the mind of the dreamer.

In contrast, the estranged individual must actually coerce himself to believe that his impressions are real. Intelligence, common sense, memories, and inferences from memories compel him to admit intellectually something which he does not feel to be evident. To the dreamer, on the contrary, the reality of what he dreams is self-evident—aside from well-known exceptions—even though the dream may contradict all his rational experience.

However, except in cases of extreme depersonalization, we can readily understand what estranged individuals mean when they say that they see the world as if they were dreaming, if we remember that they make this statement only in retrospect. For, everyone who remembers a dream after he awakens feels in it a certain alien quality. This quality is due to the incoherence and impermanence of the dream, the illogical nature of its content, and the manner in which it vanishes. In retrospect, dream figures are usually shadowy, unsubstantial, or unreal. The process of secondary elaboration not only improves the internal logic of the dream; usually, the same process alters the dream, also, so that it comes to resemble more closely a sequence of waking events. Dreams without secondary elaboration have, when recalled, more of the quality of strangeness. It may well be that this very quality leads to secondary elaboration. We arrive, then, at the curious conclusion that while they are in operation, the processes of dreaming and estrangement are basically different, and that they appear to resemble each other only in the impression which they leave behind. If we disregard the dream's importance as a portal to the unconscious and as an object of study, and if we except dreams of unusual personal significance, a dream is a "nothing"—a series of unreal images, which have disappeared from consciousness and which, even as memories, have automatically lost their content and vividness. But the estranged individual, also, feels an indifference in regard to his experiences during his estranged state. He can only recall that he was in an abnormal state. Persons severely affected by estrangement even say that their reality is less vivid than their dreams, and this is true—for estranged and normal persons do not dream differently.

Another analogy obtains between dreams and estrangement. A dreamer, one might say, is passively overcome by the dream, and the dream develops or unfolds itself *upon* or *with* the dreamer passive. A dreamer also feels that he is passively seized by the dream, for, as a rule, he cannot fix the elements of the dream in order to form deliberate judgments in regard to them. Only rarely can he voluntarily react to any of the dream elements or bring them back to mind, for the dream enters consciousness more or less as a finished picture, and it arouses only such small parts of consciousness as are necessary to receive the dream picture. These awakened parts, as soon as they are not needed, instantly fall back into sleep. The will is conspicuously absent from dreams. Scherner, in many passages of his book, depicts this lack of centrality of the ego and the weakness of the will in very plastic language. The estranged individual also feels more passive than a normal individual toward what he experiences. However, his reasons for this feeling are different from those of the dreamer: his attention is always diverted to his own condition; he becomes inattentive and his interest in other things is disturbed; so that, as a result of his disorder, he becomes apathetic and passive toward the whole of reality.

Up to the present point, we have been discussing well-known characteristics of the states under comparison. On turning our attention to "ego feeling" (which, it is true, patients do not mention of their own accord) we at once discover a feature common to both states, the dream and estrangement. In both, "ego feeling" is deficient. This is particularly true of those patients with severe depersonalization, whose ego is not invested with full ego feeling either at its boundaries or in its nucleus. These individuals feel their ego only partially and with decreased intensity and suffer a subjective loss in their sense of importance, their feeling of well-being, and the unity of their personality. However, as we shall see, disturbances of the ego in the dream and in estrangement are, for the most part, not alike. We have already drawn attention to the fact that dreams are experienced as real, and the objects of the individual's estrangement as unreal. We conclude that in the case of dreams, the ego boundary at which dream experiences impinge is invested with ego feeling, and that this is not the case for experiences during estrangement. However, neither the waking judgment of the depersonalized individual, nor the partially awakened judgment of the dreamer, is able to recognize as *false* the "unreality" of experience (in estrangement), or the "reality" of experience (in dreams). Neither individual can prevail against the abnormal cathexis of the ego boundary, which in the case of estrangement is too small and in dreams is relatively too great. This impotence in the face of a disturbance of ego cathexis is characteristic of both states.

We have, consequently, discovered two reasons why estranged individuals use the words "as in a dream" to describe their state. The more important reason is the one mentioned last—the recollection that there was a deficiency of ego feeling. This disorder of the ego is not a disturbance of consciousness, nor a feeling of giddiness, unclarity, obscurity or haziness, but an impairment of ego feeling. Before we look for its significance let us discuss a few relations between estrangement and sleep.

ESTRANGEMENT, FALLING ASLEEP, AND AWAKENING

We know from clinical observation that states of estrangement vary in their intensity and extent at different times in the same patient. Only rarely do patients complain constantly of the same degree of estrangement. Usually, the fact that they are speaking with the physician is enough to bring about an improvement in their condition. Their own interest, and their satisfaction in arousing the attention of the physician and feeling his interest, bring about an increase in the cathexis of the ego boundaries, which in milder cases appears to abolish the sense of estrangement. Usually such patients, after learning to accept their feeling of estrangement as a symptom, can describe the curve of intensity of their feelings of estrangement since the last visit. Less severely affected new patients, in the excitement of the first visit, do not feel any sense of estrangement, nor do they mention it spontaneously or at all unless direct questioning draws their attention to the fact that these states, also, are the concern of the physician. Then, as experience constantly bears out, the patients reward the physician who wishes to know about these subtle variations in their permanent condition, and who spontaneously suspects the presence of such states of estrangement, by immediately giving him their complete confidence. Even if for no other reason, an acquaintance with these states is of practical importance for physicians in general as well as for psychoanalysts.

However, although such mildly affected patients report about their states of estrangement only in the past tense, estrangement does occur even under the protected conditions of a consultation hour. Curiously enough, many such patients have merely forgotten that previously, in health, they had a stronger contact with the world and with themselves, a contact which gave a full sense of well-being but which no longer spontaneously comes to mind even as a basis of comparison.

The intensity of the estrangement depends on many factors which do not always have the same effect, but differ in their effect according to the degree of severity, or stage of development of the case. There are patients who develop feelings of estrangement as soon as they are left alone or feel themselves abandoned, whereas the presence of a person invested with libido abolishes the disturbance, or at least diminishes it to such a point that they feel practically no estrangement. Observations of this order long gave rise to the belief that estrangement consisted in a withdrawal of object libido. In some cases the estrangement sets in just when the patient meets persons who are invested with object libido, and, conversely, in other cases just when there is *no one* in his company in whom he can take an actual interest. Often merely to direct his object libido toward another person temporarily suffices to protect him from estrangement; but soon his capacity to invest his ego boundary with ego feeling is exhausted, and he is suddenly seized with a sense of the strangeness and unreality of external and internal perceptions. In most cases the severity of the estrangement also depends, fundamentally, on somatic factors. Fatigue and exhaustion or intense exertion predispose to estrangement—then, his ego frontiers crumbling under such bodily or psychic strain, the patient, gradually or suddenly, intermittently or abruptly, finds himself in a condition of estrangement. Hartmann and Nunberg were the first to show that sudden emotionally charged experiences which were followed, for only partly conscious reasons or more usually for unconscious reasons, by a so-called object loss, may produce traumatic estrangement. Theoretically, the effect of all these factors can be explained, economically, by making a distinction between two questions relating to libidinal cathexis;

namely, first, whether ego feeling can be sufficiently established at all for the ego boundary in question, and secondly, whether the libido reserve is great enough to maintain the cathexis of the ego boundary. The severity of estrangement is therefore dependent not only, dynamically, on the inhibition of cathexis at the time, but also, economically, on the magnitude of the libido supply. We can formulate this distinction, which applies in general in pathological states, by contrasting a withdrawal of libido due to an external or internal frustration with what we might call an exhaustion (*Versiegen*) of libido.

Observation teaches us that in chronic cases of estrangement, improvement, other things being equal, consists in a re-establishment of ego feeling, but that in each situation a sufficient cathexis of the ego boundary can be set up only slowly and after repeated efforts. For this reason, often, very subtle differences in ego disturbance are described in terms of whether or not the environment is sharply observing the patient or is friendly toward him. It is especially during improvement that patients describe such differences.

Analogously, we know from clinical experience that estranged persons whose condition has already improved do not always, like normal persons, regain their normal orientation toward the inner and the outer world; indeed, they feel more estranged after sleeping than at other times. Even in patients not improving, this symptom is more severe in the morning than later in the day, resembling in this respect the symptoms of depressive patients insofar as there are no exacerbations caused by the above mentioned factors of fatigue and strain. Thus, we see that melancholia and estrangement are characterized by similar daily curves of severity and similar reaction curves to strain and exhaustion. This morning increase of symptoms is directly connected with the state of ego feeling during sleep. This morning exacerbation would not have been expected on the basis of previous experience with normal individuals. On the contrary, according to our experience with healthy persons, we might have anticipated that after the libido reserve was completely replenished by sleep, the ego, in its nucleus and at its boundaries, would, at least for a time, be fully invested with ego feeling. Then, according to the severity of the case and the demands made upon the individual, the ego disturbance would reappear in the course of the day. According to this, the disturbance of libido economy would appear at awakening only potentially, and would only become actual sooner or later in the course of the day in response to the demands of the individual. In fact, such a curve is really present in all estranged persons in whom the disturbance shows any fluctuation. However, it does not become effective immediately in the morning, because the abnormally long transition from sleeping to waking postpones the mechanism of simple dependence on the magnitude of the libido reserve. In the estranged individual, as we have said above, there is a disturbance in the displaceability or, better, in the displacement of the libido, insofar as it has to invest the ego boundaries.

The investment of object representations with object libido may at the same time hardly be disturbed. The fact explains why, in spite of their estrangement, patients can work with interest and accuracy, and why they do not cease to show selection in their object relations, at least within certain limits, insofar as there is no concomitant difficulty in maintaining object cathexis. The latter difficulty may be secondary or, as Nunberg has shown, may have been the precipitating cause of the estrangement. But even in the latter case the object cathexis may persist. The very fact that it persists in the presence of a defective ego boundary causes this particular object to arouse a special feeling of strangeness. What was called "object loss" consists in this loss of capacity to perceive an object with one's full ego feeling: with the loss of the ego feeling, the narcissistic satisfaction in having the object is lost, too. Of this I have been fully convinced by a case of pathological mourning. After the death of the patient's mother all relationships, things, and recollections in any way connected with her mother were particularly strongly invested with object libido. Repeatedly, new and often very minor events from the past were coming into the patient's mind; everything connected with her mother took on great significance. The patient did not sleep day or night because of the press of ideas and associations belonging to her mother complex. These object representations were disturbingly vivid in content and deeply depressive in affect. At the same time, there was present a complete estrangement from this intensive repetition of all her past object relationships with her mother, which extended both to their ideational content and to the affect of grief itself. She said, "I have the grief but I do not feel it." Although her grief was manifest in her facial expression and in its somatic effects, the patient continually complained that she did not "really" feel her grief, an assertion which, for an inexpert observer such as I was at the time, was absolutely inconsistent with her whole condition and appearance. Years later a similar case permitted me to understand the situation: the object cathexes evoked the pain of bereavement, but the ego boundary in question[5] was without feeling, as though dead. We must therefore designate "pathological mourning" (Freud) as a narcissistic psychosis, not only because of its genesis and in its character as an unconscious identification, but also for its libidinal mechanism, a statement that holds equally true for melancholia. In recalling all the cases of pathological mourning and of melancholia in my analytic experience, I do not remember one patient who failed to express the paradoxical complaint that he felt nothing but suffering and yet did not really feel the suffering.

Though this field is somewhat remote from the present topic, I have treated it in detail here, because, for the reader to be convinced of what follows, it is important for him to recognize that there is a real distinction between *object* cathexis and the *narcissistic* cathexis of the corresponding ego boundary. The difference between the normal and the abnormal mechanism of narcissistic cathexis of the ego boundary is seen most clearly in the morning in the speed of recovery of the ego after sleep. It is because of this delayed mechanism that both estranged and depressed individuals feel an exacerbation of their symptoms every morning. And the increased difficulty of cathexis of the ego boundary is surely one reason why the restora-

. . . .

[5] Concerning the reasons for the exhaustion (*Versiegen*) of libido in melancholia, see Federn, "The Reality of the Death Instinct, Especially in Melancholia." *Psa. Rev.*, XIX (1932).

tion and strengthening of the ego during sleep fails to cause an improvement in ego feeling immediately on awakening. In melancholia there must be additional unfavorable influences, for relative improvement does not set in until evening. The investigation of these factors in melancholia is not in the scope of the present discussion. Provisionally, the morning exacerbation in estrangement seems to me adequately explained by the physiological processes in sleep. However, I have not as yet paid special attention to the problem whether, in the narcissistic psychoses, sleep itself is not subject to special disturbance.

One statement can be made which is unquestionably true: In dreamless sleep ego feeling is extinguished. I have dealt with this point in detail in "Some Variations in Ego Feeling" (Chapter 1). I first recognized the existence of ego feeling during the act of going to sleep—that is, not in *statu nascendi* but in *statu exeundi*. When an individual falls asleep rapidly, ego feeling is suddenly extinguished. A sudden disappearance of ego feeling of this nature is also found in narcolepsy. When the process of falling asleep is disturbed, the loss of ego feeling is only partial and gradual. Falling asleep is promoted if one learns to withdraw ego feeling as much as possible from the body, leaving only the ego feeling connected with breathing. Such an intentional withdrawal of ego feeling is well-known to the Yogis. But it should be used only in harmony with the regular periodicity of sleeping and waking, which in itself predisposes to the disappearance of ego cathexis. If one coerces oneself to sleep in opposition to this periodicity, sleep itself becomes an effort, and one is more likely to awake fatigued and unrefreshed.

As long as a sleeper does not dream, he does not feel his ego. Whether an unconscious ego persists, or whether Friedrich Kraus's "basic personality" (*Tiefenperson*) corresponds to an ego or to the id, are still insoluble questions. It must be assumed that even in dreamless sleep, much psychic and even intellectual work, shrewd and intelligent arrangement and construction, takes place in the unconscious. Freud has compared the unconscious with the "good folk" in fairy tales who help us with our work during our sleep. But as far as we know,

all the unconscious accomplishments during sleep are biologically centered through the unity of the body, not psychologically through the unity of the ego. Hence Freud's statement that sleep is a narcissistic state refers to unconscious
narcissistic cathexes which, if they are attached to any entity at
all, at least are not attached to the ego of waking life. It is
probable that Freud wished this statement merely to express
in an extreme fashion the fact that with the exclusion of sensory stimuli, object cathexes are withdrawn to an incomparably
greater degree than during waking life. The withdrawal of
object cathexes permits narcissistic cathexes to become object
cathexes, as when the person of the dreamer is wholly projected
and appears in the dream as another person. Here, in our discussion of the manifest expression of narcissism in ego feeling,
we must establish that in dreamless sleep this narcissistic cathexis
of the ego is absent.

When, on falling asleep, consciousness is lost, ego libido
ceases to be in the ego and all ego feeling disappears. It is
mostly a matter of taste whether one says: that the ego libido
vanishes (*versiegt*), that it is asleep, that it is withdrawn into
the id, or that it is distributed among the partial functions.
However, this narcissistic cathexis always stands ready to return to the ego, as we see from the fact that, except in pathological conditions, every stimulus which wakes the individual
immediately re-establishes ego feeling. This is readily understood if it is recalled that ego feeling perpetuates the most
primordial sensation of living substance, phylogenetically and
ontogenetically, and that its disappearance is probably a direct expression of the sleep of the cells. These are facts
gleaned from biology. Mysticism, on the other hand, would
say that the mind leaves the body during sleep and returns to
it on waking. The mind carries away all its knowledge with
it, and during dreams is supposed to reside, not in the body,
but in the place where the dream takes it. This theory is an
expression of the fact that the ego feeling in dreams is, for
the most part, a purely psychic one.

On awakening from sleep, ego feeling is established immediately. On waking from a dream, it is exceptional for the
ego feeling to be continuous with that in the dream. In health,

the ego feeling on waking is vivid and undiminished and fills body and mind with satisfaction and vigor. The ego also immediately regains its security as to its temporal continuity with its own past and its own future. This is not the case in many neurotics. They feel their inadequacy in the morning. This is true in most cases of phobia and of "premelancholia" (with this term I refer to the daily depressive moods which may exist for years before the onset of melancholia) and, as mentioned above, in cases of estrangement. Were one to inquire for symptoms of estrangement among all those who complain of beginning the day badly, it is possible that one might even find that they were constantly present. It is true that the patient does not mention them himself, because his bed and his bedroom are his fortress, remote from the demands of the day and of object relations. The estrangement first becomes fully perceptible when the individual turns toward an object. The disorder causes the full ego feeling to become established only gradually. It would be interesting to investigate to what extent disturbances and delays in the everyday habits of dressing, etc., are connected with a morning ego deficiency.

As an example of how severely a marked case of estrangement can be disturbed in the morning, I will cite a case which was materially improved by prolonged analysis. The patient's sister was in an advanced state of severe catatonia. The patient, also, had symptoms which went beyond mere estrangement, and every six months there were transitory exacerbations lasting only a few days, with uncertainty of orientation, hypochondriacal sensations, and severe anxiety, which corresponded to an abrupt but mild catatonic disturbance. This very intelligent patient understands the nuances of ego cathexis and the problem of estrangement so well, from his own experience, that he can give the most precise information concerning his condition. He can accurately distinguish estrangement for sense perceptions, for affect, and for thinking; he states that today he no longer has these disturbances, well-known to himself and to me, but that the total intensity of his ego continues to be diminished, particularly after awakening. It takes a long time before his full ego feeling is established. He feels that this is related to his sexual potency. Sometimes he is better, and then he has the same sexual excitement and general vigor in the morning which he had in his years of health. Usually, however, this normal libidinous feeling is replaced by a mixture of mild anxiety and trembling lust which he senses throughout his body and which does not permit a normal bodily ego feeling to appear. This represents a regression of ego feeling to an earlier, masochistic stage. This peculiar feeling quiets down only gradually, to be superseded by a state of moderately diminished ego feeling which, for him, is usual. All patients with severe estrangement give remarkable accounts of how they regain their ego in the morning. They are and feel strange, until they "become themselves," as far as the disturbance in the economy and mobility of their ego libido permits. I should like to add that a morning disturbance of ego feeling of this type usually causes the function of the will to be re-established more slowly in the morning.

Up to the present we have in part discussed, and in part only indicated, the relations which exist—subjectively and objectively—between estrangement, dream, and sleep. But I had other reasons for turning to this problem, and introduced the discussion of these relations chiefly for didactic purposes. I wished to use them to renew the reader's interest in the difference between narcissistic and object cathexis, in the phenomenon of ego feeling, and in the inconstancy of the ego boundary, so that he might be more interested in the subject of this paper proper, ego feeling in dreams. This subject became important to me because from the ego feeling in dreams it is possible to demonstrate the distinction between psychic and bodily ego feeling, utilizing a special method of self-observation.

EGO FEELING IN DREAMS

Dreams which one hears, reads, or recalls have undergone secondary elaboration, not only as regards their content, but also as regards the manner in which things happen in them. It is almost impossible to remember them exactly. Involuntarily one tends to recall the events of the dream as if one had followed them as an awake, unified, and complete personality and had experienced them with one's whole being. The more we have ourselves done and seen in the dream, the more strongly do we hold this belief.

Once we have begun to pay attention to ego feeling and ask ourselves or another dreamer on awaking what the ego feeling in the dream was, we will discover, first of all, that a consciousness of the self was always present and that it was the right one. The dreamer is always identical with the waking person, and knows this with certainty. This feature enables the dreamer to free himself of some troublesome portions of the ego by projecting them into other persons. The dream ego itself, however, always remains one's own ego, with a consciousness of the continuity of one's own psychic processes.

However, in the majority of dreams, and in the greater part of each dream, this dream ego differs from that of waking life in that there is a sense of one's identity (*Eigengefühl*) only as regards one's psychic processes, while the body is, so to say, ignored. In waking life, psychic and bodily ego feeling are not easy to distinguish, because both are so obviously permanently inherent in the ego. As regards dreams, however, it is quite clear to retrospective memory that these two forms of ego feeling are entirely distinguishable.

In spite of the fact that everything dreamed is experienced as wholly real, we do not—in the great majority of all dreams—feel that we are corporally present. We do not feel our body with its weight and its form. We have no bodily ego feeling with its ego boundaries, as in normal waking life. However, we are not at all aware of this deficiency of the body ego, while we would feel it dreadfully during waking life. I have already mentioned that even an estranged person need know nothing of his estrangement if he has no immediate task to perform or, for instance, if he is in the protection of his bed. But dreaming is only a very partial awakening from the state of "egolessness." The unconscious and preconscious processes, which become the manifest dream content, awaken the ego where they strike its boundaries, so that there is an ensuing new investment with ego feeling; and as long as a dream picture may have need for it, an ego boundary is never without cathexis. The evanescence of the dream and the impossibility of bringing it back to mind and considering it, are due to the fact that the narcissistic investment of the psychic ego boundaries is constantly being withdrawn as soon as one dream picture is finished and another appears.

There are exceptions to this. A scene may persist for a time; the dreamer may even recall a previous scene. Under what circumstances these two exceptions occur is a special problem. If the whole dream takes its course very slowly and in apparently re-enforced pictures, the sleep is a pathological state, a state of severe overfatigue analogous to that of a fatigued retina in which the ability to receive new images is established more. slowly, and the previous image remains longer, than normally. The consciousness of the normal dreamer regains its receptivity to new images as quickly as does the healthy retina.

The dream state ordinarily contents itself with the psychic ego and its variable boundaries: a bodily ego feeling appears only under certain conditions. When the dream picture impinges on the psychic ego boundary it awakens consciousness. Because it strikes the *psychic* ego boundary from without, as an object cathexis, it is felt as real, even though it may contradict reality. In the dream we are certain of the reality of what happens; we sense it psychically. Exceptionally, we see it with lifelike or even greater vividness. We see it as real; therefore the visual ego boundary must be to some extent awakened; but we do not have a sense of our presence as a body among bodies. It is this bodiless condition of the dreamer to which I wish to draw special attention in this article.

After awakening, one cannot usually remember where and how one felt one's body to be; even in the most interesting dream scene one cannot remember whether one was sitting or standing, the direction of one's gaze, or even the posture one assumed—this even though the dream scene may be so well ordered that one can draw it. In some dreams, the remembered events, such, for example, as seeking an object in a store, meeting a number of people, or the pursuit of an individual, directly require that the dreamer himself must have been in a certain place at a certain time, but nevertheless was there only as an observing psychic ego, or even a moving observing psychic ego, without any bodily ego feeling and without consciousness of one's body. The latter has not been awakened from the sleeping state of being without cathexis. The dream has shown no interest in the body of the dreamer. The dream awakens the sleeper no more than is necessary, and in this shows a precise selection, which may be attributed to the dream function or perhaps to the dream work. In any case, there must have been a disaggregation of ego functions in sleep which permits such a partial awakening of the ego. Thus, the dream work has a selective and condensing action both on the dream material and on the ego boundaries.

In sleep we not only recuperate from the stimuli of daily life and reactions of the ego to these daily irritants, but we also permit the ego as a whole to rest. And if sleep is disturbed by undischarged reactions, wishes or stimuli, the dream affords it additional protection by permitting only a partial awakening of the functions of consciousness and of the ego cathexis. The nucleus of ego feeling, which is connected with the function of the labyrinths and with orientation in space, need be awakened only enough to permit of the dream scenes appearing correctly oriented in space (as regards up and down). It is probable that without this nucleus there can be *no ego feeling at all,* for the intact ego apparently never feels disoriented in space. However, in order to use as little as possible of the ego feeling of the ego nucleus, bodily ego feeling awakes as little and as seldom as possible. Even as regards the ego nucleus, noteworthy exceptions do occur in dreams, e.g., a sudden turning upside down of the whole dream environment, exceptions which, as we know, are used to represent certain typical experiences.

This economizing of ego cathexis in dreams is so strict that there are even dreams of movement in which bodily ego feeling is lacking. We would all assume that a dream experience of such definite bodily character as that of flying and floating could not occur without a strong and complete bodily ego feeling. But even this is not true. I wish to demonstrate the differences, by means of this well-known and well-understood typical dream, between cathexis with bodily and with psychic ego feeling.[6]

It often happens that in flying the dreamer has a sense of his whole body, particularly when an exhibitionistic wish, a desire to show himself, is present. But even in exhibitionistic flying dreams, as in other exhibitionistic dreams, the body ego is seldom complete. Ego feeling may be distinct only for the upper part of the body, or for the arms, or for the lower half of the body, the remainder of the body being entirely without cathexis or only vague in consciousness and feeling. But particularly in these dreams, it happens at times that there is a painful sense that ego feeling is deficient, as for example in dreams of floating on staircases, in which the lack of feeling in the chest and in the arms can be quite unpleasant. However if, as often happens, the flying is done in a flying machine, bodily ego feeling is as a rule wholly lacking. The dreamer remembers the direction and course of the flight and, also, the machine, but he obtained no exact impression of the machine during the flight; he was not conscious of his body or of its position in the machine. It is still more surprising that bodily ego feeling may be quite deficient not only in these strongly displaced and symbolic representations of the sexual act, but even in direct sexual dreams. Often the feeling is limited to the sexual organs; often there is present only the specific pleasure sensation, entirely without bodily ego feeling.

Psychic ego feeling in dreams, which, as we said, is the form of cathexis regularly present, is incomparably more often passive rather than active in character. When psychic ego feeling is active, however, bodily ego feeling is usually present also. A particular type of dream associated with active psychic ego feeling is the peeping dream, which includes the bodily ego feeling of the eyes but no feeling of the remainder of the body.

In a few dreams, bodily ego feeling is present either during the whole dream or only in single parts of it. The difference between those parts in which bodily ego feeling is present and those in which it is absent is quite definite. Whoever has once

. . . .

[6] Federn, "Über zwei typische Traumsensationen" ("On Two Typical Dream Sensations"), *Jahrb. d. Psa.*, VI (1914).

become aware of it can usually tell quite definitely in which scenes of the dream he experienced bodily ego feeling. Bodily ego feeling may be very vivid and accentuated, it may be of ordinary quality, or, on the other hand, it may be expressly felt as vague and indistinct. The most extreme case of a particularly vivid bodily ego feeling with a specific quality was reported by a patient who, in childhood, had had typical somnambulistic dreams of a constant nature.

He related that he would arise from his sleep with great effort in order to save someone or something. He would have to forestall a danger. The danger would consist in something falling down and striking the endangered person or object. The sleeper would get up with the sense that it was his duty to help and to forestall the danger. This was a dream action commanded by his superego. The act of getting up was difficult; the dreamer had a sense of anxiety or oppression connected with the fact that he must get up. He would feel this oppression as in a nightmare; but, while in a typical nightmare the feeling of weight would be projected from the chest on to the incubus which weighed upon it, in our somnambulist it could be felt in the body itself as a difficulty in lifting the body. He sensed the weight of his body which had to be lifted; that is, it would remain within the dreamer's ego as a burden and an impediment to getting up and subsequently walking. During the act of walking, the bodily ego feeling was exceptionally intense.

Contrasting in one aspect to this type of somnambulistic dream—I do not know to what extent it is typical—are the inhibition dreams. In an inhibition dream a movement is intended but is held up at the last moment. Then, in the last moment before waking, a strong bodily ego feeling appears in the inhibited limb or limbs. But this somatic ego feeling in the inhibited limb differs from normal bodily ego feeling, not only in intensity, but also in the fact that the organ thus invested with ego feeling is felt as *outside* the ego.[7] Just as during

. . . .

[7] I know that this description sounds paradoxical, but the paradox is connected with the sensation, not with the description. The organ lies partially within the sensory ego boundary, but outside that for motor activity.

waking an intense bodily pain is *felt,* by the normal individual
(not by the hypochondriac), as if it hit the ego from without,
although one knows that the painful organ belongs to the body
—so the painful immovability and rigidity of the inhibited limb
during the dream is felt as striking the ego from without. Only
after awaking does the ego regain the feeling of command over
and possession of the organ.

In somnambulistic dreams, on the contrary, the feeling of
bodily weight remains within the ego. Common to both types
of dream is the fact that a contrast between superego and ego
comes to expression in them. In the inhibition dream the ego
wishes to do something; the wish, arising from the id, is concurred in by the will of the ego, and the bodily movement
would begin if the ego were not forced, by command of the
awakening superego, to inhibit the execution of the wish and
its own desire. In the end, the opposing wish prevents the execution of the previous act of will. In contrast, in the somnambulistic dream the will of the ego is incited by the superego
to a positive action which is burdensome to the ego. To summarize, in the inhibition dream the ego says "I am not allowed to do it"; while in the somnambulistic dream the ego
says "I am required to do it."

My somnambulist patient, throughout the whole process of
sleepwalking, was able to clearly observe and, later, recall another curious double orientation of the ego. During the whole
process there was present an opposing command, which resisted getting up and which retarded and impeded movement.
However, this opposing will does not, as in the inhibition
dream, arise from the superego, but from a part of the ego.
The sense of being oppressed by the task, mentioned above,
was rationalized throughout the dream by the "sensible"
thought, "You are asleep and dreaming; wait until tomorrow
morning and see if the danger cannot be removed then, or if,
perhaps, it does not exist at all." It is as if the ego were divided.
One part is very close to the thinking of waking life, while the
other part sleeps so profoundly that it can carry out movements
without waking. That this sleep must be very deep to permit
such division of the ego follows from the feeling which occurs

when the sleepwalking is interrupted by waking up, either as a result of an external stimulus or occasionally as a result of a decision of the somnambulist himself. This feeling is always one of being torn from the deepest sleep. That such an exceptional depth of sleep—that is, "being a good sleeper"—is sufficient in itself to explain the possibility of such complex muscular activity during sleep is inadequate. We know, besides, that deep sleep can be established just to allow the sleeper to express contradictory wishes and tendencies of will. All sleepwalking consists in going from the bed and returning to the bed. That this dream is a compromise is shown even in these two phases of walking. I shall discuss the somnambulistic dream elsewhere; it was introduced into the present paper only because it is the dream in which I have, so far, found the most marked bodily ego feeling—namely, the feeling of a hindering body ego, of a resistance arising from the body ego. The somnambulistic dream also forms an exception to the rule that when the psychic ego feeling is active, the bodily ego feeling is active too; for in this case psychic ego feeling was active while the body ego was passive, that is, was felt as a hindrance. During the sleepwalking, however, the body ego became active.

As a rule bodily ego feeling, when it occurs in dreams, is much less marked than in the abnormal dreams of which I have just spoken. When bodily ego feeling does not involve the whole body, but only parts of it, the parts are usually those which stand in relation with the external world of the dream, either through movements or through sensations, as I noted previously in the case of floating dreams. But it must not be thought that in dreamed movements the moving limbs are always invested with bodily ego feeling. I remarked, above, the absence of bodily ego feeling in dreams of flying in machines; the same statement applies to many other movement dreams which are devoid of any bodily ego feeling, even of the partial type. In the following study of the interpretive value to be ascribed to the different types of investment with bodily ego feeling, we shall find that the apparently unimportant, never-heeded feature, whether the dreamer does or does not feel the limb while it is being moved, is of crucial importance in the interpretation of the dream; not, indeed, for the uncovering of the latent content, but as regards the attitude which the ego takes toward the latent dream thoughts.

If the reader is convinced of the wide range of variations in ego feeling, and of the preciseness of our information concerning the appearance of bodily ego feeling in dreams, he will, I hope, share my expectation that so precise a symptom cannot be without significance. The meaning of this phenomenon can be understood only in the light of psychoanalytic methods; and psychoanalysis may be able to utilize this understanding in practical work also. Finally, our new knowledge leads us to a general problem of psychology which is so difficult that every new approach must be welcome—namely, the problem of the will.

When, purely from observation, I learned what great differences there may be in the ego feeling of dreams, I tried to list different explanations which occurred to me and apply them first of all to my own dreams, in which I could state with certainty whether bodily ego feeling was present or not. At first, I thought that I could find a reciprocal relation between the degree to which the ego is emphasized and the intensity of the dream pictures, because this relation held true in a few dreams. However, this assumption proved to be erroneous, as did a second assumption that bodily ego feeling occurs when the dream deals with the total problem of the dreamer's personality, his own fate. These two misleading relations were derived merely from peculiarities of individual dreams.

It then occurred to me that in many dreams a partial ego feeling could be explained simply, and at first without theoretical interest, by the fact that very often, in dreams, an especially strong affect is accompanied by strong bodily ego feeling. This holds true particularly for anxiety dreams, but it also is true of dreams in which the dreamer feels pity or pride. By analogy, a stronger ego feeling makes its appearance when an instinctual impulse becomes conscious in the dream, as in masochistic or exhibitionistic dreams. A careful study of bodily ego feeling as conditioned by affect and instinct would be very profitable. From knowledge gained in other fields, it is certain that we must distinguish between active and passive ego feeling, and this point proves to be useful in this instance. We have one sort of ego feeling corresponding to the active functions and another sort corresponding to the passive functions of the body. In dreams in which there is a strong affect of shame or fear, in masochistic dreams, and in exhibitionistic dreams, the bodily ego feeling is a passive one.

I suspect that definite affects have a corresponding cathexis of definite parts of the body with passive ego feeling. If such a relation can be demonstrated as a constant finding, we may suppose that, also, in dreams in which there is no affect but in which a part of the body is invested with a particular passive ego feeling, one might be able to deduce the presence of an affect which belongs to the dream, but which was not "awakened." For dreams are poor in affect; it is a necessary condition for sleep that affects be not fully produced.

As regards *active* bodily ego feeling, observation of my own dreams and the dreams of others proved that it appears when the dreamer not only *wishes* what the dream signifies, but also sanctions the dream wish or part of it with his *will*. For this reason, dreams are seldom accompanied, in their entirety, by active bodily ego feeling, for generally we are dealing with forbidden wishes which, disturbing sleep, are fulfilled in the dream. Only rarely does the ego venture to desire the forbidden. But the ego may do so partially, and individual parts of the dream action may correspond to the will of the dreamer, even though during waking life these actions might be opposed by the remaining portions of the ego. A consistent "state of mind" exists only as a phrase in books on jurisprudence, where it is supposed even to solve the problem of guilt. We psychoanalysts, and today we may well say "we psychologists," know how little undivided conviction and will man possesses, and how often, in the course of the day, the waking man wills to do something and does not do it. What he willed was his real desire. But in spite of his willing and desiring, the ego obeyed the superego, and not only did not fulfill the wish, but also repressed it. In the dream the wish awakens the psychic ego by means of the manifest dream pictures, and then the whole ego can sanction the wish in the dream, because while awake the ego wanted this wish too. Then, not only does the corresponding psychic ego boundary receive a cathexis, but the bodily ego is aroused as well. However, such an arousal does not allow sleep to persist for long. For this reason it is possible, in waking from a dream with exceptionally strong and complete active bodily ego feeling, to observe oneself and to become completely convinced of the fact that on waking one had a strong sense of still wanting what he wanted at the end of the dream. In this manner, in the past few years, I have been able to establish by self-observation the typical significance of dreams with full bodily ego feeling, just as in previous years I was able to determine the significance of this feeling in the inhibition dream. My interpretation was confirmed when it was tested by the analysis of dreams. A concurrence of the will with the dream wish is an enhanced fulfilment of the pleasure principle, and, as a matter of fact, these intensive "will dreams" are particularly pleasurable. We know, however, that the opposing will of the superego easily changes them into inhibition dreams. Actually, *the explanation of dreams with bodily ego feeling as "will dreams"* was already tacitly included in the explanation of inhibition dreams. The explanation, that toward the end of the sleep the body ego might be expected to be awakening, is invalidated by the fact that more frequently it does not do so.

The observation that a partial bodily ego feeling so often accompanies dreamed movements very well fits our explanation that active bodily ego feeling discloses the will of the dreamer. For these correspond to a volitional impulse magnified into an action. It is more curious that such movements should ever occur without bodily ego feeling. Dream analysis shows that such a lack of bodily ego feeling is not accidental. If a movement is made and no bodily ego feeling accompanies it to reveal that the patient willed it, this movement is intended to emphasize his ability, not his desire, to make the motion. The dream wish, then, refers to the ability. For this reason, the typical flight dream of an impotent man is that of flying in a machine. In this type of flying, as we recall, bodily ego feeling is usually absent. In fact, many impotent men do not wish the sexual act or an erection for sexual reasons; instead they wish that they were able to carry out the act, that is to say, that they were potent in general. This is true particularly in the case of neurotics for whom impotence fulfills an unconscious wish which runs counter to masculine sexuality, or of those neurotics in whom impotence is due to the desire not to have intercourse with particular sexual objects. Similarly, on the other hand, we can understand why some flying dreams occur *with* full bodily ego feeling; that is, because they represent fulfilment of actual willing, not merely wishing to be able to do it.

By observing bodily ego feeling, we have been able to determine the way in which "I want to" *(ich will)* and "I can" are expressed in dreams. From this we can see that this method of expression quite corresponds to the meaning of these verbs as auxiliaries of mode in the grammatical sense. For the mode of a verb expresses the attitude which a person's ego takes toward the activity or experience conveyed in the verb. In the case of "I will," the ego affirms the action and causes it to be carried out. "I can" states that, as far as the ego is concerned, the action is possible. It is therefore meaningful and logical that in dreams "I will" is expressed by the presence of active bodily ego feeling, and "I can" by the presence of psychic ego feeling only, and an absence of ego feeling. These findings should encourage us to look for other expressions of modality in dreams.

The somnambulist, referred to above, presented a special increase in bodily ego feeling, which he perceived not as active ego feeling but, at first, as a burden; and yet at the same time he willed to do the difficult thing. Accordingly, as far as I gather from his description, there was a *passive bodily* ego feeling and an *active psychic* ego feeling. His superego had commanded him to carry out the action. This curious combination expresses in a characteristic way "I should" *(ich soll)*—a volition in the service of the superego and an unwillingness of the ego. It must be added that in the course of his sleepwalking, his body ceased to be a burden and his bodily ego feeling became active. Therefore, after the resistances were overcome, and in the presence of the feeling that it was only a dream, an active will accompanied the dream activity. Similarly, in waking life, in the case of "I should," there are present, simultaneously, an activity of the willing ego and a resistance from a part of the ego. Both are expressed in the dream by the constituents of ego feeling. If we now turn to the inhibition dream—already explained by Freud in the *Interpretation of Dreams*—, my own investigations have shown that it expresses "I want to but am not allowed" (*ich darf nicht*).[8] In this the influence of the superego is unconscious; there is only an awareness of the fact that the body or a part of it, strongly invested with bodily ego feeling, cannot be moved. A muscular apparatus invested with bodily ego feeling is withdrawn from the psychic ego.

The recognition of the meaning of ego feeling in dreams gives rise to a need for a new detailed investigation of these typical dream forms. My present communication is, therefore, a preliminary one. However, it can be safely asserted that the different types of investment with ego feeling—either purely psychic ego feeling or psychic plus bodily ego feeling, active or passive, total or partial—expresses the various modalities of dream occurrences. Conversely, we shall be able to deduce the modality of the dream occurrences from the condition of ego feeling in cases where the analysis of the dream does not give it, and thereby advance psychoanalytic interpretation. The observation of ego feeling in dreams opens a new path for dream interpretation, so that we shall be able to apply the appropriate auxiliary verbs to the dream action. For, as we have shown above, these verbs express the attitude of the ego and of the superego toward the action, whereas the main verb conveys the alteration of the object brought about by means of an effector organ or instrument. That "I want to," "I can," "I am not allowed," and "I should" are expressed in the dream by the ego cathexis, fully corresponds to the processes in waking life. ("I have to," "I cannot," and "I am allowed" still await interpretation.) In waking life the whole ego and superego take definite stands in relation to an action corresponding to these auxiliary verbs; for example, in the case of "I want to," there is active psychic and bodily ego feeling, thought, impulse, and motor activity. In dreams, however, because of the withdrawal

. . . .

[8] *Ibid.*

of cathexis, both motor and thought activity are usually lacking. For this reason, the differences of ego feeling are the only means which remain at the disposal of the dream to express modality. The difference between "I want to" *(ich will)*, "I should," "I must," "I am allowed to," and "I can," which are so great in waking life, are expressed in dreams only by means of subtle, long-overlooked differences of ego feeling; that is to say, they are barely more than indicated. However, the poverty of this means of expression need not surprise us, for we have long since been taught by Freud that even the most powerful instinctual desires are often represented in dreams by a remote symbolism, in itself almost indiscernible and long overlooked.

In waking life, all power is returned to the ego, in particular the will. *The will is the turning of the whole active ego cathexis to particular activities,*[9] *whether they be mere thinking or action.* To believe that the will is only a foreknowledge of an event which would occur in any case is a completely erroneous intellectualistic conception, as Klages long since proved. The ego *as a whole* has at its disposal a certain active libido cathexis which it can send out or withdraw, and *this* is the will. Active bodily ego feeling in waking life represents the materially smaller permanent cathexis of the ego. In dreams it represents the will.

The will is not mentioned in Freud's book on dreams, for the reason that the will belongs to consciousness and to the ego.[10] My contribution aims to amplify our knowledge of dreams, particularly by showing that willing, also, can be recognized in dreams. It is consistent with the theory of dream interpretation to believe that even small differences in cathexis with ego feeling are not insignificant and accidental, but that they too are determined—determined in the same way as the modality or the latent affect which they indicate. When future studies have added to our knowledge, these determinations will also be found of use in the interpretation of dreams.

. . . .

[9] My previous theory (see "Narcissism in the Structure of the Ego," Chapter 2) that the death instinct is intimately associated with the act of willing, as I hope to show in a future paper, is probably true and does not conflict with the above statement.

[10] When willed actions appear themselves in the manifest dream content, they are derived, like thinking processes, from the dream material.

4

THE AWAKENING OF THE

EGO IN DREAMS *

Here Federn deals with the concept of "orthriogenesis," the process occurring on awakening through which one returns from the ego state of sleep to that of waking life, and in so doing one recapitulates the intervening ego states in their chronological order. In this paper precise definitions of the ego (from the descriptive, the phenomenological, and the metapsychological viewpoints) and of its topographical relationships are presented.
                                                            —E. W.

ORTHRIOGENESIS

It is probable that in sleep which is entirely undisturbed the ego is without cathexis, i.e., is cathected only as it is in an embryo (or perhaps we should say, in a sleeping embryo). From such sleep the ego of the day before awakes as the ego of the actual moment; the more normal the sleep and the awakening, the more instantaneous is the restoration of cathexis. In a moment of time the ego has to recapitulate its whole genesis. Since this phenomenon occurs daily with the coming of morning, I propose to call it *"orthriogenesis,"* [1] a word coined on the analogy of *onto-* and *phylogenesis*. Although we should have to invent a "slow-motion camera for the recording of

. . . .

*Read before the Vienna Psychoanalytical Society, November 22, 1933.
[1] *Orthrion* signifies the coming of day, daybreak in general, whereas *eos* is the word used to denote the appearance of dawn in the sky.

psychic phenomena" in order to perceive the whole process in normal awakening, it is nevertheless no mere flight of fancy to assume that such a process takes place. On the contrary, this assumption is helpful, indeed indispensable, in the more exact description and, I venture to think, in the explanation of many phenomena of dream life.

The dream ego is always only partly awakened; it possesses only a fraction of the compass and content of the ego in the waking state, the cathexis of its ego boundary is merely such as is required by the dream scene of the moment, and some of its functions are wholly absent.[2] With regard to its stage of life, we may say that in the majority of dreams the ego approximates very closely the stage which has been actually reached by the dreamer; that is to say, it is the ego of the period between yesterday and today. But in quite a large number of dreams, and in even more dream fragments, the ego which experiences them is awake only up to the point of some quite early level in its existence. Probably it is as we grow older that we dream investigators occasionally experience such dreams and this draws our attention to them; for this is a simple way in which dreams perform their function of wish fulfillment. (*"Ich träume als Kind mich zurücke"*—"I dream myself back into childhood"—says the poet.) The immaturity of the dream ego is, however, not only characteristic of this very common type of dream, but it is probably an essential part of the genesis of all dreams, with the exception of those belonging to the special category of dreams occurring at the moment when we are falling asleep.

The dream work creates pictures from dream thoughts, psychic residues from the day before and their associations, and no sooner have they, by a process of condensation, reached a sufficiently strong degree of cathexis than they arouse the wholly uncathected ego, but only up to some infantile level in its development. Partly awakened, its reactions to the arousing stimuli of the dream work are in accordance with the matu-

. . . .

[2] Moreover, some of those functions which persist may be altered in the sense of the organic disturbance set up, often for reasons of psychic economy through the changed relation between stimulus and anticathexis.

rity and range of functions proper to the ego at the particular level that has been reached. In their turn, these reactions, as the ego grows wider and wider awake, excite in it further mental reactions. Or it may happen that the ego, awakened in this way up to some infantile level and with certain of its functions awakened, may dream the stimulus with which the dream work aroused it and so, having experienced and dealt with the stimulus, may fall asleep again. If, at the excitation of fresh stimuli, it awakes once more, it is more likely to be on the level reached a short time before than on any other. This would account for the typical character of many dreams and, even more, for the similarity of dreams occurring in a single night.

This hypothesis does not conflict with Freud's theory of dreams or with his metapsychology. It necessitates a systematic picture of the essential nature of the ego (see Part II of this paper). It renders untenable the assumption of various writers (e.g., De Sanctis) that there is a special dream consciousness. Our own hypothesis supplies an explanation of the fact that almost every dream interpretation reawakens and illuminates some important phase of the dreamer's past. And further, many tendentious distortions in dreams are not to be put down to the unconscious influence of the superego in the dream work; the action of the superego is rather to be seen in the infantile ego, which has recently been formed under its influence in the course of the subject's life and has been awakened by some stimulus in the dream. Moreover, it may be not the mature superego which is acting upon the ego, but the earlier superego which belongs to the level at which the ego is awakened.

There are many distortions, however, which are quite unnecessary to explain by any reference to the superego: they occur simply because the products of the dream work are misunderstood by the still infantile ego which has been awakened, and for whose benefit the material belonging to the mature stage of the dreamer's present-day life has been worked over by the dream process.

Conversely, misunderstandings on the part of the more mature ego may contribute to the distortion and obscuring of the dream as it finally emerges. In the fact that awakening may take place on one of various levels, we have the reason why the same material on one occasion is, and on another is not, subjected to the primary processes; it explains, too, why one part of the material is so subjected, while another is not, quite irrespective of the remoteness in time of the period to which it belongs. For instance, on one occasion the death of a near relation may enter into a dream scene without disguise, because to the infantile ego there is nothing intolerable in the idea. On another occasion, however, it may be represented only in a disguised manner, because the adult ego resists it. Similarly, this is why an affect at one time retains its infantile character and intensity, while at another the devices of distortion and division are employed to render the same affect superfluous.

Possibly our new hypothesis explains, up to a point, the fact that a childhood wish is indispensable to the formation of a dream; for the awakened infantile ego reacts with its wishes, in accordance with its own nature, to the stimuli which awaken it and elaborates the stimuli in the sense of those wishes. Above all, our assumption explains the verisimilitude of dreams and brings it into close analogy with the delusions of psychosis; for the creations of the dream work impinge upon the awakening infantile ego as though they were external stimuli and are thus inevitably felt as reality. The circumference of the infantile ego lies within the thought processes of the dream work, and it makes contact with them with the boundaries of its cathexes. For orthriogenesis in dreams is like waking, not into the real outside world, but into a mental world conjured up by the dream work and experienced as the external world. We know, from other pathological processes, that various ego levels co-exist in the individual, unconsciously acting and reacting upon one another. Therefore, perhaps a dream may, to some extent, be conceived of as a mental duologue between two parts of the ego, the adult and the infantile, with its different stages and results being visually represented. Such reciprocal stimulation and reaction would account also for the separation of an affect from its source. Regression, to which the state of sleep gives rise, stimulates the pictorial form of experience. A *com-*

pleted dream represents merely the "result" of the duologue; *incomplete* dreams comprise, rather, the different "stages."

According to this hypothesis, the process known as secondary elaboration is brought to bear upon all these reactions of the ego, as it wakes from time to time, or on one level after another. The process is rightly called "secondary" because, in it, the primary mechanisms of dream work are not brought into play, but the secondary process is to some extent interpolated between different phases of the dream work.

I propose in due course to bring detailed confirmation of the hypothesis here advanced. It presupposes the understanding of an ego psychology, which I also formulate here only provisionally until it can be fully and convincingly worked out.

POSTULATES TO SERVE AS A BASIS FOR AN EGO PSYCHOLOGY

A. *Definitions.*[3]
1. *Descriptive Definition:* The ego is the lasting or recurring psychical continuity of the body *and* mind of an individual in respect of space, time, and causality.
2. *Phenomenological (i.e., subjectively descriptive) Definition:* The ego is felt and known by the individual as a lasting or recurring *continuity* of the body and mental life in respect of time, space, and causality, and is felt and apprehended by him as a unity.
3. *Metapsychological Definition:* The basis of the ego is a state of psychical cathexis of certain interdependent bodily and mental functions and contents, the cathexes in question being simultaneous and interconnected, and also continuous. The nature of these functions, and the center around which they are grouped, are familiar.
B. *Topography of the Ego.*
1. *Relation to Consciousness:* Consciousness is one of the functions united within the ego by the ego. Accordingly,

. . . .

---

[*] These definitions are printed, not as they appear in the original article, but as they were later revised by Federn himself and as they appear in my book, *Principles of Psychodynamics* (New York: Grune & Stratton, 1950).—E.W.

the ego is both the vehicle and the object of consciousness. We speak of the ego, in its capacity as the vehicle of consciousness, as "I myself."

2. *Relation to the Preconscious:* The state of simultaneous and interconnected cathexis which goes to form the ego extends, not only over what is conscious at the moment, but also over what is preconscious. Hence the ego is, in the main, a *potential* unity, which becomes actual in so far as the functions and contents pertaining to it become fully cathected and conscious. When we awake, the actual ego of the moment becomes conscious, while the rest of the ego is placed in readiness to perform its interconnected functions; we may describe it as precathected with an ego cathexis.

If we adopt this view, we must modify Breuer's theory of a diffuse, tonic cathexis of the psychic apparatus by stating that, within this cathexis, there are many functions and contents which are precathected with a more intense ego cathexis, and that, owing to this state of precathexis, they can be switched into operation simultaneously and interconnectedly. This modification is already implicit in Jung's theory of complexes. Nevertheless, we may assume, and I hope later to prove, that the continuous and interconnected state of precathexis which constitutes the ego differs qualitatively from all other complex-cathexes.

Consciousness is the "slow-motion camera for the recording of psychic processes," postulated earlier in this paper; it is as such that the ego makes use of consciousness in dreams. Hence, the ego, as it awakes, dreams the timeless, i.e., simultaneous, unconscious stimuli which awaken it as though they were taking place in consciousness and time.

3. *Relation to the External World:* The extent of the state of cathexis which constitutes the ego varies; its boundary at any given moment is the ego boundary and, as such, enters consciousness. When an ego boundary is charged with intense libidinal feeling but is not apprehended as to its content, the result is a sense of ecstasy; when, on the other hand, it is merely apprehended and not felt, a sense of strangeness supervenes.

Subjectively, we distinguish a bodily and a mental ego

feeling, and, accordingly, mental and bodily ego boundaries. That which, approaching from outside, impinges upon a mental *and* a bodily ego boundary has full reality. This reality is affectively self-evident and is subject to no further test. The "reality test" is possible only because, in the course of experience, fresh ego boundaries have been established which are no longer impinged upon by the same impression from outside. In psychosis and in dreams the more lately established ego boundaries have either lost their cathexis or it has not been restored, as the case may be. Hence the reality test is defective or wholly absent. That which, approaching from outside, impinges only upon a mental ego boundary has psychical reality (revelation). That which impinges only upon a *single* bodily or a *single* mental ego boundary is "uncanny," if experience has led the subject to expect a simultaneous impact upon several ego boundaries.

4. When libidinally cathected mental ego boundaries are impinged upon, not by objects, but by other libidinally cathected ego boundaries, affects are originated or released; their quality depends on the nature of the libidinal cathexis of the ego boundaries in question.

5

A DREAM UNDER
GENERAL ANESTHESIA *

New light is thrown on various concepts of ego psychology, especially as applied to the dream. Federn drew from his own subjective experiences during dental surgery. Vivid dream sensations are roused by the awakened mental ego, while the bodily ego, under the influence of anesthesia, remains dormant.–E. W.

Interpretation of dreams seeks the unconscious, its material and its mechanisms. Yet the dream itself is consciously experienced, and there is no doubt whatever that the dreamer himself, i.e., his ego, is dreaming. While, during sleep, there is no ego existing, the ego returns from nonexistence because awakened by the manifest dream. When in this way recathected, the dreaming ego can react to the dream, the ego can enjoy, can fear, can dislike and doubt the dream. The ego may look at the dream as at a movie or a play, or in other dreams the ego itself plays a part on the dream stage. Therefore, dream interpretation is one part of complete dream understanding, and accurate knowledge about the dream ego is the other part. Interpretation gains in certainty and value if ego contributions to the dream can be separated from the productions of dream work.

. . . .

*Read in part before the convention of the American Psychoanalytic Association, Detroit, May, 1943.

The first hint in this direction was made by Freud himself when he said that dream anxiety was the reaction of the ego to an unconscious infantile wish which became unbearable to the adult ego; this conception links the investigation of ego reactions to the problem of neurotic anxiety. Dreams are usually used in psychoanalytical case histories to illustrate that the patient's ego has changed during and through psychoanalysis. Marguerite Combes, interested in the problem of the ego in dreams, wrote a book on "Dream and Personality," [1] rich in observations, but psychoanalytically poor in understanding. Dr. French came the nearest to the writer's interests by investigating successive dreams in regard to ego attitudes. Yet no study was given by psychoanalysis to phenomenological data in respect to the degree of awakening of the ego and to specific qualities and quantities of the dreaming ego's recathexis.

Loss of ego cathexis initiates sleep and recathexis initiates dream; yet too much recathexis quickly makes dream and sleep end. Very distinctly, the mental and the somatic ego are different in regard to their recathexes. That the ego consciously consists of the bodily and mental ego feeling is one of the important phenomenological aspects of psychosomasis.

Every morning on awakening, Freud's theory of the ego emerging out from the id can be verified; therefore, the writer has introduced a new word fitting the new knowledge: *orthriogenesis.* [2] Orthriogenesis is the rapid repetition of ontogenesis of the ego and presupposes that ontogenesis and phylogenesis also exist in respect to the ego. Orthriogenesis of the dream ego is frequently incomplete: the dream ego awakens in an infantile state. Incomplete orthriogenesis easily explains many infantile and atavistic traits of dreams.

The subject of this paper is a personal experience of the writer, his own dream under general anesthesia and his own analysis of it. To avoid repeated, awkward phraseology, this

. . . .

[1] M. Combes, *Le Rêve et la Personnalité,* Bibliothèque de la Revue des Cours et Conférences (Paris: Boivin & Cie, 1932).

[2] *"Orthrion"* means "the morning" as an event in time, while *"eos"* means "the morning" as a visual phenomenon.

dream will be reported and discussed here, contrary to general contemporary practice, in the first person—according to the precedent set long ago by Freud in similar analyses.

I was occupied with observation and theory bearing on the phenomenology of the dream when I had the chance to come to the United States and, as a minor consequence of crossing the Atlantic, had to change from European to American dentistry. In this field, American radicalism is so deeply rooted that for the first time in my life I had to undergo a general anesthesia—with nitrous oxide. The dream during this anesthesia is both the subject of discussion here and the starting point of further investigation of the dream ego.

When I entered the operating room and sat down in the chair, I thought that it was a good thing to have to do with kind and courteous nurses and assistants who spoke softly and touched gently and warned me before they did anything to my helpless physical self. Such treatment encourages an obedient attitude and facilitates narcosis. It might be well to investigate how greatly the quantity of anesthetic necessary, the course of the anesthesia, and the after-effects are influenced by obedience and confidence beforehand. There was some conversation in the operating room concerning a misunderstanding over my message to my dentist that it would not be necessary for him to attend—he was not present—but my tranquil state of mind was not impaired, and the surgeon's words did not enter into the ensuing delirium.

I disliked having the lump of gum thrust into my mouth but was reconciled when I felt it was not hard but elastic. At this moment I had my last thought before the anesthetic took effect, a thought—without any fear—that I might die and that I should use my last moments to consider intensely and philosophically the end of this life and to make an important decision of some sort in regard to accomplishing something in case I should continue to live. Then I felt the strange but rather sweet taste of the gas, a slight dizziness—and I vanished as a personality. There was no disagreeable feeling while inhaling the anesthetic, no respiratory difficulty, no optic disturbances whatever. I fell asleep suddenly, as I had many years ago, and without any feeling of faintness or realization of losing consciousness. Consciousness was lost so quickly I could observe no details.

The dream did not begin immediately after the last conscious thoughts. There was an interval in which my ego lost all its mental charge—its cathexis *(Besetzung)*—and was extinguished. A short time afterward mental life returned. I did not know that I was dreaming. I had not forgotten my antecedent life and I felt myself with my own character and name. However, I lived in completely changed surroundings and I possessed a strength of will power, quickness and certainty of decision, and intensity of action the like of which I have never experienced before either awake or dreaming.

I was the chief military commander and the chief statesman of great territories, and I put in order one province after the other. In the dream I knew which country, far in the east, it was. But in remembering I cannot decide whether it was China or Greece. These provinces had straight-lined frontiers like the states of the United States of America, but the country was not America.

The time I seemed to live through while I was strenuously endeavoring to reform all these countries was very long; it appeared to last for half a year. I accomplished my task with continuous strain and tension. Everything was decided in a hurry and carried through quickly. I was very severe with myself but at the same time fully and continuously contented with the way I performed my duties. Never in my life have I felt such happiness or satisfaction with my personality and with my work. It was the strongest "feeling of oneself" and the greatest enjoyment of one's own self one can imagine. The singular events of the dream followed each other with enormous speed, all actions were carried out with perfection, one after the other, and in complete order and very quickly, since it seemed necessary to act as quickly as possible during the whole dream. Life was a glorious and victorious fight without any conceit or show. I distinctly felt that I never failed to follow the motto: "Do what you have to do."

Suddenly the glory ceased. One of the surgeons spoke to me. Immediately I tried to remember all the details but was aware of only the skeleton of the dream.[3] In similar investigations the patient should be left to awaken spontaneously and should not hear conversation around him. The awakening by another person may change a dream, and conversation hinders remembering. Therefore, complete interpretation is impossible because details are forgotten.

The principle of wish fulfillment is overt. Everything is in full contrast to reality. In reality, I was sitting incapable of moving and—as I mentioned—my attitude was particularly obedient and without any resistance. In the dream, I was acting and rushing from state to state, and nothing could withstand me. Instead of obeying the nurses like a well-behaved child, the dream made me a very masculine superman. Thus, I compensated for being fettered and for the loss of manhood and strength symbolized in having a number of teeth taken away. I cannot imagine anything more directly opposed to activity than the situation of a patient in a dentist's chair. Equally noticeable was the contrast between my role in the dream and the reality of my actual life. An exile can but watch contemporary events and criticize what happens; he cannot defend himself, his family, or his interests. Moreover, although my interest in politics is in real life intense, it is merely scientific and theoretical. I would neither enjoy a high position nor believe myself fitted for it. All these matters were totally reversed in my dream. Not only did I fight for my ideals, I myself was changed into my own ideal. Although I was chief of armies, it was no military fight; my personality conquered by its own strength and by the height of my position.

The whole dream was somewhat parallel to a dreamed monologue in Mickiewicz's *"Dziady"* ("Festival for the Dead"). The hero there dreamed in a postepileptic state of unconsciousness that he argued with God, asked from God omnipotence by strength of thought and by no other weap-

. . . .

[3] Due credit should be given here to Harry M. Seldin, D.D.S., who was present at the administration of the anesthetic and who suggested that I should record any dream I might have.

ons. Since God did not yield to his wishes, he calls him the world's "czar." It is psychologically interesting that the poet allowed his hero to develop his sacrilegious dream only in the state of a deep unconsciousness. My own dream was highly aimed but remained in the limits of the earth.[4]

I must go back to my childhood to find daydreams which correspond to this anesthesia dream. At the age of ten, I remember, I read with enthusiasm a book for boys which, as I recall it, was named "Liu-Pa-Yu." It was a Chinese story and I became very interested in the fate of the Chinese and wanted to go to the Orient myself and become Emperor of China. I was teased about this for a long time.

The other possibility, that the country dreamed of was Greece, has two sources. The first is that at the age of thirteen or fourteen I deeply resented the defeat of Demosthenes and the victory of the Macedonians over Greece. The second source is more recent. In discussions, I have frequently demonstrated the parallelism between ancient history and recent events, and made the forecast that another European-Asiatic empire might be attempted by the militarily progressive and politically aggressive northern tribe of the Germans. In the dream, I myself was the helper of all these countries. By locating my campaigns in Greece, I, myself, and not the Germans fulfilled my prophecies. (The dream happened long before the disaster of Greece.) The wish fulfillment—power, freedom, perfection, and prophecy—culminated in the satisfaction of dreaming of using my faculties for the best of all; an ideal once nourished but of which fulfillment was denied for many years.

One can expect to find that the basic mechanisms in dream production during general anesthesia will not differ from those in dream production during physiological sleep, but that there will be some psychological differences as typical consequences of the physiological differences.

A person under full anesthesia does not react to physical or

. . . .

[4] Since this paper was read, four reliable persons have written to me about dreams under anesthesia which contained cosmic experiences of the ego combined with religious, ecstatic contact with God, the Creator.

mental stimulation in such a fashion as to awaken either immediately or slowly in the same way as from physiological sleep. By extraordinary stimulation reflectory disturbances occur; one can even die but not awaken.

Dreams are influenced, and may even be started, by stimulation derived from external or internal irritation or from internal mental sources. I mention the possibility that many laymen and metapsychical authors may be correct and that psychic stimuli from other individuals might also influence the dreamer's mind. That is, there might be a hypnotic rapport established between the patient in anesthesia and the surgeon, even without the latter's intention, before the patient is put into sleep.

In any report of mental productions before, during, and after general anesthesia, it is important to determine what depth of unconsciousness was established. During the beginning and the ending of ordinary sleep, even slight stimuli affect the sleeper; during the depth of sleep, external stimuli have to be strong or have to continue for some time, gaining efficiency through accumulation. Therefore, during deep physiological sleep, the mental sources of dreams are the main ones. My dream happened in deepest sleep and not in awakening.

The main manifest dream events can be traced to stimuli and to changes of the mental state brought about through anesthesia.

I am certain of four stimuli and see a possible fifth. As I have already said, my last conscious thought was that I must seriously consider my future plans. This thought created—like an autosuggestion—my heroic course during the dream and in this regard, the dream recalls the many cases of individuals who have been able to direct their dreams during the day or evening. I would have dreamed otherwise if I had thought of some pupil or of my grandson or if I had been resistant or fearful in regard to anesthesia; in none of these cases could I have produced a dream shaped like Caesar's *veni, vidi, vici*.

While the last conscious thought directed the whole dream, a last perception determined the choice of the field in which the dream played—and more especially its form. After my awakening, the straight-lined frontiers remained as a clear visual remembrance. One might think that they are sufficiently explained by the frontiers between the states of the United States. Yet I know that while the characteristics of the map of North America were provoked in my dream, the stimulus occurred before losing consciousness. When I looked to my right side, I saw the illuminated and magnified X-ray pictures of my teeth. The pictures were quadrangular, they were hanging side by side, and I thought that they demonstrated which teeth had to be operated on. My last visual interest was given to them. They represented what had to be changed; thus the quadrangularity of the frontiers was due to the X-ray pictures of my teeth.

My identification with the surgeon was a third, recent source of my dream. What the surgeon did in physical reality, I accompanied with parallel deeds in the world of my dream. This world of my own was not limited by judgment or by reality tests; both are lacking in dreams.

This identification expressed itself by the use which I made of the fourth stimulus for my dream, the operation itself. In my dream, one province was put in order after the other; I remember that I hurried from one to the next. Repetition of an element is rather a rare dream phenomenon; usually it corresponds to a repetition of the fact represented by the element. It is probable that each extraction was transformed by the dream work (i.e., the whole unconscious mental process that builds up the manifest dream out of its latent sources) into one after the other of my separate political and military activities; I was repairing each ruined country to a sound and good state. The main mechanism in dream work is condensation, and we are not astonished to see many influences condensed into the repeated scene.

I pass over some deeper associations and interpretations[5] and only add as a fifth source of the dream my thought when I decided to have my teeth removed. As I intended a full

. . . .

[5] My military service fifty years ago, for example, was for two periods of half a year each; "Caesar" refers specifically to a peculiar situation of my elder brother sixty years ago.

and energetic repair for good, so in my dream I "repaired" my provinces.

Our interest in finding typical or exceptional features which are due to the state of anesthesia is to some extent satisfied. We have found identification with the surgeon, influence of the last conscious thoughts and the last sensory perceptions, influence of the more general disposition of mind of the week before, and influence of the acts of extraction.

By confronting these findings with the report of the dream, one might admit that there is some probability in this explanation. However, I myself have lived through this dream and am not satisfied by the interpretation, because this analysis does not render justice to the sensational singularities of this dream—to the enormous delight I had, to the great speed of the happenings, and to the tremendous strength of my ego feeling. My explanation up to this point has been incomplete because only the usual means of psychoanalytical interpretation have been used. Only the dream contents were dealt with, not the peculiar personality state during the dream.[6] This state will now be examined and explained.

During all periods of life, pathology of the ego plays an important part in all diseases. There are many pathological disturbances of ego feeling, from lack of "presence of mind" to estrangement and depersonalization, from hysterical weakness of the ego to true double personality, and from schizoid exaggeration of the ego feeling to schizophrenic diminution and regression to infantile states.

Normally, our bodily ego remains more or less the same, containing our whole body with its sensory and motor organs, but our mental ego changes continuously, depending on which functions, thoughts, and perceptions are simultaneously conscious. The mental ego feels itself to be within the bodily ego.

When, by sleep, fainting, or similar unconscious states, one's ego feeling becomes interrupted and disappears, the contiguity with the ego feeling before interruption is re-established after restoration. Therefore, the "ego" can be defined as the "lasting or (after interruption) re-established continuity of

. . . .

[6] See "Ego Feeling In Dreams," Chapter 3.

the individual's unity in regard to space, time, and causality." The "ego" defined as subject feels this "ego" as object.

These basic remarks on the ego also bear on the ego during sleep and in dreaming. However the ego state during this dream in general anesthesia was very different from that in usual dreaming.

At the moment when consciousness was lost, the ego fully disappeared; there was neither bodily nor mental ego feeling. When the dream started, the ego reappeared suddenly and lasted, with the unique intensity mentioned, throughout the whole dream. But it was only a mental ego, with no trace of the bodily ego. Both facts, the sudden disappearance of the ego and the intensity of the reawakened mental ego, are produced by the anesthesia. They do not belong to normal falling asleep and to ordinary dreaming.

In normal sleep, the mental ego awakens as little as possible, and the bodily ego does not awaken at all. When the bodily ego awakens or when the mental ego becomes stronger, with some of its critical and reasoning functions, further sleep soon becomes impossible.

By remembering where and how one was standing, sitting, lying, and moving, one can tell to what extent the bodily ego was present in some dream scenes. Usually the dream work succeeds in silencing emotional function and volition. Whenever parts of the body are clearly perceived, it is due to emotion or to an intended voluntary action which has penetrated into this part of the dream. Therefore, a dream like the one reported could not have been dreamed in normal sleep, because the dreamer would have awakened before the mental ego could get such strength. From epileptic states and from experiments with mescaline, ego sensations of analogous intensity are reported.

Freud has stated as a principle that dreaming protects the continuation of sleep by sacrificing its completeness. The aim of conserving sleep is frustrated when awakening forces become so strong that too much of the ego becomes re-established. Protection of sleep is made by the external helps of darkness, silence, covering the body, the (physiological) help of closing the eyes, and by two psychosomatic means: the increase of the "protection against stimulation" (the *Reiz-*

schutz) and the emptying of the ego itself of its full cathexis. There is a close connection between fatigue and *Reizschutz* on one hand and between sleepiness and ego cathexis on the other. One can be very sleepy without being fatigued except by the very effort to overcome sleepiness. The increased *Reizschutz* in efferent and in afferent stimulation explains the main quality of fatigue, the feeling of strain in continuing any activity or in maintaining any active or passive attention.

A high degree of mental fatigue before going to sleep shows in the pace of the manifest dream. Dream pictures change slowly; sometimes one and the same scenery remains during a whole dream which, in contradistinction to this dream in anesthesia, proceeds very slowly. Slow-paced dreaming is, therefore, a symptom of psychosomatic fatigue which has not been repaired by sleep. Sleepiness can be described as a sense of difficulty in maintaining ego cathexis.

Strong external stimuli or exciting ideas are required to ease the strain of maintaining one's ego. One can distinctly feel a moment of demarcation between states of fatigue and sleepiness alone. In undergoing the anesthesia described, no fatigue and no sleepiness whatever were felt.

The disappearance of the ego in sleep is so much of an imposing phenomenon that, among analysts, Jekels attributes sleep to the manifestations of the death instinct. Doubtless, sleep is an act of regression; but, although the death instinct tends toward regression, not every regression proves to be the working of the death instinct. Sleep makes the individual return bioanalytically to his mother's womb, a symbol of death but factually a renewal of life, and when a dream interrupts sleep, it recathects the ego as it is found in an early state of development. Jekels, in his paper, quotes Kant's opinion that only dreaming saves the sleeper from death.

Yet sleep has its great economical importance, mentally and physically. While the waking state exhausts all cathexes, sleep restores all potential and factual energies in all psychosomatic fields. Sleep is every night's rejuvenation, and more so without dreams. In a discussion, Jekels and the writer agreed in the view that symptoms and paralyses due to the death instinct can become more prominent in sleep than during the waking state because life as well, by returning to an early infantile or even prenatal state, gains instinctual intensity. There is no doubt that, instinctually, aggression and sexuality regain strength during the sleep and create dreams disturbing and protecting the sleep. It might even be that sleeping life cannot be damaged by intensified death instinct because damage threatened by death is directed against the active energetic life of waking, not against the reconstructive, quiet life of sleep. This would be parallel to the protection of sleep by loss of the ego's cathexis.

Many conflicts, wishes, regrets, fears, and many interesting impressions retain some cathexis when sleep comes. They continue to stimulate, but the ego has no boundary sufficiently cathected to react. Paradoxically, nothing can happen to the ego because of its absence, except that stimuli create dream work and this reawakens the ego. In fact, the ego under such conditions would be very vulnerable because it would lack reason, experience, anticipation, and memory. We know an ego of this sort; it is that of the hypnotized person, liable to any suggestion.

Dreams arise from the need or habit of the mental apparatus—even in a state where it lacks nearly all cathexis—of dealing with the many mental and the few physical disturbers of sleep. The uncathected state turns by dreaming into a partially cathected one. This is the dream ego, awakened merely to watch the dream and to live it through.

It is worth while to inquire to exactly what degree the dreaming ego is bound to be re-established. The answer is that the dream ego must be able to recognize, vaguely or clearly, the objects and scenes of the manifest dream. This minimum is reached, but not exceeded, by successful and perfected dreaming in which all emotion is transformed into dream scenes.

Objects and events in the manifest dream are not only recognized, they are seen and are each lived through in reality. This reality is impressed on the dreaming ego; any less superficially cathected ego would not accept it. Yet dream reality needs further explanation.

The basic characteristic of dream and of psychotic hallucination is untrue reality, a reality which does not exist for the individual in health or when awake.

Reality and visuality are caused in infancy, in psychosis, and in the dream by stimulation of the ego from outside. Ontogenetically arising from a state of nonexistence through an embryonic and infant period, the individual becomes accustomed to attribute reality to everything around the ego boundaries. In dreams, the infant ego is awakened by a world of ideas and events made by the dream work; all this is reality because of the dream ego which is awakened inside this world of picture thoughts. The ego while dreaming may not reach the period of life from which the manifest dream pictures are taken. In scenes of later life, the dream ego may be younger or older than the period represented. Neither is the dream ego's level of instincts equal and up to conscious age.

The more a dream ego is recathected, the more it participates in the dream facts, and because it feels its weakness, such a dream ego resembles the depersonalized ego.

The dream ego falls short of any activity. Even when one has to perform something in a dream, such a task is not felt either as a wanted and voluntary or as a refuted and unwillingly accepted one, but everything is done as a matter of fact, with the feeling of imposed necessity which is analogous to the imposed reality of the dream itself.

The dream ego is poorly cathected. Far from being resistant or permanent, it is unstable and it is passively exposed to the dream and defenselessly undergoing it. As it is lacking in ego functions like reasoning, volition, judgment, and use of memories, any attempt at understanding is immediately abandoned. One of the most important and least emphasized components of the dream ego's weakness is that one's mind is only partially awakened while the body continues to sleep, although this rule has exceptions.[7] The dream ego also deserves the designation of weakness because its mental cathexis is passive.

Although dreams in anesthesia are made by the same mechanisms as all dreams, in successful and deep toxic anesthesia, conditions are so different from normal sleep that important differences of dream structure could be expected. But the findings themselves could not be anticipated.

Complete anesthesia allows the dream ego to become

. . . .

[7] *Ibid.*

strongly cathected because no danger exists of being awakened, as there does in normal sleep if the manifest dream exerts too strong a stimulation on the ego, which is feebly cathected and passively exposed. In anesthesia, the dream has lost its function of protecting sleep since this function has become quite superfluous. Yet habitually, in many anesthesia dreams, mechanisms of disguise, symbol formation, and displacement are used to satisfy the wish fulfillment tendency of the id and of the ego. The dream investigated in this paper was exceptionally undisguised and clear, notwithstanding its extreme wish fulfillment.

The astonishing features center in the excessive recathexis of the mental ego without any feeling of the body which can be recollected—without any recathexis of the bodily ego. In normal dreams, bodily ego feeling carries awakening with itself, since bodily ego feeling in ordinary dreaming meets with emotion or volition of the mental ego, and if the mental ego becomes too wakeful, the body awakes with the mind and soon the dream is ending. To continue sleep, the mental ego loses, as quickly as possible, any increased cathexis and returns to an uncathected state. But, in anesthesia, no danger of awakening threatens sleep; phenomenologically, that means that no announcement of too strong stimulation compels the dream ego to withdraw any recathexis as it does during usual dreaming. On the other hand, no sleep reflex becomes stimulated by feelings of fatigue because neither fatigue nor sleepiness are felt in general anesthesia. For these reasons, the recathected mental ego can remain recathected even when it reaches extraordinary strength of cathexis, as happened in the dream investigated here.

One of the unexpected features of this dream was that the superego was recathected simultaneously with the ego. This cannot happen in any dream during ordinary sleep without awakening. The abnormal intensity of ego recathexis also explains the clearness and rationality, which contrast with the usual illogical products of dream formation. In this case of anesthesia, the manifest dream was like a chapter of a normal biography, full of Caesarean success but, thanks to the co-awakened superego, without Caesarean excesses. It is very probable that remembrances of Caesar's hurry in carrying his triumphs from province to province helped to form the dream. Many dreams in literature, in dream research as well as in fiction, biographies, and autobiographies, report vivid and long-lasting, adventurous and glorious deeds; yet the dream ego undergoes them passively, not with "conscious" mental activity, volition, and emotion. It might be that, like anesthesia, abnormal fatigue or other causes might also prevent reawakening of the body and permit, therefore, increased mental ego cathexis. However, clear and rational dreams like the one investigated remind us of the fact that it is the conflict between ego, id, and superego, and between wish fulfillment and fear, primary and secondary processes, awakening and sleep-continuing, organic stimulation and stimulus protection, instinctual stimulation and resistances, mental stimulation and opposed stimuli, which creates all irrational pictures in dreaming—even dreams' chimerical monstrosities. It is mainly because of the incompatibility between conscious and unconscious processes whenever they meet on mutual ground—and because in sleep the ego is helpless against intruding unconscious processes—that the dream becomes such a battleground. Yet, if the mental ego is abnormally actively cathected, this cathexis works as an anticathexis against unconscious processes; the ego reacts by a dream, but this dream shows the main qualities of the normal ego—volition, clearness, rationality. Such a strongly cathected mental ego has its boundaries well guarded against instinctual urges as well as against irrationalities coming from the unconscious. The mental ego reacts with its own libidinous means, with object libido as well as with narcissism. Therefore, in this dream, the objects as well as the ego feeling were abnormally strong.

The dream ego was extremely happy because narcissism as well as object libido was fully satisfied. Like an experiment, the dream shows that happiness is a corollary of ego cathexis. The dream was not a manifestation of mania because in this mental disease the superego loses its cathexis. Psychiatrically, the diagnosis of a state of amentia would be justified, if one wanted to judge an artificial, narcissistic inebriation like any waking pathological state.

One finds regularly that a dream with vivid dream scenes shows little intensity of the ego representation and feeble cathexis of the dream ego; in other dreams, the dreamer's own personality is more awakened, while the dream scenery is less vivid. This complementary relation seems to be due to some economy in the whole awakening process of dreaming. Another explanation would offer an alternative between a narcissistic or an object-libidinous wish of which the fulfillment is effected by the manifest dream. In the anesthesia dream both ego, including superego, and the dream events were exceedingly vivid, yet little memory remained of the scenery and of its visual intensity. The reality feeling of the dream events was exceedingly strong, as was the personality feeling. It is out of the question to decide whether, biologically, cathexis is increased; one has to be satisfied to ascertain the phenomenological increase of all sensations which correspond to cathexis-increase. Undoubtedly, there was not a sleeping and scarcely awakened ego in this dream, but a mental ego with highly increased vigilance, without any concomitancy of any bodily ego cathexis.

The flooding of the ego by recathexis is explained by the fact that it could not awaken as long as anesthesia continued. Yet this impossibility does not explain the fact itself. One might as well have expected a paralysis of the mental ego as of all sensory and motor functions. The easiest explanation of such, and of analogous, problems is to assume a specific affinity of the drug to the apparatus which are paralyzed.

Psychologically, there are two possible explanations. The one is that deep unconsciousness reveals the degree of the narcissism of the dreamer. This explanation will be tested when many psychoanalyzed individuals who have undergone general anesthesia are asked to report their anesthesia dream experiences. The reported case shows a great amount of narcissistic cathexis, but this dream is without value in regard to this question because of the dreamer's intense interest in ego psychology. Many scientifically engrossed dreamers unconsciously direct their dreaming to their dominating problems. Yet regardless of whether the dreamer was inclined toward the ego cathexis, the resulting dream yielded the proof of the prevalence of mental ego cathexis over bodily ego cathexis. If the ego had been reawakened by the direct influence of the anesthetic, this effect would have occurred from the beginning. But this did not happen. The mental ego was intensely recathected through the manifest dream which was provoked by the strong stimuli set by the operation. The effects of these stimuli were distinct, although through anesthesia pain by, and localization of, the stimuli were absolutely eliminated. The writer is inclined to assume that stimulation influenced the mental ego so strongly because the stimuli did not consume their energies in producing pain and sensory localization. This lack of pain and localization of stimuli is due to the paralyzing effect of the anesthetic on all sensory and motor organs, i.e., the body; because no body was felt, no body ego was recathected.

Further, the conclusion must be drawn that the body ego fulfills the task of protecting the mental ego from too intense stimulation; the body ego contains the whole *"Reizschutz."* It is easily understood that stimuli, when it is recognized whence they come and where they work, are less able to accumulate and to be condensed up to the point of disturbing or awakening the mental ego. Therefore, the fading of the bodily ego is the main reason for the development of dreams in general anesthesia and especially of dreams due to body stimuli. It is less a paradox than an amazing discovery that, with the full paralysis of the sensory organs, protection against stimuli and protection of sleep are also paralyzed. This is the reason why the stimuli could awaken the mental ego alone and could awaken it so intensely and could exert such an intense influence on the dream itself.

There are two more exceptional features of the dream which are also to some extent explained by the intensity of the mental ego cathexis—the abnormal experience of speed and of length of time lived through. Freud says that the "unconscious" is without the category of time, that time-experience is reserved to conscious and preconscious mental life. Yet we know that there exists a "head watch" by which the time is judged even during sleep; one can attribute this to preconscious functioning. By body process periodicity, the head watch gains an objective judgment of the time. Whether one feels a period of time subjectively as long or short depends on the changes of object and ego cathexis during this period and on the pleasure or dullness felt because of the changes. Occupation with many interesting tasks and pleasurable thoughts makes time speed and makes its remembrance cover a long period, in contrast to the objective judgment of time by the body ego. The enormous intensity of mental experiences and deeds combined with the lack of any interference of the body ego created the extraordinary impression of extension of time in the anesthesia dream.

The features mentioned in this dream must be checked by many investigations of dreamers of different ages and different libidinous character-structure, with different drugs used for anesthesia, with different attitudes in regard to the operations, with different kinds of operations, without operations, and with spontaneous and artificial awakenings. The usual characters of their dreams should also be known. Investigations of this kind will contribute to our knowledge of the normal and pathological cathectical reactions of the ego and of its functions.

In itself, this topic is important enough. However, it provides one more argument for the need to investigate ego cathexes in different psychoses. Many psychiatrists have recognized the anology between the mental production of the schizophrenic and of the dreamer. The main similarity lies in the identity of the falsified reality conception. Thought has reality in dreams as well as in schizophrenia, in the latter because some ego boundaries have lost their normal cathexis, in the dream because the ego is awakened from nonexistence into the perceptions of the manifest dream. In both cases, reality is due to the fact that perceptions stimulate the ego while coming from outside to its boundaries, whereas mere thoughts are inside the ego boundaries and included within the cathexis unity that is the ego. Furthermore, the schizophrenic ego suffers from the same feebleness of cathexis as the dream ego in usual sleep. By shock treatment, the feebly cathected schizophrenic ego becomes for some time fully cathected, reawakened. If we learn, by use of helpful mental treatment or by other means, how to make recathexis persevere, schizophrenia will be healed; for all psychosis bears primarily on ego cathexis.

PART II

ON THE TREATMENT
OF PSYCHOSIS

6

PSYCHOANALYSIS OF

PSYCHOSES

The differences between the treatment of psychotic from that of neurotic egos are clearly outlined in this chapter. Dr. Federn demonstrates, with case material, that the ego weakness of the psychotic patient requires psychological procedures which are in many respects contrary to those adopted in classical analysis. This chapter is based on an article which appeared in the Psychiatric Quarterly *in 1943; it has been edited and combined with an earlier preliminary report from the* International Journal of Psychoanalysis *to avoid repetition of material. (See Bibliography of Federn's writings at end of book for exact citations.) I would like to thank the editors of these journals for their kind permission to use this material.*—E. W.

ERRORS AND HOW TO AVOID THEM

When dealing with the endogenic psychoses, it is quite unjustifiable for us to confine our efforts to diagnosis and prognosis; nor is it enough, simply because the disease is conditioned by endogenic factors, to see to it that the patient is placed under care and that remedies suggested by the symptoms are applied, thereafter letting the morbid process take its course while we observe it with psychological and clinical interest. Appropriate treatment along both physical and psychic lines may have a favorable influence upon the case, in respect both to the severity of the particular attack and the course it follows, and to the onset and duration of completely or relatively normal periods and the patient's attitude towards reality at such times.

This paper will deal with two groups of psychoses, the schizophrenic and the manic-depressive. Cases include process-psychoses, stationary cases temporarily arrested with some defect formation, and pre- and postpsychotic states. These groups deserve a denomination with the ending "osis," because mental functions which disappear grossly are not lost potentially, or entirely—each function might temporarily become re-established.

The metapsychological processes in both groups are: (1) abnormal narcissistic cathexis and diminished object cathexis; (2) ego regression, through which (a) onto- and biogenetically repressed mental elements and aggregates have become conscious, and (b) the reality test becomes insufficient because of change and diminution in ego cathexis.

The two groups differ from each other as follows: (1) The quality of impairment of ego cathexis is dissimilar; notwithstanding the preceding high narcissistic cathexis, in schizophrenics there is loss of cathexis of ego boundaries, while in manic-depressives the ego boundaries are cathected with mortido. (2) Prevailing ego states are continuing separately in schizophrenia, but are alternating in manic-depressives. (3) The morbid process is interrupted by relapses in most schizophrenics but is periodic in manic-depressives. (4) The spontaneous healing process consists in defect-formation and projection in schizophrenics, but in mourning-work in melancholics. (5) The main defense mechanisms are regressive or neurotic reactions in schizophrenics but are generalized emotional reactions, spreading over the whole ego, in manic-depressives.

In the beginning, psychotic patients were psychoanalyzed mainly in consequence of erroneous diagnosis, or with the purpose of using analysis for investigation. Some of the patients investigated seemed to profit by the increased clinical interest given to them. Bleuler himself was the first to state that Burghölzli could discharge three times as many cases since all physicians had begun to deal with them on the more profound basis of Freudian understanding.

Yet these patients were not truly psychoanalyzed. I think that this was one of the reasons why they improved. The psychiatrists adjusted themselves to the patients, so as to get as much information about the patient's mental aggregates as possible, and, either wittingly or without being aware of it, behaved in such a way that the schizophrenics established good positive transferences to the physicians. Those physicians who failed in this probably soon abandoned their investigations because· they did not discover anything new.

When I began to psychoanalyze psychotic patients, all psychoanalysts believed that persons with narcissistic mental disease were unable to establish any transference to the physician. The generally accepted idea was that for this reason no psychoanalysis was possible. Nowadays, many authors know that both statement and conclusion were false. Yet there is some true basis for the belief. The transference of psychotics is quite unstable and does not warrant use of the same psychoanalytical method employed with neurotic patients. Since psychoanalysts treated psychoses like neuroses, they had poor results. They had started psychoanalyses without recognizing the underlying psychoses; they stopped the analyses when the psychoses had spontaneously become manifest or had been made manifest by analyses carried through in the usual way. Some colleagues may remember an interesting staff meeting at which they heard the complaints of a patient who had developed a catatonic state while he was being psychoanalyzed. The patient accused the analyst of having promoted his disease. Yet the analyst had neither interpreted nor encouraged the patient's free association but, rather, had been passive and listened to the patient's increasing erotic illusionary ideas. He had been allowing the patient free outlet and was taking the case history while the psychosis developed.

World War I taught surgeons that patients are harmed by routine sounding or examining of wounds of the lungs, the abdomen, the brain. Similarly, I have learned not to take anamneses in psychotic or postpsychotic cases of schizophrenia. I have watched some cases of practically cured schizophrenia for more than twenty years following the first treatment, and have observed that the patients refused to remember their psychotic states, having better insight into their pathology than I had. When they were forced to remember them, they relapsed. The patients cured of schizophrenia speak favorably of me, but they do not like to be reminded of their psychoses by meeting me. This is probably the first problem which is neglected in clinics and in private practice. Some genuinely gifted physicians, but few thoroughly trained psychiatrists, are aware of it.

The second requisite to psychoanalysis of psychotics is that there should be somebody who is interested in the patient and who will take care of him during the analysis and later on. No psychoanalysis of psychotics can be carried through without skillful assistance. The patient should be aided and protected; he should not be left to himself and his tribulations outside the analytical hours. The helper, who must have won the patient's positive transference, may possibly be the mother, sister, or brother, rarely the father, and, according to my experience, even less frequently the wife or husband. When no close relatives are sufficiently loving to devote themselves to the task for some time, a friend is necessary. Without such a harbor for libidinous relief, psychoses are not cured, or an accomplished cure does not persist, whether it was attained by pharmacologic shock, by psychoanalytical treatment, or by a combination of both.

It is not at all astonishing that most psychotics relapse at home or elsewhere when left without the continuous support of transference. Every psychosis is consciously or unconsciously focused on conflicts or frustrations in family life. With psychotics, as with children, the result of a psychoanalysis depends so largely on the helpfulness of the environment that, if a psychotic patient is disliked by the rest of his family, the treatment is as much hampered by this exogenic factor as it may be on the endogenic side by the severity of the disease. In no single case have I succeeded without the steady cooperation of the family or of someone in their place. When we remember that others besides psychoanalysts aim at achieving proper care for psychotic patients within their family circle, it is clear that our duty is to perfect our technique for the analysis of psychotics, so that it may always be available where the environment is suitable. An important desideratum is the psychoanalytical training of nurses and attendants.

Unless unsatisfactory conditions in family life are changed, the cure of psychotics turns out to have been Sisphean labor which ends in hospitalization or foster-family life. It is true that the sacrifices imposed on healthy or half-healthy family members cannot always be combined with their duties and their claims for leisure and enjoyment. Often consideration for other family members requires more attention than the care of a post-psychotic member; yet this care gradually becomes easier, and many postpsychotic patients return to usefulness and happiness. This mental hygiene work, when well organized, will prove as effective and economical as preventive care of tuberculosis. We might compare the libido with fire and electricity, helpful and dangerous powers which may be so well controlled that they can be handled by everyone in everyday life.

One of the most difficult problems in the psychoanalysis of patients with severe psychoses is the sexual problem. When a manic phase begins to develop in women, they are eager for intercourse, quick marriage, and childbirth. In manic phases, men and women always think that they love and are loved; and with their optimism, their productivity, and their over-leaping of resistance, they reach response quite easily, and this quickly culminates in married or unmarried relationships. Men and women in manic states frequently are so unable to stand any interference with their sexual desires that they return to masturbation. Masturbation is also the usual means of temporary self-consolation in middle-grade melancholias, and in young hebephrenics unrestrained masturbation occurs.

My experience has taught me that all psychotics have more chance to recover when they have moderate sexual intercourse. They are adversely influenced when, by abundant sexual activities, the source of the libido cathexis becomes temporarily exhausted; it is then that melancholic and schizophrenic periods become more severe and last longer. When treatment is successful, sexual satisfaction can be influenced and regulated to some extent. Psychotic individuals are not good parents, nor do they themselves readily tolerate the unconscious reversal of the Oedipus situation in parenthood. For these reasons, and because of heredity, sterilization by vasectomy or tubectomy is indicated. Yet, in men, the operation is complicated by a bad mental effect insofar as unconsciously it means castration; X-ray sterilization would be preferable if an unspectacular apparatus were available. In Austria, although they were illegal, I had these operations carried out with the support of Wagner-Jauregg, who fully agreed with my opinion that in young schizophrenics vasectomy has a curative effect. We disagreed in that he saw the explanation only in the diminished masturbation; I am convinced that the increased supply of libido, through the Steinach effect, has a direct influence on the defective narcissistic ego cathexis in these cases. Sterilized patients of both groups instinctively curtail their indulgence in sexuality when they are cured—this is another argument in support of my explanation.

I repeat the general conditions which should be considered in every psychoanalytical treatment: Establishment of positive transference; interruption of treatment when transference becomes negative; provision of the feminine helper; lasting psychoanalytical postpsychotic mental help and supervision; settling of the sexual problem. These general rules are not just instructions which, when followed, facilitate the psychoanalysis of a patient. They are, as I said, conditions for the treatment. In severe cases they are indispensable; in milder cases they shorten the treatment.

Patients with less severe disorders frequently provide themselves with the necessary help; the ego is able to resist full regression in schizoid cases and libidinous exhaustion in depressive cases. In these milder cases, it is sometimes possible to cure the neurosis without provoking the outbreak of the underlying psychosis. Such success is rather to be expected when the treatment is given according to pseudo psychoanalysis which has abandoned the strict Freudian rules and has compromised with Stekel, Adler, Rank, or Horney. Since many "personality neuroses," called psychopathic or degenerate, are mixtures of different neuroses, of schizoid or depressive dispositions, and of psychoses, the results of such scientifically bad methods are particularly good, and sometimes even better than the response to true Freudian psychoanalysis. The aim, however, is not to bring about help blindly, but to know how to treat mild and severe cases of psychosis with a foundation of sound theory. Neither the true Freudian technique, which Freud developed for neurotic diseases, nor the pseudo analytical measures just mentioned, are adapted to severe cases. With justifiable modifications of the technique, good results have been obtained by many of us.

My work dates back to the first decade of the century. It was in Vienna that I became deeply interested in a family in which the mother was a high-strung sadist, whom Ferri would have designated as a "degenerate mother." She suffered from severe asthma. The father died as a result of an accident which, seen psychoanalytically, can be described as suicide. There were two sons and two daughters in the family. At the age of eighteen, the younger daughter committed suicide on Christmas Eve, when she was expected to leave on a visit to friends. The thought of having no Christmas holiday in her parental home might have precipitated her decision. The elder daughter had at this period been readmitted to the hospital where, at twelve years of age, she had been diagnosed as having hysteria, and where she had been twice afterward, for many months, in an agitated catatonic state. I visited her for six weeks, and eventually won her transference by kindness, telling her pleasant stories of persons she liked and not mentioning those whom she disliked. I was well informed in regard to all her peculiarities. I promised to get her out of the hospital and did not omit chocolate. One easily wins a good transference of psychotics by using their regression to the oral level.

My wife was willing to make any sacrifice for an important task, and as soon as it was possible we took the patient into our home. We tolerated her emotional outbreaks, refusal of food when she feared poison, endless walking in her room during the nights, excessive smoking, and recounting of her hallucinatory woes. She was unrestricted, although we knew this meant risking her suicide.

I knew her past and the underlying conflicts and helped her to overcome them. In the course of the next two years she came to our shelter for shorter and shorter periods. I did not allow her to return home to her family; succeeding to some extent in influencing her abnormal mother and her kind but neurotic brothers, I induced them to permit her to live by herself. She continued her studies and became quite a good artist. I asked the teachers in the Art Academy to call me and no other psychiatrist when she became "queer" and paranoid at school. Sometimes she did not need the actual surroundings of our home but would drive with my wife for hours in a carriage, interrupting the ride many times to take unlimited quantities of whatever sweets she was greedy to have. She was then appeased and would return to her own studio. She became normal, married twice, and fulfilled all her duties. She severed all contact with us, which I then resented. There was no question of any payment, but I thought that such services deserved some devotion and gratitude. Later I abandoned this narcissistic standpoint when I realized that such desertion was right, and necessary to avoid the fear of relapsing because of being reminded of her psychotic state. The combination of transference and psychoanalytical help saved this humanly, intellectually, and artistically remarkable individual.

Later, humble, mediocre, and prominent individuals were among my patients. Every psychotic who is not feeble-minded has enough intelligence to grasp and to accept the explanation of his own mechanisms. His mental disease brings him nearer to intuition and understanding; normal persons, laymen and psychiatrists alike, have much greater resistance because of the logical, emotional, and ego components.

A brief report on the course of my first cases will demonstrate the dangers of psychoanalysis when the diagnosis of psychosis is not made in time. The tragedy is that it is the improvement that leads to the optimism of psychiatrist and patient. Sudden decisions are made by the latter, and discharges by the former are given too early. Today I know that practically no psychotic patient should be dropped from analytical care after analysis on the basis of positive transference. For a long time it has been my policy to recognize no success, and to publish no account of any case, until five years have elapsed following psychoanalysis.

My first unfortunate case of psychosis, through which I

learned a good deal, was the first of all my analytical cases. At that time no control was made officially, but I had the privilege of consulting Professor Freud whenever I needed his advice. Freud had recommended me as family doctor to a patient whom he had psychoanalyzed for hystero-epileptic attacks. He suspected a traumatic influence of these attacks on the children in infancy, for, although the mother had tried to protect them, no sufficient separation of parents and children was accomplished. The daughter was beautiful and extremely gifted. Aided by her father's wealth, she was one of the "glamour girls" in Viennese society. She concealed her hysterical moods and symptoms, so that no one suspected the underlying psychosis. Apparently because of sexual and erotic adjustment through psychoanalysis, but actually because she had reached a peak of her cyclothymia, she fell in love with a healthy, wealthy young man, who was charmed by her beauty and her vivacious, witty (in reality, sub-manic) conversation. He showed his matter-of-fact attitude two years later when he divorced her after the first openly manic phase. This marriage would never have occurred if the true diagnosis had been made in time. Even before the wedding, the girl was disappointed by the ebbing of the tide of her feelings for the man. I opposed the marriage, but her mother and I left the decision to her. She had a sincere talk with the young man, and they decided to marry.

Her life turned out to be a continuous struggle with her cycles. She was treated by different psychiatrists but always returned to me, by whom she felt understood and helped a little more than by the others. In later years she did not need hospitalization, but she was unable to achieve anything in life, as one phase of her cycles destroyed what the other had built up.

I fully agreed with her reproach that in such cases no psychoanalytical treatment should have been attempted at all unless it had been planned initially to continue for many, many years. Some of her physicians had led her to use drugs indiscriminately. Every analyst knows that patients must learn to avoid drugs during analysis; no patient may be considered cured if he returns to habitual use of drugs after analysis. Yet we cannot stop drug habits in patients who are not cured. Drug habits prove that no sufficient ego restoration has been achieved.

A similar case began with neurasthenia, with some phobias and obsessions, and ended with drug addiction and manic-depressive states. This patient was the talented youngest son of a highly gifted father, famous as "maker and shaker" of European finance. The son was a composer, scientist, business man, and writer, yet his successes were limited. The children had the same degree of vigor of instincts and drives as the father; but while in him it was invested in object libido, most of the children were abnormally narcissistic. This narcissism should have made us suspect earlier the underlying psychosis. As in most psychotic cases, the first reaction to psychoanalysis was very good. The son worked, got his degree, wrote his thesis. By identification with me, he wanted to marry; and he was accepted by a girl who had previously rejected him. He reproached me all his life that I had not warned him against marriage, and he was right. His wife had no reason to reproach me because I advised her to find her own love satisfaction elsewhere and eventually to divorce him. She did not follow my advice but always appreciated my sincerity. Because some of his phobias still persisted, I recommended him to Freud. There was no therapeutic success after two years. Freud told me that he suspected a paranoia to be the cause of the rigidity of the resistances, and that—although without success in regard to the neurosis—he may have protected him from the outbreak of his paranoia. This point of view was very suggestive to me.

No problem is harder than to judge the value of methods of prophylaxis in chronic diseases. Statistics give no answer when the differences in social and familial conditions interfere with the required constancy of "ceteris paribus." Only by understanding the intricate mental mechanisms and the organic conditions by which specific mental disturbances start and pass through different phases can we make observations and become reasonably sure of blocking one pathway of mental illness without opening another.

In the case in question, obsessions, fears, and eccentricities were improved or cured. This patient retained some rigidity in repeating the same patterns of discussion and the same problems, disregarding the lack of interest of his audience. He excused such lapses as due to the effect of drugs. Drug addiction increased during every depressed period and was never overcome during his elations. The degree of intensity of depressive and manic periods remained the same. The drug, by appeasing the amount of pain, counteracted the self-curing effect of each single depressed phase.

This patient was psychoanalyzed before he became openly manic-depressive. In the beginning of the depressed phases, he experimented with other treatments and always thought each one excellent when, with the manic phase, his optimism returned. But with every new cycle, the new method recently praised so highly was deserted. Through all cycles he retained his adherence to Wagner-Jauregg, because the latter was never influenced by the patient's "ups and downs." The only man who stopped his fears and his drug-taking was Groddeck. The transference to me never ceased, even though it was mixed with narcissistic and sadistic satisfaction gained by blaming me for the insufficiency of psychoanalysis. I had to accept this blame. Psychiatrists avoid it by asserting that they do not expect to cure such cases; because the psychoanalytic method is efficient in many cases, we are expected to help all.

Since I wanted to know more about the relationships between neurosis and psychosis I did not mind taking apparently incurable cases. I came to know the conditions which make such cases curable.

In the last two cases discussed, psychoanalysis was directed at the neurosis without awareness of the psychosis. The course might have been the same without psychoanalysis. I had the impression that in both cases psychoanalysis had fostered the onset of depression and of manic outbursts. I might have seen then (actually I realized it much later) how free association encouraged the manic flight of thoughts, and how recollection of past periods of life led to short depressions by making guilt feelings conscious. I did not at that time understand that these were hints of the threatening depression.

That we precipitate short and slight psychotic states by psychoanalytic procedure is of itself not necessarily to our ultimate disadvantage in our long combat with the unconscious. Today I use these slight outbreaks of the psychotic mechanism as indicators of deeper causes to be overcome, especially guilt feelings. But for such tactical victories one must use the strategy of immediate interruption of further free association. In my first cases I rather enjoyed, and fostered, the abundant production of unconscious material, disregarding the fact that the emotional reactions were of psychotic significance in that *the whole and not a part of the ego* was filled by a sudden and inadequate investment of libido in the manic reactions, and of mortido in the depressive ones. When the usual method is applied, disregarding manic or depressive reactions, these seem to increase so that the latent psychosis becomes manifest.

Psychiatrists who disapprove of psychoanalysis never fail to point out those cases in which psychoanalysis, far from having been helpful, created disasters. Their statements are both true and false. A series of events does not necessarily represent cause and effect. Many prepsychotic patients come to the psychoanalyst only when they already feel within themselves some uncanny menace of the threatening psychosis. The psychosis would have caught them anyhow, with or without psychoanalysis. This observation allows us to reconcile Freud's opinion, that psychoanalysis protected my patient from paranoia with the experience that psychoanalysis precipitates psychoses. When the ego is still sufficiently resistant, psychoanalysis can make conscious so many homosexual, sadistic, and masochistic trends that the forces of the repressed urges become diminished, so that, in spite of the pre-existent paranoid, schizophrenic, or manic-depressive fixation and the failure in ego structure, the psychotic state is never reached. On the other hand, when psychosis is near the threshold, psychoanalysis breaks down some ego structures and manifest psychosis results.

I think that all analysts know today that neuroses and psychoses are, as Freud discovered, the mixed results of the undermining morbid process and of defense mechanisms, with compromises, compensations, reconstructions, and symptoms of healing. Different diseases have corresponding differences in the mental "topicity" (Freud) of these mechanisms. I demonstrated a new model of topical difference in my paper regarding the distinction between hysteria and obsession.[1] Topically different disturbances do not exclude each other; but one defense mechanism frequently makes all others superfluous. When, with the progress of life, the established set of defense mechanisms, e.g., the hysterical or obsessional, is invalidated through accumulated conflicts and frustrations, then another deeper mental disorder develops. With its characteristic defenses, compensations, compromises, and reconstructions, the psychosis is born.

Patients do not die of hysteria. I have watched many terminal states of hysteria in old age, and have seen three different endings of this neurosis: Sublimation is the best; a form of narcissistic organ-disease is the most frequent; and the third is long-lasting severe climacteric or presenile melancholia from which the patients recover, having lost all or most of the hysterical symptoms.

When melancholia is the termination of hysteria, one may easily understand that this ending can be precipitated by psychoanalysis. I have the impression that melancholias so precipitated are less severe than those which occur in the natural course of neurotic struggles. Yet, quite a few hysterias end after the menopause without psychosis. Psychoanalysts must learn not to provoke latent psychoses, and, even more, to prevent any psychosis from being the terminal state of a neurosis. That is possible when families and physicians cooperate. One may say that adult psychoanalytic therapy should be prophylaxis for the aged, just as education of the child should be prophylaxis for the adult.

Recently there have been many contributions to the problem of psychosis in children. I estimate Melanie Klein's work in this field to be fundamental, although I am far from approving all of her interpretations and theoretical comments.

. . . .

[1] Federn, "The Determination of Hysteria Versus Obsessional Neurosis," *Psychoanal. Rev.*, XXVII (1940), 265-276.

These investigations must be tested by the adult lives of those individuals psychoanalyzed in childhood—as the psychoanalysis of "Little Hans" was tested later by Freud.

One more of my early experiences will be briefly reported. In 1912, a twenty year old student of modern languages was sent to me by Professor Freud. She was a pretty and clever girl, handicapped in all her activities by her obsessional state. Her neurosis had been intensified after an unhappy love affair two years earlier. Her father was a strict and honest school teacher with no understanding of the hysteria of his wife, who had divorced him, or of the neurosis of his daughter. His only son had developed into an extremely narcissistic man whose intellect was so great that he achieved a position as a judge in spite of his maladjustments. By both brother and father, the girl was neglected and exploited. Psychoanalysis proceeded with "too little" resistance. The girl lost most of her compulsions too quickly. I had to leave Vienna in 1914 for New York, and left her able to continue her studies. When I came home four months later, she received me with pride and shyness in her eyes and confided to me that she was loved by a great actor and that Friedrich Nietzsche's voice had spoken to her.

I continued psychoanalysis. Two years later her father died; four years later the patient, unable to study, committed suicide. She never needed hospitalization. I gave the report on the case in the Viennese Society. Freud approved my explanations of the development of her dementia paranoides as a legitimate continuation of psychoanalytic research work.

There were other cases which I began to psychoanalyze with a false diagnosis. Today, I might temporarily make an error in the opposite direction, suspiciously looking for signs and hints of underlying psychosis. Since all these processes manifest themselves dynamically, topically, and economically (in Freud's terminology) and not statically, early diagnosis in undeveloped cases lacks certainty.

In latent psychoses, we do not want to achieve complete analysis, proof of which would be the dissolution of transference and identification. When Freud advised trial psychoanalysis, his main object was the possibility of early discharge of cases which proved or threatened to be psychotic. However, it is very important to spot the latent psychosis as soon as possible. By such early recognition of the psychosis, our therapeutic and analytical aims and methods are changed.

Hidden schizophrenia is indicated during analysis by:

(1) The patient's intuitive acceptance and translation of symbols and the understanding of his primary processes without resistance.

(2) Quick and even sudden disappearance of severe neurotic symptoms; yet, fortunately, as mentioned above, some schizophrenics resist dissolution of the superficial neurosis.

(3) A history with periods of very different kinds of neurosis, such as neurasthenia, psychasthenia, hypochondria, early conversion hysteria, anxiety hysteria and obsessions, and severe depersonalizations.

(4) Psychotic periods of true delusions and loss of reality testing in early childhood. When one hears of such phases during the trial psychoanalysis, it is evident that the patient is in an intra- or postpsychotic state.

(5) Lasting deterioration in work, and isolation in social contacts after puberty or after leaving the regulated life at home or in school. Neurotics, on the contrary, tend to improve for some time when external conditions are changed to greater freedom, or when a new biological period is reached.

(6) Absolute prevalence of the narcissistic reaction pattern over that of object libido.

(7) Typical physiognomic signs in posture, looks, and gestures.

Latent melancholia, is indicated in hysteria and in obsessions by:

(1) States of depression occurring every morning; typically the patient frees himself by the help of wish fulfilling fantasies or sexual enjoyment. When, with advancing age, such pain-pleasure economy becomes more and more unsuccessful because reality annihilates the premises of the main fantasy, melancholia develops.

(2) A reaction pattern by which mental pain is spread over the whole ego.

(3) Early periodicity. This starts as a biological abnormality and broadens and deepens from lustrum to lustrum by mourning work for mental causes.

Mania is sometimes initially indicated by an early defense mechanism exhibiting itself for hours or days in a witty, narcissistic, and aggressive behavior, without real humor, and contrasted to a general low level of mood and many guilt and inferiority feelings.

In untreated or unsuccessfully treated cases the narcissistic ego cathexis perseveres from the pre-psychotic period through melancholia and mania, over neutral intervals, and on to the postpsychotic evening of life.

I have compared the excellent results in the case of the painter (whose life and, what is more, whose fate was saved, so that she could help herself and other people) with those in the cases of the three others who continued living miserably and making their near ones miserable too. The painter's psychosis was more severe than the others, and external conditions were by no means better in her case; but her personality was exceptionally interesting, and her kindness could be felt even through her narcissistic rages. I protected her in all her difficulties as if I were her guardian. The distance of psychoanalyst and analysand remained the pattern of our relationship, but her transference was more important to me than the progress of analysis. Analytical hours were irregularly interposed when she was willing. In the three cases with bad results, psychoanalysis of the neuroses was the leading goal. In all cases which I treated later with good results, I followed the rules dictated by the libidinous condition of the psychosis, and not those dictated by the claim for analytical thoroughness.

Subsequently, I became eager to take over those patients whose psychoses had been precipitated by the psychoanalysis of another analyst, though I myself had learned to avoid such awakening of a psychosis still asleep. Patients were sent to me by former patients and by Freud. I took some of them out of sanatoria and installed them under the care of male or female nurses in their homes or foster homes, and then began my work. In all these cases unfavorable prognoses had been made by competent psychiatrists; and my results were frequently hampered by the interference of psychiatrists who did not share my viewpoint. Later, there were young physicians at my disposal who followed my lines.

No patient can be cured unless his family wishes it, let alone in the presence of the family's unconscious or conscious hatred. No physician can cure any severe case when bed, rest, and care are lacking, or when, intentionally or not, antagonisms develop toward the task of bringing back the psychotic ego to normality and reality. Experience must be drawn, and conclusions made, from patients treated under the best conditions and with the least opposition.

Initially I lacked knowledge, even when the conditions were good, but as time went on I learned a good deal, and in the last three years of my work in Vienna I won an ideal helper, the Swiss nurse-psychoanalyst, Gertrud Schwing. At the time, I was in a position to convince the Viennese and Swiss groups to agree to her becoming a psychoanalyst, although she had no license or degree, except the "highest degree" of talent for, experience in, and devotion to, her work. During and after her training analysis with me, she learned psychoanalytic treatment of psychoses. She published our experiences in a book, *Ein Weg zur Seele des Geisteskranken.*[2] I say *our* experiences, since her proceedings were advised and controlled by me. Yet her book contains her own original contributions.

Gertrud Schwing worked in Vienna with psychotics privately analyzed by me and at the Clinic of Pötzl, who had a friendly attitude toward psychoanalysis, modified by some ambivalence. In discussions, in lectures on the occasion of Freud's eightieth birthday, and in articles, Pötzl praised psychoanalysis as a science and Freud as a genius; some of his favored assistants were psychoanalysts and members of our society. But he himself dropped his membership. In his excellent clinical lectures he taught more psychoanalysis than any other university professor, with the exception of a few in the United States and Japan. He advised psychoanalysis, but with the casual sugges-

. . . .

[2] (Zurich: Rascher's Verlag, 1939).

tion that a five-months treatment would suffice, even though there was an extremely severe obsession. No wonder that a patient twice changed analysts after five months. Once, on the request of the patient's family, he was consulted by me for a case of paranoia. He told them how happy they should be to have the case under my care, but at the same time he remarked that the patient was incurable. Unfortunately for his prophecy, the patient was cured.

Pötzl never did believe that psychoses were a field for psychoanalytic therapy. So much the more does he deserve our thanks for his assistance. When I asked him to accept Gertrud Schwing as a guest nurse to study psychoses in his clinic, he consented immediately. The good results of her work were so manifest that she was asked by Sakel to take care of his insulin cases.

I have formed the theory that in shock therapy, when a more than passing success is reached, it is due to the mental impression made by the treatment, or even by the maltreatment, and to the established amnesia. The patients awaken in a nauseous helplessness to some very infantile ego state. Piers in Elgin has published a paper about the oral level of patients in such cases. Whether they remain at this level or proceed to their normal adult states is a question which can be influenced by the mental approach. In Switzerland, the results with insulin were far better in certain institutions than in all others, because, in the successful institutions, mental treatment by trained nurses was established and the nursing staff was adequate, with one nurse for three patients.

Metapsychologically, the primary schizophrenic process appears to be a functional deficiency, or even exhaustion, of ego cathexis; secondarily, it is used as a defense mechanism. Solving outer and inner conflicts, fortifying the ego by protection, transference, identification, and, last but not least, insight into the patients' terrors and inner turmoils are the means which Gertrud Schwing used. Better results were achieved by this method, and we learned to know how and why improvement could be expected in some cases but not in others.

For treatment and prophylaxis, many more psychiatrists are needed, as well as many more psychoanalytically trained nurses, attendants, and social workers. There will come a time when the American Medical Association and the psychiatric and psychoanalytic associations will themselves promote this instruction. The wisdom of Freud in regard to lay analysis is still outstanding. I would like to see nurses trained in and through all psychoanalytic societies, or at least with their help. We cannot wait for exceptions like Gertrud Schwing among nurses, or Anna Freud among pedagogues, for thousands of such helpers are needed to fight widespread psychosis. Laws and bylaws of any group of men are temporary human artifacts compared with the laws and regulations lying in the reality of nature. The former should be changed when they prove discordant with the latter. Those who want to see the number of hospitalized mental cases reduced must improve and increase the staffs of physicians, nurses, social workers, and pedagogues well trained in psychoanalysis.

TRANSFERENCE

Neurotic patients can be psychoanalyzed successfully in spite of unfavorable external conditions. The neurotic learns through psychoanalysis to become master of his fate, within the limits of individual human power. In the psychotic, lasting success depends much more on favorable external circumstances, as we have said. Under such circumstances, psychoanalysis of a psychotic can be undertaken and will cure or improve the patient's illness. It is bound to prove unsatisfactory, though, when the rules prescribed by Freud for transference neuroses are stubbornly applied to narcissistic psychoses.

To use a familiar simile: When one is dealing with neurotics, inhibitory dams and sluices can be opened because, as the water level is low, there is no danger of real inundation. In psychoses, the same method means the opening of dams and sluices during inundation. Only in exceptional cases is that the right method, though a risky one; in most cases, it increases destruction.

The method sponsored here is not mere psychotherapy with psychoanalytical knowledge. It is true psychoanalysis, i.e., the acceptance of Freud's own definition of his method: the application of the economical, topical, and dynamic viewpoints while using free association and coping with transference and resistance. The economical, topical, and dynamic conceptions remain the same; the difference lies in resistance and transference. In psychoses, normal resistances are broken down and have to be re-established by psychoanalysis; transferences have to be managed differently. Free association as the means of bringing out unconscious material is seldom needed, because too much of the unconscious has been brought out by the psychosis. To say it in antithesis: *In neuroses, we want to lift repression; in psychoses, we want to create re-repression.*

Although it may sound paradoxical, it is nevertheless in accordance with out theoretical knowledge to assert that it is precisely in the case of the psychotic whose reason is impaired that our treatment must be addressed to his reason, in such measure as he retains it; similarly, the transference is even more important than in a transference neurosis. Psychotic patients are accessible to psychoanalysis only because, and insofar as: firstly, they are still capable of transference; secondly, one part of the ego has insight into the abnormal state; and thirdly, a part of the personality is still directed towards reality. Of these conditions the first and third are parallel, the one presupposing the other, while the second depends mainly on whether the regression within the ego is constant or is subject to temporary remissions.

Transference was the stumbling block for psychoanalysts in regard to psychoses. Freud himself said to me a few years ago: "Psychotics are a nuisance to psychoanalysis." His arguments, in brief, are that there is no transference and no healthy ego. Transference is needed to shift object attachments from the unconscious to the psychoanalyst; by becoming transferred, the neurosis enters into reality. Lack of transference in neurotics was unknown to Freud, so that he suspected an underlying psychosis when such a lack was noted. This opinion has proved to be wrong in some cases. Not every narcissism is bound to be psychotic. Freud himself detected later that the narcissistic type of libido distribution affords a foundation for aggression and independence, and this type may refuse any transference through extraordinary pride and

spite. Some analysts are apt, much more than Freud, to provoke this kind of resistance. W. Reich has called it "narcissistic
armor" which has to be broken down before positive transference can be established. Campbell is right in saying that psychiatrists see patients deformed by their treatments.

Analysts were wrong, however, in concluding that the psychotic forms no transference. He is eager to make transferences with both the healthy and the disordered parts of the
ego; these parts can either have the same object or different
ones. Such transferences can be easily lost after having been
provoked, or can last through life. The transference of the
psychotic part of the personality is sometimes dangerous and
can lead to aggression and slaughter, as well as to deification
of the object, and both aggression and deification can put an
end to any contact because of deeply rooted fears. Except in
mild borderline cases, transference cannot be used as a reliable catalytic in the elucidation by psychoanalysis. Every new
stage of development can destroy an established transference.
The psychotic does not sufficiently separate psychoanalysis
from life until his ego structure is almost restored.

This is the reason why it is preferable not to have the patient lie on the psychoanalytic couch. When the neurotic rises
from the couch, he returns to his normal behavior and to his
conscious relationship to the analyst. Not so the psychotic. He
does not fully cope with the half-reality of transference, and
thereby he confuses it with reality, and vice versa. After interpretation of his dreams, he is unable to distinguish his dreamed
intentions from his real relationships; he might run away
from home, or attack the person who provoked his dreamed
death wishes.

In many cases, if you make a schizophrenic patient adopt a
recumbent position during analysis, he will immediately begin to produce associations of a schizophrenic nature, whereas
if he sits opposite you, he will make associations in a normal
manner. Only when the patient has grasped what is wrong
with his causal sequences and intentions and has learned to
control—i.e., to dissimulate—it in his effort to adapt himself
to reality, can one for a time proceed cautiously to bring to
light material from deeper strata by means of free association.

Freud was quite right: There is no reliability in an ego which becomes the prey of illusions and hallucinations, whose precepts and concepts are themselves corruptions further forged by false projections. One accepts the transferences and egos as they are offered by the psychotic, but our method has to be adapted to them. The same conclusion is in agreement with the experience that the usual method of psychoanalysis provokes the manifestation of latent psychoses and the extension of unmistakable psychoses over larger parts of the personality.

Another reason for changing the method of analysis in the case of psychoses was the necessity of protecting the family and other persons. Any attempt to analyze a psychotic in the usual way must be made only after hospitalization. The sanatoria and clinics, however, have not cooperated with the subtle work of psychoanalysis. When treating a psychotic patient in a home, I have had to take care not to arouse fear and violence between the patient and the family. In all cases, the relatives, before coming to the analyst, had found from experience that hospitalization had done no visible good. Heavy expenses were expected for years, or for life, and the relatives, therefore, cooperated quite willingly themselves, or paid for a foster home with guardian and nurse. Sometimes a separate household was established, a procedure which was no more expensive than the stay in an adequate sanatorium. Many quiet patients were cured at home.

One of the most difficult questions is how to protect children. Many become deeply injured by living with a psychotic; on the other hand, one learns from the psychoanalysis of adults that for the child the knowledge that a psychotic parent is, or was, hospitalized is as traumatizing, or even more so, as living with such a parent. In some cases, it is better to remove the child and to leave the psychotic person in the home. Some psychotics control themselves in front of their children. When a child is already accustomed to the mother's disease and is interested in cooperating, separation would be another injury, for such a child loves the mother.

Where there are good institutions with psychoanalytically trained staff, nurses, and attendants, hospitalization is the proper measure. In this case, one hopes that mental disease will not continue to humiliate and stigmatize the patient.

In Vienna, I preferred to avoid hospitalization, in this respect usually siding with the patient himself. Manic-depressives, however, themselves ask for hospitalization during depressions, but in their manic periods resent its restraints. Whenever I could keep a patient under control during a moderate manic period, with the help of drugs, the course of the disease was favorably affected. Such a patient must be permitted to come to the psychoanalyst whenever he feels the impulse to give way to one of his quick decisions. Some patients can never forgive hospitalization, although many agree to it and recognize the necessity for it.

Twenty-three years ago, a schizophrenic with auditory hallucinations that God was calling him disagreed with his psychoanalyst in respect to hospitalization, and he escaped ten days after having been "imprisoned." His wife consulted me, and I treated him, with his former analyst's consent, in his mother's home. He recovered to the extent that he was able to resume his scientific and cultural work, and he has been supporting his family since then. By advising his wife, I directed his treatment for twenty years without seeing him. He is now working in this country, after having gone through hard experiences without a relapse. If he had agreed to follow routine procedure, he probably would have become a mental wreck like so many hospitalized cases of dementia paranoids. His wife told me recently that, far from having suffered, she has enjoyed sharing his life, although for eugenic reasons she has had no children.

In regard to hospitalization, Freud once said that the therapeutic provocation of acute psychoses through psychoanalysis might prove effective if three conditions were fulfilled: (1) thorough psychoanalytical understanding of the narcissistic mechanisms; (2) treatment carried out in psychoanalytic clinics and hospitals; and (3) cessation, by opponents, of misuse of cases which cause psychoanalysis to appear at a disadvantage.

Since then, much progress has been made in all these directions; yet it is still not advisable to provoke acute psychoses because we are still unable to prognosticate and to control their courses. I therefore often try to hinder the progress of the psychosis, and prefer to psychoanalyze incompletely but innocuously.

The psychotic patient offers his positive transference to the analyst; the analyst must nourish it as something precious in order to preserve his influence, so that the patient may regain control of his psychotic reactions through his own understanding. Transference is helpful in the analysis of underlying conflicts of the psychosis, but a positive transference must itself never be dissolved by psychoanalysis. When it is dissolved the analyst has lost all influence, because he cannot continue to work with the psychotic during periods of negative transference, as he can with the neurotic. Even with the latter, the transference neurosis and the adjustment made with the patient's ego are not the aims; they are only the means to uncover the unconscious by free association. We do not need them where free association is superfluous and the unconscious uncovers itself too much. In neuroses, the goal is to replace the rule of the id by the rule of the ego. In psychoses, the goal is the same, but before it can be attained many functions which have abnormally entered into the conscious ego have to be re-repressed and must return to the id. In psychoses the psychoanalytical use of transference is more limited, but is of even greater value than usual. The antithesis is this: In neurotics, transference is used to make repressed material free; in psychotics, to make free material repressed.

I have already distinguished between healthy and psychotic transference. The first is the same as that in the relationship to anyone who becomes a friend, helper, or lover. Such transference counteracts the dangers which the transference made by the psychotic part of the ego brings to the object, the psychoanalyst. I won a personal enemy by turning a patient's paranoid resentment into objective hatred, through siding with his family against him. Many fanatical private and political enmities are rationalized paranoid reactions, like surface forts built over subterranean powder mines. Such enmities endanger the doctor when he overrates the positive transference to his person.

When I was the physician of the Viennese military prison in World War I, I had the opportunity to see how normal transference persists during psychosis. A sergeant, an excellent, kind, courageous man, was on duty when one of the prisoners, a famous murderer called Mehalla, a basically good boy, was attacked by acute prison psychosis—became "stir-crazy." Freed from the control of his reason, his muscular strength was enormous. He broke open the door, which had previously resisted the efforts of eight men in normal frames of mind who had wanted to break out. He could not be held by his eight comrades and ran out along the corridor. When the sergeant tried to arrest him, Mehalla tore the sergeant's bayonet out of its sheath and seemed about to attack him. The sergeant did not sound the alarm, did not flee, did not use his gun; he said quietly, "Mehalla, you will not do me any harm." Mehalla recognized·the respected man and surrendered. His suggestibility—that is, his transference—persisted.

One wins the normal transference of the psychotic by sincerity, kindness, and understanding. It is a great error to believe that the psychotic accepts without protest the turmoil of his thoughts; whenever a psychotic feels that you understand him—he is yours. Frequently he offers opposition at first, but often by the next day the explanation has been accepted. One must avoid blame and severe admonition, any smiling superiority, and especially any lie. There are no white lies allowed with psychotics. To lie to a psychotic is contrary to the injunction in the Bible that one must not place a stone in the way of the blind.

For the psychotic, to be slapped in a friendly way on cheeks, shoulder, or buttocks, to be treated like a silly child, is an indignity. The very first visit to a mental hospital will soon reveal the quality of the psychological understanding and attitude of those in charge, the criterion being the extent to which the physicians and the rest of the staff have got rid of the habit of what I can only term criminal laughter by healthy persons at the victims of mental disease.

In order to establish the patient's transference, the analyst must avoid the slightest sign of depreciation or underestimation, and must give full recognition to the patient's right to have his personality respected. Medical experience and human instinct have taught me to utilize the oral fixation of many patients; it is permissible to show them hospitality and to indulge their weakness for smoking and for eating sweets. But in order to succeed, our courting of the patient's confidence must be sincere. His distrust is not simply morbid; it is the perfectly justified reaction of that part of his personality which is still normal. Before one ends the psychoanalytic session, misunderstandings should be carefully cleared up, and the positive results of the talk must be repeated in plain words. The analyst must endeavor to have the positive transference continue; without it the psychotic scotomizes him and what he says.

The experience of good transference is the chief normal reality for the psychotic. Starting from his transference, one can elucidate recently established falsifications and uncertainties. Psychotic fantasies are not always fixed, as is generally believed and as is implied in the term "fixed ideas."

I was one of the first to oppose the dogma of "no transference in psychosis." Today many American psychoanalysts have emphasized the routine of transference.

Freud described the metapsychological differences between neurosis and psychosis thus: In psychosis, the conflict between ego and id is solved by severing the relation to reality and by yielding to the instinctual unconscious, the id; in neurosis, the conflict is solved by severing the relation to the instinctual unconscious and by saving the reality relationship. This formula is a basic truth, to which all of us fully agree; but the psychotic process does not proceed simultaneously in the totality of the ego relations and of the ego boundaries. During the long period of relapses and of returns of the morbid ego changes in psychoses, the reality relationships are partially retained and even strengthened, and the id-dependences are partially diminished. On the other hand, in neurotic symptoms the relationship to reality is partially impaired, and the dependence of the ego on the id becomes, in part, greater than in normality. Freud's statement refers to the basic and general tendency, not to every actual singular phase and partial mechanism; because, as Freud added in the same papers, repairs and restitutions start immediately when the damage is done and bring together the damaged productions themselves. Freud himself frequently warned us not to become dogmatic and not to overlook the complications of phenomena and the mixtures of mechanisms.

In practice, the most important difference between transference in neuroses and psychoses lies in the factor of ambivalence. Normally, some resultant is the outcome of love and hatred, of activity and passivity, of obedience and resistance, in regard to one object. Neurotically, the ambivalent feelings toward the same object result in reaction and symptom formation. Psychotically, the contrasting emotional tendencies tear the ego into its parts. In severe catatonic reactions, the divided ego parts are working simultaneously with equal cathexes; they may stop all activities or may create stereotypy. In milder cases, the split ego states alternate in their strength, and with them alternate the positive and negative transferences to the analyst.

The same alternation is even more evident in the other group of affective psychoses. In his manic states, the patient loves all people whom he disliked in his melancholic state, and hates those whom he previously liked. The same peculiarity in transference prevails in the many milder cases of what we call cyclothymia, which do not deserve the stigma of psychosis. Very many breaks of love, friendship, or partnership, many of the customary disappointments in one's co-worker, are based on cyclothymia of one or of both individuals.

Most interesting is the outcome of marriage between two cyclothymic individuals. Very soon both become temporarily unhappy and want to separate; but they are reconciled after having lived apart for one cycle. Both remain unaware of the underlying mechanism. Each projects his endogenous change on the mate, blaming the partner for the difference in feeling. The type he loved as hypomanic he does not like at all when he feels "low." I have "cured" such diseased marriages by making both husband and wife understand that they chose each other when one was in his "low" and the other in his "high" mood swing, or when both were in their "high." In all other constellations, each is irritated by the other until the original constellation returns. When the marriage partners know that they must expect such recurring interruptions of their love, they do not become bitter against their mates, but tolerate each other or find relief in temporary vacations from married life.

Interruption in transference was responsible for the desertion of some very gifted psychoanalysts who were for a long time very close to Freud.

Cyclothymic businessmen have been observed, and it has been seen how their financial success was hindered by their "ups" and "downs." Probably all economic crises and cycles are increased because so many highly talented and energetic individuals are cyclothymic. If one could learn how to cure circular psychosis and cyclothymia, the future history of mankind might be more stabilized.

Laymen have called "hysterical" those individuals who pass easily from one ego state into another, changing their transferences and identifications. In psychotics, these different ego states, with their loves and hatreds, are independently organized. It is impossible to reunite them—before the psychotic process itself has ceased—by psychoanalysis of the causes of the change. Therefore, to use the transference of the psychotic, the analyst has to adjust to the fact that ambivalence is replaced by two (or more) ego states.

For this reason, one cannot psychoanalyze the psychotic without a helper who serves as a harbor for the patient when his transference to the psychoanalyst becomes uncertain. Gertrud Schwing found that every schizophrene craves transference to a new mother. All schizophrenes, she discovered, did not have true mothers, because their mothers themselves had never had true mothers in their infancies. What was always thought to be an increase of the hereditary factor from generation to generation has frequently been found to be recurring deficiency in the infantile libido conditions. I have defined motherhood as the "natural feeling that the fate of another person is more important than one's own." Motherhood is sublimated to devotion without hesitation; there is no feeling of duty, no sensual joy, no feeling of sacrifice. It is an instinctual behavior pattern which, in complete mothers, has resisted civilization and has created culture and Christianity.

Such motherhood is opposed by strong narcissism, which can be expected in the parents of psychotic patients.

While every neurotic patient easily transfers from his mother to the psychoanalyst, the psychotic does not do so to a male analyst. This demonstrates how the psychotic depends on reality more than does the neurotic; that is, when he is forced to transfer his mother-relationship to a man, he confuses homo- and heterosexual feelings and becomes more perturbed.

My contention that there should be women helpers for psychotic persons is therefore well founded, although the conclusion was reached as a result of simple experience. In all cases in which I was successful, I had such motherly aid; in some cases, the real mother was willing to help, because many women, although lacking in sublimated instinctual motherhood, have a great sense of duty toward a poor psychotic child. But the real mother is usually less helpful than a sister, or a nurse who becomes a sister. The relation of a psychotic becomes too possessive, and regresses easily to incest, when he is nursed by his own mother. Yet the loving cooperation of the mother is very helpful when obtainable.

Whoever wants to preserve the transference, that is, whoever wants to psychoanalyze a psychotic patient, must be very careful. Treatment of one of my most severely schizophrenic patients was suddenly stopped for a year, without apparent reason. Throughout this period the patient's sister brought detailed reports to the analyst and took away detailed instructions. In order to give the patient a male helper, he was directed to a surgeon who had been minutely informed as to how he should react to the patient's hypochondriacal complaints and had been advised to refuse any new operation. (The first catatonic period, four years before my treatment, had been initiated by two small operations which deeply wounded the patient's narcissism.) I thought I had found the cause of the loss of transference and visited the patient, but he became violent and the explanation was of no avail. Some time later the real cause was learned. By bad luck, I had recommended to the patient a male nurse whom he had known in the sanatorium during his first acute psychosis. All his hatred broke through, he rejected the man without stating his reasons—perhaps without knowing why he did so—and broke with me. Through his sister it was possible to convince him that I had known nothing about this matter, so he returned and was treated for four more years. He resumed his interest in music, became organist in a church, and had maintained his normality through all the difficulties of recent times, up to the last word heard about him three and a half years ago. All of his family cooperated with me; they had never forgotten his previous disastrous condition and the absolutely hopeless prognosis of his psychiatrist at that time. When I had asked this colleague to let me take care of the twenty-two-year-old patient, the psychiatrist had willingly consented, though asserting that he believed any psychoanalytical endeavor was hopeless but that the case was so bad I could do no harm.

One must permit patients to come at other than the customary times when they feel perturbed; but one is rarely called at night. It is dangerous to keep patients waiting, and it can be disastrous to fail to keep a single appointment. During wartime, I was once detained at a military office and arrived two hours late for an appointment with a paranoic patient, who was seen only occasionally when I came into the city. Because of this delay she had lost hope of my coming and had committed suicide, although she was attended by a nurse. I know now that in such instances one should go to the patient before the appointed time; then, I thought, as did everyone, that psychotics are unaware of such lapses.

That the psychotic transference is vulnerable must be taken into consideration; if this is not done, the transference becomes unreliable. When transference is lost, by some inner change in the patient or some error or negligence, the motherly helper permits one to continue the treatment through her, and frequently the transference is spontaneously restored, because there is no attempt to force oneself on the patient. Without a positive transference our influence is at an end, and we have to send the patient to another physician for the rest of his treatment. This procedure is exactly opposite to that which is customary, which is based on the idea that there is no need to take any notice of manifestations of dislike by a patient suffering from mental disease. It may appear paradoxical that, more than is the neurotic, the psychotic is entitled to change and to select his physician himself, and should be allowed to do so; but that is because of the vulnerability of his transference.

Many psychiatric hospitals have achieved better discipline by means of occupational therapy. Hollós, who has published an excellent psychoanalytic book on psychosis, *Hinter der Gelben Mauer,* warns us not to gain this discipline at the expense of the patient's self-expression. We should teach ourselves not to cripple this self-expression and not to silence the patient's claims for object relationship.

It is superfluous to discuss whether the close adherence of the psychotic patient to his helpers is true transference or a new attachment. Both processes are always united. In either case it is evident that the patient has longed since childhood for a friendly and loving father, mother, brother, or sister; I have found no evidence to support the theory of the English school that the objects are divided into good and bad. In the normal person, as in the psychotic, ego states with opposite feelings are focused on one object; the separation of the ego states remains unconscious in the normal individual and becomes a real split in the psychotic.

It is clear, therefore, that a psychotic patient must go to another psychoanalyst when he does not wish to continue with the one who is treating him. Frequently the motherly nurse can discover the reasons for the desertion and, by making him understand their inconsistency, influence him to change his mind. Simply to suggest continuation to him might destroy his transference to her also.

How to take a vacation when one treats psychotics is a problem in itself, and it cannot always be solved by taking the patient to the same vacation place. Nor is it good to send him temporarily to a sanatorium. One must prepare him for the interruption, or introduce another psychoanalyst. A sudden announcement of departure may destroy his improvement and his transference. One is constantly surprised by the distinctiveness of the reactions, positive and negative, of psychotic patients. They want help in order to be free from the problems which persecute them; their floating surface-productions are mostly uncontrolled results of the few problems which were traumatic. To be psychoanalyzed, therefore, is what the patient desires; to leave his disease to take its own course without aid is desertion.

THE PSYCHOANALYTIC PROCESS

Psychoanalysis reveals unconscious causes and interrelations of mental actions and reactions. This process is not continuous because resistances of patient, analyst, science, and society interfere with free association and with our readiness to combine the patient's free association with our own.

Resistance is partly manifest and conscious, partly unconscious; rational resistances have to be overcome by reason unless they screen emotionally caused resistance. The patient has to learn to sustain inevitable mental pains and to overcome emotional pains which are created or repeated through remembered materials. Some of these resistances seem quite irrational at first, but become clear by the revelation of past ego states with apparently distant, but related, experiences. Whenever some opposing resistance is overcome and insight is created, thanks to the use of transference, through analysis, new material comes to the surface, and, for a while, analysis is made smooth.

In the analysis of neurotics, free association is expected to start from the surface consciousness, maybe from details of the symptoms, from dreams and fantasies, from real life, or from transference feelings. The material produced by free association, and the resistances, are best interpreted by analogies with well-understood reactions in former and present life. The same procedure can be followed with psychotics; the difference is that, unlike the neurotic, the psychotic, in consequence of freely associated memories, may return so far into his past that he confounds present and past experience. Therefore, states which deserve the name of "mixophrenia" are more manifest than the underlying split-ego states. Yet the term "schizophrenia" is justified, because separate ego states are not united—as in normality—by the present ego, but are mixed with it; and because different object experiences are not selectively united to the right concept, but are accepted without selection by one and the same actual ego boundary.

For the psychoanalytic process, of even greater importance than interpretation is the introduction of infant situations, of traces of past experiences and complexes into consciousness by means of free association. In neurosis, one stresses and welcomes this exposure of repressed materials to the surface of present life. In psychosis, one slows down and even tries to stop such spontaneous delivery of still unconscious mental complexes, because one does not want to face any increase of the psychotic disorganization until the ego has been re-established within its normal boundaries, sufficiently invested with mental cathexis to stand the dynamic forces of the unconscious. Analytical work is, therefore, both easier and more difficult in psychotics; easier because of the greater readiness of unconscious material to appear, and more difficult because of the paradoxical strangeness of the psychotic products. If analysis proceeds with good success in psychotics, the patient himself recognizes the two processes as opposed to each other: the covering up of "the mass of repressed feelings" and the facing and analyzing of his "diseased structure." The reintegration attained by the ego is judged by such an ability to participate in the psychiatrist's attempts to investigate and to explain the psychotic reactions. Good social and occupational behavior is no proof of ego reintegration, as it is frequently based on transference and regression to an obedient child's state, rather than on the healing of the ego.

However, in every psychotic, except in cases of deepest melancholic stupor, some of the ego boundaries remain occupied with realities and with external relationships. This fact can be recognized in the patient's changes of facial expression, and it has been verified by retrospection. While the patient was in delusionary or stuporous states, events in the ward were observed and even criticized. In verbal utterances of whatever sort, sometimes the secondary normal process, and sometimes the primary psychotic process, may prevail. Most patients largely use the secondary mechanisms, reporting true and keen observations and correct judgments, but then suddenly employ primary mechanisms, with resulting absurd combinations. This is because these patients mix symbols with what is symbolized, and use objective impressions to substantiate paranoid projections and hysterical introjections. They nearly always confound thought and reality, express ideas as real, and ignore facts and their consequences—even those which they themselves have related a few minutes earlier. Reality loses importance, and ideas become reality. Analogous is the change in their emotions; in situations where the healthy or the neurotic person would have but moderate emotional reaction, the psychotic lives through all the times in which the same kind of emotion was once experienced. Sometimes such past events are chosen not by analogy but by contrast.

Any memory can be re-enacted as reality with full emotion. On the other hand, real facts meet with no emotion, because reality has lost its normal contact with the bodily and mental ego boundaries and has been reduced to the value of a casual association.

Freud studied the relationship of speech and psychosis. Sometimes a word acquires reality value, and sometimes facts shrink to mere empty words. The psychotic often speaks without any feeling when the depths of his soul should be stirred, and bursts into tears or laughter when nothing of apparent importance has been said.

Like dreams, psychotic states are sometimes difficult to interpret and sometimes easy to understand. No wonder that they seem a hopeless field for psychoanalytical interference or for suggestion based on transference. Yet the results of psychiatry, in previous centuries and in our times, and the spontaneous recoveries or improvements, incomplete and uncertain as they were and are, prove the possibility of restitution. In such restoration, mental disorder may not be removed, but the normal ego cathexis is re-established, reality testing works again, disorganization is once more limited only to dreams and unconscious processes, or to conscious ones which do not collide with reality.

By close observation, one notices that even during psychosis the ability to reason is not really destroyed; it is overlooked and neglected by the patient and by others, including the psychiatrists. In some diseases, especially in amentia and in manic and melancholic states, normal knowledge seems to have become unconscious and reveals itself in dreams. Stekel stresses the fact that moral tendencies are repressed and become the causes of neurosis and depressions. The superego of the psychotic frequently remains markedly the same as in the state of health, although its influence becomes unreasonably distorted.

Usually one discovers hints of normality in tendencies and views; the patient may indicate his residue of normality by acknowledging that he knows what other people in his situation would believe. There are good reasons for his resistances, and these reasons must be found out; he has suffered from reality and has no desire to return to it. These resistances are for the most part much stronger in psychotics than in neurotics. The neurotic is himself astonished when, notwithstanding his insight, his symptoms and abnormal reactions persist. When the psychotic accepts a normal and healthy view, he does not spontaneously see the contrast between his healthy and his deranged ideas because his reality testing does not work.

In psychoses, resistances are handled in the same way as in neuroses, depending on their nature. There is far less id-resistance than in neurotics; auxiliary forces are needed to reestablish repression.

In neurotics, the most common resistances are derived from epinosic gain and from the many anticathexes which maintain the neurotic repression. In psychosis few of these reactions are left. In the psychotic reorganization, which sometimes includes totally changed conceptions of the world, they may be at work again, but the mechanisms differ from those in the neurotic.

Resistances connected with transference are the same in psychotics as in neurotics, as long as some moral standards persist; but the transference may suddenly lose all restraint. With psychotics one must, therefore, be very careful to keep one's distance from the patient. As Ferenczi said of the child, the psychotic misinterprets words and gestures.

The resistance which is produced by the paranosic gain exists in psychotics as in neurotics. The old joke of the man who answers with the question: "All right, but then what for am I crazy?" expresses a general truth.

In some cases, resistances from the superego are still strong. There is much self-punishment and masochistic guilt feeling psychotically satisfied in melancholia and in paranoid and catatonic states.

In severe psychoses, anticathexis has almost lost all power to hinder unconscious elements from becoming conscious. I intentionally make the point that the cathexes have lost their power, not disappeared. However, in these cases, it would be foolish to analyze resistances further, to increase the intrusion of the unconscious into consciousness and to shift the border between id and ego even further into the ego. Yet we have learned, from Freud, Jung, Nunberg, Bibring, Katan, A. Reich, and very many other authors, that the psychotic's productions must be analyzed to be understood. In catatonic cases, for example, pure and simple unconscious material can be interpreted as expressing pregenital basic urges, with their object relations of earliest childhood.

Therefore, in every session, the problem rises of deciding whether to try to lead the patient back to normality or to use his psychotic state to make him cope with his deepest desires, urges, conflicts, fears, and terrors.

Before we answer this technical question, we must refute the argument that it is impossible to demonstrate to a psychotic, irrational creature the deep and obscure layers of his mind, when routine psychiatry itself is still not convinced of their existence. And this question must also be answered: Is not the psychotic quite unable to understand anything or to use anything which he might conceivably understand?

Both arguments have been proved by experience to be futile. I learned this from my first schizophrenic patient, the painter, who always said when she relapsed: "Everything is different." (*Alles ist anders.*) To the inquiry as to what she meant, she answered that the analyst must know; but seeing his ignorance she asked whether he did not see that the room was full of color. Colors were unchanged as such, but they had become three-dimensional, filling the room; so that from a red curtain the color came to her person as a transparent or opaque but substantial *red* stuff. This meant that the problem of being interested in the red color had become symbolized and materialized into something spatial and substantial; the notion "This red color interests me," was represented in a very primitive way by the apperception that the curtain *reached* her. *The thought had become substance.* The analyst explained this mechanism to her and she understood. In later years, I found my psychotic patients understood what I fear I shall not live long enough to make understood by psychologists and psychiatrists. Like the painter, the patients could feel that not only their mental egos, but their bodily egos, were touched by ideas analogous to that of the red curtain.

It is probable that in early infancy nothing is perceived as distant; everything touches, physically and mentally, the sensual surface of the ego.

Freud said that there are two ways of understanding the connection between unconscious elements and their conscious representations, i.e., logical understanding and essential experience. Logical understanding has little therapeutic effect, but the same explanation produced by the analysand from his own experience has curative value. The psychotic has little or no understanding that is logical but much that is essential. He must learn to distinguish between what he spontaneously understands and his own illusions and primitive rationalizations.

The question as to whether one should use, for further analysis, the unconscious material produced by psychotics is answered. It is dangerous to call for still deeper layers and to introduce problems into the patient's mind. When his unconscious is productive, one must help him to decipher the meaning of his astonishing products by the use of his logical understanding and self-observation and translate with him the eruptive products of his unconscious, one after the other. The translation involves three kinds of explanation: ' (1) The importance of his injuries from, and conflicts with, the external world. He himself does not suspect the detailed reactions to reality hidden in his mental creations. (2) How past ego states and situations have returned and need to be re-repressed, or recognized as remembrances. (3) How the strangeness and absurdity of his mental state is due to specific inner processes. When positive transference prevails, there are always plenty of starting points for such analysis without agitating the patient.

It is paradoxical that, in psychosis, psychoanalysis has to find the reality relationship behind the unconscious material produced, and not the unconscious behind the conscious. The difference is one, not of aim, but of distribution of the tasks. In neurosis, analysis must also find the connection in the stimulating conflicts of real life, including the transference, and, besides, must distinguish the share of past reactions in the present, and create self-control by demonstrating the phenomenology, psychology, and metapsychology of the processes.

Psychoanalysis works in the same manner when used to elucidate parapraxes. In all psychopathology of everyday life, the tasks of real life are thwarted or contaminated by unconscious elements. Almost always, one has to discover a hidden meaning in the reality relationship which elucidates the unconsciously-made error or slip of the tongue. In my 1932 lecture. on *"Die Ichbesetzung bei den Fehlleistungen,"* [3] I pointed out that parapraxes are due not to a neurotic but to a psychotic mechanism. In both parapraxis and psychosis, resistances have been diminished and have failed to maintain repression, letting unconscious processes work in fields reserved for preconscious functioning—such as speech, motor activities, and recognition. In both states the ego cathexis has become changed; in parapraxis for rather a short duration, and without warning, and in psychosis for a long duration following a preparatory state of uncertainty.

We now understand why latent psychoses are provoked by the usual method of analysis. If one combats resistances by transference, analyzes transference, and promotes free association, psychoanalysis becomes uncannily smooth. If the analyst is not warned by this feeling of smoothness, obsession and hysteria quickly disappear; the patient analyzes himself be-

....

[3] Published in *Imago,* XIX (1933), 312-338, 433-453.

tween the hours, discovers even more than the analyst guessed, and brings more material from hour to hour; and suddenly material and patient have become psychotic. This change is easy to provoke and hard to reverse; but fortunately it is not always irreversible.

Before I describe the way to re-establish resistances and make the normal ego cathexis return to the deserted ego boundaries, I wish to emphasize once more that in manifest and latent psychoses the typical analysis used in neuroses is harmful and must be abandoned, or used only in homeopathic doses.[4]

The means of re-establishing resistances are through abandonment of the usual techniques: (1) Abandon free association, because further unconscious material is not needed as enough has been offered by the morbid process itself. (2) Abandon analysis of the positive transference, because without it psychotic patients cannot be treated; negative transference, of course, may come of itself, and must be overcome by explanations, psychoanalysis, and the analyst's behavior. (3) Abandon provocation of transference neurosis, because it quickly develops into transference psychosis in which the analyst becomes a persecutor who is introduced in all kinds of delusional and hallucinated constructions, for which it seems preferable to use Bleuler's term "dereistic" thinking. This development is dangerous and may make further work impossible. (4) Abandon analysis of resistances which maintain repression, because it is not desirable to free more repressed material and more primary processes. The analyst's responsibility forbids his making the patient more psychotic.

By laying aside familiar tools of psychoanalysis, psychoanalysis itself is not abandoned; it is applied to the material and symptoms laid bare by the morbid process. Every connection of this material with traumatizing conflicts is elucidated and analyzed, as well as all resistances except the countercathexes which maintain repressions.

Distinction is made between resistances directed against

. . . .

[4] Homeopathic dosage is so small that it does not inhibit any function and provokes only very slow changes.

recovery and those against unconscious material. For instance, one endeavors to reduce guilt feelings and fears which have real objects, as well as those which are provoked by illusions and by unconscious tendencies. But phobias are left undisturbed because they protect against deeper fears and conflicts; positive relationships which give some security and pleasure are seldom analyzed. One of my patients changed his religion, became a bigot, and had phobias of policemen and of socialists during his treatment. He did not overcome these and other eccentricities until his main conflicts, which were rooted in early years, had been mastered by analysis.

In analysing a psychotic, regression must not be increased. By this precaution, we help to "encapsulate" the permanent psychotic reactions—a result similar to that observed in the process of spontaneous "recovery," which seldom implies more than that the patient recovers enough for practical purposes. Experience shows, however, that the relative capacity for the reasonable control of unreasonable ideas and reactions continues to develop of its own accord when we succeed in reintroducing the patient into a social circle and an active life. Such patients then erect a barrier in their minds against their delusional ideas, and have acquired an insight which, though it may be imperfect and is always somewhat uncertain, suffices to keep their morbid modes of thought distinct from real life. The degree to which such a patient accomplishes this objective is, moreover, a valuable index for the psychoanalytically instructed helper; it shows when danger is to be anticipated from some difficulty in real life and when the patient needs support and an opportunity to unburden himself, not only of this particular difficulty but of the unresolved unconscious conflicts.

It is evident that with the change in technique one drops the idea of the necessity for so-called perfect analysis and the hope for a clinically perfect cure. The analyst is content to see his patient return to active life, sometimes without psychotic residues, sometimes capable of permanent dissimulation of such residues. Many times the results exceed expectation and promise, but in no case can the result be trusted enough to disregard potential postanalytic care.

Freud long ago remarked: "How to deal with the family of the patient? I do not know what to say." Families have since then learned how to behave with psychoanalyzed neurotics; and families, with their psychiatrists, will learn how to behave with psychoanalyzed. psychotics. The time is near when no gap will exist between psychoanalyst and psychiatrist. Many psychiatrists already apply their knowledge of psychoanalysis to psychotic patients; the writer does not object to methods like the group analysis of Trigant Burrow and of Schilder, or to Moreno's stage method; all of these can be very helpful. Fromm-Reichmann's technique is the best psychoanalytical method so used up to the present time.

All these modifications of technique are applicable more to schizophrenes than to manic-depressives; the latter require some modification during full attacks, but the normal method of analysis is used during milder periods and intervals. But one must always have in mind the latent psychosis; the patient himself must bear it in mind, in order to help to finish the treatment.

The initiation of a depressive or a manic state interrupts free association when it is not stressed by the analyst. One gives way to the patient's spontaneous wish for conversation and discussion and prefers to smooth over, rather than analyze, resistance and the troubles of transference.

The rule that the psychotic patient should be told the truth extends to his knowledge of the psychotic nature of his disease. The manic-depressive, like all psychotics, wants to deceive himself, and he attempts to convince the analyst that his psychosis has disappeared permanently. One should not appear to agree with that opinion unless one is convinced that it is true. One's conviction that psychoanalysis can cure a psychosis will do much to encourage that belief in the patient, to the extent that recognition of the existence of a psychosis does not mean hopeless disaster. We know today that the deficient ego in a psychosis, and the dysfunctions of the ego in a neurosis, can be cured. By calling the psychosis an ego disease, every terrifying impression is avoided. To be cured, the psychotic must cooperate; and for this purpose, he must understand the nature of his "becoming different"; if he does not differentiate between the psychotic and normal ego state, he cannot be cured.

Every patient, including the neurotic, has to learn that there are two reactions toward frustration, pain, and disease. One is to outlaw and ban everything that is connected with, or reminiscent of, the causes of these troubles; the other is to know that one must tolerate them and master them, by acknowledging their causes. The one reaction means help; the other, cure. The help is illusionary and must be restricted to use in incurable cases.

When the manic-depressive has grasped the phenomenology of his disease, he can protect himself much better. There are three main facts, true for both phases, which he must know: (1) Narcissism is the source of his emotional vulnerability; therefore the corresponding task is to shift the libido from the narcissistic investment to objects; (2) the general reaction covers special reactions, as a means of defense to hide the real causes; and (3) the patient, instead of accepting frustration as pain, reacts with aggression because he wants to preserve his libido satisfaction. Later, he pays for this indulgence with absolute and lasting pain.

Both reactions cover specific conflicts by complete investment of the ego, with libido in the manic, or mortido in the melancholic. In every relapse, therefore, some distinct frustrations have to be found, analyzed, and accepted. Because this process is painful, the positive transference must be protected. By such analysis and protection, one prevents the increase in the generalized reaction and can continue analysis, in due time, in the usual way.

The greatest danger is suicide in the melancholic phase; the degree of danger can be judged by the proportion of narcissism to object libido, and of dissatisfied to satisfied narcissism, a matter which depends largely on returns and frustrations in love. In prophylaxis against suicide, improvement in the proportions between narcissism and object libido, and between dissatisfied and satisfied narcissism, represents a cure; while constant vigilance represents help. Sometimes the absolute suffering during melancholia is so great, so much greater than the sum of pleasure enjoyed in the good periods, that the "libido economist" cannot blame the suicidal patient. Yet it is the aim to thwart any patient's death—especially while his mother lives.

The change of technique described here is externally characterized by letting the patient sit vis-à-vis and by not imposing the "basic rule." The patient's actions are interfered with, the analyst is in constant contact with the family, and there is the analytical helper. At the end of the session, I have generally called the helper into the office and made the patient participate while I repeated problems and solutions brought out during the session.

Description of the treatment is more difficult than performance. It is always good to follow Freud's advice and start from the surface of consciousness. Freud gave me another piece of advice when I was an enthusiastic, inexperienced beginner. It seems trivial now, but it was very useful at that time, when resistance and transference were still undiscovered. He told me: "Always have in mind that your patient should return the next day for treatment." Today this advice is obsolete in connection with neurotics, but it still applies to psychotics, with whom no contract can be made because of the unreliability of the ego and the vulnerability of the transference.

If one begins with and elucidates one trouble, thereby bringing relief, the patient will return; explanation settles some fears or griefs. No misunderstanding must be left. The psychoanalyst shares acceptance of the psychotic's falsifications as realities; he shares his griefs and fears, and on this basis reasons with the patient. When convinced that by this procedure the patient feels himself understood, the analyst presents the true reality, as opposed to falsification. He then shows: (1) which actual frustration, grief, or apprehension is represented by the falsification; (2) which deep fear, conflict, or frustration is a primary cause of the falsification; and (3) which ego boundary changes have made the process of falsification possible.

This method is based on analytical knowledge of the metapsychological process in schizophrenia. I became certain of the truth and importance of my discovery in this field when I saw it understood and accepted by the schizophrenic himself, who is a good judge in this respect.

The ability of the patient to use falsifications as material from which to draw conclusions in a reasonable way is astonishing; but this corresponds to the main mechanism of schizophrenia. Freud spoke of primary and secondary mechanisms, combining the language of the psychology of his time with the terminology of the mechanistic theory of energy. His own fundamental general discovery was that of the defensive character of many mechanisms.

The investment of the ego boundaries with mental energy, especially with libido and mortido, is a mechanism, in Freud's sense; he himself characterized hypochondriacal symptoms and pain as accumulation of cathexis in certain organs, and he also said that in anxiety the cathexis in the ego is increased. It would seem that all these processes are mechanisms, in Freud's sense, and can be used for defense.

Bleuler found that in schizophrenics the basic process is the splitting between elements of association, and between emotion and content. The French school, starting from Janet's more general conception of physiopsychical insufficiency, culminated in Minkowsky's statement that the basic disturbance is the loss of vital contact with reality. Berze's theory of the lowering of the level of psychic energy appears to describe the morbid process in the right way.

My own investigation of the ego phenomenology, made earlier and independently, led me to a distinct metapsychological and phenomenological understanding of the basic schizophrenic disturbance. I join Jaspers in separating reality sensation and reality testing. Because the ego boundaries lose their cathexis, ideas, thoughts, and remembrances are experienced as real by reality sensation and cease to be mere thinking. Any single change of thought into something real is felt as absolutely certain and cannot be reversed by any reality testing or reasoning, and even less by the reasoning of others. Mental processes from which the ego boundaries have withdrawn meet the bodily and the mental ego from outside and must be real to the pathological ego with its narrowed boundaries.

The comparison of the schizophrenic state with the dream has been elaborated by different authors, in Germany by Kurt Schneider and his school. The basic mechanism of reality sensation is the same in schizophrenia as in the dream. One cannot argue with one's self not to take one's dream as reality. One can only recognize—seldom during the dream, but always when one awakens from sleep—that one has gone through one's own mental process as through reality.

The schizophrenic is not in a position to awaken from his pathological realities; he lives in them and mixes them with life's realities, and falsifies both. Even when the schizophrenic process has proceeded and has corrupted most memories and object representations, the schizophrenic is still able to deal reasonably with his thwarted material. That is true even for the most advanced cases. Freud's dictum that the patient is always right is more true for the psychotic than for the neurotic. The schizophrenic always proves to be right when we understand and accept his world and comprehend what his distorted expressions mean and how substantial are the motives for his actions and reactions.

While analytic treatment cannot force or persuade the patient to drop the reality sensation in his falsifications, his reason can be used to make him realize that because of his illness one part of his ego, which confounds thoughts and reality, is no longer reliable. When the patient once learns this, he has gained a great deal; gradually, from this moment, the illusions lose their power to confuse further the products of the normal part of his personality.

The next step is for the patient to learn to distinguish, by very subtle phenomenological differences, those ego boundaries with normal cathexes from those with cathexes withdrawn. At the same time, the realities which would normally be ideas and thoughts begin to be recognized as pseudo-realities.

By the schizophrenic process, previous ego states temporarily become isolated. Psychoanalysis deals with these states, in full acknowledgement of their reality, by telling the patient that they are revived child-states of his ego. When we treat a schizophrenic we treat in him several children of different ages. In this respect analysis is done in the same way as with a child. It might be worth trying to use the play method in severe cases.

By all the means mentioned so far, analysis becomes interesting for the patient and the psychoanalyst and gives to the patient more equilibrium and security. The cure itself is accomplished by finding and appeasing the instinctual and emotional conflicts which have caused the withdrawal of ego cathexis, this withdrawal occurred partly as a defense and partly because of exhaustion in consequence of too many and too deep narcissistic wounds. Analysis makes the child-states in the patient get rid of many conflicts which had accumulated unconsciously until they resulted in a breakdown of the ego boundaries. It makes the patient understand and accept the actual conflicts which awakened the old ones and were reinforced by them. It strengthens his ego states by new identification with the analyst, and satisfies his object libido by positive transference and by the analyst's help in real life. By all these means, his defense becomes superfluous, and the libido sources are enabled to restore the loss of cathexis.

My ego phenomenological concepts are in harmony with Freud's ego psychology and also with Adolf Meyer's conception of ego integration. Yet there is a difference between Freud and me with respect to the process of "losing reality." Freud said that the ego resigns contact with, and control by, reality and gives way to unconscious urges and their representatives intruding from the id. I found that it is not the "loss of reality" which is the decisive step from normality, or from neurosis, to psychosis. That step is the "gaining of reality" by what has previously been mere thought. Loss of reality is the consequence, not the cause, of the basic psychotic deficiency.

By intensive investigation of the observable changes in object conception, I became convinced that reality is not given up by the ego, but that it becomes impossible for the ego to maintain knowledge of reality because of the establishment of a false conception of reality which is stronger than any remembrance of the healthy reality concepts. In all beginning schizophrenias, including rather recent paranoia, the first false reality conception is made in thinking about something that has happened, and not during the happening itself. This first false conception is always preceded or accompanied by the patient's feeling that there is something "strange" about his own ego.

Estrangement is the characteristic first step on the way to losing reality. Yet I have shown that estrangement consists in the change of cathexis in the ego boundaries. First the libidinous component of cathexis is lost. In ordinary cases of estrangement, there is no complaint of further loss of cathexis. In the beginning of the psychosis, all ego cathexis, not libido cathexis alone, is withdrawn from some thinking processes; and by this basic schizophrenic mechanism, some products of thought are no longer inside the mental ego boundaries; yet what happens outside the ego boundaries is felt to be truly real and really true. No reality test dispels those feelings of reality. I have repeatedly observed this first stage, in which thoughts gain reality, when I have seen "cured" patients immediately after a relapse. However, even without opportunity to examine the schizophrenic process at its start, one can convince oneself of the truth of this observation by hearing reports from more advanced schizophrenic patients about their very first tribulations. The sooner psychotherapy starts after the beginning of withdrawal of ego boundaries, the better are the chances for quick improvement. In one case, a week of psychoanalysis mastered a third relapse, while the patient had needed hospitalization for many months in previous attacks.

After the first step—that of thoughts having become "real" —the next consequence is interpretation of objectively real facts by those falsely conceived as real. Many new falsifications, which, however, do not have the full value of felt reality, are the result. Then follows—as a measure of avoidance of opposed, and therefore perturbing, findings—a scotomization for the objective reality, insofar as it collides with the psychotic "reality." Only now is "loss of reality" established. Therefore I contradict Freud only in my observation that "loss of reality" is not the first step, but belongs to the "self-healing process of psychosis." The quicker the opposed and objectively right conceptions of outside events are fully discarded, the less is the loss of reality, and the better is the encapsulated and systematized falsified-reality state which results.

The process described is not the only withdrawal of ego cathexis in schizophrenia. Combined with it, but clearly distinguishable, is the mechanism of regression to a previous ego
state. Since such regression can suddenly cease or be reversed,
it cannot be caused by anything except cathexis changes. One
must assume that mature ego states reached ontogenetically,
and even biogenetically, can lose cathexes. In schizophrenia,
loss of all interest through regression sometimes replaces loss
of reality by the present ego. But in many cases, the regressive
state itself is lacking in its ego boundary cathexis and lives in
falsified partial or total realities. In every relapse, therefore,
one has to elucidate the present blurred reality conceptions as
well as the regressive ones; this differentiation involves the
most difficult part of psychoanalysis of the psychoses. Sometimes estrangement or depersonalization exists only in regression.

There exists still another form of loss of ego boundary cathexis. It is the most astonishing and the most frequently
mentioned form, but is seldom understood, because healthy
individuals are not conscious of the potential ego boundaries
in their bodies. When an inner organ loses its ego cathexis,
the self-perception of one's body becomes changed. This is a
very frequent early symptom in severe schizophrenia. Frequently, years before other schizophrenic symptoms develop,
hypochondriacal states occur, which, following Freud's explanation, are due to an increase of libido cathexis in the organ
about which the patient is concerned. By close observation of
this phenomenon, I came to the conclusion that the libidi-
nously over-cathected organ is felt to be outside the bodily
ego. When all ego cathexis is withdrawn from parts of the
body, the queerest distortions of self-perception of the body
are complained of, or merely described, by the patient; in
many cases, fear and estrangement are combined with an uncanny body feeling of one's body. As Bibring demonstrated,
paranoic misperception of the outside world may start from such
"extraterritoriality" of an inner organ.[5] Such changes of the

. . . .

[5] E. Bibring, "Ein Fall von Organprojection": *Intern. Zeitschr. f. Psychoanalyse,* 1929, 44.

bodily ego are difficult to describe; yet they are well known by the psychotic himself and are used by him for speculation and further hypochondriacal theory formation. To the psychiatrist's astonishment, the patient is able to understand the dynamic change in his own ego. All his interest in changed self-perceptions is manifestly narcissistic (or autistic, introverted, and introspective). Yet, by his understanding, a more objective interest begins to interfere with his narcissistic attitude; this serves the therapeutic aim to change narcissistic cathexes into object-libidinous ones.

In the psychoanalysis of neurotics, the patient's own personality is always involved; yet indulgence in self-inspection becomes diminished by psychoanalysis, because every accepted explanation frees the patient of troubles which make him introspective. This is even more true with curable psychotics whose morbid self-perceptions form the core of delusions and falsified thinking. Furthermore, it seems that the interest in the patient's disturbed ego function helps to restore the lost cathexis of the function.

This is an important complementary mechanism in therapeutic psychoanalysis of psychoses. It shows in the slow but steady improvement observed in every session in which a false impression was understood as such or an ego reaction was explained. In explaining, the patient's attention was directed to his ego as an object of observation and reasoning. It is certain that by every single attention of this kind the cathexis of the ego becomes strengthened and the normal ego boundary re-established for some time. These ego re-establishments persist for ever-lengthening periods. When they have become permanent, the patient's interest is spontaneously directed to the analyst, the helper, the treatment, and the normal activities which he has deserted. This is very helpful, because any increase of object libido diminishes the narcissistic vulnerabilty.

Psychoanalysis carried out in this manner consists basically in the restoration, step by step, of normal narcissistic cathexes to the ego; it reverses the step by step losses of narcissistic cathexes by the schizophrenic process.

7

PRINCIPLES OF PSYCHOTHERAPY

IN LATENT SCHIZOPHRENIA*

Dr. Federn in this chapter further differentiates between the ego pathology of the neurotic and the psychotic and gives specific therapeutic procedures to be used in the treatment of schizophrenia. The necessity of recognizing latent schizophrenia early and the significant and often misinterpreted symptoms of the disease are particularly stressed.–E. W.

THEORETICAL CONCEPTS

Scientific psychotherapy is based on the understanding of the conscious, and the underlying unconscious, psychological disturbances. While the mechanisms of neurosis are well known, those involved in the schizophrenic process are still controversial.

Every psychosis is a mental disease of the ego itself, while in neurosis only some functions of the ego are impaired. In psychosis, the main damage consists of the loss of cathexis (mental energy charge) of the ego boundaries. As a consequence, we find in this condition a narrowing of the extent of the mental ego, ideas and concepts being still preserved. But the same ideas which normally form within the mental ego boundary and, therefore, are apperceived as mere thought, at once take on the character of a false reality when they occur

. . . .

*Presented to the Staff Meeting of the New York Consultation Center on January 30, 1947, and to The Jewish Board of Guardians on March 7, 1947. Reprinted from *American Journal of Psychotherapy*, I (1947), No. 2, 129-144.

outside of the ego boundary. As the loss of the ego boundary cathexis becomes definite, this false feeling of reality takes on the quality of being beyond any subjective doubt. Yet everyone can observe that frequently with any new schizophrenic production, the ego boundary cathexis oscillates for some time and that the subjective reality of the patient's thoughts is continually interrupted. With every "swing" the patient somehow subjects to doubt the "reality" of his mental productions.

Fortunately, for long periods of time, the loss of the ego boundary cathexis and the subsequent false reality remain only partial. Furthermore, in the majority of cases, losses of cathexis are reversible, and thus the ability of correctly separating ideation from perception can be regained. Therefore, in treatment, those parts of the ego which still function with adequate distinction of thoughts and reality must be employed as allies. Only with their help can the repair of the deficient part be accomplished.

These theoretical considerations are important as a basis for the technique, especially if psychoanalysis is contemplated, whether of the orthodox type or one of the newfangled "brands."

In contrast to the situation in neurotics, one cannot, with psychotics, rely upon the ego to differentiate correctly between thought and reality. With the psychotic one must be careful not to raise unconscious instinctual and infantile material into the consciousness. Unfortunately this is inevitable once the psychosis has been established, since the ego boundaries, deprived of their cathexis, have lost their function of acting as a countercathectic agent against the pressure of the unconscious material. Although used in different ways, the means of transference and interpretation are the same in both cases. With neurosis, the psychoanalyst endeavors to make unconscious, repressed material conscious. In psychosis, he has to deal with *too much* unconscious material already brought to consciousness. Thus, the therapeutic aim here is not the release of repression but re-repression. In antithesis to Freud's well known motto: "Where there is Id, let there be Ego," we must say with regard to psychosis: "What has become the Ego's territory should be returned to the Id."

That the re-repression is possible is evident by its spontaneous occurrence after resolved psychotic episodes. To help such recovery two ends are sought by psychoanalysis:

(1) The therapist directs the patient to focus his attention upon his special conflicts which resulted in the breaking through of unconscious material. One part of these conflicts lies in the present reality situation, the other derives from material which previously was repressed. The former conflict is usually neglected and its connection with unconscious conflicts ignored by the patient. When this connection is actively revealed, the understanding of the unconscious part becomes more easily accepted. It is impressive how many resistances of the psychotic are based on definite reality conflicts.

(2) One must encourage the patient to recognize how his previous ego states interfere with his present ones. It is not generally realized by psychoanalysts that, normally as well as pathologically, ego states are repressed—successfully in normal people, unsuccessfully in neurotics and in psychopaths. Psychotic patients are able to recognize this fact; frequently they recognize it spontaneously and better than is possible with most healthy persons.

By virtue of the therapeutic influence, favorable cases react in a gratifying manner. By their own repeated attempts, the patients learn successfully to adhere to the normal adult ego state for periods of increasing length. This concept is similar to that emphasized by Adolf Meyer, in his basic goal, the reintegration of the slowly diseased personality.

Whether infantile ego states are re-repressed, or whether they are resolved through active therapy and the healing factor inherent in some psychotic processes, is difficult to say. Such a distinction would answer the pertinent question as to whether his disease is only temporarily arrested, i.e., whether the cathexis of the regressed infantile ego states has been lost again. If we are able to answer this question we could make a reliable prognosis in regard to later relapses.

Neuroses and psychoses are likewise opposed to each other in regard to the ego cathexis. In every case of neurosis, some ego boundaries are too much cathected. This is true with obsessional neurosis in respect to the boundaries between ego and superego, and in anxiety hysteria with regard to the boundary between the ego and the objective world. In conversion hysteria, the ego boundaries are enlarged to include some organic expressions into the ego. Some ego boundaries of the hysteric are overcathected with emotion. Here, too, previous ego states retain an increased cathexis through which they disturb the present ego.

Thus it may be summed up: The aim of psychotherapy is to restore lost cathexes to the psychotic ego and to drain off hypercathexes from the neurotic ego. It is, of course, easier to remove superabundant cathexes—by the therapeutic means of transference, catharsis, insight, and indulgence of the superego —than to restore missing cathexes. It is likewise less difficult to raise pathogenic and traumatic material from unconsciousness than to resubmerge it into the depths.

The differences mentioned above are explained by another basic—albeit not completely universal—distinction between psychosis and neurosis. It is one of the fundamental and unshakeable tenets of Freud that neuroses are mainly defense phenomena, while psychoses are mainly defeat phenomena, of the ego. The latter concept was implicitly stated by Freud in his explanation of the Schreber case[1]. The difference is not universal, however, because in every mental disease the conflicts between personality and instinctual drives are fundamental. Furthermore, in psychosis, too, the ego still defends itself against deeper destruction by using all remaining faculties of thought and emotion; in neurosis, the ego is not able to defend all its functioning unimpaired. Moreover, in both groups of mental illness, the ego not only defends itself against the disease but also accepts it as the source of paranosic and epinosic gain.

The above theoretical introduction was necessary in order to understand the right procedure with early schizophrenia, *from which latent schizophrenia is sharply separated.* The therapeutic aim is to prevent a latent schizophrenia from becoming a manifest one. For this reason the diagnosis of latent

. . . .

[1] Freud, "Psycho-Analytic Notes upon an Autobiographical Account of a Case of Paranoia (Dementia Paranoides)," *Collected Papers,* III, 390.

schizophrenia should be made early. Even though it may be impossible to prevent the outbreak, the attempt is worth our while since the outcome of schizophrenia is unpredictable in any case.

Most schizophrenics take a chronic-course. The personality disintegrates slowly, reality perception still controls the more important falsifications, and a rather good adjustment may last for many years with a very slow change to the better or to the worse. Therefore psychotherapy has a good chance to protect an individual against recrudescence of the disease.

Some cases appear not to be malignant, whereas others succumb as though to an actively destructive process. The constitutional forces of resistance and the scope of extrinsic injuring factors influence the course. Complicating organic factors will be dealt with later. Additional factors are inner conflicts and external emotional strain. In favorable cases, precipitating causes are usually less strong than in those ending in hospitalization. The psychiatrist, therefore, has to advise the responsible relative, the family doctor, or the social worker that a relapse is possible. Conditions which were adequate for the patient when he returned home from the institution may later become inadequate and thus harmful—because the schizophrenic himself has changed, either to a lower or to a higher level of integration.

Schizophrenia always interferes with personality development; no schizophrenic individual has matured like a normal person. Therefore we must deal with the schizophrenic patient on the level of his mental and emotional age.

PRACTICAL CONCEPTS

Psychiatry has successfully explored the pathological mental processes and the individual disturbances due to the schizophrenic disease. Unfortunately, one does not know the nature of the pathogeny itself. Although our methods of therapy, including shock treatment, do not attack the pathological cause, they offer more than a merely symptomatic relief because they improve the conditions of fight between pathological process and defense.

In those instances in which a latent schizophrenia becomes manifest, one can observe exactly a dynamic struggle between health and illness—health represented by the normal parts of the personality, and illness represented by those parts which have lost their normal cathexis, especially that of the ego boundaries. Our support of the healthy structure, as well as of the diseased parts, of the ego may arrest any further loss of cathexis. When the struggle against the first delusional threats with the subsequent anxiety in the deranged portion of the ego ceases, the strain on the healthy part also diminishes. In favorable cases it soon becomes evident that the diseased part is better controlled and guided by the healthy one.

The main help given to both parts is the establishment of a positive object libido transference and an identification with the helping personality. To the patient, transference as well as identification are gratifying and pleasurable conditions. Transference helps directly insofar as it increases object interest and channels libido away from an exaggerated narcissism.

The well-known transference improvements are as frequent in psychotics as in neurotics. Through transference and identification the patients become less vulnerable. There is a difference in the technique we apply to neurotics and to psychotics inasmuch as in neurotics we attempt to dissolve the transference and do not allow it to increase, whereas with psychotics one must preserve the positive transference and avoid provoking a negative one.

The patient needs his whole libido to maintain his imperiled functions. Therefore, in some cases, we have to be cautious in our use of transference; often the patient is induced not to direct his energy to objects, for instance, to occupational therapy, or to a job, lest this pursuit increase the narcissistic satisfaction and ultimately lead to more dissatisfaction. One must be careful not to disturb this very labile equilibrium.

J. H. W. Ophuijsen has recently characterized the transference taking place in group therapy of various diagnostic categories as a regression to the pregenital level. In prepsychotic patients we would fear provoking such a regression. When, however, in psychotics a pregenital level is already established, the transference may begin on this level but it soon progresses to include a genital component. In some respect every well-conducted institution for psychotics uses some group therapy.[2] However, many psychotics, even in a group, live as isolated individuals wrapped up in their narcissism.

When the psychotherapist speaks with a psychotic patient he must be aware that the ego levels of the patient are subject to change, as are his words and behavior. Transferences and identifications also belong to different ego levels. In transference, the patient may clearly and intelligently discuss his relationship with other people on a normal level, and the psychiatrist may use this situation to reconcile the patient with some of his difficulties. More than with neurotics, the psychiatrist must preserve the positive transference by siding with the patient in any of his conflicts.

Without staring at the patient constantly, one should watch his facial expression to notice any change in his dominant ego state. He may suddenly show some suspicion or an ambivalent feeling toward the doctor or another person; if one does not know the causes of the trouble, the patient himself usually gives his explanation when he is asked to tell about his change of attitude. One should by no means let a patient leave the office without having clarified such a change. It is inadvisable to tell a lie to the patient (even a white lie!) or to camouflage any discord or complaint that may arise.

While the positive transference creates difficulty only in paranoia, in every case identification must be recognized and resolved early, lest the patient imitate the psychotherapist too much in the process of improving. Such a patient might, for instance, want to get married or divorced, or to change his occupation. One must be careful not to mistake such an induced activity for real improvement. However, identification strengthens the healthy part of the ego directly and, in most

. . . .

[2] G. Devereux, "The Social Structure of a Schizophrenia Ward and its Therapeutic Fitness," *J. of Clinical Psychopathology and Psychotherapy,* VI (1944), No. 2.

cases, immediately improves the attitude of the diseased part of the ego. Like the child, the patient feels relieved of anxiety and of conflicts by enlarging his ego through identification with the directing adult person; his willingness to obey, his self-reliance, and his striving for normalcy improve.

With the help of such a good relationship with his patient, the psychotherapist cautiously attempts to rectify falsifications, not by criticising them, but by asking the patient to enter into all details about his illusions, hallucinations, or ideas of reference—whichever troubles him the most. Then one may juxtapose one's own explanation of the facts in question without stressing its acceptance. In advanced cases, such peaceful criticism usually is ignored; in early cases, the patient reacts to it sooner or later.

One should try to get the patient into psychotherapy at the very beginning of the psychotic phase. Usually, parents, physicians, and educators are slow in recognizing the seriousness of the patient's behavior change. In the anamnesis of the patient we often find that schizophrenia had started with a noticeable deterioration of his school marks at the time of his advanced education (college) or at the time of his work on the first important job. The student's marks in his first year or years were good; suddenly he came home with the order from the college for the parents that he be seen by a physician. If the college psychologist would correctly understand the youth's struggle against his ensuing psychosis which makes his marks as well as his social adjustment decline, the boy would at least be spared the harmful effect of being dismissed from his college. The army did much better than the schools in detecting the onset of the disease.

In elementary and high school, physicians, teachers, and mental health agencies share the task of an early recognition of mental cases. However, psychotic cases are seldom diagnosed as such immediately; they are, in most cases, labeled as behavior disorders or as development problems of the child or the adolescent. Child psychiatry and case work teach us that many prepsychotic cases of latent schizophrenia in reality are post-psychotic cases. Hence, the early childhood data must be scrutinized very closely. The help of the social worker or the psychiatric nurse is required for this task.[3] Later such help is needed to provide a good transference to a person of the opposite sex. My experience, which I published elsewhere, that a good result in an advanced psychotic case cannot be achieved without the help of a motherly woman, should be checked in regard to latent schizophrenia. My guess is that it will be confirmed.

Although the course of the disease is unpredictable, there are certain features and signs which give indication of the probable outcome, as Nolan Lewis has pointed out in a report on advanced cases.[4]

Generally speaking, the course depends on: (1.) the malignity of the process, (2.) the qualities of the personality struggling against the diseased part of the ego, and (3.) any additional conflicts as well as any damage inflicted by external factors which increase the strain imposed on the normal part of the personality. These factors work together to provoke the outbreak of schizophrenia. It is clear, therefore, that in treating latent schizophrenia our procedure must be focused on these contributing agents.

Among the pathogenic factors mentioned above, the factor of malignity cannot be reached by our science. What we can do is to strengthen the personality itself and avoid additional emotional strains on the individual who is balanced so precariously.

In regard to the malignity of the process, it may well be that this factor is not a uniform one. We may incorrectly attribute to the disease some conditions, inherent in the organism, which are attacked by the illness. This suspicion is based on the observation of organic occurrences which have precipitated the outbreak. Pregnancy and childbirth in women, as well as infectious diseases in both sexes, are spectacular in this regard. If the schizophrenia is detected during its latent state,

. . . .

[3] Gertrud Schwing, *Ein Weg zur Seele des Geisteskranken* (An Approach to the Mind of the Psychotic), (Zurich: Raschers Verlag, 1939).
[4] N. C. Lewis, "The Prognostic Significance of Certain Factors in Schizophrenia," *J. of Nervous and Mental Disease*, C (1944), 414.

the outbreak may be avoided by properly applied somatic methods and by preventive psychotherapy.

Some schizophrenic processes are initiated and precipitated by intentional reducing or gaining of weight. In most cases this change in weight is to be seen among the first symptoms. In his proprioceptive sensation of the oncoming psychosis, the patient is inclined to overdo an otherwise rational dieting. In these cases the bad effect of fasting or overeating is conspicuous. The psychosis begins with disturbances of the body ego and with hypochondriacal symptoms. In other cases thyroid and other hormonal medications precede the outbreak. Joseph Wilder[5] and other authors have stressed the importance of correcting the calcium content of the serum. Hypoglycemia is another avoidable complication which should be kept in mind by the physician.[6] I saw paranoic cases subside under such therapy after shock therapy had failed. Physicians, including endocrinologists, who prescribe endocrine preparations are not familiar with the fact that in some cases the proprioceptive ego feeling is changed by hormonal influence. Such a change makes the individual sensitive to any further loss of the ego boundary cathexis and thereby may provoke a schizophrenic episode.

Accumulated deficit in sleep is another precipitating source of damage. Chronic use of barbiturates is definitely harmful to individuals with latent schizophrenia. Frequently the manifest schizophrenic case begins in the morning with illusions and hallucinations as residues of a half-dreamy state, into which the patient's ego awakens from full sleep. This state of half-sleep is due to an incomplete utilization of sedatives or to the fact that the patient's sleep was terminated prematurely. Such persons should not be allowed to doze on but should be made to arise from bed quickly into wakefulness. In families as well as in institutions the importance of sleep of pre-psychotic cases is seldom adequately evaluated.

. . . .

[5] J. Wilder, "Organtherapie in Psychotherapie," *Nervenarzt,* III (1930), 152; and "Psychological Problems in Hypoglycemia," *Am. J. of Digestive Diseases,* X (1943), 1.

[6] F. Alexander & S. A. Portis, "A Psychosomatic Study of Hypoglycaemic Fatigue," *Psychosomatic Medicine,* VI (1944), No. 3.

A further precipitating cause can be the increase of sexual activity. The hypochondriacal fears of latent schizophrenics in regard to marriage and honeymoon are not unwise reactions to this hormonal danger. Increased sexual activities are more harmful when they are without full satisfaction and deprived of their healthy sleep-inducing effect.

Before the outbreak, slight manifest symptoms may mar the state of latency. For some weeks or months patients appear suspicious, irritable, sentimental, or exalted to a degree which retrospectively could be explained by the struggle against their inner danger. How soon a latent schizophrenic may lapse slowly, or fall suddenly, into the depth of insanity depends on his emotional strain, his libidinous frustration, and also on the unknown factor of his individual power of resistance. However, there is always a struggle before the ego gives way. The ego uses a variety of defenses to maintain its integrity. The good therapist respects and supports these defenses. This also holds true for defenses of abnormal nature, especially the neurotic or even psychopathic defenses, as far as they can be tolerated. Whenever latent schizophrenia is discovered, it is difficult to decide whether or not one should therapeutically attack a neurotic or slightly psychopathic state which, however, keeps the patient in his equilibrium without leading to a manifest psychosis.

The normal defense consists mainly of the individual's spontaneous avoidance of exaggerated strain. William C. Menninger[7] justly points to the many ways in which people compromise between mental disease and normalcy.

A frequent defense of the individual is the reduction of his activities (Anna Freud)[8], his ambitions, and even the lowering of his social status. One frequently sees an outbreak of the psychosis when the latent schizophrenic, spontaneously or instigated by another person, becomes ambitious to enter into the higher strata. It is for this reason that some schizophrenics find the rigid and circumscribed conditions in the army easier

. . . .

[7] W. Menninger, "Modern Concepts of War Neuroses," *Bull. of the Menninger Clinic*, X (1946), No. 6.

[8] Anna Freud, *The Ego and the Mechanisms of Defense*, (New York: Internat. Univ. Press, 1946).

to endure than the civilian life to which they return. Not knowing the harm they may inflict, family and friends demand of the veteran a greater activity. However, this stimulating influence in many families is counteracted by the desire, especially of the mother, to keep her son under her care and guidance.

It is difficult to pilot the family and the latent schizophrenic between these contrasting tendencies without increasing his tension. Generally, slow transition from dependency to independence is better tolerated than sudden steps, even though they may be fulfillments of old fantasies of the patient. The adult can put up better resistance against any broadening of activities than he was able to when he was a child or an adolescent. But even with adults one frequently observes how a schizophrenic episode is set off by the transition to a higher school level, or from school to a job, or to the responsible state of marriage. It is pathetic to witness such consequences of an apparently successful marriage or career. With older people it is usually the opposite. The breakdown follows divorce, material losses, or some other defeat.

The resistance against responsibilities is related to, and combined with, too close a family attachment or intense friendship. It is based on a masochistically tainted relation to people. Another group of masochistically oriented ego defenses is that of sublimations: philosophy, religion, anthroposophy, theosophy, and all sorts of esoteric mystical systems. In the latent schizophrenic such "idea systems" are used in a morbid way and their rational as well as their emotional supports can collapse easily. The psychotherapist may become well aware of their morbid nature and may want to remove them. One cannot be too emphatic in dissuading such a beginning.

This leads us to the most important self-defense against schizophrenia, the neurosis, which usually is of the hysterical or the obsessional type. The temptation of the therapist is to interfere by using rational persuasion or psychoanalysis. *No latent schizophrenic should be "cured" of his neurosis, and he definitely should not be treated by the standard form of psychoanalysis.* For thirty years cases have come to me for treatment or for consultation after having been naively, and apparently well, psychoanalyzed. Their (correct) diagnosis was neurosis. During all that time the latent schizophrenic state was not recognized. Seldom did the psychoanalyst either anticipate the outbreak or acknowledge, after it had occurred, that it was his interference that precipitated the manifest psychosis. He would invariably think the case was too difficult for psychoanalytical treatment. This kind of error is not a personal one but one made by "standardized" psychiatry. Even Bowman has recently propagated the general point of view that psychosis and neurosis differ in quantity and not in any basic quality.[9]

This writer, as well as some other psychoanalysts, has written about psychoanalysis modified for use with psychotics. Since then, typical psychoanalysis has been used less frequently with psychotic and prepsychotic cases. Yet it still happens! Therefore it is well to repeat our introductory principle: With neurotics our aim is to make the unconscious conscious, with psychotics to make the conscious unconscious again. For this reason one must abstain from taking a complete anamnesis from the patient himself, from using the method of free association, and from resolving the positive transference. Furthermore, the patient should not lie on the couch and should not be pressed into infantile ego states. Infantile ego states, immature ideation, and unconscious material come up spontaneously.

The therapeutic method with schizophrenics consists of diminishing their emotional conflicts, of cautious interpretation that gives relief, of working through of the material, and of reducing the psychotic and irrational productions to the underlying objective conflicts. With mild or early cases, as well as with pre-psychotics, one can achieve good results. The technical innovation does not contradict Freud's teaching, for he developed his method for the treatment of neurosis and not of psychosis. Freud repeatedly said that psychotics were not suitable for psychoanalytical therapy. Today his thesis still holds true when one wants to use the standard method; how-

· . . . .

[9] K. M. Bowman, "Modern Concept of the Neuroses," *J. of the A.M.A.*, CXXXII (1946), 555.

ever, it is no longer true when one knows how to modify it. One should not assume that the modified method is easier and less strict. As Freud said, "one cannot make a reliable contract with the psychotic ego." Therefore, it is only with the greatest precaution that we use a method which brings more psychotic material to the surface. The patient must also be allowed to apply for help, not only at stipulated hours, but whenever his emotional tension demands it.

In recent years John N. Rosen took an important step forward in psychoanalysis of schizophrenia.[10] He successfully treated paranoic and other delusional patients whose fully developed illness was of many years' duration. One group was in the stage of acute catatonic excitement. His treatment requires irregular hours and even continuous, day-long work. Of course, constant surveillance by experienced nursing is necessary. When his treatment becomes standardized, and when through further discoveries the biological nature of schizophrenia is better understood, we all may become somewhat less concerned when the latent schizophrenic slides into the manifest psychosis. However, up to the present time it still seems advisable to maintain latent schizophrenia in its latent state.

Latent schizophrenia frequently hides its real nature behind the cover of schizoid or criminal psychopathy. A few words may be said on this topic. The writer's impression is that the schizoid type of psychopathy *protects* the person from becoming schizophrenic when a latent inclination to this psychosis exists. The diminished intensity of all conflicts is what makes for this protection. Yet the psychopath experiences a great many conflicts, even though they may have superficial causes. He reacts to them quickly and with an uncontrolled emotional expression. Therefore, one has less reason to fear that he might provoke a psychosis in these cases by the application of typical psychoanalysis. Unfortunately, however, psychoanalysis in psychopaths is rarely feasible because it is much more difficult to establish a reliable transference with the schizoid

· · · · · · ·

[10] J. N. Rosen, "A Method of Resolving Catatonic Excitement," *Psychiatric Quarterly*, XX (1946), No. 2.

psychopath than with a latent schizophrenic whose psychosis is covered by neurosis. We have not had sufficient experience with this type to give advice because it is so difficult to maintain the transference and the necessary countertransference.

In regard to criminal psychopaths, it is generally known that there the clinical picture is usually combined with neurotic symptoms and neurotic character traits. But the treatment of criminality is not identical with the treatment of the concomitant neurosis; the former is focused much more on fortifying the superego and on normalizing the ego ideal. Success in many cases requires a prolonged identification of the criminal psychopath with the psychotherapist. This is also stated by Lindner in his valuable book on the hypnoanalysis of criminals, *Rebel Without a Cause.*

Let us hope that psychoanalytic psychiatry will never relax in its justified attempt to enlarge its realm by including psychopaths of all kinds. This attempt was successfully made by Melitta Schmideberg[11] and by her colleagues in England. Prevention of crime through psychiatric treatment of psychopathy is propagated also by Heinrich Meng in Basle.[12] Every worker in this important field will derive great benefit from *Wayward Youth,* the basic work by August Aichhorn, the pioneer of a psychoanalytically directed pedagogy. It affords satisfaction to know that the work of Freud and his followers will be carried on by the younger generation until the many unsolved problems are clarified.

Our principal conclusion seems to be rather paradoxical: Do not provoke; do not be active; do not try too vigorously to elucidate the basic conflict; master your psychoanalytic interest and your eagerness to understand your case fully; postpone your desire to obtain the history of past psychotic episodes. A psychoanalysis with daily sessions, strict rules, and,

. . . .

[11] M. Schmideberg, "The Treatment of Psychopaths and Borderline Patients," *Am. J. of Psychotherapy,* I (1947), No. 1.
[12] H. Meng, *Praxis der Seelischen Hygiene* (Practice of Mental Hygiene), (Basle: Benno Schwabe & Co., 1943); and *Die Prophylaxe des Verbrechens* (Preventive Hygiene of Crime), (Basle: Benno Schwabe & Co., 1947).

incidentally, high cost is not indicated with these patients. Every experienced psychiatrist of any orientation has learned to deal with these cases. However, as we said in the beginning, a good Freudian understanding of the dynamics, the interplay between urges and defenses, is of the greatest help to the therapist.

By an early diagnosis in latent schizophrenia, we may avoid the danger of bringing more unconscious material up to the patient's conscious awareness. An experienced psychiatrist intuitively recognizes the latent psychotic by his behavior, even when a neurosis is superimposed. It is often difficult to describe the characteristics of posture, language, and glare of the eyes. However, a hidden paranoic or catatonic stigma reveals itself by the patient's behavior and his manners earlier than by his verbal productions. Another hint for diagnosis is any information we may obtain about the occurrence of schizophrenia in the family. One feels somewhat reassured when one hears that there has been no psychotic case in the patient's family and that in the third generation the number of children has not diminished abnormally, contrary to the decrease one usually encounters.

In any doubtful case one can ascertain the diagnosis of latent schizophrenia by having a typical trial psychoanalysis of a few days' duration conducted by a trained analyst. The latent schizophrenic shows an astonishing productivity of free associations pertaining to the typical unconscious sources of anxiety. Frequently, associations are in the line of primary thinking processes, and dream interpretation is accepted without reservations. The most astonishing feature of a trial psychoanalysis is the latent schizophrenic's readiness to use and accept symbolic expression. Such excellent response frequently induces the therapist to believe that the case is an excellent object for a continued psychoanalysis. Doctor and patient join in their delight with the good progress of psychoanalysis until sooner or later the latent psychosis is brought into the open. It is one of the main purposes of this paper to warn the psychotherapist not to provoke a psychosis in this way but to interrupt immediately the course of a typical psychoanalysis and to return to a method which is more cautious and has re-repression as its goal.

Some characteristic features of free association mentioned above may be evident in an ordinary psychiatric interview. Psychological tests, especially the Rorschach, should be given to confirm or to invalidate the tentative diagnosis. Letters, articles, or stories written by the patient are also of some help, and so are paintings and drawings. Any disproportionate change in their pattern should be regarded as a danger signal.

One should be on the alert for another interesting symptom. Whenever estrangement and depersonalization linger on, the suspicion of a schizophrenic process is justified. But there are individuals where a severe estrangement or depersonalization of the inner and outer perceptions persist for years without any progressive disturbance. However, typical psychoanalysis should not be done with them. Every estrangement or depersonalization is due to the withdrawal of the libidinous component of the involved ego boundaries while some mental cathexis remains. Therefore, schizophrenic changes in either direction are accompanied by temporary states of estrangement or depersonalization. An exception has to be made with the estrangement that is a feature of severe and prolonged anxiety or terror states.

After the warning not to proceed with the usual method of psychoanalysis in individuals suspected of schizophrenia, the problem remains as to what other efficient ways of treatment are available. One useful method is that of sparing, preserving, regulating, and also exercising the mental powers of the individual. This seems to be a rather general prescription, but it involves a very distinct, deliberate, and direct advice and aid within the limits of mental hygiene. Help is especially needed in regard to the sexual life of the latent schizophrenic. Control of autoerotism, safeguarding the normal intercourse, avoidance of an incomplete satisfaction, and adequate contraception are tasks which must be attempted in spite of their difficulty. To assure contraception it may be advisable in some cases to go so far as to advocate surgical intervention by way of tubo-ligation or vaso-ligation, not only because of the eugenic aspect involved, but also because of its desirable hormonal influence (Steinach effect).[13]

Any treatment of a latent schizophrenic has to last indefinitely. When the patient is able to settle his conflicts, to tolerate his shortcomings and those of others, to bear frustration, and to accept reality, the re-educational part of psychotherapy has ended. However, no such patient is out of danger; some contact must continue, and he should know that he can call for help in case of any emergency.

The psychotherapist should not restrict his mental hygiene guidance to the patient only. With the help of the social worker he must improve the mental climate of the whole family, without taking sides unjustly. He is the defender of the patient. Yet, if possible, the psychotherapist or social worker should give psychotherapeutic advice only to one member of the family. Furthermore, it is seldom permissible to discuss the patient's problem with any member of the family or any friend of his, except in the patient's presence; the nearer the patient approaches a psychotic state, the less exceptions to this rule can be allowed. No matter how uncomfortable such restrictions may be, it would be psychologically unsound to take the risk of arousing the suspicion of the patient. This is true especially in cases where the latent psychosis is expected to begin with ideas of reference and persecution.

. . . .

[13]Harry Benjamin, "Eugen Steinach, 1861-1944, A Life of Research," *The Scientific Monthly*, December, 1945. (This effect has not been accepted generally in the United States.)

8

MENTAL HYGIENE OF THE EGO

IN SCHIZOPHRENIA*

In the following chapter the mental hygiene aspects of schizophrenia are specifically elaborated and illustrated by two case histories.—E.W.

In his *Introductory Lectures* Freud says: "Psychiatric therapy has hitherto been unable to influence delusions. Can psychoanalysis do so perhaps by reason of its insight into the mechanisms of these symptoms? No, I have to tell you that it cannot . . . We have no means by which we can make the patient understand himself." [1]

More recently, the psychiatrist has found that different kinds of shock therapy may favorably influence the course of delusional psychosis, at least temporarily. Psychoanalytical investigations have been directed more and more to the ego, particularly to the narcissistic abnormality which characterizes the fully developed psychosis. Such studies, although fruitful theoretically, have been unproductive from the standpoint of practical therapy.

Recently, my own phenomenological studies in ego psychology have brought about some improvement in both the understanding and the treatment of the psychoses in their initial and

. . . .

*This paper was presented to the staff of the Department of Psychiatry of the University of Rochester School of Medicine, Strong Memorial and Rochester Municipal Hospitals, on February 15, 1948.

[1] Freud, *A General Introduction to Psycho-Analysis,* (New York: Liveright Pub. Co., 1935), p. 227.

even in their latent states. In the treatment of latent schizophrenia, the attempt can naturally be made to *prevent the outbreak* of a psychosis.

Here we should point out the danger and temptation of believing that one can present ego psychology merely by substituting the word "ego" for "personality" or for "individual." One has to be especially careful not to use Freud's excellent quantitative or economic concept of "ego strength" merely tautologically whenever the ego succumbs to anxiety or other emotions, to some instinctual drive or wish, or to symptom formation and mental illness.

In reality the ego is a specific psychosomatic[2] unit cathected with mental energy. Everyone is conscious of his ego feelings, of the mental ego as much as of the bodily ego. Both are felt separately, but in the waking state always in such a way that the mental ego is experienced as being inside the body ego. The ego is the bearer of consciousness; yet by a unique paradox the individual is conscious of the ego. Therefore the ego differs from all other existing phenomena. In spite of all rules of grammar, and disregarding the apparent paradox, the ego is at once subject and object. As subject it is known by the pronoun "I," and as object it is called "the self." The ego has a history of development which, however elemental, is very complicated; it can be normal or abnormal, intact or disturbed, healthy or diseased. In saying further that distinct functions are exercised by the ego, I return to the habitual use of the word ego to indicate an aggregate of well known and important functions. The difference between the usual concepts and my own is that I conceive of the ego not as merely the sum of all the functions but as the cathexis which unites the aggregate into a new mental entity.

The study of the psychopathology of the ego, therefore, must start with the extraction from our clinical and theoretical knowledge of all the facts, consequences, and theories which are concerned with the ego unity itself and not with its functions.

As an example of the progress contained in such an approach,

. . . .

[2] This use of the word "psychosomatic" does not imply the attribution of somatic energy to the ego.—E.W.

I may cite the problem of echolalia palilalia, and perseveration in cases of aphasia and apraxia. The symptoms are better understood by separating the stimuli coming from the object and the responses of the patient's ego. While in normal people the ego boundary constantly changes with every new sensory stimulation or new inner intention, those having the brain lesion show an ego boundary that perseveres and does not change with every new stimulus.

The ego feeling accompanies every act of attention, which is the minimum phenomenon of the ego; plans and volitional acts are higher degrees of the same kind of ego activity.

Without entering into the theoretical and phenomenological problem of affectivity, the statement can be made that every emotion is apperceived by ego boundaries and is characterized by the kind of drive which prevails in the cathexis of the ego boundary. When a personality is called "integrated," one emphasizes by this term that some specific ego states of the individual never lose their strong cathexis but become, therefore, the prevailing attitudes of the individual. A second phenomenological feature of an integrated personality is that these prevailing attitudes and patterns of ego reaction are able, thanks to their strong cathexis, to control other ego reactions which become conscious. However, the degree of perfection of integration depends on the number of past events, experiences, and ego states which are allowed to become conscious. Many personalities are integrated only because many experiences and ego states are constantly held in repression. Repression itself can be successful or unsuccessful; only when successful does it insure good integration of the ego. Frequently the process of repression itself is attributed to the ego. Yet, phenomenologically, repression seems to be an automatism which influences the extension of the ego but has no place within the ego.

It is important to know exactly whether a disturbance is within the ego or is external to it. In either case, errors can be made which hinder the understanding of the underlying psychopathology, and thereby preventing appropriate, specific psychotherapy. This is especially true in regard to schizophrenia. By understanding possible pitfalls, our treatment, prevention, and hygienic care are re-oriented. This re-orientation starts from one specific mechanism, deficiency of ego cathexis, which can easily be found in the earliest states of this disease. Once found, the new concept can be fruitfully applied to progressive and to terminal states. Improvements and relapses are repetitions of the same mechanisms in opposite directions.

In my view, schizophrenia is characterized by four manifestations: first, creation of false reality; second, regression to earlier ego states; third, inability for abstract thought; fourth, appearance of unconscious mental material. These will now be discussed in turn.

The striking symptom of schizophrenia is the presence of delusional ideas and hallucinations. The generally accepted theory is that this symptom is based on the loss of reality. The difference between neurosis and psychosis lies in the manner of the resolution of ego conflicts which rise from the opposing forces of the id and from the claims of the external world. In Freud's opinion, the neurotic resigns fulfillment of the instincts, while the psychotic gives up reality and creates a falsified, hallucinated, and delusional world. Further falsifications in the delusional world appear in the psychotic's efforts at restitution.

In analogy to Freud's main theory of the genesis of neurosis, psychosis, too, is interpreted as a defense. My own observations contradict this theory insofar as every schizophrenia case begins, not with the loss of external reality, but with the creation of conceptions of false reality. These observations can be verified by anyone who studies the minutiae of any schizophrenic patient's earliest symptoms. Of course, in order to make such observations, the patient must have confidence in the psychiatrist and be interested in the psychiatrist's endeavor to help him, both attitudes being based on a good positive transference. Usually, the first delusions which replace real facts, and the first false interpretations which replace the reasonable understanding of real facts, bear on events of the day before. Such initial episodes happen long before external reality is lost. The method of investigation is simple. It consists in demanding the exact description of the facts. At every detail of the patient's report one shows him where he has unknowingly added or subtracted some psychologically significant data. As a result of such explanations the patient regains the true memory of the events.

These true first symptoms are not directly due to any defense mechanism. This is proven by the fact that the reality with which the thoughts are concerned is far more painful than the thoughts themselves. Of course, in every psychosis some symptoms may serve the purpose of defense; yet the psychosis itself is no defense but a defeat. It is a defeat of an ego which has ceased to be able to defend itself against the impact of instinctual demands, the requirements of external reality, and the conflicts which derive from them.

To account for such an alteration between the sensing of one and the same mental content as reality and as mere thought, the theory of the ego boundaries presented itself as a consistent explanation. In regard to the proofs for the existence of mobile ego boundaries, I refer to my previous studies of ego cathexis and ego feeling. On this basis the assumption is made that the schizophrenic loss of reality consists in loss of cathexis of the mental and bodily ego boundary. Whatever is sensed as mere thought is a mental process lying *inside* the mental and physical ego boundary; whatever is sensed as being real lies *outside* the ego boundary.

One plausible argument for the correctness of this assumption is the fact, emphasized by many authors, that schizophrenic and hypnagogic ideation are identical. The hypnagogic change at the brink of sleep consists in the fading away of the ego. This phenomenon gives to every person the opportunity to convince himself of the existence of his ego cathexis and of his ego boundaries, provided he is willing to sacrifice the pleasure of falling asleep normally.

Since in the beginning of most schizophrenias only certain regions of the ego boundaries, with the mental segments which correspond to these regions, have lost their cathexis or oscillate between cathexis and non-cathexis, mental health and mental disease co-exist. Soon however, healthy functions are contaminated by the psychotic ones. For a long time, although many functions are impaired, others are still intact and a function may alternate between the psychotic and the healthy state. Many secondary explanations and falsifications are used to create some agreement in the conflicting material. On account of this mixing of truth and falsification, of falsely thought realities and mental data still rightly conceived as such, and on account of the many illusions which result from these mixtures, we can also speak of a mixophrenic process accompanying the schizophrenic one. However, because the variance between the healthy residues and the new psychotic creations continues as a secondary process, the external reality is eventually given up. Loss of reality is, therefore, the defense of the psychotic portion of the ego and the defeat of the healthy part.

This theoretical concept leads to therapeutic innovations. In favorable cases we may help to extend the territory of the healthy ego and to lead the patient to recognize, again and again, that the reality he has created is a false one. By this method, thoughts which have gained reality return to the inside world of thought, and the relinquished external reality is re-accepted. Such improvements prove that schizophrenic phenomena are of a dynamic, not static or anatomical, character.

The knowledge that, essentially, the schizophrenic process begins with the ego's loss of the actual function of separating external reality and inside mentality gives us a new approach to the well-known regression of the ego to earlier states. It is easy to understand that the ego cannot maintain its present level when the ego cathexis is diminished or lost. Yet it is necessary to discriminate exactly between loss of the actual ego boundary and regression to previous ontogenetic and to more hypothetical phylogenetic states. The ego which has descended, through regression, to an infantile level may have its ego boundaries well cathected and be able to discriminate between reality and thought, although on the infantile level.

The psychotic regression to an infantile level leads to an entirely different conception of the outside world. The individual may, partially or totally, undergo this retrograde process so far that a narcissistic level is reached in which ego and outside world are not yet separated. Everyone knows that this kind of regression, like other schizophrenic phenomena, is not static but dynamic. The various shock treatments have demonstrated that the ego can again progress from its regressive states.

In schizophrenia there exists a second kind of regression

which is difficult to describe. In a certain respect this regressive process is in complete contrast to the loss of ego boundary cathexis and to the ontogenetic regression; to understand it one must focus on the way in which *conscious* thinking functions.

Usually we are satisfied with the knowledge that it is the function of consciousness to make the ego aware of perception and of thought content rising from preconsciousness. Yet conscious thinking does much more: It severs the memories from the surroundings in which the engrams were made. Each of our experiences occurs in one specific ego state. Therefore, every object is first perceived, not alone and by itself, but as a part of the whole setting. Every time one consciously deals with the same object, it is experienced in different ego states, usually in different surroundings. In conceiving one and the same table by repeated conscious comparisons, the different ego states in which the table was experienced are slowly severed as irrelevant, and the purified concept of the table remains. Further conscious elaborations are necessary to acquire the picture of "table" as a species. Further abstraction is necessary to develop from the species "table" the notion of the "table" which contains only the theoretically identical qualities of all kinds of tables. Still another abstraction must be made. It is also necessary to discriminate between the idea of an object as being a real one and as being only a subject for thinking. All these abstractions are the result of the isolation of the particular object from all residues of the individual events in which the object was co-experienced.

Many authors, most recently Kurt Goldstein, have characterized schizophrenic language and thought by the fact that conceptual thinking and abstract thinking become deficient and lost. This is due to the inverse process by which the special residues of the specific ego state and the surroundings in which the original experience first occurred return in their entirety to the memory. For the schizophrenic it is no longer possible to think generally of *the table;* he always thinks of *a specific table.* It is absolutely impossible for schizophrenic thinking to conceive the concept of "the table" apart from the real table. The schizophrenic process, while diminishing the cathexis of the ego boundaries as a whole, returns to every single engram the resi-

dues of the ego state, the boundary of which has experienced
the perception of the object in a real single event. The consequence is that an abnormal reality is established in regard to
the engrams of objects. To the extent that an individual becomes psychotic, his psychotic thoughts are experienced as reality and as truth. This, however, is an objectively false reality.
Paranoic thinking in particular is characterized by thoughts
which, since they could represent reality, in themselves are not
false and senseless.

It is helpful to distinguish clearly the three kinds of regressions which are due to the diminution and partial loss of ego
cathexis: regression of thought to reality; regression of the ego
to earlier developmental states; regression of the conceptual
idea to the original single experience. The fourth characteristic
of schizophrenia is the appearance of unconscious mental material and the evidence of unconscious mechanisms in consciousness. This phenomenon fits well into the theory that the
ego cathexis is weakened. Of course, while the functioning of
the ego boundaries in regard to the external world and to object representations can be observed, the assumption that there
are ego boundaries which deal with the unconscious is based on
Freud's hypothesis.

It is an important problem, and might lead to a separation
of schizophrenic cases into two groups to find out whether increased cathexis of unconscious material or decreased cathexis
of the resistant ego boundaries is responsible for the outbreak of
psychosis. However, the assumption is justified that neither the
unconscious nor the preconscious processes themselves can modify the engrams in such a way that generalized concepts, general
pictures, and abstractions are the result. Our *conscious* thinking
provides for the conceptual pictures of objects and for the objectivity of thinking, rather than its subjectivity. It therefore
seems evident that the psychosis is characterized, not only by
the regressions previously discussed and by emerging of unconscious contents, but also by an incapacity of conscious thinking to complete one of its most important tasks: controlled conceptual thinking.

By the exact knowledge of the four essential processes in
schizophrenia, we proceeded to mental hygiene of the ego, and

we are enabled to direct our mental therapy and hygiene accurately toward the varied manifestations of the illness. Some measures must spare and strengthen the ego cathexis, others must counteract regression, others must improve and even teach attentive thinking, while still others should oppose the invasion of consciousness by the unconscious, thus protecting the ego against the impending danger. To repair the harm done by such invasion remains the final step. This program will be completed by future psychiatric and psychoanalytic explorers, therapists, and hygienists.

As a paradigm I shall discuss the first group of measures, those whose purpose is to spare and to strengthen the ego cathexis. The ego structure must be adequate, not only for the usual tasks, but also for unusual acute stresses and for chronically mounting strains as well. Since the ego is a unit of dynamic cathexis, the hygienist, in consideration of the ego economy, must hinder exaggerated consumption of cathexis energies through increased wear and tear. The hygienist also seeks to help provide the ego with ample supplies of energy.

Such mental hygiene is not merely mental but psychosomatic. Organic factors exist in schizophrenia and they interfere with the dynamic approach. Yet early recognition of schizophrenia in children permits immediate reduction of all educational claims and emotional strains. In such cases, the hygienic principle is to spare the forces until later psychosomatic maturation increases the supply of ego cathexis. Because such sparing needs to be permanent, a high degree of insight and discipline of the environment is required.

Furthermore, the principle must always be followed that the healthy parts of the ego have to be strengthened by exercise, and the diseased parts by sparing. Whenever even slight disturbances set in, activities which produce strain have to be interrupted and all other claims have to be reduced to the limits of feasibility. With such precautions, the outbreak of psychosis in juvenile patients has been prevented, even though experienced psychiatrists had considered the prognosis hopeless. Of course the realms of activities must be curtailed and whole sectors of life have to be relinquished. Most individuals with chronically diminished ego cathexis and diminished reserves of cathexis do not by their own initiative demand enlarged activities. Their own restrictions frequently appear as eccentricities and idiosyncrasies, as neurotic behaviour, or as true phobias and obsessions. Frequently they seem to fit under the antiquated names of neurasthenia and psychasthenia. Very frequently slight organic diseases are hypochondriacally exaggerated and used as means of protection. No psychological therapy against this means of protection should be instituted. These are negative protective measures.

The positive means of preventive therapy are the same as those of general psychotherapy. Among them a positive transference is of chief importance, striking in its effect. Paradoxically, the psychotic patient must be allowed to choose his therapist himself, because any negative transference dooms all endeavor to failure. With positive transference it is not difficult to get insight into the individual's conflicts and to direct him to better understand his difficulties, adjust himself, and tolerate frustration.

Unfortunately, it is still the general custom to deceive a psychotic person about the nature of his disease. Yet this deception is harmful. It is much better to clarify the nature, and even the danger, of a mental disease to the fearful patient. When his psychosis is understood to be an ego disease its terror is removed. His fear of insanity changes to a conscious combat against the ego disturbance, and this struggle allies the patient with the preventive therapist. The latent schizophrenic who begins to become psychotic learns to resist the tendency of some of his thoughts to gain false reality. He resists his inclination to suddenly attribute the character of certainty to previous ideas of reference. He himself undergoes the experience that his conscious, critically directed attention is able to correct the beginning falsifications. In less severe cases, when this goal has once been reached through the help of the therapist, it continues to be exercised without further instruction. One is astonished how well candidates for psychosis immediately understand that the disturbance concerns their ego and ego boundary. They also learn to understand very well the mechanisms of estrangement and depersonalization.

Such patients come to be aware that the ego has remained

partially on an earlier level and that they like to remain on this level or to return to it. Later ego development did not fail totally, but it is much easier for them to maintain themselves in an immature state; this is the defensive side of schizophrenia. However, these individuals also have the needs of mature persons, or a need to imitate the requirements of mature persons. Therefore, conflicts and queer behavior are unavoidable, since their comprehension and emotional sensitivity remain at the level of puberty or of childhood. For instance, one cannot be astonished to hear a schizophrenic relate messages which were brought to him from certain individuals, from the stars, from the Pope, by rays, by radio, et cetera, when one considers the combined effect in such a patient of the reality of thought and of the scientific understanding of an individual in the preschool period. The ideas of influence themselves—as Freud, Tausk, and Jung have demonstrated—represent unconscious meanings.

Even extreme errors in spatial or social orientation can be made accessible to recognition by the healthy part of the ego. Furthermore, such errors can be deprived of their threatening reality when the deficient boundary cathexis is temporarily restored. However, on account of deficient concentration and attention, such successes do not persist; in many cases, what has been recognized and achieved cannot be retained. Therefore, however interesting and helpful the enlightening hygienic endeavor is, its permanent success depends on the degree to which it achieves a restoration of the normal cathexis economy.

For this task, the symptoms of estrangement and depersonalization furnish clues for our guidance. A psychosis is preceded by both symptoms. In estrangement, the ego is still functioning within its normal boundaries, but in a painful, listless manner. Objects are felt as estranged because the corresponding ego boundary is imperfectly cathected; the libidinous component of the cathexis is lacking. Depersonalization is due to a quite different disturbance of cathexis. The ego has lost its inner coherent unity. Reactive actions involving orientation in, as well as manipulation of, the real world are still performed without errors. No false reality is yet attributed to thought. But the habitual pleasurable ego feeling is lacking. However depersonalized individuals differ in their amazing complaints, they agree on one point: Their own personality has become uncanny to them because the ego is no longer felt as something automatically, i.e., preconsciously, coordinated.

Estrangement and depersonalization occur frequently in form of attacks, after precipitating causes. Under favorable conditions, these attacks terminate without leading to a psychotic state. The precipitating causes are sleeplessness, physical and mental exhaustion, long lasting difficult conflicts, and excessively frequent sexual activity or permanent sexual irritation—especially masochistic irritation. They may also be produced by continuously pleasurable excitement, especially when it leads to permanent, hopeful fantasies. Nunberg has reported cases of estrangement which occurred after the loss of a loved object; yet such cases do not terminate in psychosis.

All these factors are far from being specific. What is specific is a surplus of terror and anxiety. Freud stated that anxiety increases the ego cathexis, and by this mechanism wards off the oncoming danger, and that an accident neurosis usually ensues only in a situation of sudden unexpected danger, and not in a circumstance when anxiety preceded the real event. Yet the increase of cathexis through anxiety also means increased waste of cathexis. Because the supply of cathexis can be exhausted through prolonged terror and/or anxiety, disturbance and disease of the ego can result.

It is perhaps superfluous to repeat that the repressed unconscious contributes to the outbreak of every psychosis. Everything which, since the beginning of life, has traumatized the individual or has produced a chronic conflict adds to the danger of psychosis. There is, of course, some unknown constitutional biological factor. Therefore, ego hygiene means hygiene of the whole fate of the individual and, from the beginning, it includes protection against excess of anxiety, alleviation of anxiety states, and removal of the consequences of anxiety.

From the theoretical understanding of the schizophrenic ego disturbances, some rules of mental hygiene have thus been deduced. Others will be based on theoretical studies of the ego in paranoics, manic-depressives, psychopaths, and neurotics of all kinds.

If we conceive of ego hygiene in general terms, not limited

to the therapy of psychosis, it includes a program beginning with birth and ending with the complete maturation of the individual. Good and emotionally healthy educators instinctively provide for good mental hygiene, yet constructively good education is not the rule. For this reason hygiene of the ego must become a precise task for every hygienist in family, school, and life.

A VERY QUICK CURE: REPORT OF A CASE

Introductory Note

Federn had a wealth of unpublished material concerning his clinical cases which he had hoped to prepare for publication, but his last illness left the task uncompleted. The following case history, which illustrates the practical application of the principles of mental hygiene of the ego, has been abstracted from these unpublished clinical data. Certain details, such as the exact age of the patient, are unavailable, but it was felt that this lack did not detract from the essential value of the study.

The title, "A Very Quick Cure," is not meant to imply permanent cure of the patient; in fact, there is a reference to further treatment two and three years later. On the other hand, we can admit that a quick cure was accomplished, not only because the ego boundary, weakened in the acute attack, was strengthened, but also because the patient was provided with insight into the ego weakness and was thus enabled to practice this revised reality testing independently. Such instruction in mental hygiene provides the patient, who has gained insight into the specific ego disturbance, with lasting means to cope, by himself, with such situations in the future.–E. W.

The patient was first seen in the beginning of a schizophrenic attack. It was not, however, the very start of the disease; apparently there had been slight mental symptoms during long periods of health. There had also been organic disorders; menstruation was delayed and sexual satisfaction was achieved only before menstruation. Psychic relationship was more important to the patient than physical relationship, but there was no hysterical frigidity.

For the past few weeks the patient had felt tired. Her head was heavy; her face was frequently congested. A venesection had been suggested. She had lost interest in housework, in her children, and in other activities. She had to force herself to whatever work she had to do, and she preferred not to leave her home. During the past week she had not wished to sleep alone because infantile fear of darkness had returned. Her husband had been ill, and neither she herself nor anyone else could take care of her.

The patient used logically and grammatically perfect language. She had spontaneous insight into the morbidity of her mental state, or at least it could always be made clear to her, but this insight was not permanent. Her own attitude to her complaints and delusions showed a characteristic uncertainty; she did not doubt her own ideas when she was alone, but did so immediately on communicating them to me.

This was a case of true paranoid schizophrenia, not borderline and not latent; however, it was fortunate that treatment was begun at the stage of precipitation. Psychoanalysis, therefore, was not the method of choice, either for prevention or for preventive precipitation. The latter approach is now used because one has means to arrest and heal a schizophrenic process; yet the lasting prognosis after shock treatment or the use of Rosen's method is still uncertain. A preventive or primary method of treatment such as I use is more cautious and is no less promising. It is like repeatedly applied first aid in surgery. An individual on the verge of losing his hold on internal and external reality is induced to face both and, when the automatic cognizance of them is lost, to discern both by self-observing attention. Furthermore, the patient is taught to recognize that the psychotic false reality is alluring to him, and that it is easier to let one's self succumb to one's psychosis than to fight it off. In psychosis, the primary gain of id repression is supplanted by a secondary gain of the ego.

The patient was sent to me by a friend of hers and mine whom I had analyzed. Thus I had little difficulty in regard to transference, since the female helper so essential in these situations was already present.[3] Another favorable circumstance was the family attitude. In many respects analysis of psychotics is like that of children: therapeutic success is always easier to attain if the whole atmosphere in the patient's family is friendly to the psychoanalytic approach. The continuation of the child's treatment depends on whether it is possible to overcome the resistance of the child's family. It may be advisable or even necessary to have one member of the family psychoanalyzed; sometimes it is sufficient to have the aid of another analyst in order to appease a jealous mother or the neurotic reactions of both parents.

In this case, the psychoanalytic atmosphere in the patient's family afforded excellent conditions. Yet the patient had been treated some years before, under the same favorable conditions, by the usual method. This treatment had led to temporary hospitalization and was broken off for good.

When I saw the patient for the first time in her home I had to decide whether she should be hospitalized or whether she should be treated in her own surroundings. I decided on the latter course and took immediate steps to bar all disturbing visitors; only two psychologically oriented friends were asked to visit her. Although the danger of suicide did not appear great, the devoted and quiet servant in her house was instructed to watch her and to report any sign of aggressiveness. All sedatives and supportive drugs were removed, not only from her room, but from her apartment. Housework was recommended, but all responsibility was taken from her by telling her that until the next appointment her main duty was sleep and rest. For the first week I visited her in the home; then she came regularly to my office.

From the beginning, the patient was informed that she could call me at any time, day or night, whenever her problems became too burdensome or terrifying; my telephone service was told to connect her immediately. In this way hospitalization or continuous watch by a psychiatric nurse was avoided. All interference by her former physician and all telephone inquiries

. . . .

[3] The role of the female helper is discussed at length in another paper in this volume, "Psychoanalysis of Psychoses," Chapter 6.—E.W.

from her many relatives and friends were ended. The physician had helped to provoke the outbreak of her attack of anxiety by recommending that she go to a psychiatrist or to a sanatorium. To consult me and to be treated at home meant to the patient that she was merely "nervous" and suffered only from a psychoneurosis.

The first symptoms in the attack were sleeplessness, headache, and figures "big like mountains" which came near the patient and filled the whole world. This did not happen in a dreamy state; she was still able to chase away such cosmoplastic fantasies by speaking reasonably about simple matter-of-fact topics.

Such scenes and fantasies came more easily and were more vivid when she had slept badly the night before. Therefore, as the most valuable means of therapy, her family was called upon to protect and to respect her sleep, and I personally administered a large dose of phenobarbital at the conclusion of my first visit. On this occasion there were no further inquiries. Intervention and practical help, alliance with the patient's friend, severance of contact with her physician (although the action did not fit in with professional "ethics")—all this made the patient feel that she had gained a really interested helper. Such siding with the patient in every conflict, especially in those in which delusions are already mixed with reality, is the first step toward establishing a positive transference. When one is able to win his confidence through support in one of his problems, the patient is frequently willing to postpone all decisions, even important ones.

The second day the patient communicated more about her main conflict, although I did not encourage her to describe her chaotic fantasies. (This illustrates the difference between this method and that used in the analysis of neurotics. With free association her fantasies would have led immediately into the depths of other schizophrenic constructions.) In the evening the patient called me again because she had developed a fear that her daughter had become mentally ill. She refused to talk about her new concerns to a doctor who had visited her as a friend, but preferred to wait for me, thus testifying to her good transference. It was important now to have something useful to offer the patient; this was my first test. In this case the problems were easily solved, as I shall describe, and the menacing symptoms were soon gone. But there would have been quite a different course had I shown any immediate interest in her chaotic pictures.

Three years later, during a period of complete normality, the cosmic fantasies were explained when the patient's dreams revealed the same material. This is an example of what re-repression means; it means that unconscious products return to the dream world, they do not continue to intrude into the consciousness of the waking state.

I shall now discuss some specific delusions which occurred during the acute illness and the method by which she was helped to refuse and to correct her false ideas, rather than to accept and cultivate them.

First delusion: Suddenly she had become convinced, and was quite reasonably terrified by the thought, that her daughter had become "insane"! Theoretically, it seemed evident that she had projected her own psychosis on her daughter. If one had tried to clarify this idea of "insanity" by making her understand that this was merely a projection of her own fantasies, one would have harmed her intensely; for this would have meant to agree with her that she herself was "insane." The most important therapeutic step was to persuade her that she was not "insane," but that there existed in her a difficulty in separating thoughts and reality.

She told me that her daughter had told her that someone took away her thoughts and influenced her will; this was something that the patient had sometimes thought of herself. Although I knew that the daughter was quite healthy and that the patient's report must be untrue, I did not contradict the patient as people usually do in such cases. Instead, I insisted on knowing all the details of the occasion when the child made the statement, and I asked her to repeat exactly the words that were used. Soon the real event which had made her believe in her daughter's "insanity" became evident.

The child had missed a lesson, and her teacher had requested by telephone that the child call back and make a new appointment. The child did not want to telephone herself and said: "Whenever one telephones to a teacher one has to say 'yes,' and one cannot speak as one would like to speak." This happened in the morning. The same afternoon the patient suddenly remembered that her daughter had asked her to telephone because teachers rob us of thoughts and influence our will.

It was possible to make the patient compare her two versions of the story and to bring to her knowledge and insight the fact that it was her own interpretation which was wrong and which had caused her apprehension in regard to her child's mental state.

It is easy to guess that her consciously exaggerated apprehension covered some unconscious enmity and aggressive wishes against the child. By free association one might have verified all this. But by doing so, both the unconscious motivation and the conscious reaction would have become more vivid; the false idea would have become stronger and much more difficult to correct later. It might even have become impossible to do so. More falsifications to prove the child's "insanity" would have been added. The more the patient's own disease was projected on the child, the more evidence the disease itself would have acquired. Psychotic projection is an inefficient method of defense; however, it is continued regardless of all defeats. One can also imagine that the patient would have insisted that the daughter and not she herself should be treated. She would have admired herself for her cautious sharp-sightedness and would have refused more and more to recognize her own error.

In the same way it would have been methodologically wrong to make her understand the deeper causes of her falsification: she herself had regressed to her daughter's age, at which she herself could not have resisted any suggestion of her own teacher. "I must say what she wants me to say" was the psychotic, magic way of understanding the feeling that others were implanting thoughts in her. Thus the correct observation of the child that "one cannot speak with the teacher as one likes" changed into the statement that others are "robbing one of one's thoughts." [4]

The patient had been intensely troubled by her discovery

. . . .

[4] In other cases the feeling of being robbed of one's own ideas is due to quite another mechanism. See "Die Ichbesetzung bei den Fehlleistungen," (Ego Cathexis in Parapraxes), *Imago*, XIX (1933), 312-338, 433-453.

that her daughter had become "insane." Yet it was possible to re-establish her logical control the same evening. She re-repressed and abandoned her false reproduction and projection before a night with sleep and dream, or a sleepless night with waking dreams intervened.

It is always important to attack morbid productions on the same day on which they become conscious. That neurotic and psychotic constructions are strengthened and amplified during the night can be observed better in cases in which the psychotic process is just beginning than in those of longer duration. When new productions have been clarified beyond any doubt, then the time has come to try to clarify falsifications of older origin. Doubt and uncertainty are specific features of a beginning falsification; in advanced cases they disappear. Neurosis means doubt; psychosis means certainty.[5] As long as there is doubt, the ego boundary cathexis is still oscillating. Certainty of falsifications shows loss of cathexis; fortunately, in some cases this loss is only temporary.

Even an apparently simple delusion shows the basic disturbance of schizophrenia, the uncertainty in the discrimination between reality and thought. My theory is that this is due to morbid weakness of the cathexis of the ego boundary. The description of the basic symptoms must be completed by add-

. . . .

[5] Note: Since doubt is known to be characteristic for obsessional neuroses, or, on the other hand, may presage a psychotic delusion with feelings of certainty, this point should be clarified. First, obsessional doubt cannot always be distinguished from paranoic doubt. Second, the predominant dynamic force in obsessional neurosis is, as is well known, affective ambivalence, and the doubt concerns chiefly, but not exclusively, one's own decisions and actions. Sometimes it relates to whether something has or has not been done by the obsessional patient. Third, the paranoic doubt concerns whether or not some content is real or unreal and rests on the still vacillating strength of the ego boundary; once the cathexis of the ego boundary is permanently lost, the delusion with certainty is established. Fourth, whether the doubt concerns his decisions or the reality of some contents, as long as a patient is doubting, he is clinically considered to be neurotic. Only when the doubt becomes a certainty do we classify him as psychotic. Among cases of obsessional doubt, one is usually able to distinguish the pre-psychotic from the truly obsessional patients.—E.W.

ing that three, rather than two, mental activities confuse the material. Not only are thoughts taken for facts and mixed with them, discrimination among facts, words, and thoughts becomes impossible and are therefore inextricably confounded. In some cases, the more important confusion is of words and imaginings; in others, that of words and facts; in others, that of imaginings and facts. Yet all three kinds of misunderstandings, caused by intermingling of language (words), reality (facts), and thoughts (imaginings), are found in cases of advanced disease.

One is reminded of the different manifestations of magic thinking. Of course, when an imagining or a word assumes the quality of fact, it is understandable that it can acquire a magic influence. Of Ferenczi's three stages, magic of gestures, of words, and of thoughts, the latter two are easily recognized in almost every schizophrenic patient. Magic of gestures is frequently disguised in a defensive phobia or obsession. In this first delusion the "magic" was covered by phobic anxiety. In the second delusion, as well, an obsessional fear overshadowed the "magic" of the symptom.

Second delusion: A few days later the patient complained that her whole house was under another person's power; the power worked from a distance and was continuously very damaging and disturbing.

By free association one could have obtained material about enmities, wishes, and magic thoughts, and memories of her suspicions and of her general suspiciousness. But then her suspicions would have become numerous and more evident, the memories themselves might not have become clear; instead, her suspicion would have been transferred to the psychoanalyst and would have included him in some illusional and delusional system. However, without letting her surrender to her own associations, it was possible to follow up the way in which this typical persecutory delusion had taken hold of the patient.

She never complained that she herself "stood under the power," but that her family and the whole house were influenced. Theoretically, one could therefore assume with great probability that the opposite explanation was true, and that in reality she herself had experienced a real influence by someone and that she feared that the same person's influence would continue and would spread over her family.

It was my immediate guess that she was still wondering and doubting whether it was right to have excluded the physician who had threatened her by his advice. This would not have seemed so harmful if another specialist, consulted by that physician, had not a few days previously made a very serious diagnosis in regard to her husband. When she, her husband, and the physician went to see the specialist, neither of the physicians recognized her mental state as abnormal, and they spoke quite openly with her about her husband's illness. The diagnosis of her husband's case proved to be wrong, but had had the good effect of bringing about a complete check-up of her husband. (An intestinal operation was found to be necessary.) Her complaint meant, therefore: "I was always too much influenced by my physician, and I am afraid that he will continue to have influence on my family."

It is a general rule that the sources of recent perturbation in incipient cases lie in recent real occurrences, although the past contributes toward making the mental apparatus react abnormally by enormous aggrandizement or falsifications. However complicated both past and recent occurrences are, they have to be deciphered and brought to consciousness and to rectification. If rectification is impossible, they have to be re-repressed. However, in most cases the precipitating emotional conflict which turns the switch from one mental disorder to another mental disorder is not difficult to understand. Such conflicts can be handled by the same direct means which are used with any excited but mentally normal person. Not the morbid state itself, but the degree of its manifestation, is lowered immediately by the psychiatrist's kind and reasonable interference when a good transference has been established.

To find out whether my guess was right, the patient was asked what kind of influence she felt was exerted, whether it was a religious or a political or a mystical one. The patient said: "The last." She was asked who she believed had exerted such a mystical influence on the house. She seemed to think it over and could not find the right answer; she doubted whether she should answer at all. Then she gave the answer which had been expected. She felt that her former physician had a mystical vague influence' on her family. She could not say how this influence was exerted, but it existed.

Again no free association was used. Instead, she was asked directly for all important events which had occurred between the physician and herself. There was no hint of a love affair between them, but they had been very good friends and, as usual, a positive transference to the family physician and vice-versa had been established. When the husband's entrance into the hospital for operation had been postponed for external reasons, the physician wanted to reassure her that the operation was not dangerous and made the remark: "Well, you have him for one night more." She immediately understood that his suggestion was to use this night for sexual intercourse. She felt this was a rather free familiarity on the physician's part. The next day when her husband left the house to go to the hospital, accompanied by the physician, the doctor's words in her mind suddenly changed their meaning and became a prophecy: "You had your husband only for one more night." That meant that he would die. Of course this idea was strengthened by much repressed material; therefore she began to feel the imminent curse, and the doctor's words were interpreted as a bad omen. This was the meaning of her feeling that the doctor's influence was a mystical one.

I told her: "You believe that the whole family stands under the influence of the doctor's words," and I explained that her first thought had been the doctor's influence and that she believed in the serious diagnosis and in the nearness of her husband's death. This reasonable thought had been changed into a vague feeling that a mystical influence was dwelling over the house.

By free association much unconscious material such as death wishes and transference fantasies would have been brought to consciousness. But far from being helped, she would have become more perturbed. As with the first illusion about her daughter, it was easy to recognize that her manifest care for her family covered and compensated for unconscious forbidden infidelity and aggression. All this had to be re-repressed.

Third delusion: Since the outbreak of her psychosis she had been tormented, with some interruptions, by her difficulty in taking medicine because: "It might be poison."

This fear expressed her proprioception of being changed internally and, also, the fact that her mind became more troubled by hazy thoughts and was filled with fantastic dioramas when she could not fall asleep because she had taken an insufficient dose of barbiturate. In two attacks which occurred two and three years later, the "poison" idea was more developed and was analyzed. As mentioned before, during my first visits I did not prescribe barbiturates, but personally gave her full doses and waited in her room until she was asleep. At my request the bottles were opened at her bedside.

Fourth delusion: She suddenly believed that her husband had become blind. The source of this delusion could be found by no other means than by exact interrogation. She had had a telephone conversation with her husband in the hospital. He told her that his eyes had been examined. Then he complained because she had not come to visit him: "Why don't I see you?"

In this delusion the aggressiveness was more evident than in the others. Therefore I told her that it was quite understandable, did not involve any blame to her, and that inimical unconscious feelings against her husband were gaining consciousness. I explained that most people behave to some extent as they did when they were children; they do not like anyone to fall ill, and on such occasions children usually harbor some death idea against the sick person. I comforted her by telling her that it was a sign of her good and kind character that now, because of her husband's illness, she had become more thoughtful of her family, and that any feeling which one might call "bad" was only hinted at and had remained under good control.

No further falsification developed. After ten days she could visit her husband in the hospital and could return to her daily duties as a housewife and to her usual ways of social life.

9

PARANOID CERTAINTY

*This brief article, describing theoretical and therapeutic consid-
erations concerned with the problem of paranoid certainty, was
compiled from unpublished material found among Federn's
case histories.*—E. W.

The certainty with which paranoid patients regard their delusions presents a difficult problem, but one which can be solved
by the proper therapeutic approach. A good illustration is the
case of one of my patients, a young woman suffering from paranoid dementia. In one visit to me she stated, among other
things, that news about her had been broadcast over the radio
and that attempts had been made to poison her. Our conversation proceeded as follows:

Analyst: Have you yourself heard the radio about yourself?
Patient: (after a short pause) No.
A: How do you know that there was a broadcast about you?
P: All people have whispered about it.
A: Have you heard what they whispered?

I insisted upon her acknowledging that what she had taken
for certainty was only one of many possibilities. She was impressed that I accepted all she told me as being extremely serious and important, and worthy of consideration among the
other possibilities.

Analyst: How do you know that you are poisoned?
Patient: My bed was smelling mysteriously.
A: What kind of smell?
P: Lavender.
A: Is lavender a poison?

P: In the movies poisonous plants are put in the bedroom to poison her.

After further conversation the patient acknowledged again that when her own explanations were of only a very slight probability she indulged in taking them as certain.

She complained that she herself knows what other people think, and that others know her thoughts. In this regard it was more difficult to convince her of the falsity of her certain knowledge, for her feeling had a convincing power. However, by insisting that she report her concise thoughts, she was brought to agree that some of these thoughts are, in the beginning, only ideas with enticing probability, and that they gain certainty only when they are recalled and thought over the next day.

Can such false certainty be explained as due to the recession of the ego boundary in these cases? Does the strong cathexis of the thought itself create certainty of the thought?

To answer such questions it seems to be useful to clarify the method used by the mentally healthy person to decide whether an assumption of his be right or wrong. The healthy person compares the actual situation with analogous ones in which one or the other condition was different, or might be supposed to be different. This method presupposes the normality of the ego state, not only in the present situation, but in the situations which are thought of. If in these previous ego states the ego boundary cathexis was deficient, such trial thinking becomes invalid because in the first conditional ego situation the ideas already have a false reality.

Close investigation teaches us that the paranoic, and especially the paranoic schizophrenic, does not make even an attempt to scrutinize the certainty of his single thoughts. It appears that his systematized ideations are due to more or less incoherent single thoughts which deal with the certainty of facts and which are mixed with the ideas which have gained certainty. If everything is felt to be right about what one thinks, it is impossible to discover any error. Observing my own thinking process, I allow myself experimentally to have my own private reality, in which I assume that the combination of my ideas is right and true. If I expected general acceptance of my conclusions, I myself would be paranoid. If I preferred some ideas as being proven with certainty, not recognizing them to be merely my own assumptions, I would not be paranoid, but only stupid.

However, if I can prove the rectitude, or at least the reasonability, of my private combination of ideas, I am not paranoic and not stupid; I am an innovator and discoverer. Therefore, full proof for the certainty or probability of a person's conclusions is required before his mental health can be established. Of course, in most instances the proofs are not repeated for every conclusion, but are based on much previous mental work —learning, testing, thinking.

We can therefore assume that the complete certainty of the paranoic is due to:

(1) falsified reality resultant to the shrinking of the ego boundaries;

(2) false reality of thoughts belonging to an ego situation used in trial thinking;

(3) increased cathexis of ideas used in trial thinking.

The feeling of certainty and rectitude is also related to the feeling of truth. It is important to recognize the truthfulness of all psychotic communications. Truthfulness concerns only the relationship between one's thinking and its communication to others, not the reality situation. Since the paranoic feels that whatever he says has certainty, he always has the feeling that he says the truth. He accuses his listeners of not believing what he says; it does not occur to him that the rectitude of his mind is unbelievable to his audience. It is an achievement of therapy to make the paranoic understand that he is being truthful and, nevertheless, at the same time, may be quite wrong. The enormous stupidity of paranoic production is frequently in contrast to the cleverness and acuteness with which all hints and details are combined in the occurrences. The patient is eager to find at least a minimum of relationship in order to fit them into his systems. Such keenness is rather a good symptom for it proves that the patient still has some feeling of uncertainty, as he needs to find more and more proofs or apparent sophisms to fill the gaps in his constructions.

10

EGO PSYCHOLOGICAL ASPECT
OF SCHIZOPHRENIA*

The topic of this chapter is the breaking down of ego functions. The dynamics can be clearly understood on the basis of Federn's concepts of ego psychology. This paper offers excellent points of orientation for the treatment of such disturbances.–E. W.

The difficulty in understanding an aggregate of observations which deviate from the habitual angle of approach, or in understanding an aggregate of conclusions which are not yet standardized, is caused by the unprepared ego boundaries of the student. Yet, the function of ego boundaries is precisely the main content of this discussion, which deals with ego psychology in schizophrenia and which supplements my previous papers on theory and practical clinical applications. The task is, therefore, to adjust the reader's ego cathexis and ego boundaries to this idea and to its significance.

However, this is merely an extreme example of a common occurrence. Simply by giving a cogent title to a discourse, the mental boundary cathexis, i.e., attention, becomes concentrated on the circumscribed ego boundary which deals with that circumscribed object. By discussing the ego psychological aspect of schizophrenia, I aim to prevent interest from widening to other aspects of the problem.

However, there are other aspects that need not be disregarded, although they may lose some of their basic importance, such as:

. . . .

*Lecture delivered by invitation in June, 1949, at Winter's Veteran Hospital, Topeka, Kansas.

Bleuler's assumption of the impairment of an elementary mental function; Kraepelin's clinical picture and his theory; the modern view of the pathological process; the problem of prepsychotic personality and that of sensitizing conditions and precipitating causes; the developmental question of retarded maturation and accelerated aging, correlated with structural incompleteness and intolerance to accumulated exogenous and endogenous straining factors; and Freud's delineation of narcissistic fixation and of the defense of instinctual needs through the loss of the real world.

Without clear awareness of the ego, and without ego terminology, recognition of the ego psychological aspect was initiated by Berze, Adolf Meyer, and by K. Schneider. This aspect was implicit in the emphasis laid by both Freud and Abraham on the narcissistic character of schizophrenia. Therefore the present attempt to isolate the ego psychopathological factor as the basic fact in schizophrenia is not new—the original finding is still the main one. The disease begins with an impairment of ego cathexis; the ego boundary, in particular, can no longer be held cathected to its normal extent. This has been found in every early case, and the therapeutic use of this fact has been described previously.[1] The assumption was justified that such an impairment is not only a symptom of the initial outbreak, but continues to be the basic process during the whole course of the disease. However, there can be a temporary restitution of the ego cathexis through interruption of the process or through defensive compensation. One realizes that the impairment of the ego, which is the core of the living individual, means impairment of mental life itself—this explains the catastrophical nature of the psychosis.

Hence it appears to be a promising inquiry to elaborate the part which the diminution of ego cathexis plays during the entire course of any schizophrenic case. This alteration in ego cathexis devastates all kinds of mental functions and also creates the characteristic psychotic quality of mental production. Investigation of this process can be shared or accepted only by workers who are familiar with the dynamic aspect of the ego.

. . . .

[1] See "Psychoanalysis of Psychoses," Chapter 6.

Other investigators may remain satisfied with the knowledge that schizophrenia is merely a neurosis, more severe than others because it is a narcissistic one. Only a dynamic orientation permits the statement that psychosis is due to a decreased ego cathexis, while neurosis leaves the ego cathexis itself intact or increased and only disturbs various functions of a still intact ego.

For a better understanding of the dynamics of the ego in psychosis, the phenomenology of the healthy ego will first be discussed. It is interesting to follow the ego psychological findings of the great philosophers who have freed science from the chains of Aristotelian and ecclesiastical rules. Descartes might be quoted here. His fundamental thesis was: *"Cogito, ergo sum,"* "I think, therefore I am." This sentence contains the concept of the ego in both verbs; therefore—while accentuating the relation of thinking and being—it implies that "feeling my ego proves to me that thinking and being are mine." To this venerable but neglected wisdom modern ego psychology has returned —thanks to Freud—better equipped with psychodynamic orientation and psychogenic knowledge.

Although Freud's theory of the ego and the id is well formulated, it is not this theory but the familiar phenomenon of the *ego feeling* that proves the existence of the ego. The ego is not merely a concept and not simply a contradistinction to something else, be it the id or the object representation. There is in every individual the ego unit which remains the same, although the ego contents change rapidly or slowly, transiently or more lastingly. The ego feeling enables the individual to distinguish between the ego as subject and the whole outer world, and also between the ego as object and all representations of object.[2]

It would be simple to say that the ego feeling is identical with consciousness, yet there are ego states which are not conscious because they are repressed, and there are conscious object-representations which do not belong to the ego. When a speaker thinks of his problem, however interesting it may be, his ego feeling tells him that no interest can bridge the gap between ego and object.

. . . .

[2] Note: In handwriting at this point is: "Martin Buber, *'Das Ich und das Du.'* "—E.W.

In the idea of the body image, Schilder has found basic facts relating to the bodily ego. He states that the body image consists of the proprioceptions of the whole body, and that it changes with the body's varying postures. Yet neither the body scheme nor the body image described by Schilder are identical with the bodily ego. The body scheme represents the constant mental knowledge of one's body; the body image is the changing presentation of the body in one's mind. Throughout the changes the bodily ego is the continuous awareness of one's body. Image, scheme, and ego, all three, are themselves not somatic but mental phenomena.

One can observe one's own ego feeling in regard to extent, quality, strength, and function. In pathological cases, exhaustion and restoration of the ego feeling can be observed and controlled to some extent. It is a legitimate theory that a specific cathexis forms the ego. This well-observed cathexis is the best argument for Breuer's and Freud's theory of mental dynamics which depend on movable or fixed cathexes.

Jung introduced the concept of the ego *complex*. This complex is not identical with the ego itself, but consists of memories, ideas, and wishes connected by the affect felt in dealing with one's own ego. While all other complexes may influence the ego indirectly, the ego complex is the direct picture of one's own life and, therefore, represents the ego only as the object of one's feeling and thinking. The ego itself is the constant unit which thinks and feels itself as well as the world; the ego complex changes with ego development. Every complex when not repressed can temporarily occupy the actual ego, as does the ego complex as a whole or as a partial ego representation.

In the ego, mental and bodily ego feelings are clearly felt as separated, but always as parts of our united inner selves. They are united in such a way that the bodily ego feels the body to be outside, between the mental ego and the external world. When reference is made to "mind and body," it is really the abbreviation for "mental and bodily ego." Likewise, the "soul" means the experience of the "mental ego." Bodily and mental egos, with their relationship, ego boundaries, ego complex, and ego feeling are phenomenologically evident.

Psychology and pathology offer two additional proofs of the

existence of an affective cathexis unit: (1) The first and most convincing is presented by the pathological phenomena of estrangement and depersonalization. This is outside the scope of this discussion and will be the topic of another study. (2) Ordinary sleep gives opportunities for awareness of ego cathexis. Here is a borderline field between psychology and psychopathology, since an absolutely healthy sleep is dreamless and devoid of hypnagogic or hypnopompic transition. However, such normality or sanity is a great exception; usually, sleep gives evidence of the disappearance and reappearance of the ego, and also of its intermediate appearance on the dream stage.

Freud stated that during sleep all cathexes are withdrawn from objects into ego. This is true only from the biological aspect, because sleep is, *par excellence,* a narcissistic process and all objects are decathected. It was one of Freud's few errors to postulate that the withdrawn cathexes have returned to the ego. On the contrary, the ego itself is depleted of cathexis the moment the sleep reflex is successful. Yet, in case of emergency the ego is reawakened (recathected), as in the instance of the reaction of the nursing mother to the cries of her baby. It is problematical whether the mental night guards which awaken the ego are residues belonging to it, or whether they are object representations which have retained some ego awareness.

Aided by the withdrawal of all interest in external objects, the sleep reflex causes the ego to lose its cathexis. When this, as well as consciousness, is effaced, the unconscious processes or—as Freud named them—the unconscious mechanisms, become effective. They produce the dream, in which repressed previous ego states also participate. The manifest dream is experienced by the temporarily recathected mental ego. The bodily ego usually does not return before one is fully awakened. Most dreams occur in the interval after the mental ego has regained some cathexis but while the bodily ego is still asleep; fewer dreams occur while falling asleep, when the mental ego is still awake and the bodily ego is already asleep.

Another rather interesting interrelationship between the bodily and the mental ego can be recognized in the dreams which occur under general anesthesia. Both the mental and the bodily ego are coherent and continuing cathexis units. The bodily ego, being outside the mental ego, also has the function of protecting the mind against stimuli; it forms a second line of *Reizschutz,* to use Freud's terminology. That the body protects the safety of the mind is due to the many homeostatic processes which are maintained within exact limits between which the mind can function normally, and, in addition, the bodily ego as a dynamic unit protects the mental ego as a whole.

In general anesthesia, conditions of sleep differ from those of ordinary sleep. In the latter the bodily ego can sleep while the mental ego dreams in the interval before the awakening of both body and mind. When the dream becomes too vivid, fearful, or otherwise emotional, sleep ceases because the stimulation extends from the re-cathected mental ego to the bodily ego, till they both awaken. Then, reasonable conscious thinking recognizes the irrationality of the dream. It is understood that in schizophrenia more psychotic ideas start in the period of awakening than during the day. Not the schizophrenic, but the normal, ego awakens every morning to its full strength and dethrones the residues of the unconscious! Through its state of alertness the bodily ego hinders the mental ego from dreaming too much in the interval before complete awakening. In general anesthesia no such protection exists because the drug absolutely prevents the reawakening of the bodily ego, and so the mental ego can achieve an extraordinary degree of freedom and intensity. In normal life this would be detrimental to the general economy of the organism; the individual would be maniacal. Also normal sleep does not present such an exuberance of the mental ego as does anesthesia. Therefore, dreams under general anesthesia are experimental proof of the separability of the mental and the bodily ego.

This is also clearly evident in fainting. With few exceptions the fixed conception that fainting means falling unconscious is erroneous. Commonly, a fainting spell is filled with a series of intense experiences which, frequently, can be remembered. During a fainting spell one dreams, and may even think. Dreams during fainting combine the thinking quality of daydreams with the unconscious productivity of the night dream. At the onset of the syncope consciousness is sometimes interrupted, and when it returns the mental ego also returns. This is true for every kind of dream, be it during sleep, anesthesia, or a fainting spell. In dreams the bodily ego is seldom cathected with the mental ego. The only exception is in hysterical swooning.

In many dreams the mental ego is not in the present state, but in a past or even in a future one. There are authors who speak of the dream ego as a hallucinated one. This is an absurd assumption; the ego itself cannot be hallucinated, although the individual or an ego complex can be represented by a "hallucinated" figure in the dream. One recognizes the unique paradox which characterizes the ego; it is subject and object in one. The ego knows itself, observes itself, feels and encounters itself. Yet it is not exact to say that the ego feels itself; it would be better to say that the ego *is* the feeling of itself; this feeling is of a "middle" [3] nature, not yet active or passive. Later the ego acquires activity and passivity, depending on whether the urges forming the ego cathexis are predominantly active or passive in character.

It is important to understand that the foregoing formulations are not theory, but are facts based on observations by individuals. These observations were made in a variety of circumstances: (1) during clear consciousness; (2) during the coming and going of sleep; (3) during abnormal conditions such as hysteria.

In the last instance, hysterical patients have reported the vicissitudes of their *ego*'s losing and gaining cathexis during their fainting attacks. Edoardo Weiss has published such an observation.[4] These reports offer striking phenomenological evidence of the separability of the mental and the bodily ego. One of my own patients, who was a sincere and trustworthy person, had infrequent hysterical fainting spells. She reported that her unconscious conflicts regularly became conscious during such spells.

. . . .

[3] "Middle" is used here as the term of grammar. The Merriam-Webster defines it as "designating a form or voice of the Greek verb by which its subject is represented as both the agent and the object of action." This definition should be implemented with the notion of a static self-involvement.

[4] E. Weiss, "Agoraphobia and Its Relation to Hysterical Attack and to Trauma," *Intern. J. of Psycho-Analysis*, XIV (1935), 77.

She felt a desire to free herself from the "shell" of her hysterical sleep, and in this endeavor there was a distinct quantitative factor. She felt the severance of her bodily ego from the mental one, and was also aware of using up all her mental energies to re-establish the bodily ego. It was a feeling of having to lift a load, a jungle that had to be penetrated; the struggle symbolized her conflicts between sexuality and virtue. During this "tug-of-war" she was aware of her progress. She said that she knew exactly the proportion (a fourth, a third, a half, etc.) of the task already accomplished. There was a distinct feeling of ease when she had passed the climax of the struggle, and she was suddenly sure that the rest of the task would no longer demand the same intense strain on her vital forces and on her will-power. This feeling terminated her anxiety as to whether she would accomplish the reunion of body and mind—failing, she would have had to remain forever in anguish. In such cases both cathexes, the bodily and the mental, cease to be merely intellectual assumptions; they are actual and are experienced. The patient felt clearly that the mental ego cathexis was used up in the endeavor to regain that of the bodily ego, the lack of which was also clearly felt.

In consequence of the recognition of the essential quality of the ego as a coherent and continuous cathexis unit, some familiar and well-accepted concepts must be modified. This recognition justifies Adolf Meyer's idea of personality integration and disintegration on different levels, provided that this process is not understood to imply that the ego slowly gains its unity.

In this connection many authors have advanced the thought that ego "nuclei" crystallize to form the ego. This is an error. The ego is a united cathexis from the beginning, and for a long period the infant's ego unit, body as well as mind, still reacts as a whole. Ego maturation consists of the acquired ability to react with a part of the ego unit, while the whole of the unit remains quiescent and controls the partial reaction. The adult is able, by giving a sign with his finger, to attack or defend himself, to threaten or forbid. This indicates the difference in ego involvement between the child and the adult. The ego does not develop through crystallization but through organization. This is achieved by acquisition of typical reaction patterns and habitual emotional attitudes, notwithstanding the succession of ego levels. Both acquired ego attitudes and past ego states are to a great extent repressed. Through their access to consciousness and to the preconsciousness they influence actual decisions. The influence of ego attitudes and ego states is helpful or disturbing, depending upon their normality and fitness for present needs. Integrated personality, therefore, means maintenance of control not only of the partial ego reactions but also of different ego states. This maintenance requires the reliable and strong cathexis of the lasting, mature ego state. All psychosis is ego disease, so all psychopathy is due to characteristically abnormal psycho- and organo-genesis of the ego.

The permanence of previous ego states extends Freud's concept of ego fixation to the field of normal psychology. Because of its influence on symptom and resistance formation, pathological fixation was recognized earlier than this normal process. But the concept of pathological ego fixation presupposes the concept of a succession of ego states.

Another idea which needs some slight clarification is that of repression and forgetting. The persistence of every engram, once acquired, was accepted by Freud as a basic truth. Millions of engrams would interfere with every actual and normal reaction if they were accessible to consciousness. Their continuous retention by unconsciousness and their discontinuous, however controlled, delay through the preconscious, appear to be necessary for the normal thinking process. Yet there remains the problem of whether repression is always needed to make engrams lose their cathexis and to block their availability. By considering and watching the succeeding day-by-day ego states one recognizes the effect of the interruption of ego cathexis through the all night sleep. Every morning, when the ego is recathected through the process of orthriogenesis, many engrams acquired during the previous days are found to be no longer cathected. Only those new engrams which were related to important events, intellectual interests, or which for an emotional personal reason were included in the ego unit maintain their cathexis from previous days. The emotional reason may be a pleasurable or painful ego reaction. Many more engrams lose their ephemeral importance when yesterday's joy or pain no longer prevails. These engrams enter unconsciousness without repression through the screening influence of sleep itself.

Repression is reserved only for those painful or conflictual engrams and ego reactions which cannot be handled by sleep. It is provoked by the anxiety signals of the ego and is effected by complete withdrawal of cathexis from all connecting associations. This is in accordance with Freud's keen description of the relationship of anxiety and repression. Screening by sleep does not require the interference of anxiety. Yet, when repressed ego states re-enter consciousness or when repression to previous ego states sets in (as in hypnosis with concomitant age regression) then all engrams, repressed as well as screened, regain availability and influence.

Psychology must now also reconsider another familiar concept: narrowness of consciousness. In analysis, or in psychological experiments, free association frequently becomes impossible because many thoughts occupy the surface of one's consciousness at one time. This may be due to an obsessional holding-on to contrasting ideas, and may lead to real "hoarding." Or it may be due to some resistance which expresses itself by postponing the utterance of ideas. The theory of the method of free association is not weakened by such individual difficulties. There is still a prevailing linear sequence of ideas entering and leaving the field of consciousness. By immediate and unselected speech the thoughts entering consciousness become known and reveal unsuspected interconnections.

Freud was right in comparing consciousness with a spotlight that illuminates the dark field of preconsciousness. By a small focus of "light" one element after another becomes illuminated, or, as the poet says, consciousness lines up "on the silver thread of the memory, eternal pearls of the past." All these comparisons aptly express the narrowness of consciousness, which allows the distinct step-by-step progressive use of apperception and logical concentration on a topic, and which also prevents confusion when scrutiny is necessary and doubt becomes helpful.

Yet the concept of narrowness of consciousness is true only in regard to current associations. Otherwise, on the contrary, the field of consciousness is a wide one. Not only the line of actual thoughts, but the bodily and the mental egos are conscious.

Both may remain to a great degree unchanged—the bodily ego while the individual maintains the position, or the mental ego while the individual pursues the same interest. This constancy does not prevent the bodily ego from changing in part, depending on any alteration occurring in the surroundings, or the mental ego from changing in part, depending on any new content entering the conscious.

When Binet and Janet briefly defined consciousness by the fact that the surrounding element joined the ego, this definition itself proved that the whole ego is conscious; yet, by this insight the concept of narrowness of consciousness is modified. The bodily ego is conscious as the sum of proprioceptions and perceptions, insofar as they are united by a coherent and continuous cathexis which gives them the specific quality of the ego feeling.

As we became familiar with the idea of ego states changing in succession, we must also recognize that one experiences different ego states simultaneously. The whole content of the bodily ego is more than just one's nude body; one habitually feels one's bodily ego as clothed, and depending on one's posture, bodily ego may be felt together with one's chair or bed or such support, and including the room or the surrounding place, horizon, city, continent, and even world. This fact relates to the orienting function of the bodily ego. Such extensions of the bodily ego are conscious or preconscious. One is aware of the various enlargements of one's bodily ego; when sitting at one's desk one is conscious of all the books and other things on the desk and in the room; every single object is doubly present in one's conscious both as a "thing" invested with separate object cathexis and, also, as a part of one's enlarged bodily ego participating in the united ego cathexis.

The existence of the enlarged bodily ego with its many contents, of which one's own body is the central core, explains the fact that, normally, we are not a bit disturbed by the change of retinal perceptions caused by movement of our visual field. Thanks to the permanent ego unit the enlarged bodily ego remains the same. The surrounding objects also remain the same, although seen from different perspectives. In pathological cases of estrangement and depersonalization this phenomenon may become strikingly disturbed.

One is always aware of one's essential as well as of one's enlarged bodily ego and its contents, which are oriented in exact
accordance with reality. We may call the bodily ego that corresponds to the nude or clothed body the *essential* or the
qualified bodily ego, and the bodily ego that corresponds to the
individual as he lives in a certain place with the whole correlated world orientation the geographical bodily ego. In this regard, it is evident that a person who has migrated to another
continent has a considerably changed and enlarged bodily ego
in comparison to his previous one. Many difficulties of adjustment to a new country derive from the permanence of the previous orientation. In the range between the essential and the
geographical bodily ego there are variously enlarged states, depending on the individual's temporary situation, whether at
home, in a car, at work, etc.

One might criticize the whole concept of the bodily ego as a
superfluous repetition of the concept of the body itself, yet the
bodily ego concept is based on phenomenological experience,
not on a theoretical assumption. One set of experiences demonstrates that the *unity* of the bodily ego is felt in addition to the
sum of proprioceptions corresponding to the parts of the body.
The second set of experiences concerns the variety of bodily
ego feelings which are observed and reported by individuals, depending on their health and their moods.[5] Many disturbances
of the bodily ego consist of its narrowing or of its changed sensorial character. They are symptoms of infantilism, hysteria,
schizophrenia, hypochondria, depression, elatedness, dejection,
fatigue, or alertness, also of abnormal sexual disposition, such
as homosexuality, sadism, or masochism.

The simplest change of the bodily ego consists of an incomplete broadened or narrowed feeling, as when one is testing the
breadth of one's skull or one's chest by enclosure in the hands.
No change in the proprioceptions themselves can be assumed,
since all movements—as well as orientations—are normal.
Yet in any state of "neurasthenic" or "psychasthenic" fatigue, or
in cases of estrangement and depersonalization, the head or the
chest is felt to be thin or even almost missing. When the indi-

. . . .

[5] See "Some Variations in Ego Feeling," Chapter 1.

vidual is extraordinarily elated, on the other hand, there is a feeling of increased width. The symptom is very well defined. Practically, one should use it as an indicator of the necessity for rest and sleep, because individuals with impaired bodily ego cathexis lack the normal instinctual feeling of fatigue which guides the healthy in regard to avoidance of overdoing and of overstraining.

I would like to discuss here an observation often made about the term "ego boundary." A highly esteemed discussant of this theory refused to accept the idea that the ego has a distinct boundary because he felt that this term would indicate a strict linear, ribbonlike, or ditchlike circumference of a territory. It seems to me that this discussant is not quite free of a static conception of the mental processes. His suggestion to substitute ego periphery for ego boundary may be a good one; however, neither designation implies either a zone or a line of demarcation around the ego. Such a demarcation would be contrary to the nature of the ego itself as a changing union of components which are entering or leaving. The use of the words "boundary" or "periphery" is necessary to express the fact that the ego is actually felt to extend as far as the feeling of the unity of the ego contents reaches. This feeling sharply distinguishes everything that belongs to the ego in an actual moment of life from all the other mental elements and complexes not actually included in the ego. Because the feeling of a unit exists, there is also a boundary or limit of the unit. This is mere phenomenological fact-finding. The theory can be expressed in one sentence: One is forced to assume that the feeling of the ego unit is due to one coherent ego cathexis. The assumption is simple but far reaching and, moreover, goes beyond Freud or any of the other psychoanalysts who employ ego psychology, including Schilder, the most courageous and intuitive of all. The assumption leads to investigation beyond ego functions and ego aspects, ego contents and ego complexes. All these phenomena would never form an ego, except for their sharing in the permanent existence of a special and specific cathexis that is of a nature to be one *total unit*.

The contents are included and set apart in the relative ego

boundary, depending on changes in the surroundings. Most of the contents of any habitually enlarged bodily ego are preconscious. The preparedness of the bodily ego boundaries for any expected, or even unexpected, change aids mentally as well as bodily. The bodily ego boundaries must adapt to acceptance of the impression of changing contents without uncontrolled total ego reaction. Such an integration of the bodily ego is paralleled by the mental preparedness to changing impressions, which is called presence of mind. Mental preparedness also requires the function of the mental ego boundaries.

It is relatively easy to accept the idea that our field of consciousness permanently contains enlargements of the bodily ego. It was difficult for me to convince myself, and it will be difficult to convince others of the fact, that the mental ego also contains more than the conscious thread of associations. The difficulty is that the degree of extension of the mental ego differs individually. Some people have a narrow mental ego. The productive genius has the greatest scope of mental contents. Convincing examples have been presented to me by writers, scientists, and musicians, but none were comparable with the story of Mozart in Prague. Two days before the premiere of his "Don Juan" he had not yet started to compose the overture. His friends, the opera director and the orchestra were in excited suspense, while the genius himself unconcernedly enjoyed a gay party. Late in the evening he wrote the music without any later correction; he said that the whole musical score suddenly and simultaneously presented itself clearly to his mind. This is the outstanding and almost unbelievable example of the enlargement of a mental ego, and also proof that the greatest and most complicated production is done unconsciously. Probably some parts of the work had previously become conscious and had returned to preconsciousness.

Once the awareness of mental ego contents is accepted, one finds in oneself, and also in patients, evidence of the fact that the mental ego consciously contains materials of pictures, ideas, and conclusions dealing with specific topics. Usually, however, the contents of the mental ego are chiefly preconscious. The last associations which entered consciousness form the mental ego boundary for new associations. "Attentiveness" means maintaining an increased ego boundary cathexis for the material belonging to the current problem.

Whenever an author ventures to present some new view or new theory in psychoanalysis, he must take thought as to whether he did not, by cryptomnesia, merely repeat some finding of Freud or at least use some hint of Freud's in the direction of the apparently new departure. This procedure also holds true for the theory of the ego boundaries. Freud tried to explain the phylogenetic onset of consciousness by the assumption that some peripheral sensory parts of the mental apparatus undergo changes under the impact of their constant stimulation. Usually any stimulated organ is changed by every new stimulus and thus retains some specific trace of the new impression as an engram. Yet, one can expect that those peripheral ganglionary elements which were exposed—in an extraordinary degree and constantly—to changing stimulation will have exhausted their biological capacity for specific change. They can no longer be modified by new stimuli. Instead of developing further memories corresponding to the stimuli, they react immediately, however briefly, and return after their immediate reaction to their previous biological states. In this way, the first steps to conscious perceptions are made. Consciousness is substituted for the storage of memories. The discussion of the many problems connected with this extremely original assumption requires special presentation. Freud localized the newly acquired perceptual faculty in the grey layers of the cerebral cortex.

From a quite different angle he returned to the problem of consciousness and preconsciousness in his amazing paper on the *Wunderblock,* "the mystic writing pad." If one accepts Freud's new principles, one must attempt to apply them also to other conscious processes dealing with apperceptions and with conceptual thinking. Since disturbance and loss of conceptual thinking form another characteristic of schizophrenia, further investigation is needed in connection with the ego psychological approach.[6]

. . . .

[6] A first attempt was made in this direction by the author in his paper, "Mental Hygiene of the Ego," Chapter 8.

Freud's theory that consciousness is a peripheral process concerns the task of seeking and localizing exactly the boundary between the mind and the world of objects. Yet Freud's idea deals only with the elementary process of consciousness. The concept of the ego as a dynamic entity and of the ego boundary as its peripheral sensory organ, which I introduced, is not included in Freud's assumption and is not made superfluous by it. The combined assumptions are fitted to explain the fact that the mental ego boundary usually consists of the most recent and conscious ideas. These assumptions direct passive attention to related perceptions and associations.

Attention is directed inside and outside the ego at the same time, without any difficulty in separating them. Therefore I insist on full evaluation of the fact that every mental element has a relation to the ego boundary. When it is included into the coherent cathexis, which is experienced as ego feeling, the element is mental, is thought; when it is outside the mental and the bodily ego, i.e., is not included in the coherent cathexis unit, the element represents a real object. Without any reality test it is experienced as reality. When an element is felt inside the bodily ego but outside the mental ego it is psychologically real, in Freud's sense.

The concepts modified in consequence of the new insight into the essence of the ego can be summed up as follows:

(1) The ego is a unit long before the integration of the personality.

(2) Ego states can be repressed or fixated.

(3) In addition to repression, sleep does away with engrams through screening.

(4) Consciousness is not narrow but broad.

(5) Without any reality testing, its relation to the ego boundary decides whether a psychic element or process is experienced as real, or as psychically real, or as a mere thought.

Some theoretical formulations may be added without further elaboration.

(1) The ego is the conscious feeling of preconscious processes while the material itself remains preconscious.

(2) Volition is due to the faculty of the mental ego of shifting cathexis to specific organs and tasks of the bodily ego.

(3) Emotions are an ego function; they take place at connecting ego boundaries. The quality of an emotion is determined by the mixture of libido and destrude components which enter into the cathexis of the involved ego boundaries.

(4) The ego is the essential carrier of the individual's mental experience throughout his life.

This preliminary presentation now enables us to progress to the discussion of schizophrenia and, later, of depersonalization as ego diseases.

11

THE EGO IN SCHIZOPHRENIA *

In this chapter schizophrenia is defined as a deterioration of ego functions due to loss or to serious diminution of ego cathexis. Federn analyzes the interweaving of ego and other functions to characterize different ego disturbances in relation to an underlying insufficiency of cathexis.—E. W.

The ego's efficiency is constantly maintained by its cathexis of mental energy. One's own ego cathexis is experienced as mental energy, to which both libido and destrudo are contributory. This is Freud's theory. Like other authors, such as Monakow, Driesch, and Goldstein, I assume that a third source of energy results from the living process of the organism, and in regard to mental activities, especially from the processes of the central nervous system. Jung evaded this problem by changing his concept of libido.

Without pursuing this deep and difficult problem we are satisfied by the knowledge that maintenance of ego cathexis is necessary for all mental functioning, active or passive. Furthermore, the cathexis necessarily increases with every functional effort, with every claim from the outside world, and particularly with every task concerning adaptation and maturation. The ego cathexis, which is otherwise diffuse, is implemented by additional cathexis on the ego sector, with its ego boundary involved by such demands, depending on what specific functions are needed to carry through a specific effort or to satisfy a specific claim on the ego.

As long as its cathexis is well supplied and readily transfer-

. . . .

*Lecture delivered by invitation in June, 1949, at Winter's Veteran Hospital in Topeka, Kansas.

able, the ego functions normally. Mental functions are bound to sag, even to cease, in cases of impairment of supply or of apportionment of the ego cathexis. On the basis of our knowledge of transference neuroses, which are psychoanalytically explained by placement, shift, and withdrawal of *object* cathexis, but which also do damage to ego functions, the conclusion can be reached that excessive shifts and withdrawals of cathexis can impair or destroy an ego function. This occurs in neuroses in spite of an adequate supply of cathexis. Whether there is a lack of supply or a too great reactive withdrawal of the cathexis, the mental disturbances will be the same. Yet, correction of the disorder will depend in one case on the restoration of supply, in the other on the cessation of withdrawal.

This explains why schizophrenia as a disease and schizophrenia as a syndrome are symptomatically the same, although they take quite different courses and require different treatment. Schizophrenia is always due to a deficiency of ego cathexis, whether of supply or of apportionment. Furthermore, the causes of the deficiency in supply or of the withdrawal may be permanent or temporary. This fact is another source of the differences in the course of schizophrenia.

The causes of deficient supply are not known. However, such deficiency, as well as withdrawal of well-supplied ego cathexis, is sometimes explained by accumulated emotional strain; this may be of superficial and recent origin or deep-rooted in the early years of the patient's life. This explains why some cases yield to removal of anxiety by transference and psychoanalysis —as Fromm-Reichmann teaches—while others require deeper therapeutic probing. Rosen even tries directly to encounter and to annihilate the initial infantile conflicts. Both types of therapy are successful in selected cases.

Because of the basic divergence in etiology, no therapy can be supported by statistics. In the case of deficient supply, the probability of removing an unknown cause of a disease based on the impairment of ego cathexis must always be small; but the disease takes different courses depending on the different etiologies. When recovered or paroled, the patient may or may not continue to function satisfactorily. When the etiology is a temporary withdrawal of ego cathexis, the likelihood of relapse

depends mainly on the emotional hygiene offered by the surroundings and by the patient's own ability to adjust his course
of life to his wishes or to adjust his wishes to his abilities.

By considering the ego psychological aspect in the course of
the disease, additional problems are opened to clearer scrutiny
and brighter illumination. The future symptomatology of a case
may consist in the successive appearance and disappearance of
general functional disjunction, or of more specific disruption
and disorder of single functions. The first and basic symptom
impairs the main function of the ego. The ego unites the diver-
gent complexities of the individual and separates his impene-
trable and indivisible entity from the changing world; it
accomplishes this through the ego boundary. By constantly facing, contacting, and segregating the external world, the well
cathected ego boundary acquires the function of a sensory organ in order to feel the reality of everything outside the ego.
Cognizance of reality is therefore the main function of the ego
boundary. Whatever happens inside the ego boundary pertains
to the individual's body and mind. Of course, since one is a
part of the world, there is a mutual interrelation between the
ego and the world. Most ego experiences pour out from, and
turn back to, the outside world from which all perceptions are
originally stimulated. In this mutual flow, trespassing on the ego
boundaries is clearly felt. The basis of sanity is correct and
automatic recognition of this breach between subjective mental
individual experiences in the world and the knowledge of the
status of the world as it actually exists. Sanity means dealing
with the world and with oneself with the faculty of distinguishing clearly between them.

It is therefore obvious that in schizophrenia it is the ego that
is ill. It is also evident to the dynamically oriented psychiatrist
that the deterioration of ego functions is due to loss or to serious
diminution of ego cathexis. Yet it requires further analysis of
the interweaving of ego and other functions to characterize
different ego disturbances in relation to an underlying insufficiency of cathexis. Even in such insufficiency, a sporadic, and
even permanent, compensatory increase of cathexis for scattered
performances of the ego is to be expected. This fact should not
be used as counter-argument against the general insight into

the economy of schizophrenia, which shows it to be due to *de*crease of ego cathexis.

Deficiency will show up first by irregularity of those functions which need perfect investment with ego cathexis. These are the functions dealing with the ego's struggle for the individual's existence.

The ego dependencies, defined by Freud, are also the ego's battlefronts. Every single dependency needs cathexis investment in its endeavor to maintain the ego function—normal, strong, quick, and exact. The best known dependency is that concerning the world of objects. All previous experiences must be used intelligently to cope with external forces, whether they be aggressive or friendly, whether defense, aggression, flight, or evasion is needed. Therefore lack of cathexis causes the ego to be inadequate in dealing with these forces.

Thinking is trial action which precedes action itself. Adequacy in thinking presupposes separation of the trial from the action, and of the object from its representation by thought. This separation requires proper functioning of the sensory organs, which are mental and bodily ego boundaries for reality perception.

The initial schizophrenic disturbances of intelligence[1] are due to the lack of cathexis of the mental ego boundary. Instead of appreciating and using the trial action as such, the schizophrenic feels it is definitely the real object and action; some thoughts have acquired the character of reality. The next consequence is that ideas representing the object are confounded with the object itself. Then, the newly synthesized engrams coming from the external world are falsified. The product is distorted, and external reality is confused with falsified ideas about that reality. For a short time the falsified reality can be partially denied, concealed, and controlled, especially when the physical surroundings continue to be perceived without distortion. This is due to the greater resistance of the visual bodily ego boundary. In advanced cases, the surroundings are also falsified with progressive loss of ego cathexis. The patient be-

. . . .

[1] Preliminary schizophrenic symptoms of a hypochondriacal and neurasthenic nature are frequently overlooked.

lieves in the false reality without question. When the normal ego boundary cathexis is restored, through therapeutic influence or spontaneously, the false reality ceases, and thought again becomes thought. The schizophrenic constructs his false reality as something natural and evident, while its gross grotesqueness allows the psychiatrist to recognize it immediately as a symptom.

In paranoia, the imaginary is less striking at the onset. The absurdity of the series of falsifications lies merely in false constructions from justified premises and in logical conclusions from rightly perceived facts. Later, however, the individual loses his capacity for logic and self-criticism, arriving at absurd conclusions and paranoiac systems; nevertheless, these still carry through some fine thread of logic which seduces normal people into putting faith in them. Litigious paranoiacs, in particular, may plan and carry through their lawsuits without error of logic or jurisprudence.

Every paranoiac ideation pertains to the idea of reference. At first such an ideation is similar to that of a neurotic. This parallelism diverges sharply when the ideas acquire the paranoiac mechanism. In both cases the facts may be the same and may also be trustworthy. What the patient says and thinks contains no false reality. He was "looked at," as he claims, in the office, in the train, or on the street. His reactions to the supposed attitudes and his observations of them were exaggerated but appropriate. It is known that people have a friendly or an inimical or a critical attitude. Praise, blame, suspicion, and even prejudice are ever present. No encounter is made in a strictly neutral spirit. Therefore, it is not impossible, although highly improbable, that the repeated "references" really happened. Even a paranoiac absurdity such as thinking that the frequent appearance of a low-flying plane has the purpose of watching one's nightly masturbation is, physically, not impossible; likewise it is possible that a personal message was printed in the editorial in the morning paper, or that an admonition was broadcast by the Pope over the radio—all this is physically possible, although actually impossible to assume. It is more acceptable that the believer in God as a father should feel that God's will was revealed to him personally. The degree of irrationality and improbability of these ideas depends on the patient's degree and critical use of knowledge. Some paranoiacs are able to rationalize their assumptions well and to use only arguments which can be supported rationally. What is true in regard to ideas of reference is also true in regard to suspiciousness and to jealousy.

The cardinal point in paranoia is the false certainty[2] which is attributed to the persecutory idea even before fabrication of false realities. What the healthy mind would consider as possible becomes probable and then certain to the paranoiac. Likewise, what is impossible to the normal is possible here. Conceptions of probability and improbability are no longer understood. The scale of non-existence, impossibility, improbability, uncertainty, possibility, probability, certainty, and existence is annulled. The differences between these states have altogether lost their importance. All ideas and conclusions are "felt" as certain. False certainty is to the paranoiac what false reality is to the schizophrenic.

The basic difference between false certainty and false reality is that false reality means substitution of a false world for the real one, while false certainty merely means changes in judgments about the world. Furthermore, a false reality brings about enlargement of both bodily and mental egos, while a false certainty brings about enlargement of only the mental ego. However, the two conditions have three points in common:

(1) Everything that is real is certain.[3]

(2) Reality and certainty are tested as well as directly felt.

(3) They cannot be proved by one individual; the consensus of other persons is necessary.

In regard to the third point, the schizophrenic regularly presupposes that the explanations of such paranoiac ideas are overevaluated. This explanation makes the object cathexis of the idea, and not its relationship to the ego, responsible for the false certainty. False reality was explained in the same way and also

. . . .

[2] In the paranoid, as contrasted to the paranoiac, a false probability is established, rather than a certainty.

[3] This principle was expressed in Freud's words: "There can be only one scientific truth because there is only one reality." Freud was opposed to all "as if" syllogisms.

by the assumption of an act of projection. The latter explanation refers to the relationship of the hallucination to the ego.

In regard to the paranoiac false certainty, additional phenomena clarify the relationship of certainty and reality. Although all thinking is trial action, there is a noticeable difference between typical schizophrenic and paranoiac thinking. Schizophrenic thinking accompanies and influences the patient's behaviour and his choice of reactions. His false ideations, therefore, form his actual life. In the healthy individual, the thinking processes function partly to accompany and direct his actual behaviour and partly to plan for future actions. Paranoiac thinking is mostly of the latter kind—it means planning. It is a coherent trial action anticipating the future ego situation on the basis of the memory of past ones. The character of planning explains the aggressive and systematic qualities of paranoiac thinking.

It appears that the character of planning in paranoiac thinking correlates its false certainty with false reality due to loss of ego cathexis. Healthy thinking constantly tests and proves every new conclusion by the experimental use of other ego states which are concerned with the same problem. Many of these experiments are not repeated, but are used with accepted and habitual certainty. This does not lead to false conclusions because healthy thinking apperceives the real facts without falsifications.

In paranoiac planning the conditions are different. The paranoiac, like the schizophrenic, remembers ego situations which contain falsified realities. But every false reality gives certainty to the paranoiac thought, because what is felt to be real is also felt to be certain. Also, these easily made assumptions and completed falsifications all acquire the certainty of reality. Therefore, in the last analysis, there is no basic difference between the processes of falsification of reality in schizophrenics and of falsification of certainty in paranoiacs.

Although in early paranoia facts themselves do not undergo falsification by the loss of the ego boundary cathexis, the patient's own thoughts in any given situation are remembered as parts of the reality and therefore are later felt as certain, just as is reality. Such absolute certainty abolishes critical and logical scrutiny. Rationalization plays its role by fitting in results of the feelings of certainty. "The dice of thinking are loaded."

The consequences of falsified certainty reach even farther than those of falsified reality. Falsified reality gives some false bases of action; however, when these activities are not provoked, or if they are hindered, when provoked, the false data may be ignored or repressed. But the influence of false certainty is interminable; more and more false certainty accumulates and goes on to interfere with intelligent judgement. The proper use of experience and anticipation in thinking is not possible in the face of disrupted ego boundary functions. The automatic knowledge of when associations which come from the preconscious should be applied is confused between tangible external reality and thoughts. Thinking, under these circumstances, becomes futile. The individual then renounces clear thinking and uses his associations for wishful fabrication of fantasies and castles in the air. Intelligence and critical scrutiny, through which the level of the reality principle was reached and is maintained, become faulty and return to subserve the pleasure-pain-principle. The devastating influence of the loss of the function of the ego boundary increases because, with the continuation of the disease beyond the actual conscious ego, more and more preconscious ego states offer their falsified reality conceptions. Great, also, are the consequences of the mingling of the elements of falsified and true reality.

The ease with which the feeling of certainty is established, further accounts for the lack of desire to correct errors or nonsensical expressions. At first sporadically, later diffusely, and in advanced cases generally, no need is felt to rectify the performance. For this reason mental skills and faculties eventually deteriorate. In the typical dementia of the schizophrenic this deterioration is due not so much to the loss of his achievements as to the loss of any need to use them. In late stages it may completely break up the element of language and the three Rs.[4]

. . . .

[4] They can be re-established by any form of shock treatment that—like a miracle—temporarily re-establishes the lost ego boundary cathexis. To see an apparently almost illiterate moron change into the author of a subtle love letter is a convincing demonstration of the power and value of the ego cathexis.

Scientific knowledge or artistic abilities which the patient had acquired degenerate to a repetitive and apparently haphazard productivity, even though impulses and drive for creation continue. The falsified certainty about the perfection of all performances suppresses any motive for improvement, self-scrutiny, or learning. Through his generalized subjective self-satisfaction the schizophrenic becomes unaware of the poverty and impairment of his performances. The catatonic stereotype of schizophrenic art, however, derives from many sources.

The loss of ego boundary cathexis thus results in the following:

(1) Impairment of distinguishability of thought and object.

(2) Falsified reality of thoughts.

(3) Falsified certainty of judgment and conclusion.

(4) A generalized false certainty as to the quality of the acts.

The schizophrenic process penetrates the preconscious mind. Almost all important preconscious ego states progressively lose the cathexis of their boundaries and cease to function with exactitude and rectitude. The normal ego works without error preconsciously, because in the preconscious engrams and anticipations deriving from outside experiences are already well separated from engrams deriving from thoughts and ideas. In entering consciousness perceptions automatically join perceptions and thoughts join thoughts, while the preconscious ego state is included in the actual cathexis unit of the present ego.

This is not so with the schizophrenic. Too many of his preconscious engrams are falsely stored and falsely labeled as to reality, certainty, and rectitude. In the midst of a host of erroneous and falsified engrams few correct residues of experiences and reactions are still employed.

A typical kind of preconscious falsification is responsible for the symptom in which the patient feels that ideas have been taken away from, or were imposed on, him. Both delusions offer the picture of projection of an inner process on another person. The underlying mental process is simply the forgetting of something that one has known. For the healthy, such forgetting would require a psychoanalytical explanation. The schizophrenic knows the explanations from his own experience. His forgetting may follow his thinking of a certain person. By succession of thought he gets the certainty that the forgetting was caused by the content of the preceding thought. Therefore he declares that the person concerned was the cause of the blocking of his stream of associations. No real projection[5] has taken place. Because the idea of the other person has acquired reality, the patient does not comprehend that his thoughts about the person, not the person himself, are the causes of the loss of his ideas. An analogous mechanism is at work with implantation of an idea.

One can easily understand that a schizophrenic patient who has thought of another person in correlation with himself cannot help but feel that his next thoughts are implanted by that person. Yet there are cases in which any thinking of a person is sufficient to make the patient attribute to him the causation of the next ideas or of the loss of these ideas. It is another manifestation of falsified certainty. Any sequence in regard to time is, with certainty, felt as a causative sequence. The insane seem to take sides with critical epistemology.

It is even more astonishing to witness the preconscious deviations, resulting from the loss of ego cathexis, in regard to skills which were acquired in infancy and childhood and which have become habitual and automatic in the adult. Normally, a person reading is unaware that syllables and letters are building up to form words: the interruption from one line to another is unobserved; the engrams of previous word perceptions, their spelling and understanding, are the work of the preconscious, which enters consciousness when needed; the whole is a smooth continuity. When the preconscious ego function diminishes, some patients suddenly find reading difficult because they become aware of the lines, single words, syllables, and letters. The conclusion is that the preconscious organization of reading is an ego function and depends on the full cathexis of the ego unit in which it is included. When the ego boundary which deals

. . . .

[5] True projection is due to unconscious mechanisms. This is not simply a problem of terminology. When one refers to the thought of a person transformed into the real person by the mechanism of the loss of the ego boundary cathexis, one might say that this is the most frequent form of projection. It would serve clarification to give this process a new name like "reality attribution" or "regression to reality."

with the language loses its cathexis, the letters and syllables cease to be merely means of thinking: they become real objects.

Disturbances in the visual field are more striking. I have observed cases, otherwise mild, in which the preconscious act of accommodation and focussing required conscious attention to avoid blurring of vision. Here the ego functions acquired in the first half-year of life lose their united cathexis. In all these cases the diminution of cathexis has narrowed the ego boundaries to an earlier stage to which there has been regression.

Ego regression is well known to be responsible for the revival of early narcissistic and other libidinous phases of archaic thinking methods. Infantilism of the ego is due to regression to a state when it was not yet well separated from the id, the superego, or the external world. This fusion with the world through regression is quite different from the falsified reality which has been described. False reality production is an initial stage of schizophrenia, regressive narcissistic fusion is a late stage. It is now reasonable to assume that the process of ego regression is also due to insufficiency and diminution of the ego cathexis. More and more, the dynamic approach suggests that maturation is due, not only to the evolution of the constitutionally preorganized organic mental qualities, but also to the development of the bodily ego and the mental ego. There cannot be a sharp division between the two processes. The organic factors require the perennial investment of mental cathexis for their proper functioning; then this cathexis must prevail through all of life. The ego is not a statically functioning aggregate. Because the ego is an active unit of the individual's life, a unit built up and kept alive against opposing forces, the maintenance of its mature state consumes mental cathexis continually. For this reason, regression of the ego means that the investments of cathexis necessary for maintenance are no longer available. The typical ego regression of the schizophrenic can therefore justifiably be ascribed in part to this deficiency.

In the early stages of the illness, fixation also plays its part. In this instance some previous ego states have not been sufficiently decathected during the process of maturation, but have been repressed. As the disease progresses, these repressed ego states and ego reactions reach consciousness and enter the actual ego. This explains why there are many archaic and infantile ego reactions in schizophrenia, with their primary processes interfering with the normal secondary ones. The repressed material which has come up from the unconscious also interferes with the use of normal preconscious material. As a rule, the healthy ego is protected against any flagrant intrusion of unconscious material and mechanisms. There are exceptions, however, in conditions of mass psychology or when there is an excess of emotion or instinct. To a mild extent the unconscious shows its influence by parapraxes: errors, slips, forgetting, etc. In these situations the unconscious does not enter consciousness unchanged.

Because of this, it has been reasoned that there are special forces of the ego which hold the unconscious down, damming the overflow of the unconscious from spilling into consciousness, as it were. Such dams are understood to be dynamic, not static, maintained by emotional cathexes such as shame, guilt feelings, anxiety, and feelings of righteousness. The author doubts this view and does not think that protective forces can hold down the unconscious by their direct influence. There is no proof that specific boundaries of the ego are cathected with energy to repress the unconscious or to maintain this repression. Then again, repression is instilled by anxiety, as Freud has found; anxiety phenomenologically means inhibited flight, and flight is a process of evading, not damming, and of coping with the intruding dynamisms. An additional argument against special protective forces is that the unconscious rules during the night, while the ego sleeps. The reverse is true during the day. If the ego could dispose of some cathexis to fight off the unconscious directly, then no neurotic and cultural compromises with the unconscious would ever have developed.

While no direct fighting off is involved, a number of different methods are used by the conscious and preconscious mind in the struggle with the unconscious.

(1) Words and symbols are interposed between the products of the unconscious and conscious thinking. Through words and symbols, the unconscious products are understood and are dealt with by the secondary processes.

(2) The ego seems to have its attention constantly diverted;

i.e., it seems to have its boundaries more strongly cathected in the lines bordering on the outside world.

(3) The ego, when it is normal, must accept, and wants to accept, instinctual drives. This acceptance must be modified or refused when the ego is forced to do so by the superego or by the standards which have been set up by the ego itself.

(4) Repression is accomplished mainly by anxiety and a process of flight. This results in cathexis withdrawal which interrupts any link of association to undesirable products of the unconscious and to total ego states as well.

(5) It is probable that pleasure automatically fosters, and pain inhibits, the instinctual drives. Anxiety is the most important kind of pain working in this way. One can say generally that this is the only mechanism which directly fights off the unconscious. This mechanism was recognized by Freud in his second theory of repression, when he said that the anxiety signal puts the pain-pleasure principle into action.

These complicated reactive means protect the ego against the unconscious, partially by reflexlike automatisms, and partially by being established and fortified and defended by the shifting of cathexes to positions where they work as countercathexes. It is obvious that these complicated methods of partially accepting and partially using or warding off the unconscious need a constant supply line of cathexis.

The process of shifting cathexis is also partly automatic and partly purposeful. It depends on situations conditioned by the ego's dependency on the id, the superego, and the outside world. Some tasks are repetitive, and therefore regularly expected, some arise suddenly out of unexpected emergency situations. In every instance a high degree of ego cathexis is always needed to fulfill the task. When, therefore, an acute or even a permanent deficiency in ego cathexis develops, normal dealing with the unconscious is altered. In schizophrenia this ego cathexis deficiency allows intrusion of the unconscious.

Total loss of ego cathexis is present only in extremely deteriorated cases. Otherwise many functions of the ego and many ego boundaries remain cathected, although meagerly so. At best they are sluggish and ill-defined. The partial diminution of ego cathexis explains a typical trait of the manifold schizophrenic picture: the increase in the degree of sensation and the result-ing heightened emotional and impulse irritability.

Ordinarily, cathexis of the ego, and especially of the ego boundaries, works as countercathexis against all kinds of stimu-lation. Every single ego reaction remains controllable. The sen-sations provoked through stimulation are themselves moderate, pleasurable or painful. Cathexis weakness, on the contrary, im-mediately permits undue response. Adolescent schizophrenics feel every aggressive impulse, and also every aggression from outside, excessively. The same is true in regard to emotions in other age groups. Catatonic reactions implying positive rage or negativism may be induced by the slightest emotion.

The ego psychological aspect of schizophrenia is not merely of theoretical interest; its therapeutic value is important and can be tested in early stages of the disease as well as in ad-vanced stages. It is paradoxical but true that rational insight is an effective therapeutic weapon against apparent dementia. Psychoanalytic insight was recognized as one tool in the treat-ment of neurotics. The psychotic strives even more keenly to un-derstand his disease.

However, in psychosis, the earlier rational insight is applied, the more effective it is. The psychotic learns to gather every change into his own ego experience, and he thus becomes able to accept without terror what he has recognized without amaze-ment. Through his fearless interest he can eventually re-establish his normal ego. By overcoming his abnormal ego reac-tions he achieves the therapeutic goal: called, most generally, re-repression.

12

DEPERSONALIZATION*

This chapter, the third of the three lectures given at Winter's Veteran Hospital in Topeka in 1949, all published here for the first time, gives a dynamic understanding of the syndrome of depersonalization, a phenomenon which Federn analyzed in minute detail. Feelings of depersonalization may constitute a disease entity per se.–E.W.

In Chapter 10, schizophrenia was surveyed anew from the ego psychological aspect. The gist was that schizophrenia is due to a lack of ego cathexis, and therefore should be labeled with the term "ego disease." A different, but closely related, group of ego diseases includes estrangement and depersonalization. In this group the loss of ego cathexis differs from that in schizophrenia. It is probable that the loss is more specific in that only the *libido* component is deficient; furthermore, the bodily ego is more affected by the loss of cathexis than is the case in schizophrenia.

Up to now "ego diseases" were not recognized and diagnosed as such because, generally, the psychological role of the ego was overlooked. For this reason the concept of the ego remained hidden behind such notions as "the individual," "the person," or "the integrated personality." Internal medicine is in a similar situation in regard to the heart. Symptoms of heart failure may be localized in other organs whose functions are disturbed by the primary deficit. Thus the stomach may be blamed when,

. . . .

*Lecture delivered by invitation in June, 1949, at Winter's Veteran Hospital in Topeka, Kansas.

due to impaired circulation, food is no longer appreciated. In the case of estrangement, when outside objects lose their appeal, one's object libido, mood, or mind are held responsible instead of the ego.

As might be expected, in very advanced diseases of both the ego and the heart symptoms are correctly localized. When a real breakdown of the ego leads to depersonalization, the patient says to himself: "I am no longer Me," or "I have been deprived of my Self."

On the other hand, many people frequently mention that their egos needed bolstering or that their egos were inflated; psychoanalysts say that their patients' narcissism was wounded. In speaking so, however, both patients and psychoanalysts have in mind the psychological function not of the ego, but rather of the whole personality, and also self-evaluation, pride, and mental health.

The personal pronoun substitutes for the name of the individual but does not specifically indicate his ego, which therefore acquires a certain "anonymity." It seems a paradox to speak of the anonymity of the ego, since it is constantly referred to in conversational sentences. One should, rather, speak of an "incognito" of the ego. Amidst a crowd of everyday activities "His Majesty, the Ego" conceals its omnipresent [1] and unique power.

Normally, there is no more awareness of the ego than of the air one breathes; only when respiration becomes burdensome is the lack of air recognized. Today psychiatry commences to understand that a disturbance in the functions of the ego is an ego disease. Similarly, cardiology began a hundred years ago in connection with circulatory studies.

In practical life this is irrelevant. No one needs to know or to

. . . .

[1] This term, and not the weaker term "ubiquity" is purposely chosen because omnipresence is one of the attributes of God. Not only for narcissistic motives, but also logically, man is "the measure of all things." Therefore, man was forced to form conclusions out of his own experience in regard to the world in which he lived. As in his own body he felt his ego, so he assumed that in the cosmos is a cosmic ego—named "God" or "World-Soul." At first man also believed that the cosmic ego had a bodily ego, as himself. Later, the cosmic ego was thought to be merely psychic or mental.

feel the functioning of his ego, provided that it functions normally. Even in the short periods of an absolute blank, when consciousness is without any clear thought, the ego and the identity of the individual remain intact. To recognize specific ego symptoms one must select mental disturbances in which the ego disease is isolated or accompanied by concomitants such as hysteria or anxiety states.

Depersonalization and estrangement are both monosymptomatic ego disturbances. Cases show a great variety depending on the extent of the symptom. In each disease the symptom is defined by its name. The term "estrangement" is even more precise than "depersonalization." For the latter the right name might be "ego atony," with the meaning "loss of *inner* firmness of the ego." However, since the ego is the necessary support of the personality, when it cannot function as before the patient feels his self changed, even to a vanishing point. Therefore, depersonalization may be defined as the subjective experience of the disruption of one's ego.

As the phenomena of estrangement are easier to understand and describe than those of depersonalization, some diagnostic clarification in regard to the latter is still desirable. The diseases are mingled because both interfere with perception. The change in self-perception concerns both body and mind; the bodily as well as the mental ego can be attacked by both diseases.

Both estrangement and depersonalization can be partial or total. Total estrangement is a rare occurrence, and total depersonalization is even rarer. If help is delayed, the memory of his panicky state may upset the patient for many years. Sometimes a severe phobia of a recurrence of depersonalization persists together with a slight ego disease, and if this phobia is combined with fear of insanity, it resembles a pre-schizophrenic hypochondria. Sometimes it becomes difficult to differentiate between nosophobia and hypochondriasis; however, in both cases the course of the disease will depend on whether the ego cathexis is re-established.

Fortunately, partial estrangement and slight depersonalization are much more frequent. Light attacks are taken either as merely an interesting symptomatic complication which enters into the picture of a neurosis or a schizoid state, or as happenings in an otherwise healthy individual. The condition indicates that fatigue and exhaustion of short duration, intoxication, or emotional excitement have interfered with the regular ego cathexis. To accuse such etiological factors reminds one of the pre-analytical etiology which was opposed by Freud. Yet, in regard to the supply of ego cathexis, the old explanation was justified.

Slight or short estrangements are noted by the patient as shades of vividness of perception. Other patients ignore the initial change and do *not* complain unless terrified by sudden coldness and unfamiliarity of perception. Generalized and extreme estrangements are exceptional. In the majority of cases they occur in distinct situations: riding a train, leaving the house, in the office, sometimes only on certain street corners, and with specific objects. Usually estrangement begins with respect to one person, and may happen only once. In many cases it is restricted to reading or listening to music, even specific music, to a special job, or to the usual occupation of leisure time. Such restricted symptoms justify the assumption that partial or specific ego boundaries can become deprived of their normal cathexis.

All phenomena of estrangement, as well as of depersonalization, show one and the same paradox. Although perceptions, apperceptions, or proprioceptions have changed, intelligence and senses as well as skills and adjustment remain intact. This paradoxical feature is even more striking in depersonalization. The patient may announce with complete belief that he is unable to see, to think, even to breathe, to stand, to walk or move his hands, to love or to hate any person; he complains that no actuality of life is left to him. Yet he accomplishes all this normally, and frequently he himself adds: "I know I do think, I do see," and so on. Then he breaks out in despair to say: "Language has no words to describe my state, but it is as I say. Insanity would be a relief." The literature contains many examples of patients' excellent descriptions. They use similes and symbolic language because they find that the usual expressions are unsatisfactory. As language is a social instrument of interrelationship and communication, and as his own ego is the individual's domain and does not interest others, language has few general words related to egoism and egotism and the "I," and none relating to an ego state.

Even the term "ego state" met resistance when introduced. Audiences had difficulty in understanding its meaning. Hence the speaker learned that unpreparedness of the ego boundary is a main cause for the usual misunderstandings as well as the usual resistances met in psychology. The many conscious and unconscious plagiarisms which occur have their merits in that they prepare the ego boundaries of the public and popularize the original works. Innovations, be they in science, politics, or the arts must be "brought thrice" or more. The first presentation offers new engrams which become preconscious, the second influences the ego boundary, and the third is necessary for confronting the enriched ego boundary with the new knowledge. Freud himself felt this and gave seven almost complete presentations of his doctrine.

There is no doubt that the estranged patient feels more isolated than does the neurotic, and this isolation is accentuated by his difficulty in expressing his discomfort. His intelligence is bewildered by the contrasting symptoms. Many patients try to be their own psychologists, which keeps them occupied and alert and draws them out of depressive reactions. Although many of them profess to think that death would be preferable to such miseries, they are not suicidal.

No pathology is found in any of their organs. All senses function with great exactitude because they are stimulated by the estrangement itself, and only ego relationships are interfered with. Whether vision or hearing or object-related thinking is disturbed, unfamiliarity is always the result. It is improbable that the senses and the mind, which differ so much from each other, should undergo the same species of disturbance. It is much more probable that the uniform, but multisegmental, disturbance is situated in the ego boundary, which we have found to be the sensory organ for all apperception of reality. Therefore, the apperceptive process accomplished by the ego is impaired. This impairment is purely functional; our assumption is that it is due to some deficiency in cathexis. Through Freud, we have learned to recognize the quantity of libido shifted in all organismic functions, possibly including the entire area of the autonomic nervous system. One recognizes the accession of a libidinal component to any function by its erotization, warmth, and pleasurable connotation. It is precisely this connotation which is lacking in each of the numerous manifestations of estrangement. This justifies the assumption that estrangement is due to loss or withdrawal of the libido component from the cathexis of the ego boundary.

This conclusion, however well-proven theoretically, contrasts with the subjectively felt evidence of the patient himself. He does not recognize any change of his ego; he cannot say more than that the external objects or his internal experiences underwent a mysterious change. Psychology recognizes that the phenomenon of projection also applies to the ego itself. What really happens to the ego is felt to proceed from outside its boundaries, as a change in the quality of the thoughts as well as of the objects. Without the broadening of the meaning of "projection" this term could be applied only to the unfamiliarity of external objects, not to that of thoughts.

The projection of a functional loss of the cathexis of the ego boundary was exemplified for me through my own experience with the boundaries of my bodily ego while undergoing a local anesthesia. It was necessary to block the left mandibulary nerve. Not only the gum and the teeth, but also the cheek and both sides of the lower lip and part of the upper lip were anesthetized. This was felt as a triangular gap in the left walls of the mouth cavity. Cheeks and lips, when touched by the finger from outside or the tongue from inside, no longer belonged to the body. The bodily ego was indented; it could not be reconstructed from memory. I was not aware of the foreign dead parts which lay there in place of my own flesh. They could not be used to fill the defect. It could be clearly recognized that the bodily ego is formed by the proprioceptions transmitted through the sensorial nerves, plus a uniting cathexis. No paralysis of the sensorial nerve was felt as such, only an amazing vacuum in the body. This vacuum can be compared to mental defects in organic brain lesions. The analogy to estrangement showed as sensitivity slowly returned. Then gum, lips, and cheeks with mucosa, bone, and skin, were paraesthetic; any object coming in contact with the lips and cheeks—finger, instrument, or tongue—was felt as strange and different from normal. One clearly recognizes that this strangeness was due to impaired function of the sensory organ of touch.

Therefore one can conclude that the occurrence of estrangement demonstrates the existence of a mental sensory organ. Since no physical organ is involved, a mental organ—the ego boundary—must be presupposed to be implicated whenever objects are blamed for causing the sensation of coolness, strangeness, unfamiliarity, colorlessness, shallowness, or lifelessness.

"Gestalt psychology" has postulated that estrangement is due to interference with some holistic quality of apperception. To say that the whole personality reaction is changed holds good when one adds that every severe ego disturbance involves the whole personality. Psychoanalysts who explain external estrangement as withdrawal of libido from the object themselves share the self-deception of the patient and do not recognize the projection. Nunberg offered this explanation but modified it by adding that the patient has also lost his ability to love, especially his narcissistic love. Freud remarked, in a discussion, that a patient of his experienced estrangement when he lost himself in too strong an identification with another person. Oberndorf and Wittels also enlarged on the importance of fixated early identifications. All kinds of traumatic or developmental interferences have been held responsible for the occurrence of estrangement or depersonalization, yet none of the causes can be accepted as specific. No specific causation can be expected, because estrangement and depersonalization are neither psychoneuroses nor psychoses; they are quantitative disturbances like Freud's other actual neuroses.

From this point of view, estrangement is only the extreme prototype of some not yet fully studied disturbances of the ego. The libido has typical components. One can expect that both subtle and coarse differences will be found in all experiences, depending on the prevalence or lack of specific cathexis components and aggregates of components—passive and active, feminine and masculine, oral, anal, exhibitionistic, sadistic and masochistic, and emotional. These need to be recognized as variations in both healthy and diseased ego states. Such investigation will terminate many controversies in psychoanalysis and psychology.

Apart from this broader outlook into the future, some clinical questions can already be answered today on the basis of the pathology of the ego boundaries.

Estrangement and depersonalization may be merely actual neuroses, or they may be initiatory phases of neuroses or psychoses. The difference in their course depends on the underlying disturbance in cathexis. Just as was demonstrated in regard to schizophrenia, in some cases the lack of supply of libido, or in others its withdrawal, has altered the function of the ego boundary.

Fortunately, most attacks are due to a brief withdrawal provoked by anxiety or other neurotic implications. Yet, in many cases withdrawal or poor supply of the libido component turns into a schizophrenic withdrawal or a deficiency in the supply of the whole cathexis of the ego boundaries.

The symptoms of depersonalization and estrangement are different, and patients know exactly how to differentiate between them. This can be tested frequently, because very often both cathexis deficiencies show up in the same person. They are differentiated dynamically by the fact that in estrangement only the ego boundaries have lost their libido component, while in depersonalization the core of the ego is deprived of libido. It may be that other components of its cathexis unity have also become deficient. Since the peripheral and structural cathexes of the ego have different functions, the symptoms of the structural deficiency lack the character of estrangement.

Our knowledge of the normal ego offers some cues to the understanding of the ego in depersonalized people. Normally, there is the feeling of unity in regard to continuity, contiguity, and causality of the individual's experiences. In depersonalization these basic functions are disturbed, usually all of them at once, exceptionally only one or another of them. Generally there is an acute attack; sometimes, however, a chronic state. Even more than in estrangement, words fail here to describe the positive aspects in this "uncanny" mental situation. Its negative side, more easily described, is a loss of basic security and self-certainty.

Insufficient continuity manifests itself in the inaccurate feeling for time, past, present, and future; the passing of the moment is also vague. A state of mind or an event cannot be differentiated as permanent or as lasting only for a moment. Slighter disturbances cause the person to live through past times as if they were present, and vice versa. The *déjà vu* belongs to this category.

With this vagueness comes uncertainty as to the historical sequence of memories, frequently combined with a clouded feeling as to whether one has experienced something oneself or whether another person may not have been the actor. Uncertainty is also felt in regard to whether one has or has not personally lived through experiences which one knows have been those of another person, who may be living or a figure from fiction or history. In these cases the cathexis deficiency lies in those ego states in which identification with the other individual or figure took place.

The loss of inner coherence of the ego is, therefore, not fortuitous but follows the traces of the genetic ego development. Freud said that pathological splits in the personality are predrafted by cracks in the normal ego.

Identification means inclusion of the mental representation of the other personality into one's own enlarged ego boundaries, bodily as well as mental. The ego states with the identification are preconscious or unconscious. Normally, when they enter consciousness, the ego boundaries are sufficiently cathected for there to be no doubt in the normal conscious mind about what belongs to each of the two personalities. If cathexis becomes deficient, depersonalization is felt in this respect; the memory of the person may also be felt as estranged, sometimes with the connotation of extraordinary clarity. Such extreme clarity of certain memories or ideas is frequently mentioned by the depersonalized individual. It is probably due to a compensatory attempt to counteract the vagueness caused by libido deficiency by shifting cathexis to the circumscript ego boundary and to the object.

Another symptom of depersonalization deals with the contiguity of the mental ego. These patients complain that their feeling and thinking have become extraneous processes and do not belong to them any more. Extreme sexual and aggressive fantasies come into their mind unbidden and uncontrollably. Not only fantasies, but also intentions and impulses which are opposed to their dominating attitude, are suddenly present and felt as within, but not integrated with, the ego. In a neurotic person with an ego still intact, the same ideas would become obsessional and compulsions would develop. In the depersonalized individual, they are not incorporated as they should be by the cathexis unity of the ego.

In the area of the bodily ego, movements of the hands and even the most familiar procedures such as breathing, eating, and walking have, to the patient's astonishment, become disconnected and are experienced as happening of their own initiative; they are no longer automatic or wilfully initiated. Yet patients who have experienced estrangement in another period of the ego disease declare that these poorly connected functions are not estranged.

More frequent is another symptom of depersonalization which demonstrates the bipartite structure of the ego, bodily and mental. The patient complains that he feels he accomplishes activities only with his bodily ego, without the participation of the mental ego, except when he suddenly becomes aware that it is doing its work only by routine. However, the mental functions are intact and do their needful share. Such a state can last days or weeks or years and is viewed as a form of apathy, which, as a symptom of depersonalization, serves as a defensive mechanism allowing the patient to ignore his ambivalence and to be indifferent to the unsolvable conflicts which have aggravated him and drawn constantly on his ego cathexis. Depersonalization in itself is not a defense mechanism. In such cases apathy could also be described as automatization. Every normal automatism means that reactions or actions proceed preconsciously. In depersonalization one becomes aware of them as they spread over areas which are otherwise consciously controlled and directed by the mental ego.

One of my patients, who remained depersonalized after his

first and only attack of schizophrenia, described in his own terminology the lack of participation of his mental ego. He differentiated two states in his daily feeling and personal life, one in which he was "Out," and the other in which he was "In." This did not mean extraversion and intraversion. His state of being "In" was a general automatism and apathy due to the disconnection of his mental ego from his bodily ego, his activities being performed mainly by the latter. In this case no defensive mechanism complicated the pathology of the case. It became clear that some provocation from object libido for an individual or activity sporadically interrupted his state of apathetic automatism. Before treatment this happened inadvertently. It was possible to dissolve the mechanism by focussing our common interest on the movements overstepping the threshold between both states. During treatment, when a positive transference and counter-transference were attained, the patient learned to come "out" longer and longer until the states of depersonalization disappeared. They have not recurred for five years. No one knows whether the case would have taken the same course had it been treated as a neurosis and not as an ego disease.

Less frequent than these states in which the individual feels his mental ego to be lacking in interest or half sleeping, is the opposite condition in which the bodily ego is uncathected. The individual may either miss his bodily feelings and his bodily ego intensely or enjoy the fact that he is merely a spiritual being. Such cases begin very early in life and are manifested, not only in asexuality or impotence, but also in narcissistic pride in the highly intellectual and refined conduct of life. The diagnosis of depersonalization is suggested by the vagueness and uncertainty of their self-analysis and the lack of genuine feeling. They live ascetically and think in abstractions. But they do not know whether they actually feel themselves to be as they describe or only believe that they do so. This kind of depersonalization is due to sex rejection in the earliest years before true repression can be used. The defensive attitude hinders the acceptance of the bodily ego by the mental ego.

Even in chronic and severe depersonalization the disturbances are partial and temporary. The depersonalized patient is irritable and sensitive, almost like the allergic person, to the slightest emotional or external stimuli. Depersonalization in regard to the enlarged bodily ego is most striking. Any change of an object in the room, or any sound, is sensed by such an individual as happening within themselves, and they must control their automatic repetition of the movement seen or of the sentence heard. The patient cannot tolerate the slightest unexpected activity or speaking, and family members complain that he seeks solitude to an impossible degree. Quite innocent remarks or gestures disturb him deeply without any idea of personal reference, such as is seen in the neurotic. It appears that in a catatonic person certain movements, as well as rigid postures, are motivated by a persistent depersonalization.

Since changes in the surrounding room are able to provoke the depersonalized reaction, it can be expected that the patient will be even more strongly depersonalized when he himself moves about. In slight cases such feelings can be mastered by increased attention paid to the change. This exemplifies the general rule that a shift, willful or provoked, of ego cathexis to the disturbed function is used to prevent a depersonalized feeling. Therefore, such patients must follow the curves of the train or car in which they ride with great attention. In severe cases they cannot do so any more; they ride with closed eyes and immobilized body. Even so they sense the changes of direction of the vehicle and react to every single one with a depersonalized feeling. One of these patients could tolerate the ride through the tunnel of the subway but was very frightened by seeing people move on a platform which was passed by the train.

It is probable, but difficult to prove, that enlarged content of the mental ego is also susceptible to such stimuli. Empathy and telepathy seem to be caused by this feature. The patients observe, to a disturbing degree, their own identifications, which are complained of as losses of their emotional independence. Any suggestion given by another person is felt to be seduction. Depersonalized feelings may also be induced by reading, listening, or seeing a movie. Those slightly depersonalized may still find relief from a radio or movie performance. In severe cases, however, the patients keep away from such excitements. Usually such details are not revealed spontaneously by the patient, due to his fear of being thought crazy or a liar. His own fear of insanity comes from this dread of being held insane, apart from the uncanny nature of his disturbances. In fact, any interruption of the inner coherence of the ego cathexis can progress and lead to schizophrenia. Therefore, depersonalization frequently covers a latent schizophrenia, although the diagnosis may remain uncertain for a long time.

Before ending the symptomatic description, a unique observation may be reported. The disrupture of the ego cathexis in the following case had the effect that hysterical stigmas became conscious to the patient. Her hysteria had been present for seven years anteceding the depersonalization. When the latter condition set in, various conversion symptoms continued but were described differently than before, insofar as the organs with the hysterical symptoms were felt to be independent parts of the body. This was manifest in a globus and in stomach troubles. At the same time she became aware of the extreme narrowness of her visual field and of her hemi-anesthesia. The conclusion is permitted that neuroses are also related to disturbances of ego cathexis which have not yet been studied sufficiently.

Depersonalized patients find relief for some hours after a dose of barbiturates. The danger of developing drug habit and true addiction is great. The use of benzedrine or of both drugs combined is helpful; anxiety, discomfort, and mental pain are interrupted for some hours. It is questionable whether any curative effect can be attained or whether psychotherapy is rendered less difficult. It might even be that these drugs precipitate the outbreak of a latent schizophrenia.

In the severest cases, the patients require an immediate relief with morphia on account of the extreme fear, anxiety, terror, and restlessness. Their extreme disintegration is without any disorientation or mental incapacity; rather, such patients are overalert. They can neither be alone nor tolerate company. Unable to describe their state of mind, they feel as though on the verge of insanity, losing their memory and their "Self." The writer himself has not seen these states, but knows them only by the anamnestic reports of patients and from the literature.

The complaint of vagueness, inner insecurity, and change in depersonalization differs from the complaint of strangeness and unfamiliarity in estrangement. In none of the cases is the reality of the experiences denied. Therefore the writer does not agree with Oberndorf, who changed the name "estrangement" into "de-realization." While no object is deprived of its reality, the reality of the object is deprived of familiarity. Some estranged patients say that their perception or mind cannot come close to the object; something is between. Estrangement of inner processes has, of course, no relationship whatsoever with reality. Every patient immediately drops the word "unreal" when he is offered better terms. With this remark we come to the topic of inner estrangement.

Inner estrangement is not part of depersonalization, although frequently inner processes, by being isolated through depersonalization, can also be felt as estranged. Yet, the difference between the impaired function of an ego boundary and the coherent ego unit is so important that it is better to unite external and inner estrangement as one ego disease and to separate depersonalization.

Both disturbances commence suddenly. The onsets of slight depersonalization are frequently overlooked and are called by laymen "nervousness," or, in severer cases, "nervous breakdown." The first estrangement is never overlooked. The patient is almost stricken by the thought of a person or memory which is felt to be strange and unfamiliar. He himself is in a state of surprise, having been unprepared to encounter the object or thought which became strange. The reason for the withdrawal of libido from the ego boundary was well explained by Nunberg. In the interval between the last previous thought given to a person and the present one, the positive relationship has changed, owing to some real or imagined frustration or disappointment in respect to the person.

Although the estrangement in regard to external objects is better known to psychiatrists and patients, it seems that the thought of the object is more frequently estranged than is the object itself. In many cases emotion is also felt as estranged. Inner estrangement might spread over almost all of the mental processes, fantasies, memories, judgment, and planning. Estrangement of the subject's own voice combine inner and external estrangement.

One might say that inner estrangement is due to awareness of an otherwise unconscious mechanism. The normal countercathexis of the ego boundary, like the guardian of a threshold, hinders the object representation from entering the mental ego. In a healthy ego, when the thought of an object becomes painful, the countercathexis becomes increased to meet it. But when the libido cathexis decreases, the painful thought or memory becomes estranged. Normally, when the libido is withdrawn from the ego boundary, the object becomes forgotten and repressed. Estrangement of thoughts is therefore a sign of unsuccessful repression and increased consciousness of a mechanism which is otherwise automatic. Therefore estrangement of mental elements has its normal corollary in repression; while depersonalization has no normal equivalent except sleep. Deficiency of sleep is one cause of depersonalization.

Estrangement of emotions is frequently found to be a part of an inner estrangement. One would not expect such a disturbance because neither the affect theory of James-Lange nor of Freud can explain it. Laymen and psychologists are accustomed to attribute affectivity to the total personality.

Only my own theory of the affects tries to give a consistent explanation for this symptom. Emotions or affects are sensations developing between ego boundaries which come close to each other. In every emotion two ego states influence, or are influenced by, one another; to influence, as well as to be influenced, has a sensory element which becomes conscious. To speak of inner ego boundaries means no more than the fact that the ego senses itself, not only as an indiscriminate whole, but also as having a thousand different "shades" of feeling, depending on which aspect or state or sector of the ego comes uppermost in influencing the others. The quality of the cathexis is also involved. Affect, or emotion, is the word for which "shades" of feeling was used symbolically in the previous sentence. The quality of the emotion depends on the cathexis compound in the respective ego boundaries. It is very natural that libido deficiency in the cathexis of one ego boundary or of both does not change the emotion itself but only its impression. Whenever emotion is experienced—whether normally felt or estranged—the contents of the ego remain preconscious, while the sensory impact of the cathexes which met for mutual mental influence becomes conscious.

This theory accords well with Freud's statement that three parts are discernible in emotion, two sensory and one motor: (1) The individual senses the emotional quality; (2) emotion acts on the body and stimulates musculature and glands; (3) these stimulations contribute a further sensory impression to the individual. It is evident that a motoric part due to the cathexis energy can be expected together with a sensory part due to the qualification of the ego boundary as a sensory organ. When the ego psychological aspect of mental diseases has been accepted and carried through, the problem of abnormal emotions will also be approached on the basis of the theory of the ego boundary cathexis. The meaning of unconscious affect will be clarified, and countercathexis through emotional dams will be included in the problem of cathexis-shift. Many special questions will be answered, but not the general question solving the essential nature of any cathexis unit in itself. The answer is only hinted at by the postulate of "an inwardly directed function in the central nervous system."

While these broad problems are merely brought to light and still remain far from a complete survey, additional observations and results in the clinical field can be reported.

In the discussion of estrangement all sorts of ego psychological implications come up. One of the fascinating features of the ego is that while being one unit it is also felt as two separate units, the bodily ego and the mental ego. The bodily ego perceives, while the mental ego apperceives. In external estrangement, perception and apperception are both felt to be estranged. Deadness and coldness of impression pertain to estranged perception, unfamiliarity to estranged apperception. The character of greater distance pertains to both. Oberndorf has already stressed the perceptive side of estrangement and has approached the concept of the ego boundary by speaking of the "integrity of that part of the body which registers the stimuli of external sources."

Usually disturbance of perception is felt more sharply than

that of apperception. However, the latter absorbs so much concentration that the patient's other problems are neglected. Oberndorf and other authors therefore thought that estrangement is due to lack of interest. However, although loss of interest contributes to the symptom, it is not the cause, since objects of no interest can be so intensely estranged that the patient begins to weep. That uninteresting surroundings have become strange is more perplexing than the loss of interest for a specific person. On the other hand, many estranged objects remain in the field of interest.

In regard to apperception there is no merely external estrangement. Some patients themselves state that not only their present perception but also the memory of past impressions has changed. Past engrams are felt to be far distant in time and space. The object becomes unfamiliar, not only in its present appearance, but also in the matter of recognition and in regard to the whole history of its relationship. The correct facts and localities are remembered, but without vivacity or warmth; all knowledge has become lifeless.

When present experiences as well as memories become monotonous in this way, the patients' moods are tainted by indifference and even depression. Their depression is of the reactive type. Hence, sporadic and circumscript estrangements are the ego pathological side of a neurosis. Being itself an actual neurosis, estrangement is linked to the transference neuroses. This is in accordance with the mechanism of withdrawal of cathexis and with the causation-frustration or loss of the love object. Some "complex-conditioned" emotions may also be felt as estranged. There is "something" felt between the emotion and the personality sensing it.

Yet there are cases in which the "complex-bound" estrangement is not the whole disease. More complete disturbance of the cathexis economy develops. Afterwards, no thought occurs without a quality of distance and strangeness, no emotion is felt any more as warm or genuine. To his own amazement the individual feels strange to himself, and even his principal ego reactions, love and hate, shame and pride, are estranged. Such intense inner estrangement does not belong, nosologically and clinically, to the group of neuroses but to that of depressive psychoses. Depersonalization, as disrupture of the cathexis unit of the ego, belongs nosologically as well as clinically to the group of schizophrenic psychoses.

Happily it is not the case that every intense estrangement leads to depression, or every depersonalization to schizophrenia. All forms of both disturbances can occur as intrinsic ego diseases and can cease without leading to a fully developed neurosis or psychosis. On the other hand, the different forms can themselves intermingle or follow one another.

Unsolved nosological problems are:

(1) Are deficiencies in ego cathexis due to its lack of supply or to its withdrawal?

(2) Which components of the cathexis are involved, and why is a specific one lacking or increased?

(3) Which mental functions are most disturbed and why?

(4) Has an abnormal complex determined the localization of a disturbance?

(5) Is the ego boundary or the ego unity involved, and why?

This enumeration demonstrates that our knowledge in special ego psychology and ego pathology is still in an early stage. Yet generally, symptoms, disturbances, and cathexis vicissitudes can be better coordinated on the basis of the ego unity, the ego boundaries and their cathexes.

Because of incomplete nosological and etiological data, we know little about the course of the cases, whether with or without therapy.

Both disturbances can be symptomatic or true diseases. As symptoms they accompany a neurosis and contain a warning that the state of ego cathexis should be considered while one is analyzing. As disease, they may lead to schizophrenia and offer the therapeutic problems of this psychosis, which has been discussed in previous papers of mine.

Some—or possibly many—psychiatrists proceed immediately with the diagnosis "schizophrenia" whenever any delusion or any depersonalized state is observed or anamnestically reported. Other psychiatrists are cautious enough to make such a weighty decision only after repeated delusions or persistent depersonalization. They then proceed with ECT and report excellent results. Yet these results are statistical, not therapeutic. Most of these cases would have regained their mental health with any other treatment, even without any.

In these diseases therapy is largely a matter of mental and physical hygiene of the bodily and mental ego. Since fatigue and exhaustion are etiological factors, the patient has to help restore the lacking supply of cathexis by rest and moderate work. Yet it would be wrong to insist upon prolonged bed rest; the ego does not necessarily recover when the body is resting. Furthermore, both supply and investment of ego cathexis are stimulated by working. It is therefore a rule, taught us by experience, to stimulate the patient to activity but to prevent all fatigue. Any exception to this rule is punished by immediate loss of the improvement won in a long period of days or weeks.

Whether extraordinarily prolonged sleep offers chances for the ego's regaining its cathexis reserves is beyond the author's knowledge. Yet *sleep*—the other course of nature's feast—must be protected by all means. If sedatives are needed, it is an old rule to give them by descending, not ascending, dosage. Nights without the administration of the same or a related chemical compound have to be interposed regularly.

The third practical rule is the avoidance of exaggerated sexual activity, and especially exaggerated masturbation.

The last point leads to an important etiological factor. In hebephrenia and schizophrenia, as well as in depersonalization, the sexual hormonal economy and sexual activity play a dominant role. In depersonalization this role is paralleled by the devastating influence of long states of anxiety. Both factors are connected with exorbitant sexual fantasies, especially of a sado-masochistic nature, without the relief and the pauses which complete sexuality offers. In these cases sexual masochism is terminated only by exhaustion. To improve such habits needs the keen and devoted work and understanding of the mental hygienist. Any severity or, even more, any threat would ruin the whole endeavor.

Positive transference to the helper and the family are main desiderata.

On the basis of present knowledge, diagnostic and prognostic separation is very difficult. Following Freud's advice, the only way is to make a trial psychoanalysis. Nowadays this is usually impracticable because there are not enough psychoanalysts available either in hospitals or in private practice. The Rorschach test is used as a substitute and is helpful for diagnostic and prognostic purposes. However, the use of the Rorschach is questionable because it can be carried out by an ambitious psychologist in an inconsiderately energetic and even sadistic manner. I have seen such testing provoke the outbreak of a latent schizophrenia in the same way as does application of ordinary psychoanalysis. For all these reasons, psychoanalysis and the Rorschach test as means of diagnosis should be reserved for the psychiatrists. For the purpose of therapy, the education of many more physicians and qualified laymen is needed. Therefore clergymen, teachers, social workers, lawyers, and psychologists should be trained to become psychoanalysts, as Freud advised twenty years ago.

13

EGO RESPONSE TO PAIN

In this chapter original observations of the ego reactions to mental and bodily pain are discussed and analyzed. The paper offers the therapist a novel orientation for dealing therapeutically with states of suffering. This chapter and the one entitled "Manic-Depressive Psychosis" were prepared from an unpublished manuscript which was found among Federn's papers and was apparently intended for a chapter in a projected book. The material was of such basic interest and value that I felt it must be incorporated in this volume. Since it was in the form of only a rough draft, I have transposed and edited the material rather freely and have divided it into the two papers for greater clarity.—E.W.

A normal person in distress does not want to increase his suffering; he wants to get rid of it. He is happy when he finds that there is no actual reason for him to suffer. If he discovers that the causes for his suffering lie in a disorder of his physical self, or in events outside his mental self, he tries to find out how they can be, or at least might be, removed or terminated.

The immediate effect of any frustration is mental pain. Any frustration, and particularly one which might culminate in the loss of a love object, creates sadness in the emotionally healthy person. Thus sadness is the normal initial emotional reaction to frustration.

In childhood the emotional reaction to the pain of frustration is always *generalized*, causing the ego to experience a slight or severe feeling of unhappiness. In later years the ego has learned to bear many pains as such, without generalized reaction. Any prolonged unhappy emotional reaction which embraces the entire ego is termed a bad mood, or distress, while if it is felt only by a part or sector of the ego, it is called grief.[1] In childhood both bad mood and grief are normally brief. In adult life they are of longer duration; this is a main feature of maturity.

Normally, everybody tries to abolish mental pain, just as they would physical pain. The pain-pleasure principle described by Freud induces the mental apparatus to react primarily in such a way that pain is diminished and pleasure increased. Two normal ways out of the mental pain from frustration follow the pain-pleasure principle. The first is to shift the libido, from the object which through frustration has become painful, to a new object. The second is to occupy the mind with familiar objects which are known, either in reality or in fantasy, as pleasant; this form of reaction is called self-consolation. Both pathways are identical psychodynamically; so far as the economic compensation is concerned, it makes no difference whether the libido investment is directed towards a new object or is added to that of an old one. There is a very exact economic proportion between mental pain and its compensations. The positive effect can be reached by a relatively small joy related to the object if that object was very important to the individual; that is, if the whole ego or much of it is interested in the object. If only a small sector of the ego is involved, the joy itself has to be greater.

Sadness is the painful ego state created by ceasing to love. If the love object was very important, the consequence of the loss quite frequently may be that love turns into hate, which may neutralize the love or alternate with it. This hate can give some satisfaction and diminish the sadness through the pleasure in seeking revenge; it may spread over other objects and influence the person's attitude pattern. Such reactions begin in childhood and undergo total or partial repression, through

. . . .

[1] If a part of the ego is still able to think about the sorrow and to perform other functions, only a sector of the ego is occupied with the unhappy reaction, regardless of its intensity. The term "bad mood" (which unfortunately may have the connotation of "petulance") is to be interpreted as indicative, not of a minor intensity of reaction, but of its generalized quality, so that the sufferer is unable even to think about his grief.

which ambivalence is unconsciously either remolded or intensified. There are many individual shades in these reactions; some people continue to grieve for a lost love object without any hate.

We frequently forget that any kind of compensation should normally begin not immediately, but rather after the pain has been tolerated for some time.[2] The amount of pain "due" for each loss varies individually in regard to duration as well as to intensity. An object which does not deserve some grief and pain when it is lost was not worth loving or possessing at all. Therefore, whoever wants to obey the pain-pleasure principle without restraint resigns from any really blissful object relation. This is the psychology of "corruption through continuous amusement," of *"panis et circenses,"* for the masses as for the individual. The addicts are psychopaths characterized by infantile adherence to the pain-pleasure principle.

But there are still other ways of dealing with pain. The easiest way to avoid any state of pain is immediate *repression.* A more difficult way is to split off that part of the ego which is still interested in the object; this leads to scotomization,[3] which means unawareness of the entire sector of the world to which a frustrating object belongs. The process is completed unconsciously; in regard to the object itself, the consequence is *denial.* While repression and denial are means to avoid any reasonable and positive normal reaction to frustration, *negation* is the conscious and reasonable reaction. It is the voluntary decision to refrain from any further investment of libido in the negated object, the object as well as the frustration being fully realized.

Everyone has to learn to restrict these three reaction patterns—repression, denial, negation—as much as possible to the

. . . .

[2] An old mystic poet said: "Wollt ich dem Leid entrinnen, wie sollt ich Lust gewinnen? Gott lenkt durch Lust und Leid die Welt in Ewigkeit." ("Were I to try to escape grief, how should I gain joy? God, through joy and grief, guides the world eternally.")

[3] This term was introduced into psychoanalytical literature by Laforgue and was accepted by Freud. However, twenty years earlier Stekel had already spoken of the analyst's "mental scotoma" for those conflicts and complexes of the patient from which he suffered himself.

single frustrated libidinous desire and its object. When restricted in that way, all three reactions are normally useful. They spare the individual prolonged pain, yet they allow him to meet other similar objects without fear of, and resistance against, another libidinous investment. The individual retains the courage to risk frustration while hoping for the fulfillment of his dreams.

Whoever is able to react to a frustration by negation has in this way obtained greater experience in coping with the reality of life. He still remembers the past frustration and asks himself about the reasons for it—whether it was caused by his own guilt or by qualities of the object itself. Thus any frustration becomes a warning not to be as confident as before and teaches him how to cope better with the dangers of new frustrations. He is endowed with what Horace calls the *"bene praeparatum pectus"*—the well-prepared heart. When frustration has this result, there is no gap between the pain-pleasure and the reality principles. The first has become the servant of the second.

From the point of view of remaining objective, courageous, and clear-headed, denial is less adequate than negation of a frustration. It is impossible to deny the frustration without also denying the object itself and other similar objects; thus, through denial, no new experiences are gained and a sort of idiosyncrasy is established against the sector of the world containing the object. But as an immediate mechanism of ego defense, denial is more effective than negation. The individual sacrifices knowledge in order to gain quietude of mind. Such sacrifice indicates that the amount of pain from frustration was too great, and we must therefore grant that denial or scotomization is a very expedient mechanism from the economic standpoint of the pain-pleasure principle. Most people are prompt to react in this way. The striving for objectivity, especially in matters where one's own libido is involved, is rare and heroic. However, there are still many who are unwilling to sacrifice knowledge for quietude.

Successful repression is even better than denial as a protection from the effects of frustration. Actually, repression hampers both objective observation and rational thinking more than does denial, but it is not felt as a disturbance. It is maintained with less countercathexis than denial and is therefore less taxing.[4]

It is good to see the positive sides of repression and denial, because psychoanalysis impels us to emphasize their morbid aspects. It is normal to begin the new day having forgotten the frustrations of the past one as much as is permitted by common sense and by important object relations. Every night's sleep should extinguish the pains of the previous day, and every morning should reawaken the ego free from the past day's burden. Normally—i.e., in normal periods of the life of a mentally healthy individual—the night's sleep means successful repression of the pain of all transitory frustrations. However, as long as the continuation of the striving for fulfillment is justified by reality and permitted by the superego, frustration has to be accepted as not being transitory. When sleep does not fulfil the function of repression, all pain of frustration survives, and it accumulates.

Anna Freud has described as a defense mechanism the restriction of ego activities. We may remark that it is not an isolated reaction; whenever a frustration is dealt with by one of the normal reactions, part of the ego activity is put out of action to a certain extent; thus when there are a great number of frustrations normally reacted to, marked restriction of ego activity ensues.

Up to now we have discussed the reaction to mental pain in normal people. When we consider the complication of this reaction by fear, we approach the study of neurosis and psychosis. Whether the individual is fearful because he was already neurotic at the time of the frustration, or whether the fear has been produced by the impairment of sexual drives

. . . .

[4] It might be well to note the difference between denial and repression. Repression is the deeper process; the repressed material is relegated into the system Ucs, into the id. In contrast, denial· is unawareness of a section of the ego, of a field which belongs to the preconscious; scotomization is a blind spot in the retina, and the retina is ego territory. Denial, in my opinion, is an ostrich policy—"I don't want to see." Negation is a normal attitude when, with adequate motivation, a person decides not to invest in an object.—E.W.

through the frustration, is irrelevant; in any case, fear irrationally increases all reactions and makes them overflow all limits. In the process, the originating frustration may even be repressed and lose its importance. Phobic mechanisms set in, and all associations with the object are feared and are therefore inhibited or severed. Countercathexis of great realms of activity is increased in order to hinder any reappearance of anything related to the frustrating object.

In scotomization, sectors of the world containing the frustrating object are no longer acknowledged. If fear was involved in the frustration, the processes of denial and repression are not finished when the object itself is severed. Libido cathexes are further withdrawn, until all memories which are or were related to the object are repressed; furthermore, repression blocks out the era of life in which the frustration took place, including even a great part of the period before the event. It is understood that the extent of expansion of such consequences depends on the size of the conflict and on the degree of fearful pain created by the frustration. Repeated frustration in childhood can result in an impairment, or even the loss, of all object libido or in the discontinuance of entire components of sexuality. Through intense instinctual frustrations, the whole character is changed and the sexual development ceases. By identifications, or with the entrance of more mature components of sexuality, it may make another start later. When no such repair is made—spontaneously, by helpful environment, or by psychoanalysis—coldness and dullness in all object relations is established for life. Vanity and interest in money are the only gauges for value. Sexuality is separated from the personality, and no libido is shifted to other aims. Because of their lack of sensitivity and interest, individuals with such impairments are frequently called schizoids. Yet they do not deserve this name, since their deficiency is due much more to exterior frustration than to heredity.

Repression is a part of normal as well as of abnormal development. The difference between mental health and disease depends mainly upon whether or not repression in childhood has been successful. The process has succeeded when not only the frustration but also the emotional reaction, especially the complication of fear, is removed from consciousness. The more normal the adult, the less he continues to have childish fears. His childhood neuroses are also fully repressed. The inability either to overcome or to repress the fear leads to neurosis. In this way we come to the conclusion that the more repressions are due to anxiety, the more the field is being prepared for neurosis; and the more they are due to mental pain alone, the more normal the individual remains. This conclusion should be tested clinically, because it deals with the most important question of disposition to neurosis.

Which kind of repressions prepare for psychosis? Could we find an answer to this question it would also establish and define a disorder characteristic for, and common to, all prepsychotic stages. We accept here the differentiation between psychosis, prepsychosis, and prepsychotic personality which was proposed by Kretschmer.

There is no doubt that mental pain and fear play an etiologic role as important in psychosis as in neurosis. Since psychoses are generally thought to be mental disruptions which are more severe and deep than neuroses, it would be easy to satisfy ourselves by believing that the determining factor is quantitative—that greater degrees of mental pain and fear than are present in neurosis are responsible for psychosis. The idea is reinforced by the fact that the highest degree of mental pain becomes manifest in the psychoses themselves. So far as fear is concerned, it is uncertain whether it is greater in occasional deliria and severe phobias or in psychotic states. This approach, however, cannot be the right way to solve the problem; the initial rather than the terminal states should disclose the essential differences to us. In general, it is my impression that the preneurotic individual is less disturbed than the prepsychotic one. Frequently a person who can compare his own neurotic and psychotic experiences tells that the psychotic state actually relieved him from the mental pain, as well as from the fear, experienced during a prepsychotic neurosis. But it is nearly impossible to compare the degrees of pain and fear in different individuals, and some states of fear and pain cannot be compared.

In any case it is not permissible to conclude, from a difference in the diseases after they are developed, an analogous difference in their causes. We therefore discard the idea that whether the individual becomes psychotic or neurotic depends on a quantitative difference in the mental pain and fear which was inflicted upon him, and which he had to endure before the disease. We become aware of another kind of difference, a qualitative difference in regard to the acceptance or non-acceptance of suffering.

There is a slight but very important distinction between "suffering from a pain" and merely "feeling a pain." Suffering is the direct experience, included in the ego boundaries, of the mental pain caused by the painful event or object or by, respectively, the memory and the object representation. Through such suffering, the ego has realized the full intensity of the event. The next time the idea returns, the pain is no longer felt to the same degree. This is the most elementary primary step in normal grief and normal mourning. The acceptance of pain is the tribute we pay to normality.

The individual who is to become depressed does not pay the tribute. He feels the afflicting object as something that pains the ego boundary from outside. He may suffer the pain inflicted on the ego narcissistically, but he does not suffer it directly within his ego boundary as does the normal person. Therefore, whenever the event or the memory of the event returns it is felt by the unchanged ego boundary with the same intensity as the first time.[5]

Usually such an individual reacts, not with the simple suffering of pain, but with anger and aggression. The thought of the painful event or person is recalled repeatedly by the aggressive anger, and the pain is never either absorbed or isolated. The repeated return of the same pain from the same source, in its original intensity, accumulates into much more hurtful emotion. In this way a vicious circle develops from the simple primary failure to accept suffering from pain. Complete depression is the consequence of such senseless accumulation

. . . .

[5] Inside the ego the pain can, so to speak, be digested and assimilated in this internal organ. Eternal grief is caused by failure of the ego to carry out this "digestion"—that is, to undertake the mourning work.—E.W.

of mental pain, and depression creates further accumulation. Why it is possible for such states of depression to subside is more enigmatic than why they subsist. It seems probable that in such states the suffering of pain, which from the beginning of its development was not accepted, is now forced upon the ego. In this way the ego is able to change its attitude toward painful ideas, to accept them and to end them. All this sounds paradoxical, but can be explained by the fact that through suffering the person learns to enjoy pleasurable experiences again. The vicious circle previously referred to ends in this way; continuous mental pain creates apathy, and apathy precludes the aggressive reaction which hitherto provoked the return of the same painful thoughts.

The elementary constituents of morbid sadness and depression which have been described can be checked by anyone familiar with self-observation. Everyone can recognize for himself, in his unavoidable reaction to painful experiences, the difference between feeling pain and suffering it, between whether he lets the pain hurt the ego from outside, like an object, or from inside, like a part of himself.

In mild cases, psychotherapy can improve the false ego-reaction without deep analysis: Transference must be used to induce the patient to identify himself with the psychotherapist, who uses the methods which should have been used in childhood to teach the child the right reaction toward his early pains. In severe cases, long analysis and transference identification are necessary to change the morbid elementary reaction. Most depressed individuals cannot understand that it is possible to accept frustration. The Book of Job beautifully expresses the refusal of such acceptance by the depressed.

Some persons seem to end their grief by sudden rebellion against their pain. This apparent rebellion is in reality a sudden conscious, no longer automatic acceptance of the suffering, as if the individual were to say to himself: "All right, I have suffered this frustration, but I shall find new aims and new sources of pleasurable satisfaction." In most cases, when an individual makes the attempt, he immediately finds some satisfaction for some parts of his personality which have been neglected on account of his grief. He has in this way acted volitionally and the result is usually to overcome the sadness automatically. However, if external conditions are not favorable, a relapse into deeper grief frequently occurs. The morbid depressive reaction is finally deserted only when the primary reaction to pain ceases to go the morbid way, with its end roads leading to exalted flight from, and fearful submission to, the pain.

And yet, with the insight into the elementary reaction which has been described, our knowledge ends. We do not yet know why and how the acceptance of mental pain into the ego enables the individual to overcome the pain. We can only use metaphors taken from the organic functions, assuming, for instance, that the pain is "consumed and digested by the ego." Such symbolic terms are still necessary to circumscribe processes as yet undescribable. We have to use symbols descriptive of organic life because we proceed to problems of emotions and affects, where the merely economic and mechanical terms no longer suffice.

I dare to proceed to a theoretical explanation of why this acceptance into the ego ends sadness, while pain which is merely felt as an object continues. One reason might be that the acceptance is a conscious process on which a full amount of interest, i.e., libido cathexis, is directed; while the mere "feeling" of pain is a preconscious process, and only that feeling becomes conscious, but not its causation, which is outside the preconscious. Making the cause of the pain conscious is therefore a psychotherapeutic help in regard to both unconscious and preconscious processes. The individual who consciously accepts the pain—and its causes, the frustration or loss of object—practices what Freud called "working through" in psychoanalytical therapy.

But we still have not found an explanation—we have only described the fact that consciousness is an element of therapy. We are reminded of Freud's theory that consciousness developed because peripheral parts of the central apparatus were exposed to stimuli so numerous and so varied that they became hardened against all of them and no longer retained traces of the stimuli in the form of memories of the stimulating objects. The hardened portion of the mental apparatus uses up the entire energy of the stimulation in repeating for a short time the object or event that stimulated it; the organ of consciousness then returns and is opened to new stimulations. In the same way, consciousness might absorb so much of the energy of the painful stimulation that the residual memory could be tolerated.

However, it is possible, and seems probable, that beyond this effect of consciousness there is another difference between "feeling" pain objectively and "suffering" it. I offer the postulate that there are two different kinds of mental pain. The first is that familiar to us in the pain-pleasure principle. It is a specific sensitivity of the ego and is experienced by any ego boundary, as long as it retains its libido cathexis, when a libidinous claim is frustrated. Frustration or denial are both the negative fulfillment and attainment and the positive specific stimuli of the libido of the ego boundary, which must be regarded as a specific sensorial organ. From this basic psychological conception, we can conclude that any libido cathexis of a mental function must endow this function also with the capacity of a sensorial organ which feels pain or pleasure as a change of quality of the libidinous cathexis.

The second kind of mental pain has no pleasurable counterpoise; it is produced in the individual himself by the destructive forces which are turned outward as hostility, aggression, and destruction, and inward as auto-destruction. It was Freud's conviction that all these kinds of destruction are due to one and the same principle, the death instinct. I join his opinion, and have termed *mortido* the energy produced by the death instinct.

From the beginning Freud defined sexuality in the new broad sense, as *"Lust-trieb,"* and considered its award to be pleasure; but in his new theory of instincts he overlooked drawing the inherent conclusion that the award for the death instinct is pain. This gives us the formula: Beyond pain and pleasure which correspond to fulfillment or non-fulfillment of libido, there exists pain which corresponds to the fulfillment of the death instinct. There is no expression for the non-fulfillment of the death instinct, which may cease but which cannot be frustrated as can libido.

However, to assume that the ego reacts to the cessation of mortido cathexis with exultant relief and a joyful new grasp on life seems a very probable explanation for the free expansion of libido cathexis and for the elation of the individual after the end of a depressive period.

Freud's reduction of the many instincts to Eros and Thanatos—sexual instinct and death instinct—has been criticized and rejected by many, including certain eminent psychoanalysts who prefer to stick to Freud's first distinction between sexual instincts and ego instincts. Non-analysts are not convinced that there is no proof for the old division into self-preservation and preservation of the species (the latter expressed by sexuality) as the main constituents of instinctive life. Freud argued that every instinct to preserve life is in itself constituted of some components of both Eros and Thanatos. Eros unites and ties together the living elements and preserves the living structures in continuous antagonism to Thanatos, which endeavors to separate these elements and structures, to kill them, and to bring them back to the inorganic phase of death out of which all life developed. According to this concept, all ego instincts are characterized by their localization; self-preservation may then be considered due to the pre-established order of the contest between the sexual and the death instinct in every organism.

But we can avoid many superfluous arguments and describe the facts more distinctly if we apply a triple classification of the instincts without deserting Freud's dualism of love and death instincts. The manifold processes of life are performed by drives which correspond to Freud's definition of instincts— they have specific objects, specific aims, specific organs; they re-establish a state of existence which has been disturbed by some stimulation. Although it is possible to demonstrate in every one of these instinctive actions an erotic and a destructive element, it is much more practical not to combine them as "self-preservation." The sexual instinct which furnishes libido cathexis, together with the death instinct which furnishes mortido cathexis, are distinguished by the specific awards for fulfillment, which are lacking in the instincts of self-preservation.

There is no doubt that the biological functions which are stimulated instinctively—such as eating, which includes chewing and swallowing, and all excretory functions—also have a pleasurable award. The psychoanalytical theory of the instincts explains this award by the libido component which is anaclitically dependent on these biological functions. And yet many non-analytical authors did not accept this; they emphasized the existence of *"Organlust,"* which Bühler, among others, thought to be non-libidinal. Accurate self-observation and weighing the communications of analysands demonstrate that there are two components in this biological pleasure, one due to the organic functions and the other to the anaclitic libido. In regard to pain, we can also separate the displeasure created by non-fulfillment of biological functions from the destructive pain in traumatic degrees of frustration.

Another difference between the sexual and death instincts on the one hand, and the life-preserving instincts on the other, is that the former can accumulate and be shifted to other functions and aims, while the strictly biological instincts remain attached to their respective organs. When, for instance, hunger or thirst become so strong that the whole organism is involved and the ego overwhelmed, it is the destructive and libidinous components which irritate and stir all sectors of the personality.

A third difference between death and sex instincts and the strictly biological instincts is that they are felt in different ways, the latter being felt merely as needs or as irritations of a hue which is specific for a specific function. Quite different are the feelings engendered by libido and mortido. Even our language is reluctant to apply the concept of libido *to,* and use the terms "instinct" or "drive" *for,* such organic needs as urinating or defecating. In the excretory function especially, the well-distinguished libido component is very great in some individuals and nearly lacking in others. Freud himself has explained all hysterical and neurotic organ-symptoms as due to the double function of the organs in expressing libido cathexis and organic need.

14

MANIC-DEPRESSIVE PSYCHOSIS

In this chapter new points of view in regard to depressive and manic states are presented. The relation of these states to addiction and to the tolerance capacity of the ego is particularly interesting.—E.W.

The symptoms of manic-depressive psychosis are typical and well known, and but little dependent on the prepsychotic individuality. At the peak of either phase, the gap between genius and average person, wise man and fool, is leveled, and difference in background and education is erased. Before this kind of psychosis, human values fade away as before death itself. Just as organic matter is coagulated both by freezing and by boiling, so are all the features of normal mental life blotted out both by depression and by mania. And, in analogy with temperature and organic life, only in the middle layers of emotion can a prosperous mental life develop.

Freud's investigations of manic-depressive psychosis are presented mainly in his papers on "Mourning and Melancholia" and "Civilization and Its Discontents." In the latter, he had the daring to trace the origin of these diseases back to an assumed "First Crime," the slaughter of the Forefather. This assumption explains the disease as a complete repetition of the reaction pattern "prehistorically" acquired at a time when it was justified by the enormous emotions preceding, and roused by, the crime. The rather perplexing theory gained probability when it was found that strong unconscious patricide material was present in psychotics of this group.

At the time when the manic-depressive pattern is acquired, as well as later when it is unconsciously repeated, the manic phase is due to the triumphant satisfaction from the achieved patricide; the depression is due to the ordeal of remorse the patient suffers after he has gained insight into the futility of this triumph—which ended his hate, while his love regained strength through his memories. Once this reaction pattern is acquired, any guiltful success of sufficient intensity can provoke a manic phase which will be followed by a depression. These patients suffer a setback after exultation; in this rhythm, with the manic phase preceding the depressive one, the death is felt as due to fulfillment of a death wish, which is later on regretted.

A second rhythm, in which the manic period follows the depressive one, is probably more common than the first. It was explained by Freud, in "Mourning and Melancholia," by analogy to pathological mourning. In the depressive-manic rhythm, the regretted death—which had previously been wished for—can be enjoyed once a sufficient amount of mourning grief has been bestowed on the loss. Both rhythms are the unconscious repetition of a previous traumatic event, when an important love object was lost through death. In both forms, the death wishes are unconscious and have to be unearthed by psychoanalysis; the intensity of the disease depends largely on the resistance against their acknowledgment.

It is not easy to understand Freud's concepts in regard to mourning, or its similarity to, and difference from, true depression. Three main topics—narcissism, mourning work, ambivalence—were combined in his fascinating clinical essay. He distinguished pathological from normal mourning, and pathological depression from the exaggeration of a normal emotional state. One might think that feeling miserable on account of a death is an elementary phenomenon needing no further explanation. However, any pathological mental misery is no simple phenomenon. Both physician and relative may well feel desperate in their incompetence to deal with, and their inability to understand, the person overcome by such misery.

The normal person tries to rid himself of suffering and is happy when he finds there is no actual reason for him to be distressed.[1] Depressive persons behave in an opposite manner and thus show their illogical relationship to their own disease. Every such person attributes to himself conditions which are manifestly outside his self. He feels that he is responsible for, and guilty of, everything, especially his disease; on the other hand, he also "rationalizes" his suffering, but by irrational thought, by projecting the causes into the outside world. Illogically, and without any reasonable probability, he is apprehensive of the return of long past disasters and "indulges" in the expectation of new ones. The proverb, *"Qui s'excuse s'accuse,"* is reversed; by accusing himself the patient attempts to find his punishment as well as to do away with the riddle of his guilt.

In the manic phase, on the other hand, the irrationality is found in the paradoxical way in which the pain-pleasure principle is carried through to its climax and in the lack of rational causes for the elated contentedness. Normally, a pleasurable state of mind is maintained and indulged in until a kind of boredom sets in and demands another cause for pleasure, or some rest. The manic person, on the contrary, continuously deserts his happy ideas, one after the other, as if they were painful to him; and, indeed, they do become painful, through his fervor in comparing them with still more pleasurable ideas and because of his fear of their coming to an end.

The manifest manic state is also related to the psychology of the addict. There are many types of addiction; drug addiction shows its structure most completely. No addict can stand his craving for satisfaction for any length of time. While the manic is able to shift his craving for mental pleasure from one object to another, the addict is chained to his specific addiction. When it is frustrated he must do everything he can to obtain satisfaction or else he succumbs to the greatest despair, and to a suicidal state of panic.

While the manic and the addict are characterized by their eagerness to avoid—that is, their impotence to tolerate—the *impending* frustration, the depressed person is characterized by his impotence to tolerate the *experienced* frustration. Many

. . . .

[1] See "Ego Response to Pain," Chapter 8.

people become addicts in order to avoid depression, and many addicts become depressed when their addiction is frustrated. Persons with mild depression frequently try to overcome any beginning depressive state by some addiction; usually it is for alcohol and nicotine, but it may be for any of various drugs.

Transitory states of addiction lie intermediately between the manic and the depressed. A manic person who cannot satisfy his impulse to feel pleasure by a flight of thoughts frequently goes through a state of impulsiveness, a sort of addiction, before he breaks down into a depression. And depressive states frequently end with some addiction or impulsiveness which terminates in a manic phase. It is possible that many a chronic addiction began as such an intermediary phase, which became fixed in order to avoid the manic-depressive states themselves.

The addict is suffering too great a pain in his ego. He not only feels the pain resulting from frustration, he also suffers the frustration itself as pain; there is a race between the suffering by frustration in his ego boundary and the painful frustration by the object. The addict does not suffer *about* himself as does the depressed person, nor *outside* himself as does the manic person—his ego itself suffers terribly through his craving.

Patients of all three groups (manic, depressive, addicted) can be cured only when the elementary deficiency common to them is overcome—their deficiency in regard to the ability to bear and suffer mental pain. By examining the reaction of the ego to mental pain as a basic disturbance of emotional equilibrium, we learned that the equilibrium can be restored by various normal means. In discussing the elementary failures in restoration, we had to consider the pathology of fully developed depression, and we found it easier to understand this pathology if we followed Freud's way of explaining melancholia and depression through the study of pathological mourning; this, through normal mourning; and that, through sadness.

The tendency to exclude mental pain brings harmful and even disastrous consequences when uncontrolled. The beginning of all mental morbidity is cowardice before, and fear of, mental pain. To turn immediately to another object is an easy way out. To substitute fantasy for reality is a more dangerous way, which becomes even more harmful when the fantasies are built mainly to satisfy narcissism. Whoever wants to remain mentally sound should stand a good deal of the pain of frustration, or of the despair created through the loss of an object, before he begins to compensate for the loss and to master the pain.

The manic and the depressive states are two opposite entities of reaction to frustration. In the way a child reacts, his terminal states are already foreshadowed. Whether the individual will become sick, or whether he will merely have an altered reaction pattern, will depend on the volume of emotional strain to which he is exposed through life. However, the child who, when frustrated, stumbles on immediately to a new object, or to a fantasy, is reacting in the same way as he would later in a developed manic state. In order to avoid the haunting memory, to avoid any possibility of approaching it, the manic mechanism is to leap from one idea to another, from one object to the next; interest remains with these imagined objects or ideas only as long as they are joyful and promise success. Because the child has neither criticism nor objectivity, he is able to avoid mental pain in this way without any difficulty. In adult mania, the joyful ideation usually contains some objective planning; however, this planning, just as in childhood, lacks criticism and true objectivity. Whenever critical judgement tries to intervene, be it that of the individual or that of others, we can observe that the cathexis of the idea is so strong that it overrules any criticism. But as soon as there is any doubt or difficulty, and especially as soon as any connection with the repressed frustration is unavoidable, the entire chain of thoughts and plans is immediately deserted and another one is adopted; sometimes it is difficult to find such a new chain, and in this case intercurrent fear and unrest are immediately felt.

Thus, inability to stand frustration is characteristic of the manic state, as it was characteristic of the beginning when any painful idea was quickly deserted; those individuals concerned deviate from the normal ways of dealing with frustration by seeking comfort too quickly. Depressive persons, on the other hand, deviate by their inability to seek any comfort at all. Their repression is insufficient, their denial and negation do not prevail, their phobic mechanisms are inadequate to prevent dwelling on the experienced mental pain. Children reacting in this way already show, to a slight degree, the essence of depression. The inner reasons for a child's black moods are: first, too much narcissism; second, lack of strong pleasant object relations; and third, inability to identify quickly and intensively with another person. Typical environment offenses are more painful to children of depressive tendencies than to normal ones. Perhaps prevention of later development of disease should begin at these early stages, by helping the child to overcome his midget depressions. By the cumulation of temporary black moods, a habitual sadness can develop which results in a structural depression.

Apart from the dire therapeutic need, the study of the psychoses is important because they are the field in which any basic theory of instincts must be tested. German psychiatry emphasizes that the essence of schizophrenia consists in: (1) a specific schizophrenic mentality, and (2) some progressive destruction of the personality. From the psychoanalytic point of view we speak, not of destruction, but of the prevalence of the destructive instinct. This does not manifest itself in schizophrenia, all phases of which are explained by loss of libido cathexis and regression, but it is quite apparent in both phases of manic-depressive psychosis. In the manic phase the destructive instinct is directed outward; in the depressive, inward. Freud's theory is that destructive and death instincts are one and the same. The deepest general theoretical assumption is that this group of psychoses represents abnormal manifestations of the death instinct itself, while all other neuroses and psychoses, including the schizophrenic group, represent abnormal manifestations of the love instinct. By this assumption the difference between the two main groups is precisely defined, and the possibility of the combination of both groups in one person is explained. Reactively, of course, both instincts are involved in both groups of diseases, just as they are in normal life.

In one of his last papers Freud hinted at the probability that individuals differ in their instinctual constitution: the proportion between death and love instincts, and the absolute intensity of both, characterizes their personal constitution from the instinctual aspect. It is not said that manic-depressive individuals are constitutionally endowed with more death instinct than others, but during the disease itself the death instinct increases. That explains a fact which has impressed us, that in spite of the leveling influence of the manic-depressive states, the individual's prepsychotic instinctual constitution is shown in one feature, namely, the amount of cruelty and aggressiveness which is directed toward the outside world in the manic phases and inward in the depressive ones. This prepsychotic feature accounts, in the depressive or manic phases respectively, for the danger of suicide or of assaults and for the intensity of self-torment or of tormenting others. The intensity of the disease itself is probably shown mostly in the depth and length of the phases. Patients who prepsychotically showed a kind and generous personality may retain something of this quality even in the choking grip of the manic-depressive states.

It is difficult to estimate to what extent manic-depressive psychosis may be based on heredity, on the habitual reaction pattern, and on both. It has been proved by family research that heredity plays its role in severe cases. We do not know, however, which are the hereditary elements; it is probable that disposition to depression is inherited, while the manic reaction is a secondary consequence. The cyclothymic alternation of elated and depressed moods is certainly a familiar hereditary phenotype. Since both tolerance and intolerance of mental pain depend largely on biochemical central nervous processes, and probably also on differences in quantities of cells, heredity may play its role through these factors in the individual with a basically abnormal reaction to mental pain. However, the unbiased observer might conclude that the emotional mental deviation may express itself in the biochemical state just as well as the unknown biochemical deviation may express itself in the emotional state.

There is no contradiction between our belief in the success of psychoanalytic treatment in severe cases of recurrent manic-depressive states and our belief in the importance of the hereditary factors. Heredity does not absolutely determine the disease; the strain of the occurring offenses appears to be the provoking factor. The old astrological fatalists used to say: *stellae ducunt, non trahunt*—the stars lead us, but do not drag us. The same is true in regard to heredity, the scientific basis of modern fatalism.

PART III

NARCISSISM

For the third section of this book I have selected two highly technical expositions which have not previously been translated into English. They are intended for the readers who wish to acquire a deeper theoretical understanding of Federn's conceptions of narcissism. "The Ego as Subject and Object in Narcissism" was read at a meeting of the Vienna Psychoanalytic Association in June, 1928, and was published by the *Internationale Zeitschrift fuer Psychoanalyse* (XV, 343-425) in 1929. "On the Distinction between Healthy and Pathological Narcissism" was published in *Imago* (XXII, 5-39) in 1936; this paper was based on papers read in Oxford in 1929, Lucerne in 1934, and Prague in 1935. I would like to thank the editors of these journals for their kind permission to translate and edit this material.—E.W.

15

THE EGO AS SUBJECT
AND OBJECT IN NARCISSISM *

"Natura non facit saltum!"

Variations in ego feeling are experienced by normal people and, particularly, by persons who feel the external world to be estranged. As I have discussed elsewhere,[1] this fact permits us to recognize, by means of self-observation, one libidinal component of the ego. The ego must be conceived of as a continuous experience of the psyche and not as a conceptual abstraction. Communications of patients concerning such self-observations constitute important material for the study of the functions of the ego. Such inquiries do not merely investigate interesting phenomena of estrangement, but rather do they touch upon the fundamental theories of psychoanalysis. They represent empirical proof for the correctness of Freud's doctrine of narcissism. Likewise, it should be possible to demonstrate, from the study of the various kinds of depersonalization, the reality of other libido processes inferred by psychoanalysis. Without such, or other, new evidence the libido theory would time and again be designated, by its adherents as well as by its opponents, as a happy "heuristic" idea, not be taken as a description of reality, in spite of its fruitful development and perhaps because of the very resistances which the idea arouses. Hence everyone would consider himself justified, according to
. . . .

* From a paper read before the Vienna Psychoanalytic Society, June 27, 1928.
[1] See "Some Variations in Ego Feeling," Chapter 1, and "Narcissism in the Structure of the Ego," Chapter 2.

283

his personal predilection and evaluation, in applying another theory of psychodynamics.

The actual observation of libido processes requires the co-operation of many psychoanalysts who are also interested in the phenomenology of these processes and whose writings should complement each other. The writings must also be mutually understandable. This requires the use of an unequivocally uniform terminology.

My earlier papers merely expected the reader to differentiate conceptually between ego libido and object libido, and to distinguish whether the term "narcissism" was used with reference to the subject or to the object. Briefly, the main conclusion was that feelings of estrangement in perceiving the external world ensue when the ego boundary *loses* some of its libidinal cathexis (subjectively recognizable as ego feeling), despite the persistence of object cathexes (subjectively recognizable as investing of objects with significance).[2] With this statement I contradicted the previous explanations of estrangement (and of all states of depersonalization) which implied, on the contrary, an increase in narcissism attended by a decrease in object cathexis. Nunberg came close to the correct interpretation when he spoke of an "injury" to narcissism by the loss of object libido. To my knowledge, only Minkowski, who is not a psychoanalyst and who uses the psychology and terminology of Bergson, arrived at the same conception as I did.

Since we designate as narcissism the "cathexis of the ego by libido," I stated briefly that estrangement is based on "impoverishment in narcissism on the part of the ego boundary." To my surprise, experts on libido theory and Freudian metapsychology were quite unable to comprehend my explanation, so that they were unable either to accept or to reject it. To these readers the term "narcissistic cathexis" always meant a libidinal preoccupation *with* the ego, a concentration *on* the ego. Since patients with feelings of estrangement are very much preoccupied with their own states, this would indicate a concentration of libido on the patient's ego, and thus an "increase in narcis-

. . . .

[2] The object representations also may lose their cathexes, depending on the course of the disease, the onset of which is marked by depersonalization.

sism." How then could Federn speak of a "decrease in narcissism?"

A remote cause of the misunderstanding is that many readers and some authors have indiscriminately accepted "estrangement" and "object-loss" as synonymous, and expected the terms to be explained identically. But whereas "estrangement" constitutes a specific occurrence, a particular mental sensation, "object-loss" is an expression with many meanings.

It seems more important to me to reach an agreement about the use of the term "narcissism," especially whether it is correct to use it in a vague manner, to indicate any strong affective reaction of the personality.

Actually, in every affective reaction there is also a stronger ego feeling which cathects more intensely that ego boundary with which we apprehend the object in question, on which the stimulus from the object impinges. In reactions of diminished affectivity this ego boundary is less cathected with libido. This statement seems to be self-evident, but is substantiated only by the fact that it is possible for the object no longer to be apprehended with any affect at all, when estrangement ensues because the ego boundary has been completely deprived of libido.

The term "ego boundary" shall not designate more than the existence of a perception of the extension of our ego feeling; I was misunderstood by some who thought I implied that a boundary surrounds the ego like a belt, and that this boundary is rigid. The opposite is true. These boundaries—i.e., the range of functions of the ego which, invested with ego feeling and thus cathected by libido, still belong to the ego—are always changing. But a person senses where his ego ends, especially when the boundary has just changed.

I wish to anticipate a second objection which would rest on an obvious misunderstanding. My investigation calls special attention to the ego *boundary* by starting from its perception by oneself. However, I am not at all of the opinion that ego feeling exists only peripherally. The sensation of the ego *boundary* is more easily perceived because the latter changes almost continuously, while simultaneously all of consciousness is filled with ego feeling. In my opinion, it exists from the very beginning, though at first vague and poor in content.

It is not only as a metaphor that I here refer to the impressive undulations of the cleaving ovular cell, or to the change in the whole body of the amoeba while it emits or retracts a pseudopod. At the beginning of life, the living substance reacts as a whole. This impression became most clear to me many years ago, when I observed highly organized protozoa. After a granule of starch has passed the gullet, the big nucleus immediately loses its brightness, while the whole protoplasma, fibrils and vacuoles, is simultaneously set in motion; at once the food dissolves in the protoplasm—a primordial picture of the alimentary orgasm postulated by Radó.[3]

This unity disappears in body and mind because, with progressing adaptation, division of labor proceeds in the formation of tool-units. The specialized organs must themselves be protected in their function from disturbing stimuli, and have to protect the whole organism from continuous disturbance through their independent absorption of such stimuli as are adequate to them. But if Freud ascribes to the ego the function of unifying the manifold component events, he implies that this achievement is aimed at the restitution of a state which previously was permanent. This is in agreement with the ultimate aim which Freud postulated for all drives; namely, to re-establish a former state of things, either directly or indirectly. The detours constitute differentiation and evolution.

The term ego "boundary" should therefore imply that, in contrast, ego feeling is a totality. Accordingly, the libidinal cathexis which constitutes the ego feeling must likewise be centrally coherent.[4] Ego libido actually corresponds to the amoeba which Freud used as a simile. The existence of a multiform ego boundary, which at any given moment differs in degree of cathexis of its various parts, in no way contradicts the inner coherence of

. . . .

[3] S. Radó, "Die psychischen Wirkungen der Rauschgifte," *Internat. Zeitschrift f. Psychoanalyse,* XII (1926), 498.

[4] Figuratively speaking, the ego has a mental center to which all mental ego functions connect; however, the connection of ego function with the id is not established through the mediation of the nucleus of the ego, but occurs according to the various drive components of the id which supply the ego functions with mental energy.

the ego. We must maintain both concepts because there exists estrangement, not only in regard to the external world, but also in regard to many mental processes, including: all cognitive processes such as remembering, thinking, reasoning, and judging; affective attitudes such as hoping, fearing, wishing, worrying, grieving; and thought processes which influence the imagined or real external world, such as deciding, beginning, terminating, commanding and obeying. The various instances of estrangement—i.e., those which are not complicated by a deeper psychotic or neurotic disturbance—prove that these normally affective strivings and experiences may continue consciously in the individual, without impinging on the libido cathected boundary of the ego, or, more precisely, without the boundary of the libido cathexis of the periphery of the ego reaching them. (Non-psychoanalytic psychology expresses the difference with the words: The feelings become sensations). That this is not a question of *loss* of affect we recognize by the facts: first, such a patient acts partly as if he still had the affects; and secondly, he misses them and states that he himself (that is, his ego) has changed and that for this very reason he no longer feels his affects.[5]

We may ask next whether we are justified in calling the libidinal cathexis of the ego boundaries "narcissistic." "Erogeneity of the ego" or simply "ego libido" might be just as correct. The first of these terms seems to be consistent but has the disadvantage of blurring the antithesis between ego and the "erogenous zones." Furthermore, we associate with "erogenous" the idea of organ pleasure of a specific nature, while the erogeneity of the ego, inasmuch as it feeds the ego feeling, appears to be particularly desexualized and general. We had better reserve the expression "erogenity of the ego" for the ego which is sexualized, in antithesis to the ego during the waning of sexuality.

. . . .

[5] H. Nunberg, ("Über Depersonalisationszustände im Lichte der Libidotheorie," *Internat. Zeitschrift f. Psychoanalyse,* X [1924], 17) and myself (see "Narcissism in the Structure of the Ego," Chapter 2), have adduced arguments in proof of the fact that the specific ego feeling rests on libidinal cathexis and not on cathexis with another kind of drive energy; for the sake of continuity I refrain from enumerating further arguments here.

Freud says: "It is possible that for every such change in the erotogenicity of the organs there is a parallel change in the libidinal cathexis in the ego." [6]

However true it is that the ego must have an erogenous cathexis in order to be felt as ego, and much as the term "Eros" is enticing for this use, I consider it more advisable to employ the term "ego libido." The term has generally been used in the sense of narcissism, but is not quite identical with it. Since it is a question, not only of terminology, but of factual doubt, I wish to quote a passage by Freud in which he characterizes or defines the concept of narcissism. In his paper, "Instincts and Their Vicissitudes," in which he clarifies these most difficult problems he had just come to comprehend, Freud states: "Originally, at the very beginning of mental life, the ego's instincts are directed to itself and it is, to some extent, capable of deriving satisfaction for them on itself. This condition is known as narcissism and this potentiality for satisfaction is termed auto-erotic . . . At this period, therefore, the ego-subject coincides with what is pleasurable . . ." [7]

In this characterization the stress is laid on the satisfaction experienced in one's own ego (mind and body, individuum) in contrast to the external world. The context motivates this emphasis. Thus, although "the ego's instincts," mentioned at the beginning of the passage, certainly include the libidinal cathexis which feeds the ego feeling, it is not certain that a definition of ego feeling would include the autoerotic satisfaction which, according to the subsequent words, are part of narcissism. We shall come back to this point later.

In any case, the healthy ego feeling is a pleasurable feeling, but does not have the character of a state of special satisfaction, nor, to be sure, that of a state of special dissatisfaction. In general, it becomes an actually pleasurable feeling only through intensification originating in the id, or through the addition of libido cathexes which had not previously been part of the ego. At any rate, the passage quoted is not in disagreement with the use of the term narcissism for the function of the ego libido to

. . . .

[6] Freud, "On Narcissism," *Collected Papers*, IV, 41.
[7] Freud, *Collected Papers*, IV, 77f.

which we turn our attention.[8] I said before that the simile of the amoeba is especially fitted for the ego feeling; Freud used the same simile several times in order to make narcissism understandable. Also, Freud's comment that "narcissism is the libidinal complement of egoism" applies to the ego feeling as well, the lack of which makes a person so unable to enjoy anything that he is truly characterized by the words: *"Und er weiss von allen Schätzen sich nicht in Besitz zu setzen."* [9]

However, we establish complete accordance between our conception of ego feeling and the above quoted characterization of "narcissism" if we realize that the ego feeling is fed precisely by that part of the ego libido which constitutes narcissism, without, however, being autoerotically satisfied. Such a state of lack of satisfaction does not need to bear the character of displeasure, but has the quality of an *agreeable fore-pleasure* because, from the economic point of view, it is a matter of quantities which have been fragmentized by distribution. That is to say, the term "agreeable fore-pleasure" actually does full justice to the quality of the experience of healthy ego feeling.

This discussion was necessary in order to show that we have used the term "narcissism" for the investment with ego feeling without transgressing the conceptual content intended by the discoverer of narcissism, although his definitions proper always include also the relation to the ego as love *object,* as, in the most incisive instance, in the phrase: *"loving oneself,* which for us is the characteristic of narcissism." [10]

· · · · · · ·

[8] The following passages from Freud's *Collected Papers* also justify my use of the term "narcissism": first, from "The Libido Theory," V, 133, "The libido of the self-preservative instincts was now described as *narcissistic libido* . . ." (but not the continuation, ". . . it was recognized that a high degree of this self-love constituted the primary and normal state of things."); and second, from "One of the Difficulties of Psychoanalysis," IV, 349, "The condition in which the libido is contained within the ego is called by us 'narcissism' . . ." (but, again, in the conclusion of the sentence the object relation of the ego is stressed).

[9] Goethe, "Faust," Act V, Scene 5. Literal translation: "And he does not know how to take possession of all treasures." Bayard Taylor translation (New York: The Modern Library, Random House):

"And he knows not how to measure
True possession of his treasure."

[10] Freud, "Instincts and their Vicissitudes," *Collected Papers,* IV, 76.

I was thus justified in introducing the term "ego feeling" (*Ichgefühl*)[11] into psychoanalytic literature in my paper. "Narcissism in the Structure of the Ego," [12] but I might just as well in this context speak of "ego libido" or of "objectless narcissism." The latter term would also indicate the drive-dynamics in the ego feeling, viz., that it constitutes the stage of fore-pleasure of the libido.

It may seem amazing to speak of "objectless narcissism," since it has become customary to consider and designate object libido and narcissism as absolute antitheses. But they are not antithetic conceptually, because certain types of narcissism, disregarding the ego feeling, always have the ego or parts of it as their object. In actual antithesis to each other are "object cathexis" and "ego cathexis"; the first term indicates that the object, and the second that the ego, is that which is cathected by the libido, that which is experienced with pleasurable desire. It is the purpose of the present paper to describe this antithesis.

We come nearer to what I believe to be the correct conception of the observed material if we make an assumption in regard to the origin of the ego feeling which differs somewhat from Freud's view. Assumptions which are arrived at non-psychoanalytically are permitted with regard to these problems as they have not yet been investigated by psychoanalytic methods and, perhaps, may never be investigable by this method.

It is Freud's basic assumption that ". . . it is impossible to suppose that a unity comparable to the ego can exist in the individual from the very start; the ego has to develop . . ." [13] This assumption derives from the non-unitary nature of the "id." I hold, however, that an ego feeling is present from the very beginning, earlier than any other content of consciousness. This hypothesis corresponds to that of many philosophers and

. . . .

[11]This word (the German original) appears in Freud's paper "Mourning and Melancholia," *Collected Papers*, IV, 155: "The melancholiac displays . . . an extraordinary fall in his self-esteem (*Ichgefühl*), an impoverishment of his ego on a grand scale."

[12]See Chapter 2.

[13]Freud, "On Narcissism," *Collected Papers*, IV, 34.

psychologists[14] and to the view shared by many biologists that a germ of consciousness—I would like to call it a rudimentary ego feeling—pertains to every protoplasmic organism, even the lowest one, and thus to every living being.

I should like to adduce two more observations as indirect argument for the assumption that an ego feeling exists from the very beginning. It sometimes happens that for a short time we lack conscious ideational content; nevertheless we sense our bodily ego and also, distinctly, a psychic ego feeling. The latter is empty of mental and emotional functions. Since these are certainly gradually acquired, it is unlikely that the psychic ego feeling alone would remain preserved if it had not been present from the very beginning, though undistinguished from the mental content. In addition, self-observation shows that in the process of falling asleep or of fainting the psychic ego feeling is the last to disappear. The fact that it vanishes last speaks in favor of the view that it was present at the first. In consciousness it was always connected with a content of sensations, later of representations as well; and while these changed, a psychic ego feeling must have been present as a continuum in the changing state. This ego feeling first creates the ego by encompassing all experiences and experience traces, and then, due to the libidinal cathexis which is continuously fed by the drives, it waxes with the ego.

Finally, an argument from biology supports the view that the erogenity of the ego is present from the beginning. We know that those chemical influences, which later feed the libido functions as hormones, act in a formative way on the whole organism prior to birth; there is no reason why they should not also furnish to the psyche, from its awakening, the libidinal element which manifests itself in the ego feeling.

The gradual build-up of the ego occurs through the new acquisition of entire groups of experience-representations and their memory traces, which are drive-cathected from the id; they derive from internal and external impressions or from reactions to them. These are standardized partly in a hereditary and

. . . .

[14]T. K. Oesterreich, *Die Phänomenologie des Ich in ihren Grundproblemen,* (The Phenomenology of the Ego in its Basic Problems), Leipzig, 1910.

partly in an acquired way, and the ego, in spite of their dependence on the individual forces of the id, disposes them in given order, integrates them, and attaches them to itself. The ego feeling, the primary ego libido, encompasses every such new acquisition. The expansion of the ego boundaries consists in this process of annexation along with ego feeling, and we have only to recall the familiar phenomenon of regression in order to understand the manner of their later pathological shrinking.

This time of ego development is the period in which primary narcissism rules. For, while the incorporation into the ego proceeds, each ego state achieves autoerotic satisfaction by way of the newly acquired functions and representations. In other words, while the ego comes into being and grows, pleasure is derived from ego-felt experiences, of which those that are actually autoerotically accentuated—first of all those of one's own body, but also those of the visual and auditory perceptions—are, in accordance with the pleasure principle, more strongly cathected with ego feeling. In the ego feeling of the adult the erogenous zones still show themselves to be particularly sensitized. However, the entire ego, too, is the object of this primary self-love, in as much as the entire body is enjoyed entirely, in the many movements performed with autoerotic pleasure and in the pleasures of touching and looking which begin early. It is more difficult to obtain a clear idea of the primary narcissistic cathexis of the mental functions, which to the adult appear wanting in libido, what we call "dry." However, the observation of the ego pleasure with which children make a game of them, and the fact that neurotics and psychotics invest a great deal of libido in these functions, do not leave any doubt that they, too, are cathected with both ego feeling and primary narcissism. The states of depersonalization mentioned above confirm this view.

We understand now why "primary narcissism" at its peak, with its strong id derived drive and pleasure energy, very much overshadows the simple ego feeling. One's own ego feeling as such becomes perceptible only upon the repression of the autoerotic experiences and experience traces, with the predominance of the interest for objects. But even for the adult ego feeling is so much obscured by autoerotic, and even more by object libidinal contents of consciousness, that only in the case of variations and disturbances could it attract the attention of self-observing persons and of the researcher.

In so far as "primary narcissism" in the child encompasses his own individuality, we can—once our attention has been directed to it by Freud's discovery—convince ourselves directly of its existence through observing the behavior of the infant. The fact that in the child narcissism is even more clearly apparent than in animals and also, probably, than in primitive man, is due to the circumstance that the human offspring is spared for a long time from the danger of the external world and the continuous fear of it, because the human being has, of all creatures, the longest period of dependency. Observation of a spoiled pet, however, will also disclose unequivocally narcissistic behavior.

In so far, however, as primary narcissism encompasses the external world, we cannot observe it but can only deduce its presence. It is therefore more difficult to conceive this part of the libido doctrine as reality-description, and it is usually held to be mere theory. For in the adult's conception of the external world, the object cathexes so much outweigh primary narcissism that the latter can be experienced only in states of devotion and rapture, the highest degrees of which we call ecstasy and mystical union[15]—where, as some philosophers express it, the "realm of freedom begins" and the *principium individuationis* with the laws of causality seems to end.

Yet Hanns Sachs' paper on narcissism, the first to follow Freud's presentation, dealt with that type of narcissism which refers to objects of the external world, and the repression and projection of which lead to the animistic conception of the world as found in primitive man. In the stage of primary narcissism, the child and primitive man behave in a different way

. . . .

[15]In her paper, "Zufriedenheit, Glück und Ekstase," (Contentment, Happiness, and Ecstasy), Helene Deutsch has pointed out the re-establishment of a narcissistic unity and the expansion of the ego and its boundaries. *Internat. Zeitschrift f. Psychoanalyse*, XIII (1927), 410-19.

than later, after the establishment of the ego boundary, when the objects of the external world are *felt*,[16] not merely recognized, as being outside the individual. In the first place, children experience some of the changes happening to external objects as if they had happened to themselves, and therefore react with anxiety and anger, with pleasure and distress, although "nothing has happened to them," according to the adult's conception. Secondly, however, they are independent of the happenings of the external world because they have the capacity to substitute for it their continuously cathected representations of that world, which are experienced with full ego feeling.

Hence, in the stage of predominant primary narcissism the ego boundary coincides with the child's entire conceptual world, from which current consciousness singles out a small part which in its context does not yet correspond to reality. We may suppose that the mental processes of this period occur in the form of primary processes; the occurrence of displacement, condensation, and substitution by the opposite is amply demonstrated later on by the individual use of words and by neologisms. But even at this early stage the distribution of the intensities of libido cathexis corresponds to the interest in the external world. That which the child desires more strongly and frequently, early and consistently obtains the correct designation, and such a designation becomes more solidly rooted whenever a need is satisfied. Therefore, just as with primitive man, a kind of reality integration can take place in spite of the narcissistic cathexis of the external world, because the narcissistic cathexis is not diffused equally over the entire conceptual world, but, depending on the strength of autoerotic satisfaction of the erogenous zones achieved by an object, a stronger cathexis is concentrated on the representations of this particular object. The repetition and more intensive cathexis of the desired and the vital object representations are at this stage still quite in accordance with the pleasure principle.

Thus, from the very beginning, the primary ego feeling also includes the external world, which expands steadily through
. . . .

[16]Compare "Some Variations in Ego Feeling," Chapter 1.

new experiences. Its various sections, that is, their representations, are cathected with narcissism, not equally, but in varying intensity, as are the parts of the body. Nevertheless the object cathexis is of a purely narcissistic nature and not yet that of object libido. Those things which are more intensively cathected narcissistically assume the character of objects only through the union of the libidinal desire with the function of the self-preservative drives. But their representations are felt as *belonging to the ego,* although the objects are desired as means of satisfaction by the self-preservative drives and by the libido. Only when the small child feels the *ego distance of the object,* has primary narcissism lost its exclusive validity for the function in question. For instance, as long as both the representation of the mother's breast and the delight of sucking are *cathected with ego feeling,* it is true that the pleasure of sucking and the appeasement of hunger are longed for, and the breast is sought as the means to these ends; but, although the mother's breast is actually craved, it is not yet external to the ego feeling. Only when it is experienced as alien, as *withdrawn from the ego feeling,* does it receive an object libidinal cathexis. The concept of the ego feeling in this way facilitates understanding of primary narcissism as it is applied to the representations of the external world.

Hence in primary narcissism there are no object cathexes uncathected by ego feeling. Whatever seeks satisfaction and whatever gives satisfaction—the former being the subject, the latter the object, of the libido—is bodily, and is in its mental representation cathected with ego feeling, that is, with integrated ego libido. As long as the child does not yet have a representation of his own ego, the ego exists only as subject, and only as subject experiences itself in its parts. Primary narcissism may therefore be designated as the subject level of the ego.

The development of object cathexes *outside* the ego puts an end to the exclusive dominance of primary narcissism. However, we must not imagine this period of narcissism as ending with a particular event—as the textbooks of history imply in, say, separating antiquity from the Middle Ages. The external world is not suddenly discovered as something separate from the ego and thereby, also, the ego as something different from the external world. The object level of the ego has to be delimited for every individual relationship. At first, one object after another is laboriously acquired as such; in the case of more intense drive excitation—for instance, in affect due to a deprivation—the primary narcissistic cathexis may quantitatively overshadow the object cathexis to such an extent that any kind of "objectivity" is bound to disappear.

Before discussing the role of the ego feeling of the individual at the object level, I would like to draw attention to a difference between the ego libido transformed into ego feeling and the primary narcissism, a phenomenon which can be clearly observed also in the adult. Breuer first formulated the hypothesis that we have to distinguish between resting and mobile cathexes. Otto Gross advanced the same basic idea in his doctrine of the primary and secondary function.[17] In his metapsychological writings Freud acknowledged Breuer's idea as representing deepest insight.[18]

So far we have discussed ego feeling separately from its autoerotic reinforcement in the stage of "primary narcissism." The question arises whether these two components are not also different from each other with regard to rest and mobility. The observation of the adult teaches that the ego feeling in the ego boundary concerned increases whenever attention or volition is directed toward an object. If we have assigned the character of fore-pleasure to the ego feeling, the mobility of the libido cathexis becomes understandable because with every such increase the tension of fore-pleasure increases and seeks satisfaction (end pleasure). On the other hand, we have taken for granted that it is precisely the autoerotic satisfaction by which very important portions of the ego are more strongly cathected with narcissism. It does not make any difference whether a drive increase from the id or a stimulus from the outside disturbs this state of satisfaction directly or over various preconscious or unconscious routes. In either case the fore-pleasure factor in primary narcissism, and thereby the ego feeling of the

. . . .

[17]O. Gross, *Die Cerebrale Sekundärfunktion* (The Cerebral Secondary Function), Leipzig, 1902.
[18]Freud, "The Unconscious," *Collected Papers*, IV, 121.

ego boundary in question, will be enhanced. Therefore, we may surmise that in every mental act the movable cathexes derive from the fore-pleasure tension of the unsatisfied libido, and the resting ones correspond to the satisfied quantities of libido.

Yet this distinction cannot be the correct dynamic explanation of Breuer's view, because the libido must certainly lose its energy with satisfaction. The cathexes do come to a state of rest following their satisfaction, but they cease to exist, they do not continue as "resting" ones. The autoerotic satisfactions—and similarly, later, the object libidinal ones—thus only result in points of rest in the fluctuations of libido. As points of rest, however, they have a special significance: namely, since once obtained, satisfaction is sought again from the same representations and processes, these points of rest will always be cathected anew with libido which seeks satisfaction. The libido will appear as "resting" only inasmuch as it does not flow out in other directions but finds its gratification at these points. Therefore we can speak in general of *apparently* resting cathexis whenever no greater amount of libido flows out from a psychic element, or vanishes upon satisfaction, than flows toward that element. ("Element" is used as a general term for every kind of individual mental apparatus or mental process which is cathected with libido).

The observation of the ego boundary allows further conclusions in regard to the problem of resting and mobile cathexes. We know that in general, in the waking state, the entire ego boundary remains constantly cathected with ego feeling. Hence we may conclude that, on the whole, a certain amount of unsatisfied libido (of the fore-pleasure type) remains in the resting state, although unsatiated. This amount is quite different for different individuals and for different elements and functions in the same individual. Only if this lasting cathexis undergoes an increase will it have the tendency to flow off. This is a general assumption underlying the libido theory and it is confirmed once more through the observation of the ego feeling.

In order that more than this measure of libido be maintained in the resting state, its flowing off and its satisfaction must be prevented. Observation of the ego boundary in depersonalization shows that object libido is prevented from flowing off if the ego boundary withdraws from the objects in question or from the libidinally cathected functions. Thus we see that one way of maintaining libido in the resting state is the withdrawal of the encountering libido cathexis, which in depersonalization is recognizable in the divestment of the ego boundary of ego feeling. May I point out here that Freud postulated the same mechanism for the origin of repression, insofar as in this phenomenon the cathexis is withdrawn by the preconscious.

According to Freud there are still other mechanisms which prevent the libido from flowing off; however, they do not belong to the present subject. The preceding discussion was important for this topic because it showed that the withdrawal of the ego boundary—more precisely, the withdrawal of the ego feeling—prevents the flowing off of the libido which had cathected the representation abandoned by the ego. In the analysis of the states of estrangement and depersonalization, I found (as did Reik and Sadger later) that terror and anxiety experiences bring about the states of estrangement, i.e., the withdrawal of the ego boundary. We may, therefore, assume that primitive man was forced to detach his ego from the external world and to abandon primary narcissism only laboriously and under the pressure of the frightening external world. The child follows the same development, but it is substantially facilitated by the powerful protection of father and mother.

What role can we ascribe to the ego libido (the ego feeling) and to the ego boundary in later development? In our discussion we shall distinguish the relationship of the individual object cathexes to the ego boundary from the total development of the ego boundary. According to Freud, this development consists in the transformation of the pleasure ego into the reality ego and, again, the transformation of the latter into a purified pleasure ego as a reaction to the intrusion of the object.[19] As far as I was able to think through this part of metapsychology, the acquisition of the object cathexes corresponds to the first process, and the abandonment of the previous ego boundaries corresponds to the second process.

. . . .

[19] Freud, "Instincts and their Vicissitudes," Collected Papers, IV, 78.

The ego boundary withdraws from objects whenever the child experiences disappointments from them, whenever he finds that they are not subservient to his wishes, and whenever he undergoes pain, grief, anxiety, and even fright from them. The process is hereditarily determined to such an extent that I do not know whether the most accurate observation of the healthy person will be able to point out external causes. Perhaps the nightly interruption of the ego feeling in sleep, which is so easily observable, is sufficient to bring about the *gradual* change of the ego boundary in the healthy person. In any case it plays a significant role. In pathological cases, such as in all kinds of transitory or permanent estrangement, the traumatic origin is demonstrable; the estrangement is noticed suddenly, whether it ensues following a single frightening experience or a chronic severely injurious one.

In addition I should like to note, diverging somewhat from Freud, that—speaking in the image chosen by him—the development of object cathexes cannot be merely a matter of pseudopods which the narcissistic libido-reservoir, like an amoeba, extends toward the objects. The process must always be one in which the total ego libido withdraws from the objects leaving behind only object cathexes. It withdraws from the objects which had been narcissistically cathected in early development, as well as from those acquired only later upon transitory contacts, at a time when the ego boundary had already withdrawn to leave the external world as a whole lying outside, and only parts of that world, though large ones, remain narcissistically cathected and pertaining to the ego. *Object cathexes ensue when the ego boundary again withdraws from the object representations, that is, from the memory traces of the object engrams.* Then, on the one hand, we have the ego which is cathected with total ego libido and, in contrast, the individual object representations in increasing numbers, which are ordinarily cathected with small quantities of libido but, nevertheless, can be cathected from the id with strong intensities. Psychoanalytic experience indicates that these object cathexes, isolated from the ego, have their own regular vicissitudes of libido and that, for instance, repression, the failure of which leads to symptom formation, concerns these representations.

Self-observation, with which many communications of other authors are in agreement, necessitates a new assumption in the libido theory. Observation of the ego feeling confirms the fact that the *libido of the ego boundary* (recognizable as ego feeling) and the *libido of the object representations* again fuse, at least in all psychic acts which are fully experienced. Thereby they either achieve satisfaction (for instance, that of simple recognition), or they induce, in the case of incomplete satisfaction, further conscious and preconscious psychic processes with or without contact with the ego boundary (that is, with or without further contribution on the part of the ego libido). Whether such unions of ego libido and object libido may also occur without our conscious awareness is, I emphasize, an important psychoanalytical problem.

In every unification of ego libidinal boundary and object representation, a transitory enlargement of the ego boundary ensues; hence my discussion of the further relationship of ego libido and object libido reverts to Freud's conception of the encompassment and abandonment of objects. (The individual object representation is, of course, only the simplest example; the process usually occurs in an analogous manner in complicated processes and functions.) The only difference between my view and that of Freud concerns the origin of the object cathexes.

In all conscious unions of ego libido and libidinal object cathexis, not only do we have awareness of the processes but we also feel the vividness and reality of the perception or of the thinking, or of the affect as well. As, for a particular ego boundary, the intensity of ego libidinal (primary narcissistic) cathexis may vary from the most vivid ego feeling (at its highest degree in mania or enthusiasm) to the divestment in estrangement, so also the satisfaction and the sensation of full experience may occur in all degrees of intensity. What Schilder designates as "ego distance" and "ego nearness" of a process cannot be explained in terms of extent of separation from the ego; neither can a process be conscious to a varying degree. Instead, the libido intensity of the ego boundary is variably great. The fact of becoming conscious is contained in every union of ego libido and object libido. However, there is more in it than a mere becoming conscious, because conscious awareness is maintained even in the case of complete estrangement. Since the ego feeling is a feature of the ego's being permanently conscious, the difference between a process which is conscious and one which is fully egotized could be only a quantitative one. More likely there are two distinct functions operating on the ego boundary, one concerning also the core of the ego, and thereby causing the quality of being conscious, and the other causing only the ego boundary feeling.

Thus we have presented the issue by stating that the narcissistic cathexes recede from the external objects, and also that, more and more, the thinking functions and the affective reactions develop and occur preconsciously outside the ego feeling, though always and in every ensuing experience to be encompassed anew by the ego boundaries and by consciousness.[20]

What, however, happens to the old narcissistic boundary of the ego while the field of the object cathexes, which are encompassed at any given time by the ego boundary, is enlarged and with it the extent of the ego boundary itself? The answer cannot be derived theoretically but can only be gleaned from experience. One thing is certain: No rational division, as it were, occurs between the cathexes of the ego and of the object representations, nor do bodily and psychic elements and the external world each obtain their own specific cathexis.

If development took such an orderly course, the problems which keep us occupied could be resolved in a few sentences. Indeed, the old associationist psychology would not have had to be enlightened at all by psychoanalysis. It would have been adequate to distinguish representation, sensation, perception, feeling, etc. and their further combinations and integration. The stabilization of integration would keep everything functioning in well devised channels which could be investigated from physiological or experimental psychological points of view. The psychic agencies thus developed would awaken each

. . . .

[20]By comparison with later papers and with personal communications, it is apparent that here Federn had not yet formulated the concept that the ego feeling encompasses the preconscious. True, the single contents of the preconscious are not conscious at every moment; but the conscious feeling of disposing of the preconscious material is in agreement with Federn's later formulations.—E.W.

other, keep each other in suspension, let each other sleep, and also work against each other (for instance, if contradictory messages were to arrive) so that they could act also as inhibitory functions. But, by and large, they would not only accomplish the tasks assigned to them in an orderly manner but would also get the better of the "mob" of drives, unless somewhere an official fell ill or the communication system between the offices failed to operate. Behold the mental picture of the microcosm of the mind, as it was originally drawn after the contemporary European governmental organization by the old academic psychology.

Psychoanalysis has destroyed all vestiges of this idyll. In pursuing the comparison it would be interesting to investigate to what extent the mental picture it has created of the mind corresponds in turn to the social order at the time of its origin. Here we want to stress only two novel features in the new representation of the mind (I do not call it a picture because there are too many dimensions to it). In the first place, continuing to speak in terms of the simile, we understand that there are *public, private,* and *concealed* processes; and secondly, we consider that from the drives upward, and perhaps even among the drives themselves, there is stratification which is, however, neither uniform nor permanent.

Obviously, and on the surface, the ego feeling separates the external world from the ego, and the psychic ego feeling sets off the body from the psyche. Clandestinely, as it were, the narcissistic cathexes with ego feeling of many representations of the external world persist, they change and develop, they are given up and again are newly invested. Most deeply hidden, even from one's own consciousness, the entire world of primary narcissism remains extant, as dreams and psychosis reveal; for, the primary narcissistic ego (which comprised external world and individual) is repressed and becomes unconscious in its totality. The infant's image of the world and ego feeling have become completely unconscious in the adult, but evidence their existence by the fact that they may return in psychoses. I believe this is a new conception since usually only repression of the object representations and their elaborations are discussed.

Thus, in the establishment of the new ego boundary three things occur:

(1) The external world is *egotistically* grasped through the object cathexes: reality adaptation of the ego (of the reality ego) to the world.

(2) The external world is *egocentrically* encompassed by the ego through narcissistic cathexis: annexation of the representations of the world to the ego in conformity with the individual's wishes.

(3) The previous ego is repressed: unconscious continuation of the *ego-cosmic* ego.

This pictures side by side, in Freud's words, the reality ego and the purified pleasure ego—and also, not mentioned by Freud, the continued existence in the unconscious of the primordial ego which encompassed the world and the ego narcissistically and which Trigant Burrow has designated as the "preconscious." [21] We shall discuss the latter when we examine the ego feelings and ego boundaries which delimit the superego. Here we shall deal with the relation of the conscious ego boundaries to each other and to the object cathexes.

As we pointed out earlier, the ego boundary becomes continually more mobile and encompasses increasingly more functions and more representations. The release of the external world from the ego feeling has had as its goal its conquest and mastery; for this purpose all abilities and skills of mind and body are applied, and to the extent to which they are conscious, and not estranged, the ego feeling encompasses them. Thus, at the stage of the reality ego and the purified pleasure ego, the ego boundary, in regard to the latter, becomes much more multiform and richly structured than it had been at the stage of total narcissism. With the maturation of body and mind, both the bodily and the psychic ego boundaries expand gradually. Pathological cases reveal that, not only in early development, but also later on, entire ego boundaries with their corresponding narcissistic cathexes may be repressed, since in exceptional cases such mid-developmental ego states are main-

. . . .

[21] The term is quoted in English in the German text, in order to indicate the special meaning in which Burrow uses the term.—E.W.

tained. Moreover, what we call fixation is a state correlated with a more rigid formation of a specific size and boundary of the ego. As we learn from cases of exhibitionism and masochism, if a specific component drive accentuates a particular ego boundary, this boundary will be more strongly cathected. As it is not possible then to enlarge it by slow development, repression is needed in order to progress past such stages. (Freud has spoken analogously of the peace-ego and the war-ego of the war-neurotics.) From a certain age on, which differs individually, such spells of repression in regard to the ego boundary cease completely and it undergoes further changes only gradually with newly acquired functions: the person remains the same. The basic experience that an amnestic period is brought to a close by specific events is therefore due, not only to the repression of interconnected object representations, but also, and mainly, to the repression of one drive-component and of the ego boundary which is cathected by that component in a characteristic manner. As stated above, this is the case especially in regard to the mental functions, but at times also in regard to the body and its functions.

Such a strongly fixated ego boundary often is not repressed because it and its cathexis has become unpleasant, just as primary total narcissism could not become devoid of pleasure; rather, the displeasure is due to the circumstance that *two narcissistic ego boundaries cannot co-exist without confusion*. Adults who quickly and frequently fall back to earlier ego states, with other ego boundaries, evidence insecurity and shame which make them highly uncomfortable. As a matter of fact, the repression from consciousness becomes necessary precisely because the individual could not consciously relinquish the previous sources of pleasure. It is probable that only a distressing external event can inaugurate and make possible the repression of the object representations concerning this event and the associated ego state and boundary. The postulate that object and ego cathexes are usually repressed simultaneously is in agreement with our general observation, stated above, that in every psychic occurrence object cathexis and cathexis of the ego at the ego boundary concerned are united.

Here we are in a position to indicate more precisely which

is the "ego boundary concerned." In every experience, the object representation, with its libido cathexis, unites with the narcissistically cathected representations of the same object which pertain permanently to the ego. The question raised previously —"What happens to the narcissistic ego boundary with the acquisition of object cathexes?"—we have answered by saying that it persists and it changes further. It is true that the newly acquired object cathexis has arisen because the narcissistically cathected ego boundary receded from the resistant or painful objects, or because the ego boundary only transitorily encompassed the new perception with ego feeling, so that the object representation could remain extant without ego feeling but invested with new object cathexis (stemming from the id). However, in accordance with psychoanalytic experience, in this case, too, nothing gets lost that has once been acquired. The fact that a new experience which remains extant as an object representation was gained with a withdrawn or immediately withdrawing ego boundary does not prevent the old representations, stemming from an earlier time and cathected with ego feeling, from persisting in memory; therefore, for the same object we now have two imprints (*Niederschriften*), as Freud called them in another connection, or engrams, in the sense of Semon. The one is narcissistically tinged, indistinct and does not accurately correspond to reality, except in the mind of geniuses, and even there it is always mixed with infantile elements; the other is fairly correct, recently acquired, and very accessible to rectification by new experience. Both unite in the experience because both are called into consciousness currently by a *perception* or by a *word image* which belong to both. *The more the narcissistic representation, or group of representations, corresponds in content to the object libidinal one, the more easily is the libido satisfied in their realization and unification.*

I know that this entire presentation will be difficult to accept. But self-observation makes it possible to distinguish, as they arise, the ego cathected contents from the object representations; the differentiation is easier in the wish invested mental processes than in the conceptual ones because the contents of the former are more strongly cathected with ego libido. Attached to both are libido quantities which are unified in the experience. Once one has observed the process as it occurs in wish invested groups of representations, one recognizes the same process in everyday thinking or acting. "Comprehending" means that a new representation element is invested with ego libido and assigned to an existing, orderly group. If there is no stronger, i.e., narcissistic, cathexis in the preconscious when an object representation arises, only the ego feeling (libido cathexis) of the ego boundary, as we now know it, is experienced as it flows to meet the emerging representation. If the ego feeling, too, is missing, estrangement ensues, as has been discussed before. Thus, the *narcissistically cathected* representation is *not the same* as the representation *cathected with object libido*.

Summarizing, we may state: The ego libido continues as a unity throughout the whole life in the ego feeling and in the cathexes which stem from autoerotism and strengthen the ego feeling. But this is possible only because the representations thus cathected no longer have the character of reality which they had at the stage of the exclusive domination of primary narcissism. They have surrendered it to the object impressions which impinge upon the ego boundary from the *outside*. For this purpose the memories of that stage at which they still had the character of reality, the memories of what I called above the *"ego-cosmic ego,"* had to be *repressed*. From the economic point of view, this complicated development was possible because there was a corresponding decrease in the libido supplied by the id to the old narcissistic cathexis, in its totality, as the libido needs of the real objects increased to the same degree.

Thus we see how both the central ego libido, with its changing boundaries, and the object cathexes, which build up in isolation, continuously evolve in this entire developmental struggle of reality adaptation versus the archaic, pleasurably narcissistic ego formation. The contiguity of the libido cathexes is interrupted by the isolation of the object cathexes and by the processes of repression. But we know that pathologic and physiologic alterations in the economy (sleep, dream, psychoanalysis, ecstasy) can restore the discontinued contiguity for a shorter or longer period.

Our exposition has also shown that every fully experienced

(not estranged) mental process unites currently, in a transitory way, the cathexes separated through the developments described: those of the reality ego, whose boundary is turned toward the apprehension of reality, that is, toward perception and motility, including speech; those of the purified pleasure ego, whose narcissistic boundary was described earlier; and those of the object representations. Thus, actually, reality adaptation must have disrupted, in every direction, the original narcissistic libidinal unity in such a way that it can be restored only through *cathexis displacements* which are *adapted* to the external world. Based upon the observation of the ego boundaries, another insight is gained which surprisingly demonstrates, even in the complex mental acts, the correctness of Freud's definition of the drive—that it tends to restore a previous state of things.

As we saw, the repressed "ego-cosmic ego" is not included in this restoration of the narcissistic unity, for an understandable reason. In the "ego-cosmic ego," reality and representation are *not* differentiated; therefore the adaptation of the mental contents to the reality of the current happenings of the external world, as conveyed by the external perceptions, would be disturbed by this "ego" and possibly by other spontaneous representations which are conceived of as real by the "primordial ego." If the "primordial ego" were not permanently repressed, the whole task of development—i.e., the correct reproduction, both permanently, and at any given moment, of the occurrences of the *external world* by the pictures and concepts of the *mental* occurrences—would be continuously confused and disturbed by unfamiliar, archaic, and early infantile representations regarded as real.

If, therefore—in the dream and in mental diseases—the repression of the "ego-cosmic ego" is lifted partially, phantoms actually enter the mature ego which developed later; they have the character of a physiologic regression to an early stage of the ego. Consequently, we can well understand that in a mentally diseased person hallucinations and delusions about himself and other people may emerge, while he still adjusts to the real world with his *remaining normal ego boundaries*. The ego boundaries in the dream and in the psychoses have not yet received attention, or certainly not enough. The awakening of the "primordial ego" in the dream is implied, though not *expressis verbis,* in Freud's metapsychological studies, in his theory of dream, and in other writings. There it is described as regression (historical and physiological); consequently, the concept presented here hardly differs from that of Freud.

Moreover, I would not have proffered this explanation, which seems fantastic at first sight, were it not for the interest we must take in the cooperation of the repressed "ego-cosmic ego" in the formation of one of the great agencies of the ego —namely, the "superego." Both primary and secondary narcissism and the roles of the ego as subject and object in the superego must be delineated with as much precision as possible.

I know that many psychoanalysts believe such investigations to be more or less skillful mental acrobatics, and see in Freud's concept of the superego no more than an excellent formula for integrating reactions, which were formerly examined separately, on the basis of their common denominator, demanding and inhibiting. Other psychoanalysts take just the opposite position, regarding the superego as if it were another person who had lodged himself in the psyche as a kind of dragonnade, and they find no cause for wonder at the formation of such a foreign body; on the contrary, they are glad to have obtained in the "superego" a scape-goat, as it were. Other authors, however, notably Alexander, Fenichel, Glover, Jones, and Odier, have worked hard to reach an understanding of the formation of the superego. Clear and meaningful though Freud's presentations are, one has to work through them to fully acquire their significance.

To the extent to which I was able to observe others and myself, I recognized Freud's concept of the superego as a description of reality and did not consider it merely a theoretical formulation.

First let us cautiously draw conclusions from self-observation of the ego feeling in regard to the subjective delimitation of ego and superego. Every such conclusion must be drawn with great circumspection, since both one's own observations and the observations of others are always subjective. Once the ego feeling as an object of self-experience arouses more psychological interest, we shall collect more material for comparison and also be able to utilize more correctly the earlier communications; for whatever has been described in the literature of all schools as self-knowledge, self-contemplation, and self-education refers to the relation of superego to ego. One thing is certain: be it demanding, prohibiting, or permitting, the superego, in its conscious as well as in its unconscious operation, always deals in the first place with the ego. In the process, both experience "moral" pleasure or displeasure, according to the gratification or non-gratification of the libido invested by the superego in the ego and vice versa. I am inclined to believe that the superego itself does not have any executive power at its disposal. Yet the libidinal attachment of the ego to the superego is so great that pleasure may become bliss and displeasure torment. Under the influence of this pleasure and displeasure, the ego accepts the superego's orders according to the latter's libidinal cathexes, and it experiences its own executive function as its "I ought." However, I am not sure yet whether "I must" implies an executive power of the superego. The structure of the superego is probably different in different character types. The superego may also deal with other persons not directly, but through identification of the ego or the superego, or both, with the "egos" and "superegos" of the other person.

What do we feel in regard to the ego boundary turned toward the superego? Ego and superego are separated by a particularly sharp boundary. This statement suggests a curious and extremely important implication of the ego feeling. We clearly experience the fact that the ego feeling can cathect a boundary which borders, not on the external world, but on an inner world, or, more precisely, on another boundary of the ego. We remember here that cases of depersonalization have furnished us many examples of pathological states in which an internal process of the ego is experienced as estranged. Thus we see that a particular type of estrangement occurs if the ego feeling (the ego libidinal cathexis) recedes from an ego boundary which borders on another ego boundary rather than on the external world.

This curious finding, arrived at not by speculation but via the self-observation of persons suffering from estrangement, leads us to new insight into the nature of affects. In the estrangement of the inner world, which is a form of depersonalization, the patient no longer senses his affects as connected with his ego. Therefore, according to our conception, we may conclude that many or all *affects* operate *between two ego boundaries* which touch on each other. Thus, to formulate a theory of the affects it will be necessary to examine the individual affects with regard to this kind of special localization, and to determine in general the function of the affects in the libido economy which, as we have seen, operates at the ego boundaries.

Let us now return to the problem of the ego boundaries between ego and superego. There are specific functions (considering, deliberating, affirming, denying, praising, blaming, and the like) which in the healthy person are strongly cathected with ego feeling, whatever their object. If these functions have the self as object, the ego also feels itself as an object of such self-preoccupation. With others as objects, it is the ego, as well as the superego, which usually exercises these functions. Probably different people behave differently in regard to the self as object. The ego of a simple, naive person leaves occupation with the self to the superego to a larger extent than does a contemplatively or scientifically inclined self-observer.

One would think that in the process of self-supervision the ego might well feel itself to be the object of supervision by the superego; in the other functions mentioned above, however, the object, is not truly the ego itself but rather the *representations* which one has formed of the ego. More precisely, they are object cathexes—that is, the cathexes of representations of the ego, of the qualities of the ego, and of the judgments about it. So far, this seems correct, even self-evident. However, in clear recognition that a good part of secondary narcissism has such *representations of the ego,* one's thoughts about one's ego, as its object, I wish to draw attention specifically to the fact that, not only is the cathexis of such object representations which refer to oneself particularly intense, the ego also feels itself as object of the functions[22] (in a way similar, say, to that in which an animal notices or senses if one speaks of it). In other words, ego boundaries come in contact. It is a special task of self discipline to ignore or eliminate the sensation of being the object of one's self-observation if one attempts to know and guide oneself.

Such internal contact, however, by no means exists only between ego and superego, but it occurs at all the various boundaries which are cathected with ego feeling, as soon as the ego or a part thereof becomes the object of one of its functions. Again, it is through the organization and higher development of the psyche that narcissism ceases to be autoerotism and turns into a distinct libidinal relation of a subject to an object; both lie inside the ego but seem most frequently to be differentiated functions or parts of the ego. To avoid the misunderstanding that I do not recognize, nor accept theoretically, the antithesis between ego libido and object cathexis, I would like to emphasize once more the difference between true object cathexis and the cathexis of the ego as the object of narcissism. The object cathexes are isolated libido quantities invested to a varying degree of stability in the representations of concrete objects and in other elements; the narcissistic cathexis is a stronger cathexis of an ego boundary, but is always contiguous to the total ego libido of the entire ego.

Let us recall here that Freud considered the relation of the ego to itself described here, to be the original one, both for narcissism as a whole, for the "loving of one's self," and for the component drives of sadism and scopophilia. From this relation evolves the active and passive attitude toward the object (loving and being loved, the pleasurable tormenting and

. . . .

[22]In this paper I intentionally use the general term "function" because, for the sake of comprehensibility, I wish to avoid discussion of non-libidinal forces both in and outside of the ego. I have two reasons for this: In the first place I do not yet know enough about the relation of libido to the other drives to discuss it systematically; and secondly, such a systematic discussion would be incomprehensible to the reader, or at least could not become a living reality for him, as long as the new findings and conclusions have not yet been accepted by him.

being tormented, pleasurable looking-at and displaying oneself). We differ from this conception in that only with the higher development of the ego can we imagine a proper "loving oneself." Prior to this, in the stage of pure psychic autoerotism, which is the original expression of primary narcissism, we recognize only the sensation of craving for pleasure and its satisfaction in one's own person, not yet a *directing* of the libido toward oneself. Stemming from the early autoerotic total experience, the libidinal unity and the pleasurableness in the ego feeling persist; utilizing the psychology implicit in classical Greek grammar, the thought may be expressed by saying that primary narcissism has the character of the "middle voice" and that only later, after the ego meets with itself time and again in innumerable relationships, does it reach a *"reflexive"* form. We may express the situation more precisely, on the basis of studies of estrangement, by saying that the ego feeling cathects from two sides innumerable (preconscious) processes which occur outside the ego.

For instance, what we call self-complacency always requires a concentration of ego feeling at a boundary with which the individual encompasses his own qualities, functions, and achievements. In the person who is self-complacent, insecurity develops if the ego boundary which functions as object is as strongly cathected as the one which functions as subject of narcissism. As mentioned before, the lasting simultaneous cathexis of several ego boundaries on reaching a certain degree of intensity and extension results in confusion. Some cases of *embarrassment neurosis* and of *blushing* have this mechanism.

If I have succeeded in accustoming the reader to the concept of ego boundaries contacting each other, I can now answer the question concerning the narcissistic cathexis of the superego. According to what has been said, it is clear that as soon as the organization of the ego develops the functions of moral evaluation, demand, and rejection, these functions will operate between two ego boundaries, affectively and narcissistically, so that whenever the superego goes into action these functions become cathectable with ego feeling from two ego boundaries. If, however, this statement described the process of cathexis exhaustively, the special emphasis of the superego would properly characterize no more than a special task of the ego; it would not, as Freud really wished, designate the specific double-structure of the ego in the broader sense. Indeed, this doubleness could be simulated by the fact that the delimitation of ego feeling comes to awareness with particular conciseness and distinctiveness between the ego and the functions comprised by the superego.

Thus, the superego would be sheathed, as it were, in the ego, but would be no more than a specially developed group of functions of the ego, sharing its center with the ego's other peripheries. This connection could become so tenuous that, as has been said, a double structure would be simulated. We are aware of the grandiose antagonism of ego and superego, which Alexander[23] has made impressively vivid by calling it reciprocal over-trumping and outwitting, and which led Nietzsche to speak of the "self-hangman and self-judge." Thus in the case of a stronger libido cathexis (primarily a sadistic one), the boundary between ego and superego leads to division in the ego, so that one becomes aware in oneself of that double structure which appeared questionable at first.

Could such doubleness perhaps come about merely by the excessively strong libido cathexis of this group of functions? This renders the corresponding ego boundary oversensitive to frustration, while at the same time the conditions for satisfaction are particularly difficult since for this purpose self-evaluation would have to acknowledge all *ego ideals* as achieved by the real ego. Disappointment, the absence of satisfaction, would cause the two boundaries to be permanently experienced as cathected with libido, creating irritation, pain, and agonizing bitterness on the one side, and a state of stirred-up emotionality on the other. The most grandiose projection of this libidinal cathexis tension is Dante's *Inferno!*

There are narcissistic injuries of another, not a moral kind, the infliction of which the ego cannot overcome; it remains painfully encroached on itself. The discrepancy between an ego created in fantasy and the actual person can be profoundly

. . . .

[23] F. Alexander, *Psychoanalysis of the Total Personality*, (Washington, D. C.: Nervous & Mental Disease Monograph Series, No. 52, 1930).

injurious to narcissism, and yet the sensation of ego unity does
not get lost, except in cases of hysteria, i.e., under abnormal conditions; the ego feeling maintains the unity between the real
egocentric ego, its fantasies, and the reality ego.

The superego alone is separated so definitely from the ego
that such sadism can break out between them. Not until severe
psychoses develop can the superego dissolve in the ego. We
do not speak here of deficient arrangement of the functions of
the superego. In the normal person harmony is established
through a certain reciprocal moderation and yielding; in the
obsessional neurosis we see the neurotic detours to this objective; in mania the libido cathexis of the ego is increased to such
an extent that by comparison the superego is cathected weakly
and is incapacitated; in melancholia the opposite obtains; in
pathological senescence the superego frequently loses the supply of libidinal cathexis from the id earlier than does the ego.

Thus, I conclude from my conception of the superego that
the strict supervision on the one side, and the intense fear of
this supervision on the other, must greatly accentuate the
boundary between ego and superego, but that the two are distinct entities from the very beginning, and, hence, that the
double structure actually exists.[24]

He who remembers some of his own dissonances and arguments between superego and ego, especially he who has experienced the torments of self-reproaches of a striving personality,
has learned that the ego feeling vacillates between ego and
superego in a peculiar manner, to be experienced in no other
situation, and that one cannot simultaneously be ego and superego—if one may use the expression. In order to change from
one ego feeling to the other, one must pass, as it were, through
a void, empty of ego feeling. One has lost the sensation of one's
ego before one gains that of one's superego, and vice versa.
How can this be explained?

One must assume that the ego and the superego actually
. . . .

[24] Latin grammar, as teacher of psychology, reminds me of a rule which I
learned almost fifty years ago. It is certainly peculiar that precisely those
words denoting functions of the superego (*piget, pudet, paenitet, taedet
atque miseret*) are inflected not in the first but in the third person, as
being of unknown origin, i.e., arising from the depth of the unconscious.

correspond to *two* ego feelings, that is, to *two unities of ego libido*, each homogeneous in itself, but not with the other; they do not have in *consciousness* a central contiguity. The fact that such contiguity neither is, nor can become, conscious (thus, that it is not preconscious either) does not exclude the assumption that, individually, ego and superego peripherally cathect common contents with libido, that both have an analogous distance from, and potential connection to, the object cathexes and the reality ego.

Freud resolved the riddle of conscience by uncovering the superego and by deriving the unconscious superego from identification with the commanding and prohibiting persons of childhood. We must assume that this identification develops with particular intensity and particularly early and that it can be traced back to the time of the primary narcissistic unitary ego. Since at that time the ego still reigned supreme, the inhibiting and commanding persons were also cathected with ego feeling (every command is, as a matter of fact, only a prohibition of doing differently and of omitting). As was discussed before, the primary narcissistic ("ego-cosmic") ego formation was repressed because it was in disagreement with reality adaptation; I now supplement and delimit my earlier exposition by adding that a portion of narcissistic ego cathexis remained unrepressed—that portion which concerned the parents, primarily the mother. The latter repression was omitted for the same reason that the former took place: because the maintenance of the parental agency in the ego not only did not contradict but rather corresponded to reality adaptation. However, a separation ensued between *that* ego which left the parents outside of its ego feeling and *that* ego which had absorbed the parents in itself. The latter became the superego. This explains the particular egoticity, as it were, of the superego, and also shows that the findings of various psychoanalysts (Klein, Rank, Jones, Clark, Burrow) in regard to the formation of the superego in the period *prior* to the Oedipus stage do not contradict the Freudian doctrine. The particular strength of the superego could thus be ascribed not only to the phylogenetic and ontogenetic impact of the father's sadism but rather to the power of both parents *and* to the supreme omnipotence with which primary narcissism once invested the child. Hence philosophy and the introspection of the righteous man lets Kant ascribe the same reality, and pay the same devotion to the categorical imperative as to the starry sky. Both were once experienced with the same ego feeling. But while the character of "egoticity" of the external world, being useless, sank down into the unconscious, that part of the external world which had so early begun to dominate the ego, being useful, continued to be maintained and invested with ego feeling; however, this part was not in the egocentric ego but had another center. In order to avoid confusion, the representation of the original persons was repressed; only the inhibiting and direction-giving power remained in consciousness. This nucleus represented psychically no more than the first inhibitions; therefore it was enlarged by many identifications until a useful, often an excessively strong, superego was formed.

I think it may be comprehensible now why ego and superego should have two ego boundaries so sharply separated from each other. A concept of the superego as an abstract formulation for functions which belong together has to be rejected.

While we have found an ego boundary between ego and superego in the normal person, curiously enough we are unable to establish the existence of such a boundary between mental and bodily ego. Perceptions of one's own body may, of course, become estranged if its parts are objects of seeing, hearing, and so forth. One's own voice is very frequently estranged. In psychoses of a hypochondriac type the ego feeling can be missing from a great variety of organs and functions. Schizophrenic patients often know more about their ego boundaries than do normal persons, just as they understand symbols for which the healthy person has no conscious interpretation. For instance, they are often aware of the depth of their bodily ego feeling. A patient of mine advanced this as the reason for his inability to use the organs which lacked ego feeling: "I will again be able to breathe right when I shall feel myself from tip to toe." Yet he did not complain of estrangement! Similarly, the healthy person has no feeling of estrangement when, in the process of slowly falling asleep, the bodily ego feeling disappears before the mental ego feeling. This fact does not contradict my earlier explanations. Estrangement develops only if (preconscious) functions which operate outside the ego no longer reach the ego. Decreases in the ego feeling proper (not in the boundaries) are not noticed as such; one has to concentrate one's attention on the phenomenon.

These discriminations should enable us to differentiate exactly between estrangement and depersonalization. (Occasionally the two terms are used indiscriminately.) If a process which takes place outside the ego reaches it from the preconscious without being invested with ego feeling in the process of becoming conscious, the sensation of estrangement is experienced. If representations which ordinarily pertain permanently to the conscious ego, those of the body in particular, lose their ego feeling, depersonalization ensues. That occurs in the phenomenon of splitting in abnormal awakening and in hysteria, as I have discussed previously. Then the body is felt as belonging solely to the external world, outside of the ego, and bound only by memory to the (historic) ego; it is really depersonalized, yet it is not experienced as estranged but as a new phenomenon never yet experienced. This extreme degree of depersonalization, which I described as only a transitory stage in awakening, came about because at that moment not even the reality ego had been established. The exact investigation of depersonalization proper will therefore permit certain deductions also in regard to the reality ego, just as the observation of estrangement enabled us to make inferences in regard to the "ego-centric" ego, as we called the narcissistically cathected ego. We may conclude that bodily and psychic ego feeling are subjectively a unity, divisible only through observation of the withdrawal of the ego feeling from the body. Thus the body has a three-fold position: it is part of the ego (not only known to be so objectively, but also experienced subjectively); it lies between ego and external world, because its organs mediate the impressions of the external world; and it is a part of the external world, because via the organs which are turned toward the external world, impressions of the body as object also impinge on the mental ego. This three-fold psychological role of the body seems to be important for the understanding of conversion. Incidentally, three groups of *Weltanschau-*

ung correspond to these functions: the idealistic, the monistic, and the materialistic; they are types of self-concepts. The fact that the idealistic mode, more than the others, makes a person happy is due to the circumstance that it re-establishes the primary, narcissistic conception and that it also meets one of the most powerful desires of secondary narcissism—namely, to love and exalt one's own body. Actually the entire ego libido derived the name "narcissism" from this beloved object. This name was most appropriately chosen to convey the idea, disturbing initially, that the antagonistic ego drives obtain libido from the sexual drive.

I have termed the turning of the libido from the outside toward one's own body as secondary narcissism, on the assumption that the beautiful Greek boy, with the awakening of love, first sought external objects, and only secondarily became the victim of the beauty of his own image. He thought he could at last embrace a beauty worthy of himself, then found himself and death. But, if we analyse it, should this kind of narcissism be designated as "secondary"? Did it re-establish the stage of loving oneself which is reached in early childhood? Rather, had not the beautiful boy remained at this earlier stage? Otherwise his self-image would not have appeared more attractive to him than some shepherd or shepherdess! Freud, however, designated "loving oneself" as the first stage of instinct-vicissitude; hence, certainly, as "primary." From what has been said, it follows that in the Freudian sense "primary" and "secondary" relate only to the history of the processes which lead to a particular cathexis, not to the kind of dynamics with which I have dealt here. We may say that primary narcissism is always objectless, that it is the source which feeds the ego feeling in the form of objectless, but always object-ready, libidinal striving, and that any investment in objects in narcissism is secondary. With the latter comment I depart from Freud's terminology but not from his views.

When I originally gave the lecture on which this paper is based,[25] the following were among my theses: 1) *primary* nar-

. . . .

[25]An abstract of this lecture, containing thirteen theses, appeared in *Internat. Zeitschrift f. Psychoanalyse*, XIV (1928), 572.

cissism is of ego libidinal nature, *secondary* narcissism is of object libidinal nature; and 2) the ego boundaries are not rigid, but are, at any given time, determined by the circumstance that psychic processes impinge upon the unitary primary-narcissistic cathexis; the unitary ego feeling is maintained through a contiguous narcissistic cathexis.

I must modify the first thesis, in regard not to content but to terminology. The term "secondary narcissism" was applied by Freud to the turning back toward the ego, or toward groups of representations or functions pertaining to the ego or having the ego as content, of a quantity of libido which had previously been turned toward an external object. I do not feel entitled, and it would also cause confusion, to use the term "secondary" to indicate object relations in narcissism, although the facts which are designated by the word "secondary" in both the first and the second sense coincide with each other not entirely and not in all cases.

I can formulate the thought of my first thesis more correctly in the following way: a) the ego feeling is maintained by objectless ego libido, which corresponds to the fore-pleasure of the drive; b) narcissism begins as *"middle voice"* and becomes *"reflexive"* libido. In later development, too, "middle voice" and "reflexive" narcissism are to be differentiated.

With this formulation I use new terms for newly emphasized qualities, and the term "secondary" remains reserved to indicate a preceding and different investment of a narcissistic cathexis.

We may ask now, in what way does an *object* cathexis become a secondary narcissistic one? This may be the result of the expansion of the ego feeling to cover object representations. As a matter of fact, this is a transitory occurrence in every kind of topical psychic process. Once libidinal satisfaction or tension reduction of any other kind has been achieved, object and ego cathexis may have changed in character: the ego libido may encompass more elements of object representations than previously, and may do so permanently, or the opposite may obtain. The process is repeated innumerable times. For instance, identification comes about when the ego feeling permanently encompasses the entire group of representations concerning a person. Such transformations also take place unconsciously. On the other hand, as I stated above, ego libido may recede from representations and functions, so that even later in the topical experience they are less intensely cathected than before. Identifications may be relinquished. Thus, if the ego libidinal cathexis has decreased and the experience is reactivated by external perception or unconscious internal stimuli, the previously familiar object or the pertinent memory assumes the character of "strangeness." The beloved person actually impresses us as strange if we suddenly "do no longer care" for him; that is, if we have divested his representation of the ego libido with which it was formerly cathected. That the object cathexis may continue to exist for a long time regardless of such a changed situation is shown by psychoanalysis, which deals with unconscious and preconscious object cathexes. In cases in which object cathexes were repressed, or have faded because of libido displacement, the vague narcissistic image may be maintained for a long time. There is only a quantitative difference between the experience, known to everyone in everyday life, that a person previously loved may suddenly appear strange, and the other extreme of pathological estrangement. In his paper on "Neurosis and Psychosis," Freud raises the question as to: ". . . what that mechanism analogous to repression may be by which the ego severs itself from the outer world." [26] The divestment of the ego boundary of ego libido, and the resulting estrangement, proves to be the answer to this question. It plays a role every day in all detachments from non-repressible objects. There is an entirely different way in which object cathexes may be transformed into narcissistic ones which cannot be observed directly, but can be deduced, in the narcissistic neuropsychoses and the psychoses. Here the libido has been withdrawn from the objects by the id, and we now find increased ego libido, after an *unconscious* transformation of libido quantities.

It is certainly easier to influence the former process. The fact that detachment and new attachment of object cathexes may result from change of the ego boundary makes the curative

. . . .

[26] Freud, *Collected Papers*, II, 254.

effect of re-experiencing and remembering in psychoanalysis understandable. But where the libido is withdrawn from the external world by the id, psychoanalysis is helpless; actually, psychoanalysis can effect renewed attachments of object cathexes only if sufficient external ego boundary is still cathected strongly and permanently enough. Therefore, therapeutic results are not possible in severe melancholia or mania, nor in the catatonic, where ego libido is concentrated on inner processes.

If it is true that frequently narcissistic "images" of the objects exist in addition to the object cathexes, and that the ego and superego have ego boundaries which are separate, which, however, cathect some of these images jointly and more intensively with ego feeling and narcissism, then Jung's "complex theory" obtains support. Unconsciously all "imprints" are connected through numerous associations, through memory traces of experiences, through repressed experiences from earlier ego states with different ego boundaries, and also by way of the id, through the memory traces which the development of the libido, and especially of the individual component drives, left behind. Together they form the *complex* which, viewed from the side of the ego, encompasses a variety of internal and external ego boundaries; and which, considered from the world of objects, represents a variety of objects and persons of the external world. In the topical experience all these various cathexes are gratified or tension is reduced some other way, via the contact of the object representations with the ego boundary. Therefore, it makes good sense to speak of complex-readiness, complex-satisfaction, complex-effect, and so on. Since complexes are for the most part unconscious, they are not accessible to self-observation, the scientific use of which was implicit in the theme of this article. But the doctrine of the complexes is pertinent in this context, and we see that it is a construction which correctly renders reality.

In conclusion I should like to emphasize: This exposition is a description of reality insofar as it deals with the ego boundaries and with the dynamics of narcissism. The assumption of the balance of cathexes of the ego boundary and of the object representations is an hypothesis which enlarges upon Freud's theory. I feel that new findings demand theoretical supplementation. However, I suppose that by now I have imposed more than ample new ideas upon the reader.

If to some readers these findings seem strange, I should like to offer a theoretical explanation for this sensation based on these very communications. To experience an act as satisfactory, the cathexis of the object representations and the narcissistic cathexis of the pertinent ego boundary must agree. However, there is no narcissistic cathexis as yet for new impressions, unless one succeeds immediately in establishing identification, as may happen in the case of a captivating lecturer. Ordinarily, new ideas need a certain length of time to obtain libido from the ego feeling of their public, on the one hand, and as object representations on the other. Only then is the reality-ego capable of distinguishing critically whether the concept of reality as presented was correct. In simpler words, in the face of new ideas there is no comprehension without empathy; if this is lacking, prejudice clings to the old ideas.

16

ON THE DISTINCTION BETWEEN HEALTHY AND PATHOLOGICAL NARCISSISM *

When Freud discovered ego libido and introduced the concept of narcissism, a new field was opened for psychoanalytic investigation. However, this new concept has increased the difficulties of understanding theory and terminology. It also demanded of the psychoanalysts that they revise what they had learned unless they were to rest content with word-knowledge and faith in authority. Previously it had been easy to consider the basic distinction between the ego drives and the sexual drives as the basis of the dynamic conception of, for instance, the neuroses. Now the ego itself became a libidinally cathected agency, and the concept of "narcissism" replaced Bleuler's "autism" which had hitherto served to designate the pathology in introversion and estrangement from objects. However, "autism" indicates that the goal of the strivings or of the concern lies in the inner world of the individual, ordinarily of the sick one; while the term "narcissism" refers to the goal *and* origin of the cathexes not only in autistic processes and states but in others as well. It implies that the cathexis is of libidinal nature, and that it is not only turned toward the inner world but that it has pertained to the ego from the very beginning, and emanates from it.

As a result of this new conception, Freud's theory of instincts no longer can distinguish non-libidinal drives from libidinal ones by their derivation from the ego. Rather, they must be

. . . .

* From papers read in Oxford (1929), Lucerne (1934) and Prague (1935).

differentiated by their goal which, genetically and observably, appears partly as even destruction of the ego—as death. Logically, there should be a term, analogous to libido, for the cathexes supplied by this drive. Accepting the theory of the death instinct, I propose the term *mortido* for the energies of these cathexes; Edoardo Weiss, to avoid any commitment regarding acceptance of the death drive, has preferred the term *destrudo*.[1] Obviously, the latter term, in its turn, is prejudicial in the sense of the assumption that the only originally destructive tendencies are those that were turned toward the external world, and that they are the ones which attempt to destroy the inner world by their redirection toward the latter. Since the decision in this alternative will not be up to psychoanalysis, but to bioanalysis or even to pure biology, no argument need arise in regard to this terminology. It is not lack of precision if, often, several of our terms are applicable to the very same phenomenon. The psyche has been divided analytically only for better conceptual comprehension; the phenomena themselves cannot be partitioned into sections and labelled accordingly. This is why, for example, someone who misunderstood analysis needed the complementary synthesis; the misunderstanding consisted in mistaking the term "psychoanalysis" for dissection of the analysand's psyche into its component parts, while it actually refers to the kind of intellectual work in which analysand and analyst are engaged.

Hence, in discussing our topic, we shall not expect opposite terms to always have antithetical meanings in the same sense, but they must permit correct distinction of the differences in the processes to be distinguished. For instance, when Freud differentiated the erotic type from the narcissistic one, this did not contradict the libidinal nature of narcissism; the word "erotic" in this case was used in its common everyday sense.[2]

The characterization of this "narcissistic type" does not imply that it is pathological or abnormal, but it does imply the qualification that it is never met with in pure form. In a discussion

. . . .

[1] See E. Weiss, "Todestrieb und Masochismus" (Death Drive and Masochism), *Imago*, XXI (1935), 396.

[2] Freud, "Libidinal Types," *Psychoanalytic Quarterly*, I (1932).

on this subject, Freud cited Falstaff as a specimen of nearly pure narcissism; this figure, however, because almost too normal, is rather a borderline case of normalcy and would hardly be considered an ideal in real life. In the description of the "narcissistic type" the emphasis is on self-assurance, which is the basis of activity and particularly the reason why aggressions can imperturbably be directed against the outside world. Thus a strong narcissistic cathexis has here been recognized as the normal, useful, and necessary countercathexis by virtue of which object cathexes are asserted with active energy. We may say that ego libido supplies our normal countercathexis to our normal object cathexes. It is partly freely displaceable or fixated, and partly has been absorbed in the character structure.

Here, and in other constellations, narcissism and ego libido are antithetic to Eros and to object libido; likewise, the narcissistic injury is antithetic to the suffering resulting from frustrated object libido. If, however, from here on one were to insist on using the terms rigidly in their dictionary sense, then narcissism could never be said to relate to an object, be it a "something in the external world" or an object representation. In reality, a great deal of ego libido is anaclitic toward the ego drives, in the old sense, and thus is not only connected with the ego but also turned toward the object or the object representation. This expresses, in terms of the libido theory, what the psychologists, especially Schilder, have said about the ego being contained in the act. Accordingly, there is narcissism which has nothing to do with objects, and another kind which does have an object; or, more precisely, one may be narcissistic either without object cathexis or, as for instance in narcissistic object choice, precisely with libidinal object cathexis but without any subsequent transformation of narcissism into object libido. In either case one remains completely within the range of the normal and healthy. As I discussed in more detail in an earlier paper, all secondary narcissism has as its object the ego, or what has been incorporated into or enclosed by the ego.[3] Here the antithesis between object libido and narcissism no longer lies in the relatedness to an object, but in the nature of the

. . . .

[3] See "The Ego as Subject and Object in Narcissism," Chapter 15.

object, namely, whether it is a part of the external world or of the ego; the strict distinction becomes untenable—quite in consonance with the actual psychic happening—if, and to the extent that, the ego encompasses parts of the external world. Once, however, we have come to distinguish ego cathexis from object cathexes, we shall commonly use the term narcissism precisely for that ego cathexis which enters into relationships with the external world and with the object representations; in fact, it is only important to recognize and to emphasize that these cathexes are of ego libidinal nature, since it is self-evident that the ego is cathected with ego libido to the extent to which libido pertains to it. In instances of narcissistic behavior which puzzle us, we have the task of separating the healthy and normal from the pathological and abnormal.

Although narcissism was first recognized in its pathological form, it is unquestionably not a pathological residue of the past but the normal essential means for establishing the living psychic coherence of the ego. Thus it was described by Freud as a *normal* reservoir of libido. Subsequently, many psychoanalysts emphasized the pathological features in narcissism, partly in order to interpret correct Individual Psychological findings from the point of view of the libido theory. The pathology of all narcissistic attitudes, the narcissistic cathexes, the narcissistic injury, was emphasized once more in the sense of "autism." It was said frequently that the narcissistic cathexis would interfere with the interest in treatment and recovery, that it would frustrate any interest, or that excessive narcissism would render transference more difficult or impossible; the technical prescription of Reich was to destroy the "narcissistic armor." However correct all this was and still is, the statements were much too general to lead to explanatory connections. Besides, we should not forget that every anxiety, every feeling of shame, every feeling of guilt, is a narcissistic process and that a narcissistic component is inherent in every instance of sadomasochism, masochism, and exhibitionism; hence, that the term "narcissistic" ordinarily merely replaces a known specific concept by a general one. A distinction must also be made between normal narcissism and those narcissistic relations characteristic for the psychoses. In the latter, the return to the fixated narcissistic stage makes futile the application of psychoanalysis as developed technically for the transference neuroses.[4] In the case of psychoses it is a matter of a different comprehension of reality on the part of the patients; also their unconscious conflicts have hampered their ego development or met with an ego which was maldeveloped for endogenous reasons. The pathological narcissism of the psychotic will not be the subject of this paper. Here I want only to discuss individual criteria for the distinction between pathological and normal narcissism. I hold this to be useful, because the concept and the term "narcissism" should not unjustifiably become restricted to the realm of pathology.

In all probability we gain during every psychoanalytical treatment a sure and nuanced impression of the extent to which the narcissism shown by any patient may be considered normal or pathological, and, in the latter case, whether the pathology lies in its increase or in its use. We also notice any abnormal decrease of narcissism below the level which we expect

. . . .

[4] Even today, (i.e., 1936—E.W.) Freud himself has a very skeptical attitude toward the analytical treatment of psychoses, and therefore toward my communications concerning good results in incipient and advanced schizophrenia. But experience time and again confirms the fact that the schizophrenic patient transfers as quickly as, and no less reliably than, neurotic, and some healthy, persons. His transference, though, is dissolved immediately if one adheres to the technique of analysis of the neuroses. If one avoids this, the psychotic is—in principle—analysable by virtue of his transference. Nor is his more intense and deviant narcissism an impediment; it simply forces the analyst to enter into the deviant comprehension of reality. The increase in narcissism affects only one part of the ego, or, more precisely, the infantile, restricted ego. Often there are several infantile ego states existing facultatively at the same time; these must be recognized in order that one may establish contact with them, as one does with a child. Many newer—that is, more lately acquired,—stages and contents have lost their narcissistic cathexes in part, or even completely, and have become material accessible to psychoanalysis, while the unconscious has become more accessible and yields, without resistance, much material no longer repressed. Both object libidinal and narcissistic cathexes are transferred in varying proportions; the latter in most cases through the renewal of earlier identifications. The analysis of the self-observation of a secondary narcissistic nature which has the abnormal mechanisms as its object gains a major value. At any rate, every analysis of psychoses leaves behind a strong impression of pathological narcissism.

in the normal individual. Such a decrease is characteristic in states of estrangement in which, however, secondary narcissism in the form of self-observation so frequently sets in compensatorily that some analysts mistakenly still consider it as the reason for the estrangement. There also exists a neurotic soberness and coldness which derives from lack of narcissism; this is found in incipient psychosis, unless anxiety is in the foreground, and also in neurotics with very minor states of estrangement.

The abnormal increase in, or investment of, narcissism shows itself, in general as well as in specific instances, in the behavior not only of an analysand but of any person. For example, it would be interesting to discuss in detail how few people are able to extend a greeting or a hand-shake in welcome or in farewell, not narcissistically, but with mere object cathexis, as one would expect an individual with a normal attitude to his fellow men to do automatically. In the neurotic analysand these little "symptomatic mannerisms" are multiplied and intensified in a very characteristic way. We see the same phenomenon in many other symptomatic signs; in even greater measure we hear it in the cadence of inflection and accentuation of his voice, either in whatever he says or in only individual sentences or specific themes as determined by complexes; a mere slowing-down of the pronunciation often betrays the intrusion of a second, more narcissistically cathected ego boundary upon the one previously active. With certain individuals, one can discern in every drawl a second and a third innervation, emanating from what the speaker wishes to "represent." Increased narcissism is discernible in the manner of judging events which are in themselves unimportant; in the manner of reaction to the arising mental contents, especially to repressed material; and above all in the interpretation of the attitudes of the environment toward the patient, particularly those of love objects, and vice versa. It is evident to everyone, except to the patient himself, that the inability to judge objectively is nearly always caused also by, and can be considered an objective criterion of, narcissism. Both W. Reich and the school of Individual Psychology have found general viewpoints which often permit a correct distinction and have made many detailed observations.

In order to evaluate narcissism—be it only according to our

impressions—we also must investigate, as always in matters of economy of libido cathexis, whether the individuals in question have a different total amount of libido available. In fact, it has always been assumed to be so. The expression "character, full-blooded personality," [5] as also the term "sensuality" as used by many authors, has in the layman's language always designated a particularly great amount of available libido. For the analyst such an assumption is complicated by his knowledge that there also exist libido quantities which are fixed or repressed, or which have become unavailable through organic repression or other structuration, and that it is precisely these quantities that determine the strength of the personality and character; whereas the "free" surplus of libido is what becomes manifest to observation of others and of oneself. Yet the existence of these maximal quantities of libido can be concluded only indirectly and theoretically.

Psychoanalysis therefore resorts only rarely to the assumption of a larger or smaller quantity of total libido; its practice and theory deal with the change in the investment with, and cathexis of, libido, and with the dynamics and economy, not with the statics and quantity. When Freud published the distinction between narcissistic and erotic individuals, he probably did not have the total quantity of libido in mind but the manner of its investment and its comparative increase in one or the other direction. In any case, he has expressed his opinion that certainly the proportions of the libido distributed to the ego, to the object world, and to the superego are constant for every individual only within broad limits; if that is the case, the borderline between normal and pathological increase or investment should also differ in individuals of different types. Accordingly, Eidelberg may be on the right track in ascribing specific dispositions for specific neuroses to the libidinal types.[6] It is furthermore understandable that the interest in quantity of libido has induced younger analysts to examine experimen-

· · · · · · ·

[5] In German, *"Natur, Vollnatur."*—E.W.

[6] Eidelberg, "Zur Theorie und Klinik der Perversion" (On theory and treatment of perversion), *Jahrbücher f. Psychiatrie und Neurologie,* L. (1933).

tally (Bernfeld and Feitelberg[7]) or theoretically (Eidelberg) the possibility of finding methods to measure libido quantities.

Presumably no analyst doubts the existence of great constitutionally determined differences in libido quantities. We do not know specifically whether the quantity of narcissism also varies constitutionally. If we further probe the role of constitution, the narcissistic psychoses are but evidence for the fact that a given libido quantity proved insufficient to supply both narcissism *and* object libido. Surplus as well as deficit of libido may obstruct the normal distribution and investment, and thus either may cause a predominance of narcissism. It may be, moreover, that it is the necessary compensatory mechanisms of countercathexis which operate excessively in constitutional surplus, whereas they fail to operate in constitutional deficit, and that only in this way does the pathology and abnormality of the libido distribution become evident; even an explanation of the opposite consequence is conceivable in these complicated economic relationships. In addition, the factor of constitutionally determined quantity would explain their higher rate in certain ethnic groups or human types, whereas the factor of the conditionally determined libido quantities would explain the more than merely apparent higher rate of neuroses, specifically of narcissistic neuropsychoses, at the critical periods in everyone's life.

Despite the scanty result, the above discussion was presented for the sake of completeness. Now we return to our topic, which is at least more accessible psychoanalytically, namely, to the theoretical elucidation of the distinction between normal and pathological narcissism according to its manifestations. My previous studies have opened an access to the direct observation of narcissism, inasmuch as I discovered an index of normal narcissistic ("middle voice") cathexis in the "ego feeling." We also learned, from certain symptoms appearing in a variety of psychic processes and functions, to recognize increases as well as decreases in the ego feeling, that is, in narcis-

. . . .

[7] Bernfeld and Feitelberg, "Ueber psychische Energie, Libido und deren Messbarkeit" (On psychic energy, libido, and their measurability), *Internat. Zeitschrift f. Psychoanalyse*, XVI (1930).

sistic cathexis, and thereby the existence of different "ego boundaries." Topographically, the ego boundaries are the carriers, one could even say the mental organs, of narcissism, although the sensations, urges, and excitations stemming from the narcissistic libidinous processes pertain to a variety of erogenous zones and functions. Accordingly, a pleasurable ego feeling is the "certificate of origin" of the narcissistic cathexis of a bodily or mental ego boundary; in the former case narcissism is, as a matter of fact, an expansion of the autoerotism from which it stems; the quantities of libido which constitute narcissism are probably smaller in normal ego feeling than were those of the original, permanent autoerotic cathexes.

The term "ego boundary" should be understood in its literal sense to mean that we feel how far the ego extends, or, more correctly, the point beyond which the ego does not extend. As regards the bodily ego feeling, this means that the ego boundary does not always coincide with the body boundaries—it may either not fill them up or may extend beyond them. The latter situation is well illustrated by the driving motorist who always extends his bodily ego to the fenders of his car. Through boundaries of the mental ego feeling, on the other hand, we become aware of the fact that we experience emotions, thoughts, perceptions of all kinds, memories, and our own speech and motion as entering into the ego area from the outside, and that they belong to the ego and continue to pertain to it until they are in turn replaced by others.

With this we would have done no more than describe in different words entering into consciousness, continuing in it, and disappearing from it, were it not for the following phenomena: first, in the case of deficient libido cathexis of the ego boundaries, psychic experiences are conscious as usual and yet estranged; and, secondly, normally much which becomes conscious remains in consciousness as part of the external world and separated from the ego, whereas other contents by becoming conscious are absorbed into the ego. The difference is due to the fact that there is a variety of ego boundaries, but only one boundary for entrance into consciousness. Thus a phenomenon may connect with the ego only at the intellectual boundary, while lacking contact at all other ego boundaries; thus it is recognized and considered as belonging to the external world, although it occupies the intellectual ego boundary of the moment. A third reason which compels us to distinguish consciousness from the ego boundary implying inclusion in the ego lies in the fact that in us are a great number of various non-conscious ego states, with a variety of contents and boundaries, which may become conscious but which preconsciously or unconsciously always share in influencing our feelings and thoughts. Briefly, there are unconscious and preconscious ego boundaries, and therefore we must not identify consciousness with ego boundary.

The uniformity of a character rests on the existence of some firmly established, invariable ego states, in which the main boundaries are unchangeable as to their content and extent; it also rests on the manner in which they are cathected with libido—they become conscious as a result of various impressions, particularly on occasions arousing analogous affects. The more such invariable ego states have been formed or predisposed in a person; the more these reaction-foundations of the ego nonetheless attach new contents and reaction-directions to individual ego sectors and their ego boundaries; also, the easier certain individual non-typical ego states enter consciousness from the past in a reality-adjusted selection—the richer is the individuality.

There is a great deal of narcissistically invested libido stored up in all these ego states, with their actually or potentially ready attitudes, reactions, contents, and boundaries. These are, as was mentioned above, the countercathexes which permit the ego to cathect objects with sufficient stability and to endure frustrations from them. What we call "inner resources," "to be at peace with oneself," and "equanimity" rest on these narcissistically gratifying inner cathexes in the ego states which though past, are ready to be awakened. The analysis of resistance is directed particularly toward these ego states, insofar as they are not normal ones, and actualizes them in the transference situation. Psychoanalysis concerns itself with these ego states methodically, although it apparently aims at evoking unconscious material indiscriminately. The attention given to the arising ego states corresponds, therefore, to the importance of the uncovering in general as well as to the significance of the uncovered material. Hence considerable narcissistic participation and satisfaction may become manifest upon the emergence of each new layer and may seem to be even more intense in appearance than it actually is, without being pathological. Gradually more and more object interest is established, free of, or accompanied by, but little narcissism. This makes the points of excessive narcissistic cathexis more conspicuous. The existence of such excessive narcissism can be recognized from the circumstance that on seemingly quite unimportant occasions the person's interest in his own current or previous ego is manifested apart from his direct object interest; frequently it occurs so far in advance of object interest that the reason for the special narcissistic investment becomes understandable only later.

Thus we find an unusual narcissistic investment of the ego in the ego, and also a particularly intense narcissism in the ego states themselves; often the investment is very emotional, full of self-pity, pathos or self-flattery and obvious self-aggrandizement—affects which may be covered up by compensatory opposite affects but will be noticeable nevertheless. Narcissism is manifest in such affects, and the fact that it becomes manifest in the affect is evidence that it is no longer of a normal kind. Affects have this in common with object interests; they appear in the relation of the ego to a stimulating something. In the case of object interests the ego enters into relationship with a libido cathected object; in the case of affects, with a libido cathected process of the ego itself. The object interest may take a simple and immediate course with stronger or weaker libido cathexis and corresponding consumption of cathexis, or this course itself may thereby be the object of the ego's interest; in the latter case a narcissistic process of cathexis, and its satisfaction, or frustration, was added to the object libidinal one.

We shall not designate every such narcissistic concomitant process as abnormal, much less as pathological, because in this way we would earmark as exceptional what is the norm among many people. However, the mentally healthy and normal people enjoy their narcissistic satisfaction, if at all, only after the act. They are so preoccupied with the object and the overcoming of difficulties that they have no libido left for self-inspection. For Faust, "to be self-pleased" signifies the end; the fact that he rejects it so strongly proves, however, how great the temptation is. It is almost impossible to perform the "know thyself" only with inwardly directed object interest devoid of interested subject-love. Hence we shall establish the overcoming of narcissism in object libidinal interests and struggles as an ideal goal, but not as the norm. It is a different matter with narcissism that becomes manifest in affects and appears as the kind of sentimentality described above.

The relation of the affects to the drives has not yet been elucidated psychoanalytically. MacDougall's theory postulating that the affects are specific reactions of the psyche to the various drives is justified in principle; in particularities, the pertinence of its application will depend on the pertinence of the underlying theory of drives. According to Freud, the affects are centrifugal processes; this does not mean that Freud did not know or recognize the centripetal, sensitive nature of the affects; the passages in question clearly speak of both directions of the processes of discharge of excitations. But since the centrifugal direction was not yet universally known at that time—nor is it today—it was emphasized in Freud's writings. In another place Freud designated the affects as normal processes parallel to hysterical attacks. Analytically, we often speak (as Grüninger did first[8]) of affect cathexes as we do of libido cathexes, of economy, displacement, investment, or repression. Recognizing that there are changing ego boundaries cathected with libido, viz., with different kinds of libido, we understand better, economically, topically, and dynamically, the nature of the affects. We must add here that ego boundaries may also be cathected, totally or in part, with mortido (destrudo).

Affects always develop between two ego boundaries acting on each other, and differ according to the kind of drive cathexis of the ego at these boundaries: it may be libido of different

. . . .

[8] U. Grüninger, "Zum Problem der Affektverschiebung" (On the Displacement of Affects), Zurich, 1917; *Internat. Zeitschrift f. Psychoanalyse,* VII (1921).

kinds, active or passive, mortido (or destrudo) of different kinds, active or passive: at specific ego boundaries, one of which may pertain to a previous ego state which is entering consciousness—that is, to the more adolescent or infantile ego. Therefore, affects are the mutually developing sensations which the drive cathexis of the ego arouses in the drive cathected ego. In this way we understand the manifold nuances of affects of the same kind, their manifold mixture and shading, their displaceability, and the simultaneously centripetal and centrifugal nature of the discharge of their excitation. We must assume that they arise precisely at the ego boundaries because, frequently, the affects are subject to specific and very peculiar sensations of estrangement. The affect of shame, for instance, arises if a sexually, and especially an exhibitionistically, cathected ego boundary acts on an ego boundary cathected with anxiety. Grief develops if an ego boundary cathected with mortido (or destrudo) acts on one which is cathected with object libido. Freud once interpreted hatred as the relation of the (total) ego to the object, and added that the drive itself could not hate.[9] Therefore we should supplement our definition of such affects as are directly concerned with the external world with the statement that an affect may also develop if an ego boundary is affected by an object cathexis. But on closer scrutiny we find that hatred is one of the cases in which the affect-exciting object brings the current ego boundary—cathected with aggression, with active mortido—into relationship with previous ego states in which the ego boundaries have been cathected in the same manner; for hatred always "rises"; it is already prepared, and merely renews itself in the current ego state. Other ego boundaries with libidinal cathexes may complicate the feeling of hatred for the object concerned. Ambivalence, too, becomes possible by diverse cathexes of two ego boundaries.

Although anxiety and terror are so intimately tied up with feelings of estrangement (as terror arouses estrangement which, on the other hand, precedes or accompanies intense feelings of anxiety), and although so many authors considered them the causes of estrangement, I find no statement and remember no

. . . .

[9] Freud, "Instincts and Their Vicissitudes," *Collected Papers,* IV, 79f.

experience of my own to the effect that anxiety itself was estranged. This is so because anxiety develops *in* the ego,[10] not
at the ego boundary. This is not true for fear, nor is it true for
the bodily sensations accompanying full-fledged anxiety; for
both, feelings of estrangement may exist. It might be justifiable to subsume anxiety under the unitary conception of affects, because one sees anxiety develop in the total mental ego
when the bodily ego comes under the sway of imminent death
or under the full impact of the death drive. However, there are
no peripheral boundaries between bodily ego and mental ego
at which the ego cathexes would act upon each other as they
do at different boundaries of the mental ego. Therefore,
wherever relations between bodily ego and mental ego have
to be described—as, for instance, in conversion and in the somatic components of anxiety and of other affects—one first has
to do justice to the complicated topographic relationship between mental ego and bodily ego, which demands particularly
careful observation. However, I shall not consider this my task
here, although the subject matter of narcissism would require
the previous solution of this problem for the very reason that
narcissism is genetically connected with autoerotism, and that,
in its manifestation as perversion, its object is one's own body.

We have not transgressed our topic by discussing the affect of
anxiety. The interrelation between anxiety and libido—narcissistic as well as object libido—is as important clinically as it is
theoretically. If there is no narcissistic cathexis, the reaction
to sudden danger will be apathetic terror and paralysis, but
not the very peculiar sensation of anxiety in which the ego feel-

. . . .

[10]Likewise, it is striking that estranged persons do not complain that their
will is estranged, although they complain about its disturbance, withdrawal, and intractability, and objectively it often appears to be more
disturbed than are the affects, concerning whose estrangement the patients
complain so much and so variously. Thus, this experience, unless it is
based on insufficient observations which will have to be corrected, would
indicate that the function of volition pertains to the total ego, and not
to the ego boundaries, as I pointed out in another paper ("Ego Feeling
in Dreams," Chapter 3). The motor activity—as executive organ and
executive function—must be clearly distinguished from volition (function) and organ.

ing, on the contrary, is greatly increased. Thus anxiety is the best example to illustrate the way in which libido cathexis and mortido cathexis merge in the unity of an affect.

On the other hand, the affect of guilt feeling, in its pure form, is experienced in an entirely different manner. Consequently, it will not do to designate the feeling of guilt (and also, frequently, the feeling of shame) as social anxiety, whereby the feeling of guilt is considered predominantly anxiety in the face of punishment (and shame predominantly anxiety in the face of depreciation and abandonment). Since we speak here of "anxiety in the face of something," [11] it is apparent that, properly, we are dealing with the addition of fear. Via the genetic and experiential engrams, the fear of punishment has become tied up with the entirely different affect of guilt, both unconsciously and consciously. In the case of strong guilt feeling, the true affect of anxiety also occurs regularly for unconscious reasons—among them, probably, those assumed in *Totem and Tabu*, the objections of the professional anthropologists notwithstanding. It is the biological task of the ego to act throughout in the interest of the individual; likewise the ego enjoys as its own success all success and pleasure which the individual gains from the ego's achievement, and it painfully experiences the failures as its own misfortune, and the counter-attacks of others, insofar as they are retaliation, as its own punishment. But not every feeling of guilt contains components of anxiety and punishment. For example, one may have feelings of guilt for not having yielded to an upsurge of hatred, without any motivation for social anxiety or fear.

The feeling of guilt demonstrates clearly that affects develop as feelings of tension between two ego states. In fact, it was this particular affect which first made me aware of this topographic condition. In relation to an object representation, two ego states join; in the case of an unconscious feeling of guilt, both are past ego states; in the case of conscious guilt feeling, one is the current ego state and one (or several) stem from the past. The instinctual cathexis of the current ego state differs from that of the past. If the difference increases to the point at

. . . .

[11]In the German original, *"Angst vor etwas."*—E.W.

which they become antithetic, and if a significant relationship and a significant reaction are concerned, the feeling of regret is transformed into guilt feeling. We are used to applying the term guilt feelings only when the antitheses of the cathexes are subjected to ethical judgment—that is, when social condemnation and fear of punishment augment the antitheses. However, close scrutiny reveals that the same type of affect, although of lesser intensity, springs from every kind of antithetic behavior, given subjective significance and reaction. As soon as one's own past behavior no longer has one's own approval, a slight feeling of guilt is experienced, side by side with intellectual self-judgment.

If the antitheses in question are accentuated morally to a high degree, as is the case whenever an intense feeling of guilt arises, and if, in particular, an ego attitude of love or hate has yielded to an opposite one, there is a strong feeling of unbalance, of unadjustability, of inability to reach a solution, of the antithesis of cathexes; we experience as guilt feeling, with regard to the past reaction, the state of tension generated by this incompatibility. The intellectual labor which dissects the reaction in its details, its motivations, its justifications, its inevitability or omission, its good and bad consequences, again brings the subject matter, in all details, into contact with both ego states; this is brought about by every intellectual act, regardless of whether the past reaction constituted an act or an omission, and even if either were no more than intended or contemplated. The unbalanced state is in itself tormenting; the reproaches of the superego exacerbate it; both lead to the well known end-state of the need for punishment, the compulsion to confess, to self-condemnation and readiness for atonement—a state which externalizes the unbalance toward the external world and thus liberates the ego from the inner dissension inherent in the feeling of guilt.

Such antitheses of attitudes occur even in early childhood whenever the child in his current ego state adopts the attitudes of his educators; they also occur later on, whenever he identifies himself with them. Gradually all ego states of these identifications merge into the superego, which has sharp boundaries toward the "ego," the latter being only partially influenced by identification. Edoardo Weiss has published observations according to which the superego may originate in a traumatic manner. This can only mean that feelings of guilt which have arisen as a result of intense conflicts, rather than chronic and minor ones, are retained in memory and that the strengthening of the superego is experienced as contrition. Accordingly, whether the superego develops before the Oedipus period seems to be a sham problem; feelings of guilt exist much earlier, but only gradually and much later does the superego obtain its sharp boundaries toward the ego, which have been prepared by the same cathexes as the ego's. From then on feelings of guilt develop, as a rule, between the interacting boundaries of the superego and the ego.

The feeling of guilt, no more than anxiety, is not merely an unsettled conflict of aggressive tendencies between superego and ego, or between two ego states. The contacting boundaries must also be partly cathected with libido. Without this libidinal component, we find the self-hatred of melancholia instead of the normal feeling of guilt, or—as in pathological mourning—an indifferent, estranged guilt feeling. In this respect the feeling of guilt may be counted among the narcissistic affects.

The topography of the development of affects between two ego boundaries, as discussed above, makes it clearly understandable that both centripetal and centrifugal discharge of excitation pertain to the affect; my own use of this term is orientated toward the ego, while Freud in using it wanted to emphasize the fact that, in analogy with motor activity, the affects discharge excitations into the somatic system, that is, to the muscles, blood vessels, and glands, both ductless and secreting. Precisely this typical consequence of increase in affect, which, as a matter of fact, can be controlled or reduced completely or partially (controlled in motor activity, reduced in innervations of vessels and glands), agrees with our conception of the affects. In the encounter of ego boundaries, drive cathexes are freed or are turned from the resting state to discharge, and if their energies have not been used up in the psychic experience, they are transferred into the somatic system.

Therefore, the readiness for excitation and discharge of affects also depends upon the state of libidinal tension, bodily as well as mental—in toto, as well as in particular instinctual areas.

It is also quite evident that the affects, like the drive processes, are partially "resting" and in tension, and partially are mobile, increasing and discharging. As the ego meets with itself at drive cathected boundaries, these not only receive, like sense organs, the stimulus of the impression of the other drive cathexis, but there occurs also a sort of libidinal satisfaction—under inadequate conditions if the drive cathexes differ in kind, under adequate conditions if they are of the same kind. In the former case the affect is a complicated one, frequently somewhat confusing, and in spite of its libidinal nature it is somewhat painful and tormenting; in the latter case it is simple, either pleasurable or unpleasurable, and is self-increasing. Every discharge of an affect contains a component of pleasurable satisfaction, because libido quantities are merged and dissolved, and an element of unpleasure, inasmuch as cathexes are not in agreement with each other. The solution of drive cathexes in the affect is not complete; a new sensation[12] comes about, different from each participating drive cathexis, precisely the peculiar affect itself; it still contains excitation energy which im-

. . . .

[12]Every affect is a characteristic sensation apart from topography, dynamics, and economics. It is the specific mode of sensation of the manner in which the adjustment at the ego boundaries occurs, whether it fails or succeeds, is rapid or delayed, expands or shrinks, and depending precisely upon the specific, highly differentiated types of drive cathexes involved. Every affect has its course of discharge, in which the ego boundaries often change—particularly if, in the affect, a libido adjustment occurs between them. In the affects one can find again the justification for the first economic theory of pleasure and pain. Actually the feeling of guilt with its unsettled tension is exclusively tormenting; this is not true for anxiety of minor degree, and certainly not for compassion. The latter arises between one's own ego and an ego boundary which includes the pitied individual; the tension of the unpleasurable feeling dissolves in pathos, pity, *Weltschmerz*, depending on whether the other ego is included in one's own, whether one's own ego loses itself in the other, or whether the ego boundaries expand to a universal extent. The pleasurable nature of the affects depends on the qualities of the drives which cathect the ego boundaries; this is particularly clear in the feeling of shame, the pleasurable component of which stems directly from sexuality.

parts itself to the entire ego in so far as the latter does not regulate and curb its expansion.

The fact that the affects come into being at the ego boundaries does not mean that the drive cathexes—similar perhaps to electric tensions—are only peripheral excitations. It is always the entire ego, or individual functions or parts of it, which are libidinally cathected; the term "ego boundary" merely serves to express the concept that the cathexis unit which constitutes the ego always has a sharp delimitation, including specific functions and contents and excluding others. The fact that there exists a precise ego feeling also speaks against Schilder's theory of varying "ego nearness" and "ego distance" in normal mental life. In any case, we are justified in speaking of the affect cathexes of an ego boundary, although this seems to contradict the interpretation, given above, that the affect in general arises only from the encounter of drive-cathected ego boundaries. Every affect is a phenomenon that has arisen dynamically and contains energies of cathexis which at any given moment imbue the ego within its boundaries with a specific quality of feeling and excitation, and which continue to act at the same or other boundaries so that further affects can arise by a new encounter of an ego boundary cathected affectively or instinctually—there is no end to the possible complications. The surplus energies flow off into the somatic system. When we consider that the affects arise from an encounter of the ego with itself, we understand that the study of narcissism had to lead us to this examination of the affects; we understand also that in non-analytical literature many manifestations of narcissism are described in terms of the affective qualities of self-complacency, coquetry, vanity, and pride, while the ubiquity and significance of the libido extant in the ego is not recognized. Jung's classification of character structures into introverted and extraverted types did justice to the significance of narcissism.

We now return from the examination of the affects in relation to narcissism to the behavior of the patient when in analysis former ego states emerge. It is normal that more or less strong affects arise at these occasions; sometimes they take time to become manifest and intense, at other times they erupt so suddenly that they then take hold of the rest of the ego more or less intensively, totally or partially, only to fade away again or to be disposed of in some other manner. The ego participates in each such dramatic occurrence, either joyfully or with suffering, and defending itself with libido cathexes which either continue to exist in an unsatisfied state or are satisfied and come to rest. In the case of increased narcissism, however, the ego is, in addition, particularly concerned with the process of disposing of the affects and participates in it narcissistically; it is up to our subjective judgment to determine which degree of narcissistic participation has to be considered as pathological. To the individuals concerned, this participaton is so natural and such a matter of course that they become aware of the abnormality of their behavior only by having their attention directed either to less narcissistically cathected processes in their other fields of experience or to the conduct of other, less narcissistic persons. Increased narcissistic investment is unhealthy in several ways: it increases affectivity, and with it subjectivity as well, in a diffuse, useless manner; it falsifies all kinds of conceptions; it consumes libido which should benefit reality adjustment and the objects; it prevents relationships with other persons; it offends these others, while both sides, unless analyzed, fail to understand the causes or to know correctly the reasons; increased narcissism makes people experience everything doubly, as it were, and thus it produces an abnormal life rhythm. We shall come back to this later in discussing the distinction between normal and pathological narcissistic phantasies. On the other hand, however, strong participation in one's own experiences, affirmation of one's own affective reactions, and satisfaction with one's own personality—that is to say, attitudes we must call narcissistic—are useful and healthy bases for relations with the external world, as we have pointed out before in general; specifically, they are the narcissistic countercathexes to the multitude of object libidinal attachments.

I started here from the observation of narcissistic behavior during analysis because this situation frequently permits us to comprehend, to examine, and even to simply notice the details of the cathexis processes; otherwise we evaluate our impressions only through empathy or according to our background of experience. However, narcissistic behavior during analysis does not differ from that which is constantly demonstrated in life in general and, of course, also in our own lives, provided we observe or analyze ourselves in a sufficiently objective manner. When we find the narcissistic reaction to be exaggerated or different from that which we expect in normal behavior, we should not immediately think of unchangeable anomalies of character, constitutionally or otherwise endogenously determined, but of reactive anomalies, the particular genetic causes of which we must discover; they are partly complex-determined, in Jung's sense, and partly typical and general reactions to typical and general influences since early childhood.

The fact that an individual acts out his experiences excessively in a narcissistic manner may betray a kind of ego weakness—in fact, paradoxically, it may indicate a lack of normal narcissistic countercathexes. In addition, such behavior frequently is the continuation of the general behavior of the parents toward the little child who was not permitted to develop, nor to experience his development, naively. This behavior of the environment is perpetuated, not only in the superego, but also in the ego in the form of self-observation. I am referring to this familiar constellation, which is not an original psychoanalytical insight, only in order to point out that we may use the term "ego weakness," which for a time was applied so liberally, also in regard to the behavior of the ego boundaries insofar as it is typical for the individual; moreover, we may be able more precisely to characterize the specific kind of ego weakness. Whether the excess of narcissistic reaction described above could be designated as ego weakness is a problem I leave undecided; it may signify a continuous readiness and an excessive preponderance of the ego which need not have developed as a reaction against one's own weaknesses, as the typical Adlerian mechanism would have it.[18]

. . . .

[18] Nor will intense affectivity revealing itself in violent affective reactions be judged as ego weakness by common standards. Not everyone will agree with Nietzsche who designated as "robust" that conscience which does not react easily, however brilliant and broad in meaning this paradox may be.

However, we are in a position to gauge the lability and stability of the ego boundaries, and we shall speak of ego weakness whenever the former excessively outweighs the latter. On the other hand, one can recognize an abnormal ego rigidity or ego weight in excessive stability. An ego formation in which the ego boundaries can change rapidly and easily but remain stable at any time if a standpoint must be held or defended, should be considered ideal. Although these differences have been repeatedly described by the characterologists, I discuss them here because in order to understand them one must pay attention to the ego boundaries and the narcissistic countercathexis.

We find, then, different resistances toward internal and external influences upon the ego in each individual at different times and states of readiness, and constantly in different individuals. We have discussed the internal influences in another context, although not exhaustively; the external ones derive chiefly from other individuals or from the ideas of others, principally in the same manner as we learned from Freud's group psychology. There are persons who at any time expand their ego boundaries to include every new impression; hence they are ready always to absorb new and different objects into the ego—in other words, to cathect them with ego feeling, with narcissistic libido—and to thus engage in always new identifications. To such uninhibited expansion of the ego boundary there is not always a corresponding equally rapid and uninhibited withdrawal. Individuals with a steady and solid ego boundary are unable to understand those with a soft and mobile boundary. The possibility of absolute resistance of the ego boundary is evidenced by the existence of the group of professions from the executioner down and upward to Tamerlane and his like. The consent of the superego to such activities—the moral question, that is, which does not concern us here—is made possible by the division of responsibilities in the social order. In contrast, the compassionate character, sensitive as a mimosa, is never able to keep his ego completely to himself. A brilliant physician and analyst has called such persons "identification-acrobats."

The resistance of the ego boundaries—the durity of the ego

—is prerequisite to cruelty as well as to justice, to steadfastness, and to objective understanding; lack of resistance of the ego boundary is prerequisite to pity, to social feelings and humanitarianism, to empathy and conciliatoriness. Ego boundaries expanded to a common identification may obtain an extremely strong narcissistic cathexis without prejudice to the simultaneous continuation of the individual ego boundary—for example, in nationalism, in religious and political associations, or in military units—and, through their resistance, provide the individuals with a much desired strong support. This characterological classification hence becomes much more complex because in the same individual certain ego boundaries may be very resistant, while others are less. Persons whose ego boundaries are extremely resistive to religious influences may otherwise yield to any other strong influence. This is due to the fact that the narcissistic countercathexes are of different strength and not connected in the same manner with the various ego fields, in relation to different groups of objects or opportunities for identification and their conscious and unconscious effective components.

It seems self-evident that the ego, this mighty and always ready cathexis center, must have a specific biological task, and hence be more than the psychologically artificially isolated area common to the functions of body and mind. To identify this task would almost seem to me superfluous and banal, were it not that I remember my own amazement at the result when I clarified the question for myself, and had not as brilliant a thinker as Rudolf Goldscheid[14] urged me to put it down in writing. The ego has the biological function of attending to the interests of the living being it regulates (that is, defense, attack, nourishment, housing, and so forth up to the sexual, to love, and to the most refined individual cultural needs) and must attend to them automatically and unconditionally, though, in civilized society under restraint by the superego and in directions imposed by all the tendencies previously absorbed into the ego. For biological reasons, the family ties, which derivate from nest-building and parental care in animals,

. . . .

[14]Austrian social-philosopher (1870-1931).—E.W.

belong among the interests of the individual, and therefore attending to them belongs among the spontaneously accepted ego functions. This biological function of the ego undoubtedly demonstrates that egoism is the necessary and justified basis of all individual existence. This formula corresponds with actual observations and exempts us from the hypocrisy of disowning egoism and yet being continuously obliged to practise it, and it also removes the incompatibility of egoism with altruism, doing away with the frequently sophistical arguments of whether in the last resort altruism is nothing but a kind of egoism. Thus, the biological function of narcissism, which Freud designated as the libidinal process parallel to egoism, also becomes evident.

The ego has to accomplish difficult tasks; due to the cathexis of the ego functions with libido, the ego obtains narcissistic pleasure premiums in all its functions. In the animal, and in simple conditions of human society, the individual's strength and capacity just suffice to carry out the task of biological self-assertion; accordingly, the ego has cathected with libido only the egoistic biological functions, in the narrow sense. In fact, this accomplishment appears to be a sufficiently large and difficult task to many persons in culture and society; hence the obduracy with which they defend themselves against any expansion of their ego boundaries constitutes for them a natural and normal act of self-protection. With the expansion of opportunities for achievement through cultural development in all directions, the individual, in community with others and participating functionally in community achievements, has also acquired abilities which go far beyond those of the single individual. Accordingly, the ego boundaries could expand, and functions which far exceed the narrow self-interest could likewise obtain their narcissistic cathexis and be invested with the narcissistic pleasure premium. Consequently, that individual appears harmonious who has well balanced the compass and amount of his interests, abilities, and narcissistic cathexis. Thus the theory of narcissism and its application for the understanding of the ego becomes, if not a new starting point, a new foundation for understanding social integration and integrative ability.

For the purpose of our topic, we recognize that lability of the ego boundaries, unless it is tied up with special achievements and abilities of the individual, must involve conflicts and shortcomings which may lead to neurotic disturbances. On the other hand it may originate as a consequence of neurotic conflicts and as compensation for object libidinal deprivations. Yet lability of the ego boundaries is certainly partly also constitutionally predisposed; we find it, as a rule, in markedly infantile individuals, and also, particularly, in those who are bisexual. Masochism, which is causally and probably also constitutionally determined by infantilism and bisexuality, makes for greater passivity and easier destructability, hence for greater mobility of the narcissistic cathexis of the ego boundaries. The bisexual disposition permits more rapid identifications with individuals of the same sex, also because it interferes with the heterosexual object libidinal relations. In woman, a predominantly masculine disposition interferes with the normal sexual use of feminine passivity and thus predisposes to a masochistic attitude of the ego and, thereby, to lability of the ego boundaries.

As we stated earlier, readiness for identification is a consequence of cultural development. It is unquestionably true that civilization offers a relatively great protection against the severe adversities of life—cold, hunger, and enemies who threaten death, castration, and slavery. By such protection a softening of the resistance of the ego boundaries became permissible and was achieved. On the other hand, only the further progress of civilization has permitted, and also effected, the restriction to the individual ego of the familiar ego boundary expanded to the group ego, which existed phylogenetically through long periods of time. The existence of this group ego, however, did not indicate a weakness of the ego boundary, but a permanent and very resistant expansion of the ego, encompassing the homogeneous mental ego feeling and probably also the bodily ego feeling. Therefore we may state that civilization gave rise, first, to the resistance of the ego boundary in the group ego and, later, to the resistance of the ego boundary in the individual ego, and that finally it permitted the special expansion of the ego and a particular lability of its boundaries to certain individuals—of whom some have been soft-hearted, kind, and humanitarian, and others only weak. On the other hand, we witness again and again regressions to the ego boundaries of a group ego, though an expanded one, which always prove particularly resistant.

Another kind of ego weakness is to be distinguished on principle from the lability of the ego boundaries; we became aware of it, too, through the concepts which have been presented here: ego feeling, ego boundaries, and narcissistic countercathexis. We are referring to a process which is responsible for the stability or lability of the ego attitudes. As a rule we may consider this process as normal, if the total ego remains in psychic equilibrium—that is to say, does not lose its narcissistic cathexes—in spite of the occurrence of a special achievement, for instance, an intense affective engagement. It is pathological, on the other hand, if almost the entire ego feeling—that is to say, a surplus of narcissistic cathexis—is concentrated on these boundaries, and the entire ego submits without resistance to the affective engagement. Naturally this does not apply to unusually grave events. But even under such circumstances, it will make a difference whether the ego has been affected only secondarily or whether, as it were, it suffers in its structuring cathexis which is felt to maintain the ego. We find two terms for affects of the same kind in linguistic usage, depending on whether the affects have overwhelmed the total ego or whether its stability has remained intact. For example, Freud once suggested, without ever coming back to the question, that anxiety and fear are distinguished by the fact that fear has an object while anxiety is an objectless mental state. This is not so. The most significant difference lies in the circumstance that anxiety takes hold of the total ego, and fear only of a part of the ego at that boundary which is turned toward the feared object. In fear, the sensation of danger exists only at the ego boundary threatened by that danger. The seizure of the total ego by the feeling of danger, or, as I stated earlier, by hallucinated terror, interferes with observation of the direction of the object from which the danger threatens. Furthermore, a feeling of fear may be intense without becoming anxiety, and a feeling of anxiety may have low intensity; yet the latter is anxiety, because the entire ego has been seized with a feeling of danger, though only a faint one. Another difference between fear and anxiety runs parallel to this one. If one compares both feelings, both contain the conception of terror; Adler, too, described anxiety as hallucinated danger. But anxiety is the feeling of a *flight inhibited* by the conception of terror, fear the feeling of *self-defense inhibited* in the same way. The anxious person therefore experiences, "senses," the threat of danger always as coming from behind; the person in fear has the threat before his eyes, actually or mentally. Thus anxiety may join fear or fear may join anxiety, or the one may transform into the other.

The same antithesis between seizure of the entire ego and of only one part of the ego is expressed in the word pairs: "rage and anger," "agony and pain," "grief and sorrow," "temper and mood," and perhaps also in "expiation and penitence," "revenge and retaliation," and "passion and love." Whether the ego participates only at one ego boundary or in its entirety is the difference which decides whether something merely happens to the ego or whether something overwhelms it. In the first case the ego can resolve the imposed affect-excitation within itself, with the aid of the other ego boundaries; in the other case, the overwhelming excitation must first have taken its course.

Identifications are differentiated in the same manner; they may involve the entire ego or only one part of it. The mechanism operative in either kind of identification is probably a different one. Only the identification involving the entire ego deserves the name "introjection of the object," which was introduced by Ferenczi;[15] this kind of identification stems from unconscious oral or intestinal incorporation, or from unconscious phantasies of return into the womb. These ego expansions go deep and far back into the past. Those occurring

. . . .

[15] In later discussions with the editor, Federn rejected Ferenczi's term "intro*jection*," since nothing is "thrown" into the ego in the phenomenon of identification. He preferred to call this phenomenon "internalization of an object." The expansion of the ego cathexis over an object is what Federn would call "egotization," which is the translation of Federn's term *Verichung*, or *Einichung*.—E.W.

later, ordinarily through identification, rest directly on the extension of the ego boundaries, mental and bodily, so that they now include the other person within themselves. The same phenomenon also occurs in every object relation or interest in an object, but then in only a transitory manner at the ego boundary which exists at that time. In the case of identification, the expansion of the ego boundary is lasting and occurs at a steadily increasing number of ego boundaries. This is a slow process of gradual union which takes place repeatedly, but each time involves only part of the ego. Fixated in infantile development and unconsciously, the feeling of belonging to the loved persons repeats itself in these identification processes; it always implies an extension upon them of the ego feeling, that is, of the narcissistic cathexis of the ego; the expansion of the bodily ego feeling of the child who snuggles close to the protecting figure, or who is held and carried by him, is also repeated.

Fusion with another person through clinging and embracing occurs with strong libidinal cathexis, which contains genital, sensual, and tender urges, tactile and muscular libido (for instance, from the clinging drive described by Hermann), and other components. Through the inclusion of his person in the ego of the loved person with whom he thereby feels identified, as one, the small child feels not only fearless and protected, but also of increased bodily size and freed from the experience of the weakness of his ego. And yet even such early identifications are determined by purpose and are partial, unlike the first ones which involve the entire ego. On the other hand, it is probable that every total identification is based on the phylogenetically fixated unity of the individual with the universe—that is, the primary narcissistic cathexis unity, which, as we pointed out earlier, may be renewed at the occasion of the expansion of the ego boundaries into the group ego. It may be assumed that the formation of a strong superego is partly predisposed phylogenetically; yet the extremely great differences among individuals in regard to the strength and totality of the superego in its action on the ego suggest the assumption that in ontogenesis, too, there is a wide variation in the depth at which the mechanism operates and in the strength of cathexis in the identifications which contribute to the formation of the superego.

I have not hesitated to speak, repeatedly, of satisfied and unsatisfied narcissism; this distinction, which does not appear in either Freud's first paper, "On Narcissism: An Introduction," [16] nor in his later writings, was forced upon me by the observation of narcissistic behavior. (However, I am no longer the only one aware of it, and I need not draw others' attention to it.) To distinguish whether narcissism is healthy or pathological it is doubtless most important to know that its satisfaction is possible, the manner in which it occurs, and then, in the individual case, to ascertain the success in achieving satisfaction and on what this success is contingent—knowledge, as it were, of the conditions for successful love in narcissistic cathexes. Nevertheless, one feels a resistance to using the same term for the satisfaction of object libidinal desire and of narcissistic tension. It is also noteworthy that long before we were interested in the possibility of satisfaction of the narcissistic need, the lack of that satisfaction and the disappointment in, and denial of, narcissistic pleasure was widely known; for a time it seemed to be an almost fashionable interpretation in psychoanalysis. Everyone was pleased if he had found a "narcissistic injury" to have been pathogenic. The consequences of failure of narcissistic satisfaction had attracted attention earlier than the ordinary state of satisfaction; as indeed, it is usually only the lack of something to which we are thoroughly accustomed that makes us aware of its existence.

The difficulty is due somewhat to an obscurity of the terminology and, remotely, to a difficulty in understanding the libido theory, but essentially it is due to the nature of the narcissistic cathexes, to the ego libido itself. The difficulty in terminology I mentioned before: it is assumed that the concept of narcissism implies the lack of an object, whereas libidinal satisfaction implies the union with, the reaching of, an object; or, again, in autoerotism it implies the increase of forepleasure up to the achievement of end-pleasure, if in the absence of an object, yet at an erogenous zone through an erotic

. . . .

[16] Freud, *Collected Papers*, IV, 30 ff.

or sexual process by which the goal of the sexual drive is reached. However, narcissism is autoerotism raised to the mental level; its subject—and in secondary narcissism its object as well—is the ego, or a part or a function of the ego, and, as we discussed above, the ego boundaries are analogous to the erogenous zones in bodily libido processes.

At this stage of theoretical conceptualization of the libido we are faced, as always at the point of transition from the bodily to the mental field, with an insuperable difficulty: as soon as we want to replace by specific terms the very general expressions which are hardly more than figurative illustrations, we either have to apply to the mental field concepts suited for somatic phenomena, or vice versa. The use of the term "erogenous zones" to describe the mental experience of the ego boundaries,[17] must not induce the reader to misunderstand my presentation as implying that somatic-libidinal processes occur at the ego boundaries in the same manner as at erogenous zones. However, we know of processes and states in the mental ego —sensations of exaltation and satisfaction in the mind—whose analogy to erotic and sexual occurrences has always been demonstrated by language, poetry, music, and philosophy, and whose actual connection with sexuality has been discovered and demonstrated by psychoanalytic libido theory, descriptively and genetically, clinically and in normal psychology. It will be a further task of psychoanalysis and biology to find out to what extent and detail the mental processes parallel the bodily ones, and how many somatic phenomena may and must be transposed to the mental level—how far we may get, as a matter of fact, if we apply *the libido theory to the limit*.

. . . .

[17] I am well aware of the fact that the expression "ego boundary" also has a too geographical and bodily implication; this has been a considerable obstacle to the acceptance of my findings. However, we do not speak as mind to mind, but as beings oriented by the senses, and we have to be satisfied with designations which orient three-dimensionally. The reader of good will, whose resistance has been overcome, will succeed in translating terms correctly to the corresponding mental experience as intended by the author, and thus he will be able to follow the subsequent progress of our understanding.

From the heuristic point of view, it is enticing to push the transposition far, but this is of scientific value only in so far as facts become known which cannot, at present, be interpreted otherwise.

Such a fact is the existence of ego libido which allows us, like Narcissus, to gain pleasure from our own ego and, also, to injure ourselves or to suffer narcissistically as a consequence of object libidinal frustrations or disappointments. The ego libido constantly pervades the ego. Its lack creates the obvious impression that the individual finds no true satisfaction either from himself or from objects; whereas an increase of ego libido makes the individual excitable to the point of hypersensitivity and joyful tension. We must assume, furthermore, that ego libido can be satisfied through fulfillment of the claims on one's own ego, i.e., approximating the ego ideal, and that it can be injured to the point of loss of ego libidinal cathexis, if, time and again, such satisfactions fail to materialize; but we must not assume that this satisfaction is comparable to that in object erotism, because we do not know of any process which corresponds to that of sexual union with the object.

The obvious—but, as far as I know, not yet explicitly formulated—interpretation for all these phenomena seems to me to be that ego libido, from simple ego feeling to most intense narcissistic tension and self-absorption, always maintains the character of *fore-pleasure*. This corresponds to the essential nature of autoerotism, from which narcissism stems and to which it is analogous. Nevertheless, autoerotism can reach end-pleasure, in imitation of normal sexuality. The mental ego lacks adequate organs for this purpose. Whenever a person tells us of an ecstatic, mystic, or artistic exaltation of libidinal satisfaction to an orgasm-like state, we usually learn of simultaneous autoerotic end-pleasure. It is not impossible, of course, that processes similar to end-pleasure and orgasm exist in the mental field also. (See Radó's "alimentary orgasm," and W. Reich's explanation of epileptic seizures.) I myself am inclined to assume that all wish fulfillments are attended by cellular processes which, with the union of female and male elements and energies, belong among the sexual ones. But this pursues the libido theory to the limits; the idea is not demonstrable, it is, in the sense of Plato, only *alethes doxa* (true belief), and not *episteme* (real knowledge).

If we stay within the framework of established and verifiable knowledge, we may say that the narcissistic cathexis achieves no more than fore-pleasure which actually does not constitute full satisfaction. Therefore, we have agreed with, and simultaneously explained, the view of Freud and later authors that it is not correct to speak of satisfaction of narcissism. However, after this clarification, we are justified in using the term if we take into account that fore-pleasure also provides a certain amount of satisfaction. As a matter of fact, civilized mankind lives, to an extraordinary degree, in a state of somatic fore-pleasure tension, due to the cultural restriction of sexual gratification which has resulted from the substitution of the rut periods of the animal world by a perenniality of the sexual drive. People find much and intensive satisfaction, or rather—since that term is incorrect—much pleasure in this state. Fore-pleasure, which in the normal sexual act increases progressively until end-pleasure is reached, may last a short or long time at any stage. Hence, one may also speak of more or less pleasurable satisfaction of fore-pleasure. The same is true for narcissism, which may, in certain persons, provide pleasure in different affective experiences and, as we know, at different ego boundaries, at variably or perpetually different levels. The ease with which some people in most uninteresting occupations live is based on healthy narcissism. Sublimation, too, rests essentially on the substitution of ego libido for autoerotism, on the subsequent inclusion, into the mental ego as well as the bodily ego, of the aim of the drive which is to be sublimated, and on the cathexis, with mental ego feeling, of the achievements which become valuable by sublimation; the mental ego feeling incorporates into the function the libidinal component which stems from the sublimated drive. Thus we understand that the fore-pleasure tension contained in narcissism should be conducive to all processes of sublimation; sublimation is its permissible investment, resolution, and reversal to the object in accordance with cultural demands.

Obviously, in the case of narcissism, we should not speak of direct satisfaction if the fulfillment of narcissistically cathected desires, the realization of narcissistic attitudes, and the confirmation of narcissistic self-elevation occur through others. Rather, it is merely the condition under which, at any given time, the level of fore-pleasure may become and remain high, which depends on all of these and on other similar opportunities and fulfillments. Now we are able to add a theoretical interpretation to the impression, mentioned early in this paper, that in practical work with patients we are able spontaneously to spot normal and non-normal expressions of narcissism. The higher the level of fore-pleasure cathexis which must be reached and maintained, the more numerous are the conditions which have to be fulfilled, and the greater becomes the danger of failure. Hence ensue unrest, commotion, and search for restitution of the missed feelings of fore-pleasure.

The lowering of the level of libido is an unpleasant experience; it is understandable that other opportunities for libidinal cathexis are sought through further libidinal excitation; the ego boundaries become labile; moreover, the unsatisfied libidinal cathexis more readily expands to include the entire ego. We do not know how autoerotic libido is converted into ego libido, nor what enables ego libido to maintain a higher or lower permanent level of fore-pleasure in the form of narcissistic cathexes. We can only assume that in this kind of fore-pleasure—as in somatic autoerotic processes—libidinal excitation, and thus libidinal energy, is consumed and that the cathexis level is always re-established anew by the body (through glandular hormones and sexual stimuli) and by the mind as well (through object libidinal stimuli and through object libidinal cathexes which seek and find satisfaction), and that thus a certain degree of fore-pleasure is always re-established. To this purpose narcissism also directs the investment of object libido. In addition, it is understandable that whenever fore-pleasure must be maintained at a permanently high level, the readiness for anxiety will be greater; in fact, we can observe this in pathologically increased narcissism. This constellation creates a vicious circle as anxiety probably uses up libido and allows the ego boundaries to become more labile; and in turn, anxiety probably increases the libidinal cathexis. We can further see the difference between healthy and pathological narcissism in the circumstance that for the former it is sufficient to establish and to maintain a comparatively low level of fore-pleasure, and the level may be raised at any given moment that the conditions are fulfilled; one may guess that in addition there is no need of excessive libido displacement or, possibly, of undesirable libido cathexes such as, for instance, excessively perverse ones, or ones that are conflictual in regard to their object. The maintenance of a sufficient amount of countercathexes of a narcissistic and object libidinal nature toward the displacements and increases may also be mandatory. The permanent narcissistic level which is experienced as well-being in the ego feeling is probably relatively high in normal narcissism.

We have expressed in the intricate language of the libido theory what the novelists are able to render far more vividly by describing restless, self-searching, and excitable talk and behavior, or what, in psychological and medical books, is communicated in a few sentences in the descriptions of certain psychopaths. The psychoanalyst, indeed, should not see his task as consisting in the observation and description of these modes of behavior, but rather in the understanding of the dynamics involved and of the relationships with the rest of the libidinal economy. Therefore, it seemed to me of practical importance to emphasize that narcissism is fore-pleasure, and to make it clear that, first, such narcissistic fore-pleasure varies on a scale from the beginning of excitation to end-pleasure and, secondly, that the degree of satisfaction depends on this, as well as on the intensity and extension of the libido cathexes. All of this does not transcend the teachings of Freud concerning the goal inhibited drives. Clearly such drives may remain fixated to intermediate goals in the ego and only indirectly approach the object, or they may remain fixated to external objects and thereby indirectly approach a goal set in the ego. Whatever, in the form of resistance, inhibits the achievement of the goal may, through this goal inhibition, itself become the libido cathected intermediate goal; frequently this is the road to sublimation.

The original goal has been renounced for good; the new goal appears more beautiful and more desirable, but is unattainable. Just as the handsome shepherd-boy's love was not satisfied by any other object and he perished because he found the object in himself, so in the same way this tragedy is repeated, though less violently, in every narcissistic love; occurring between two ego boundaries, it seeks fulfillment in vain in the reflection in the mirror. By turning away from the original goal, it has *lost the opportunity of full satisfaction.* This, however, is precisely the reason why narcissistic love accomplishes so much for cultural and individual aims; at the same time, anaclitic to other instinctual aims, it achieves with these a kind of gratification and end-pleasure. The conditions for this achievement, which so far have been discussed theoretically and in general terms, we shall now discuss in detail.

When Freud, in 1908, read his paper "The Relation of the Poet to Day-Dreaming," [18] he had not yet developed the concept of "narcissism." The significance of the facts on which this concept rests, however, had already been recognized by him. He described the way in which object interests and ego exaltation, as goals of daydreaming, become tied up with unconscious infantile wishes. The concept of narcissism as a germinating idea is expressed in the following passage: "It seems to me, however, that this significant mark of invulnerability very clearly betrays—His Majesty the Ego, the hero of all daydreams and all novels." [19] The conclusion, presented here, that narcissism of every kind is fixated at the fore-pleasure stage, adds significance to Freud's opinion that the aesthetic pleasure in the appreciation of poetry acts as a *fore-pleasure premium* which in turn facilitates the understanding of the dynamics underlying the effect of writing. The temptation of fore-pleasure creates in the reader the same kind of narcissistic mood that induced the poet's phantasies and motivated him to write.

Independent of theory, we may investigate the problem of the conditions for satisfaction, in phantasies of love, greatness, and

. . . .

[18]Freud, *Collected Papers,* IV, 173.
[19]*Op. cit.,* 180.

ambition, which always unite contents and goals that are clearly narcissistic and those that are directed toward the object. What can be recognized in the conscious phantasies must also be valid for the narcissistic cathexes, as we may assume that there is always an unconscious content tied up with them which corresponds to the satisfaction of drive, libido, and affect in the cathexes in question.

The mood of fore-pleasure, as discussed before, is clearly recognizable in all conscious phantasies; the *first* alluring pleasure stimulus, it draws the individual into the mood of reverie. This is the direct derivative of the autoerotic pleasures with which the small child, and probably even the infant, innocently combines his phantasying. The more this innocence is interfered with by outside influences (exerted partly by education and partly by the experiences upon the return to the world of objects), and later by the superego, the more additional conditions have to be met so that the pursuit of the narcissistic phantasies may prove uninterruptedly pleasurable and satisfying to a sufficient degree.

The narcissistic phantasy[20] is slanted more and more toward real tasks, interests, relations, desires, and activities. These inter-

. . . .

[20] In the strict sense of the term, narcissistic phantasies are those in which, not only experiences are imagined with narcissistic emphasis, but the person of the daydreamer himself is experienced in these situations. In hysteria this kind of phantasy formation is so characteristic that a hysterical individual may experience all of life only indirectly, with a phantasy ego. His object libido is only feigned; he does not possess it in his own person but only through assigning it to the imaginary figure which he makes live his life. Freud has called attention to the fact that the hysterical identification rests on claims held in common. Vice versa, one may also find—always, I surmise—that the ego figure of these phantasies has arisen through identification with persons in whom the desired claims are fulfilled. This kind of phantasy formation is in great part unconscious and uncovered only by analysis. Such phantasies permit us to understand well, from the economic point of view, why object libidinal gratification may satisfy narcissism—since only by this means can identification reach the goal of fulfillment of the desires and claims, so that only the phantasied object libidinal satisfaction transforms the phantasied ego person into the ego ideal which is narcissistically desired.

ests have a goal, and, in order to reach it, more and more complicated and intellectually demanding ways and detours are devised. These are goals of self-preservation, of enrichment, of self-assertion, of social achievements for others, of gaining friends and adherents, up to the phantasy of leadership or discipleship. The more actual intellectual work is accomplished in the procedure, the more the processes and the difficulties are laboriously combined in accordance with reality, and the paths toward the goal examined critically, even scrupulously, in the light of reality, the more does phantasy turn into useful planning and pondering endowed with a normal narcissistic component. Nevertheless, imagination and planning are to be considered narcissistic phantasies whenever the intellectual work is based on an unreal premise in regard to the position and opportunities of the daydreamer which, however, is accepted as real, though the further elaboration of the plan may then be ever so precise and even creative. In this kind of phantasying, the narcissistic satisfaction may become so great that the fore-pleasure approximates end-pleasure in intensity; moreover, it is always contingent on the phantasied achievement of the goal to which the narcissistic striving for pleasure has attached it.

Again we can observe the fusion of narcissistic and object libidinal striving. Their joint course toward a goal which satisfies both is found in all, or at least most people's actions and accomplishments and creative activities. In action, the cathexis of the object libidinal striving is more intense than in phantasy and thought, but the satisfaction of the object libido is often conditional upon the simultaneous satisfaction of the preformed narcissistic phantasies (Adler's "graph of life" and "role playing"). These phantasies are partly unconscious; Freud followed them to surprising depths in the analytical exploration of people who founder on success. In addition I wish to point out that the narcissistic premium is not conscious in many object-libidinally cathected actions because the narcissistic cathexis has taken a detour via the identification by means of the ego expansion; these vicissitudes of libido have been discussed frequently in another context. Precisely in practical proceedings, the deficiency in narcissistic components becomes evident in

soberness and in the matter-of-factness which is often a necessity rather than a virtue, since in these instances, not only narcissism is missing, but adequate object libido as well.

A third type of gaining satisfaction in narcissistic phantasy
is usually considered the only one in discussions of narcissism.
It is probable that it constitutes a regular unconscious element
in phantasying. If it is conscious, it is rather ridiculous and
has preserved the greatest measure of the infantile state of
being in love with oneself. The entire phantasy then consists of what we before designated as the premise. Regardless of any opportunity, let alone practicability of fulfillment,
the reverie indulges in timeless sham events, actually substituting for the present. The time factor, especially, distinguishes the moderate kind of phantasy, described above,
from the absurd, almost purely narcissistic kind which concen-
trates on pleasures and self-flattery in the images of life; in the
former, being slanted toward reality, at least the time necessary for reaching the goal is gauged correctly. It was from a
young and otherwise exceptionally talented American that I
heard the crudest consolation, and greatness, phantasy of the
second kind. Skipping all intermediary links, he phantasied
over and again that during his lifetime a colossal statue was
erected on an island, depopulated expressly for this purpose,
in his honor as the greatest ex-president of the United States.
The more the phantasy indulges in self-flattery, the more it
draws on exhibitionistic instead of normal object libido, so that
there probably is always an element of unconscious exhibitionistic phantasies active which, as a residue of earlier exhibitionistic masturbation, were repressed in part and in part underwent
an inadequately sublimated psychic elaboration.

The danger of such phantasy activity—that is, of pathological
narcissism—lies in the circumstance that such individuals become so spoiled through the easy achievement of a high degree
of fore-pleasure that they lose the capacity for real and complete achievement. At every attempt they digress from the preparatory stage into gaining narcissistic fore-pleasure. That probably everybody playfully retains a "Reservation for the Pleasure
Principle," and may do this with impunity, was pointed out by
Freud.

We may now summarize the characteristics which distinguish healthy narcissism from the pathological type:

1. Healthy narcissism is employed as countercathexis to the object strivings and for their support (for example, hope, ambition), but not as their substitute. The more narcissism functions as such a substitute, the more pathological it becomes.

2. The ego boundaries are resistant in normal narcissism; the ego is sufficiently stable due to the adequate narcissistic countercathexes.

3. The affects are resolved without sentimentality, though with intensity—that is, without renewed investment of narcissism.

4. The level of the fore-pleasure satisfaction resulting from the narcissistic cathexes is not too high; whereas the level of such fore-pleasure inherent in the permanent ego feeling is in general as high as possible.

5. The satisfaction in conscious and unconscious narcissistic phantasies is conditional on real object libidinal discharges, although the converse conditionality is not lacking. In pathological narcissism the latter predominates (this belongs in the context of "1.").

6. The contents of conscious and unconscious narcissistic phantasies are more in accord with reality, less infantile, and cathected by fewer perverse infantile sexual components.

7. The latter point is further confirmed by the fact that the promise magically established in these phantasies becomes more grandiose and more impossible in the same measure as the contributory narcissistic attitude deviates from normality.

I think that we are not enough puzzled by the fact that it is possible to experience and enjoy something completely impossible as reality in the absence of any constitutional tendency to insanity, outside of a fugue or any other abnormal state of consciousness. The simultaneous achievement of pleasure can be explained satisfactorily by the conscious and unconscious connection with autoerotic libido processes. The problem, however, lies in the phenomenon that the character of reality is achieved in consciousness, not nearly but completely, though limited to one's own subjectivity and hence valid for one's own ego exclusively. This problem is solved by my assumption that those phenomena are experienced as real which meet an ego boundary from outside; they are experienced as mentally real if they impinge only on a mental ego boundary, and as completely real if a bodily ego boundary is also involved. Phantasy is content with the mental reality and can afford to be so because daydreaming excludes objectivity.

However, the exclusion of objective validity from phantasies does not mean that wish phantasies are not fed by any object libido. Although we explained at the beginning of this paper why rigid antitheses do not exist between the two forms of libido investment, we shall now attempt to clarify the lack of any antithesis in the essential nature of, and the presence of such antithesis in the use of, ego libido and of object libido.

The character of fore-pleasure in narcissism, which we have demonstrated, emphasizes an important distinction, but does not denote an absolute difference between the two types of libido investment. Object libido also brings abundant fore-pleasure, and narcissism, if it becomes a bodily perversion or mental self-absorption, also achieves a satisfaction of the type of end-pleasure.[21] Economically we have formulated the difference, though only a relative one, in the maintenance of the stages of fore-pleasure; dynamically both are libidinal forces; mortido enters into the service of both, or it opposes both. An actual distinction can be found only in regard to topography. In the first place, there are separate object representations which are cathected with object libido, in contrast to the unitary, although continuously variable, ego, which is cathected with ego libido but also invests object libido in the objects or in their representations (egoism) and invests ego libido in the ego or in parts of the ego (narcissism). What occurs in all egoistic desires and actions is that ego and object (or object representation) meet at the ego boundary immediately. On the other hand, in narcissistic desires, the ego, as object of narcissism and

. . . .

[21] The peculiar kinds of self-absorption of the religious, especially of the Buddhist, meditation all but abolish the difference between the two forms of libido, the antithesis between ego and object being in part overcome and in part ignored.

simultaneously as subject of egoism, is once more inserted between ego and object. Hence object libido[22] is also—immediately—concerned with the ego; narcissistic libido is also —only indirectly—concerned with the object. From the genetic point of view, taking the dynamic, economic, and topographic aspects into consideration, it is unthinkable that there could exist any object libido not invested by the ego in an object, according to conscious and unconscious needs and experiences; that is, on the basis of numerous ego situations (including hereditary engrams). On the basis of other needs, experiences, and ego situations, the investment and, even more, the satisfaction are inhibited by the ego and superego. All this is true also for the investment of narcissistic libido.

Hence we see that it is not narcissism which determines the ego structure, but the ego structure which determines what has to be designated as ego libido and what as object libido. Overcoming narcissism therefore does not mean to let craving and acting emanate from the id, but only to renounce the multiple participation, or at least the interpolation of ego participation. For many years the child simply renews previous ego situations with all narcissistic and object libidinal reactions on meeting with the same or a similar object. Maturation, as well as traumata and education, results in a decrease of the narcissistic cathexes and in as immediate as possible investment of object libido in objects, so that previous ego situations are not renewed in their entirety, nor is each individual one renewed. The object representations are subject to the same development.

If this is so, this investigation may lead us to understand and to appreciate the work of *consciousness* in one particular area.

. . . .

[*]It is also erroneous to designate as narcissistic the desire to be loved. It corresponds to pure object libido of a passive nature. Only if it does not relate to the object immediately, whether in reality or in phantasy, but is interpolated as love phantasy between ego and object, is it narcissistic. Freud rightly considers the high increase in object libido an impoverishment of the ego of the person in love; but this is correct only so far as it concerns immediate object libido which cathects one ego boundary more than all the others. In most instances, through being in love, the entire ego of the lover receives more narcissistic cathexis, which must be conceived of as normal countercathexis.

We have found the same difference between normal and abnormal processes for the entire ego, for its parts, and for the phantasies: as a rule, ego libido is invested as counter-cathexis to object libido. The less close is the tie of ego libido to object libido, the more normal becomes the investment of both. We have demonstrated that this separation is never completely successful. We may now pursue further this difference between normal and abnormal into the individual conceptions and memories of the external world. As I demonstrated elsewhere,[23] starting from a different point of departure, two kinds of experience-traces of objects are preserved in our preconscious and unconscious memory: those connected with the experience situation (or, more precisely, with the situations in which we met with the object) and others which contain only the object. Accordingly, the former pertain to the ego *and* to the object and have the object representation included within the ego boundary—more precisely, the ego boundary is expanded over the object. The purer are our object representations, the more our thinking becomes objective and free from subjectivity and from the dominance of the ego. The pure object representation, in turn, is freed from the narcissistic component, left by its inclusion within the ego boundary. We know that this liberation occurs through the introduction of the time factor, and through the comparison of several ego situation memories which contain the object and which are separate from each other in time. This task, however, is achieved exclusively through *conscious* thinking; otherwise one does not progress beyond object memories which are tied up with, and falsified by, the ego and which are always narcissistically cathected. Conscious thinking, of whatever content, but particularly of formerly narcissistically cathected content, results in objectivity and correct conception of reality, since it leaves behind pure object representations.

This function of consciousness also clarifies the effect of working through in psychoanalysis. It frees a person from pathologically invested narcissism which falsifies reality.

. . . .

[23] Federn, "Die Ichbesetzung bei den Fehlleistungen" (Ego Cathexis in Parapraxes), *Imago*, XIX (1933).

WRITINGS OF PAUL FEDERN

1901 "Zur Reform des ärztlichen Spitalsdienstes," *Wiener klinische Rund-schau*, XV, 276-278, 293-294.

1912 Contribution to: *Die Onanie: Vierzehn Beiträge zu einer Diskussion der "Wiener Psychoanalytischen Vereinigung,"* Wiesbaden, Verlag J. F. Bergmann, pp. 68-82.

1913 "Beispiel von Libidoverschiebung während der Kur" (Abstract), *Internationale Zeitschrift für ärztliche Psychoanalyse*, I, 303-306.

1913 "Ein Fall von Pavor nocturnus mit subjektiven Lichterscheinungen," *Internationale Zeitschrift für ärztliche Psychoanalyse*, I, 556-559.

1913 "Beiträge zur Analyse des Sadismus und Masochismus:
"I. Die Quellen des männlichen Sadismus," *Internationale Zeitschrift für ärztliche Psychoanalyse*, I, 29-49.

1914 "II. Die libidinösen Quellen des Masochismus," *Internationale Zeitschrift für ärztliche Psychoanalyse*, II, 105-130.

1914 "Über zwei typische Traumsensationen: (1. Vorbemerkung 2. Über den Hemmungstraum 3. Über den Flugtraum)," *Jahrbuch der Psychoanalyse*, VI, 89-134.

1914 "Lust-Unlustprinzip und Realitätsprinzip," *Internationale Zeitschrift für ärztliche Psychoanalyse*, II, 492-505.

1914 "The Infantile Roots of Masochism," *New York Medical Journal*, C, 351-355. (Abstract with discussion: *Journal of Nervous and Mental Disease*, XLI, 596-599; *Medical Record. N. Y.*, LXXXVI, 822-824.)

1915 "Some General Remarks on the Principles of Pain-Pleasure and of Reality," *Psychoanalytic Review*, II, 1-11.

1919 "Zur Psychologie der Revolution: Die vaterlose Gesellschaft," *Der Oesterreichische Volkswirt*, XI, 571-574, 595-598; Enlarged reprint: *Zur Psychologie der Revolution: Die vaterlose Gesellschaft*. Wien, Anzengruber-Verlag. 29 p.

1919 "Einschlafen und Einschläfern," *Wiener klinische Wochenschrift*, XXXII, 1243-1244.

1919 Review of: "Alfred Adler, Das Problem der Homosexualität, München, 1917," *Internationale Zeitschrift für ärztliche Psychoanalyse*, V, 220-221.

1920 "Zur Frage des Hemmungstraumes," *Internationale Zeitschrift für Psychoanalyse*, VI, 73-75.

1920 Review of: "Bernhard Aschner, Die Blutdrüsenerkrankungen des Weibes, Wiesbaden, 1915," *Internationale Zeitschrift für Psychoanalyse*, VI, 89-90.

1921 Review of: "Ulrich Grüninger, Zum Problem der Affektverschiebung, Zürich, 1917," *Internationale Zeitschrift für Psychoanalyse*, VII, 497-500.

1922 "Schema der Libidoaufnahme zur Begutachtung und Indikationsstellung" (Abstract), *Internationale Zeitschrift für Psychoanalyse*, VIII, 486-487.

1922 Review of: "Albert Moll, Behandlung der Homosexualität: biochemisch oder psychisch?, Bonn, 1921," *Internationale Zeitschrift für Psychoanalyse*, VIII, 84-86.

1923 "Die Geschichte einer Melancholie," *Internationale Zeitschrift für Psychoanalyse*, IX, 201-206.

1924 "Varendonck †," *Internationale Zeitschrift für Psychoanalyse*, X, 203-204.

1924 "Masturbation," *Journal of Sexology and Psychoanalysis*, II, 251-266.

1926 "Einige Variationen des Ichgefühls," *Internationale Zeitschrift für Psychoanalyse*, XII, 263-274.

1926 —"Some Variations in Ego Feeling," *International Journal of Psycho-Analysis*, VII, 434-444.

1926 "Freud'sche Psychotherapie," *Deutsche Zeitschrift für Homöopathie*, V, 546.

1926   Contributions to *Das Ärztliche Volksbuch*, edited by H. Meng; three
(1924) editions, Stuttgart, 1924-1929: "Der Arzt im Dienste der Gesundheitspflege." (Others are incorporated in the *Psychoanalytische Volksbuch*.)

1926 Contributions to *Das Psychoanalytische Volksbuch*, edited by P. Federn and H. Meng; first edition 1926; second edition 1928; third edition 1939:
"Stellung der Psychoanalyse zur übrigen Psychotherapie."
"Die psychoanalytische Heilmethode."
"Schutz vor Nerven- und Geisteskrankheiten."
"Körperliche Hygiene des Geschlechtslebens."
"Seelische Hygiene des Geschlechtslebens."
"Hysterie und ihre Behandlung."
"Funktionelle Störungen des Geschlechtsaktes." (With H. Meng).
"Psychoanalyse und Medizin."
"Märchen - Mythus - Urgeschichte."

(1929) "Uber einige Fortschritte der psychoanalytischen Forschung." (With E. Weiss).

(1930) —"Psychoanalytical Method of Treatment," *Medical Reform of Reviews*, XXXVI, 421-433.

1927 "Die Wiener Diskussion (über Onanie) aus dem Jahre 1912," *Zeitschrift für psychoanalytische Pädagogik*, II, 106-112.

1927 "Narzissmus im Ichgefüge," *Internationale Zeitschrift für Psychoanalyse*, XIII, 420-438.

1928 —"Narcissism in the Structure of the Ego," *International Journal of Psycho-Analysis*, IX, 401-419.

1928 "Psychoanalyse," Reclam. *Praktisches Wissen*, third revised edition, Leipzig, Reclam, 1928.

1929 "Über einen alltäglichen Zwang," *Internationale Zeitschrift für Psychoanalyse*, XV, 214-221.

1929 —"An Every-Day Compulsion," *International Journal of Psycho-Analysis*, X, 130-138.

1929 "Das Ich als Subjekt und Objekt im Narzissmus," *Internationale Zeitschrift für Psychoanalyse*, XV, 393-425.

1929 "Die Diskussion über 'Selbstmord,' insbesondere 'Schülerselbstmord,' im Wiener Psychoanalytischen Verein im Jahre 1918," *Zeitschrift für psychoanalytische Pädagogik*, III, 379-389.

1929 "Selbstmordprophylaxe in der Analyse," *Zeitschrift für psychoanalytische Pädagogik*, III, 379-389.

1930 "Der neurotische Stil," *Abhandlungen aus der Neurologie, Psychiatrie, Psychologie und ihren Grenzgebieten*, LXI, pp. 194-201; Reprinted (1932) in *Almanach der Psychoanalyse*, 1932; 15-26.

1930 "Psychoanalytische Auffassung der 'intellektuellen Hemmung,' " *Zeitschrift für psychoanalytische Pädagogik*, IV, 393-408.

1930 "Neurasthenic Core of Hysteria," *Medical Review of Reviews*, XXXVI, 140-147.

1930 "Die Wirklichkeit des Todestriebes: Zu Freud's 'Unbehagen in der Kultur,' " *Hippokrates*, III, 341-366; Reprinted in *Almanach der*
(1931) *Psychoanalyse*, 1931, 68-97.

1932 —"The Reality of the Death Instinct, Especially in Melancholia," (Remarks on Freud's book, *Civilisation and its Discontents*), *Psychoanalytic Review*, XIX, 129-151.

1931 "Zum 6. Mai 1931," *Zeitschrift für psychoanalytische Pädagogik*, V, 233-240.

1931 "Über die Wirkung sexueller Kräfte in der Seele," *Sexualnot und Sexualreform: Verhandlungen des IV. Kongresses der Weltliga für Sexualreform*, pp. 123-134.

1931 "Eduard Hitschmann zum 60. Geburtstag (28. Juli 1931)," *Internationale Zeitschrift für Psychoanalyse*, XVII, 420-423.

1932 —"Sixtieth Birthday of Edward Hitschmann (July 28, 1931)," *International Journal of Psycho-Analysis*, XIII, 261-264.

1931 "Vom Nationalgefühl," *Almanach der Psychoanalyse*, 1931, 97-101.

1931 "Der Lebensmüde im Krankenhaus," *Österreichische Blätter für Krankenpflege und Fürsorge*, VII, 77-86.

1932 —"Weariness of Life in Hospital Patients," *Mental Hygiene*, XVI, 636-649.

1931 "Psychologie der Familienfürsorge," *Jahresbericht des Wiener Vereins Settlement.*

1932 —"The Settlement Method in the Education of the Psyche," *Neighborhood,* V, 63-74.

1932 "Das Ichgefühl im Traume," *Internationale Zeitschrift für Psycho-*
(1933) *analyse,* XVIII, 145-170; Reprinted in *Almanach der Psychoanalyse,* 1933, 96-130.

1932 —"Ego Feeling in Dreams," *Psychoanalytic Quarterly,* I, 511-542.

1933 "Die Psychosenanalyse: Zur Indikation," *Internationale Zeitschrift für Psychoanalyse,* XIX, 207-210.

1933 "Die Psychosen-Analyse: Zur Technik," *Internationale Zeitschrift für Psychoanalyse,* XIX, 444-449.

1934 —"The Analysis of Psychotics: On Technique," *International Journal of Psycho-Analysis,* XV, 209-214.

1933 "Sándor Ferenczi," *Internationale Zeitschrift für Psychoanalyse,* XIX, 305-321.

1933 —"Sandor Ferenczi," *International Journal of Psycho-Analysis,* XIV, 467-485.

1933 "Die vier Frongesetze der Zwangsneurose," *Internationale Zeitschrift für Psychoanalyse,* XIX, 616-620.

1933 "Die Ichbesetzung bei den Fehlleistungen," *Imago,* XIX, 312-338, 433-453.

1933 "Zunahme der Süchtigkeit," *Die Bereitschaft,* XIII, 77-79; Reprinted
(1935) in *Almanach der Psychoanalyse,* 1935, 54-60.

1933 "Zunahme der Süchtigkeit," *Sozialärztliche Rundschau*

1933 "Frigidität," *Wiener klinische Wochenschrift,* XLVI, 671.

1933 "Verhalten des Hausarztes gegenüber den Neurosen," *Wiener klinische Wochenschrift,* XLVI, 1462-1463.

1933 "Zirkuläre Freundschaftsbeziehungen," *Wiener medizinische Wochenschrift,* LXXXIII, 470-472.

1933 "Nachbarhilfe für Arbeitslose," *Blätter für das Wohlfahrtswesen der Stadt Wien,* XXXII, 21-23, 41-43, 49-51.

1934 "Das Erwachen des Ichs im Traume: I. Die Orthriogenese, II. Thesen zur Ich-Psychologie," *Internationale Zeitschrift für Psychoanalyse,* XX, 109-112.

1934 —"The Awakening of the Ego in Dreams: I Orthriogenesis, II. Postulates to Serve as a Basis for an Ego Psychology," *International Journal of Psycho-Analysis,* XV, 296-301.

1934 "Mental Factors in the World Depression," *Journal of Nervous and Mental Disease,* LXXIX, 43-58.

1936 "Zur Unterscheidung des gesunden und krankhaften Narzissmus," *Imago,* XXII, 5-39; partly reprinted, as "Ichgrenzen, Ichstärke und
(1937) Identifizierung," in *Almanach der Psychoanalyse,* 1937.

1937 "Die leitungslose Funktion im Zentralnervensystem: Eine Frage der Psychologie an die Physiologie," *Internationale Zeitschrift für Psychoanalyse,* XXIII, 250-274.

1938 —"The Undirected Function in the Central Nervous System. A Question put to Physiology by Psychology," *International Journal of Psycho-Analysis*, XIX, 173-198.

1940 "Hysterie und Zwang in der Neurosenwahl," *Internationale Zeitschrift für Psychoanalyse und Imago*, XXV, 245-263.

1940 —"The Determination of Hysteria Versus Obsessional Neurosis," *Psychoanalytic Review*, XXVII, 265-276.

1940 "Psychoanalysis as a Therapy of Society," *American Imago*, I, 65-80.

1942 "Some Suggestions on the Mental Hygiene of Soldiers," *Mental Hygiene*, XXVI, 554-559.

1943 "Psychoanalysis of Psychoses: I. Errors and how to Avoid them, II. Transference, III. The Psychoanalytic Process," *The Psychiatric Quarterly*, XVII, 3-19, 246-257, 470-487.

1944 "A Dream under General Anesthesia: Studies in Ego-Cathexis," *The Psychiatric Quarterly*, XVIII, 422-435.

1945 "The Psychiatric Social Worker's Concern with Shock Treatment," *The Newsletter of the American Association of Psychiatric Social Workers*, XV, 13-17.

1946 "Employment of Neurotics," *Journal of Clinical Psychopathology*, VII, 803-813.

1947 "Principles of Psychotherapy in Latent Schizophrenia," *American Journal of Psychotherapy*, I, 129-144.

1947 "Professor Freud: The Beginning of a Case History," *Samikṣā I*, 305-311.

1948 "Freud Amongst Us," *The Psychiatric Quarterly Supplement*, XXII, 1-6.

1949 "Mental Hygiene of the Ego" (Abstract), *American Journal of Psychotherapy*, III, 290-291.

1949 "Mental Hygiene of the Psychotic Ego," *American Journal of Psychotherapy*, III, 356-371.

1949 "Zur seelischen Hygiene des Ichs," *Die Psychohygiene: Grundlagen und Ziele*, Bern, Verlag H. Huber, pp 17-24.

1949 Dedication (to August Aichhorn): *Searchlights on Delinquency*, New York, International Universities Press, pp. vii-viii.

1949 "Psychoanalytic Prevention Versus Therapeutic Psychoanalysis," (with H. Meng), *ibid.*, pp. 26-34.

1952 —"Psychoanalytische Prävention contra therapeutische Psychoanalyse," (with H. Meng), *Monatsschrift für Psychiatrie und Neurologie*, CXXIII.

INDEX